D0882456

THE WARSAW RISING OF 1944

SOVIET AND EAST EUROPEAN STUDIES

THE WARSAW RISING
OF 1944

JAN. M. CIECHANOWSKI

CAMBRIDGE
AT THE UNIVERSITY PRESS
1974

Published by the Syndics of the Cambridge University Press
Bentley House, 200 Euston Road, London NW1 2DB
American Branch: 32 East 57th Street, New York, N.Y. 10022

© Cambridge University Press 1974

Library of Congress Catalogue Card Number: 73-79315

ISBN: 0 521 20203 5

Printed in Great Britain by
Alden & Mowbray Ltd
at the Alden Press, Oxford

CONTENTS

ABBREVIATIONS

AK   *Armia Krajowa* – (Home Army).

AL   *Armia Ludowa* – (People's Army).

CBKP   *Centralne Biuro Komunistow Polskich* – (Central Bureau of Polish Communists in the U.S.S.R.)

GL   *Gwardia Ludowa* – (People's Guards).

KRN   *Krajowa Rada Narodowa* – (National Council of Poland).

NSZ   *Narodowe Sily Zbrojne* – (National Armed Forces).

PKP   *Polityczny Komitet Porozumiewawczy* – (Political Consultative Committee).

PKWN   *Polski Komitet Wyzwolenia Narodowego* – (Polish Committee of National Liberation).

PPR   *Polska Partia Robotnicza* – (Polish Workers' Party).

PPS   *Polska Partia Socjalistyczna* – (Polish Socialist Party).

RJN   *Rada Jednosci Narodowej* – (Council of National Unity).

SZP   *Sluzba Zwyciestwu Polski* – (Victory for Poland Service).

ZPP   *Zwiazek Patriotow Polskich* – (Union of Polish Patriots in the U.S.S.R.).

ZWZ   *Zwiazek Walki Zbrojnej* – (Association for Armed Struggle).

ACKNOWLEDGEMENTS

In December 1968 I was awarded a Doctor of Philosophy degree of the University of London for a thesis entitled: *The Political and Ideological Background of the Warsaw Rising, 1944*. This work is an abridged and revised version of that dissertation.

I am much indebted to Lt-Gen M. Kukiel, K.B.E., Ph.D., for permission to use the Archives of the General Sikorski Historical Institute in London, and to Maj-Gen T. Pelczynski for allowing me to study the documents housed in the Archives of the Polish Underground Movement Study Trust in London.

I am deeply grateful to Mrs R. Oppman, M.A., of the General Sikorski Historical Institute, and Mrs H. Czarnocka, of the Polish Underground Movement Study Trust, for their kindness, consideration and the patience with which they dealt with my many requests for documents and data.

I gained much from the interviews and discussions concerning the Warsaw Rising which I had with the following persons: the late Gen T. Bor-Komorowski, who was Commander of the Home Army from 1943 to 1944, Lt-Gen M. Kukiel, K.B.E., Ph.D., the war-time Polish Minister of National Defence, Lt-Gen S. Kopanski, Chief of Staff of the Polish General Staff in the years 1943–5, Maj-Gen T. Pelczynski, Chief of Staff of the Home Army in the years 1941–3, Col K. Iranek-Osmecki, Chief of Intelligence Service of the Home Army in the years 1943–4, Col J. Rzepecki, the Chief of the Information and Propaganda Bureau of the Home Army in the years 1940–4, Col F. Demel, Chief of the Operational Department of the Polish General Staff in the years 1943–4, the late Col S. Juszczakiewicz, who was Deputy Chief of the Personnel Department of the Home Army in the years 1943–4, Maj Z. Miszczak, the Head of the Eastern Section of the Home Army's Intelligence at the time of the insurrection, Mr Z. Stypulkowski, the Member of the War-time Presidium of the National-Democratic Party, and Mr J. Braun, the Member of the Council of National Unity in the years 1944–5.

I take special pleasure in paying tribute to Col J. Bokszczanin, Chief of Operations of the Home Army from January 1944 to July 1944 and the last Chief of Staff of the Home Army, for his candid, exhaustive and illuminating written and oral evidence concerning the plans of the Home Army Command for the Warsaw insurrection.

I was also fortunate enough to benefit from correspondence and discussions on Poland's war-time politics with Mr K. Popiel, the war-time leader of the Polish Labour Party – *Stronnictwo Pracy* – and a leading member of the Polish Cabinet in London in the years 1940–4, and Mr K. Sieniewicz, the last Secretary General of the Polish Labour Party.

My thanks are also due for the helpful criticisms, suggestions and encouragements of Professor K. B. Smellie, Professor J. K. Zawodny, Professor R. F. Leslie, Professor H. Seton-Watson, Professor P. Skwarczynski, Mr S. K. Panter-Brick, Mr H. T. Willetts, Mr J. Kulczycki, Mr Z. S. Siemaszko, Dr J. Betley, Professor B. Czaykowski, and Dr J. Zielinski.

I have also profited greatly from lengthy discussions concerning the military aspects of this work with Col Z. Jarski.

My greatest debts, however, are to Professor L. Schapiro and Dr Z. A. Pelczynski for their kind advice and encouragement and for their incisive and scholarly criticisms; and lastly to my wife who has helped me in so many ways that I find it impossible to express adequately my profound gratitude.

Finally, however much this work owes to other people's help and advice only the author is responsible for its contents and conclusions.

INTRODUCTION

The purpose of this study is to examine the political and ideological background of the Warsaw Rising and to trace the course of events which led to its outbreak. It is an attempt to establish when, how and why the authors of the insurrection decided that Warsaw should be freed from the Germans 'by Polish effort alone twelve hours before the entry of the Soviets into the capital'. It will examine the political and ideological anatomy of the Polish underground state, whose leaders decided to stage the insurrection. The term underground state is used here to denote the political and military organisations of the Polish resistance movement loyal to the exiled Government in London.

This study is not concerned with the course of the rising itself and only those purely military affairs and events are discussed, which had direct impact on the policies and decisions of the pro-London authorities. To exclude military problems altogether would have tended to obscure rather than to reveal the political aspects of the insurrection, the opening of which was intended by its authors to coincide with the climax of the Russo–German battle for the Polish capital.

Further, in order to place the events and decisions leading to the insurrection in their wider political context it is necessary to conduct a number of preliminary inquiries into the main spheres of Polish political life and diplomacy during the Second World War, to examine the genesis and development of the underground state, and to determine to what extent the decision to fight in Warsaw was consistent with the basic attitudes and plans of the pro-London leadership in Poland and abroad. Relations between the pro-London and Communist-inspired resistance movements must also be studied to establish the origins and causes of the bitter struggle for power in post-war Poland which developed between them during the last years of the German occupation and to assess the effects of this conflict on the policies and decisions of the pro-London leaders. Similarly, it is necessary to analyse the insurrectionary operations conducted by the Home Army – *Armia Krajowa*, AK – east of Warsaw in the spring and summer of 1944 and to decide to what extent the outcome of these operations influenced the Polish determination to fight in the capital. The Home Army formed an integral part of the Polish Armed Forces loyal to the exiled Government. Relevant aspects in the diplomatic field are attitudes of Churchill, Roosevelt and Stalin to the Polish question and to the Polish Government in London, especially after Stalingrad and the Teheran Conference when it became clear that Poland would be liberated from the Germans by the Soviet rather than Anglo–American forces. A review of the main diplomatic developments regarding Poland in the years 1939–44 is required if we wish to assess the impact of these developments on the policies and actions of the pro-London authorities and to discover whether the Polish Government made diplomatic preparations for the insurrection. At that time the exiled Polish Government was still recognised by both London and Washington as the lawful Government of Poland, and Churchill was seeking to bring about a Russo–Polish *rapprochement*.

This study is based primarily upon unpublished Polish documents relating to the plans, aims and activities of the exiled authorites and the leaders of the underground state. It is also based on the author's interviews with, and letters from highly-placed witnesses of the events and questions under examination.

At the same time, when examining the evidence, both documentary and oral, certain reservations must be borne in mind. First, as E. H. Carr put it: 'No document can tell us more than what the author of the document thought – what he thought had happened, and what he thought ought to have happened or would happen, or perhaps only what he wanted others to think he thought . . .' Secondly, it must be remembered that all the documents consulted reveal mainly the Polish side of the story. Indeed, lack of access to the Soviet war-time documents makes it very difficult, if not impossible, to write a comprehensive history of the political background of the Warsaw Rising. Through the Polish documents, however, it is possible to trace the decisions and actions of the highest Polish authorities, which culminated in the outbreak of the insurrection, and to analyse their motives. These are the aims of this study.

Finally, evidence collected from surviving witnesses must always, for obvious reasons, be treated with caution; it is very difficult to evaluate it precisely. The author decided to use such evidence in the hope of recording certain vital fragments of the history of Polish war-time politics.

The main difficulty in preparing a study on this subject is that, essentially, it is still topical, and provokes emotionally-charged reactions.

J.C.

Baltic Sea

L A T V I A

LITHUANIA

0   150 miles
0   250 km

Gdansk (Danzig)

● Kaliningrad
(Königsberg)

● Wilno

Pomerania

E. PRUSSIA

White Russia

GERMANY

Vistula

Narew

Bug

Warsaw

● Kowel

Silesia

Lublin

Volhynia

U. S. S. R.

Krakow

San

Western Ukraine

● Lwow

C Z E C H O S L O V A K I A

RUMANIA

H. A. Shelley

| pre-war frontiers |
| Curzon Line |
| Ribbentrop-Molotov Line |
| Oder-Neisse Line |

1

The Big Three and Poland:
July 1943 – July 1944

1. The collapse of Poland and formation of the Polish Government in exile

The German attack on Poland, which precipitated the outbreak of the Second World War and finally led to the destruction of the Third Reich, began on 1 September 1939. Within a few weeks Polish regular resistance collapsed, in spite of the heroism of the Polish Army, and Poland found herself once again under foreign domination.[1] At the end of September 1939 Poland was once more partitioned by Germany and Russia. The Red Army entered eastern Poland on 17 September in accordance with the Nazi–Soviet Pact concluded on 23 August 1939, which provided for the partition of Poland in the event of war.[2] In August 1939 Hitler and Stalin decided to co-operate in the destruction of Poland as her frontiers were unacceptable to them both. Germany was not reconciled to the terms of the Versailles settlement in Eastern Europe, while Russia resented the loss of territories ceded to Poland by the Treaty of Riga. Stalin tried later on to justify his pact with Hitler in terms of political and strategic expediency.[3] But, to the Poles the Red Army's entry into Poland appeared as an act of treachery, a 'stab in the back'.[4]

The defeat of Poland began for the Polish nation a period of oppression, terror and destruction, which lasted for almost six

[1] For a comprehensive account in English of Polish political life in the inter-war period and causes of the Polish defeat see: A. Polonsky, *Politics in Independent Poland 1921–1939* (Oxford, 1972); A. Gieysztor et al., *History of Poland* (Warsaw, 1968), pp. 637ff; and H. Roos, *A History of Modern Poland* (London, 1966), pp. 98ff.

[2] For the text of this treaty see: *Documents on Polish–Soviet Relations, 1939–1945*, vol. I, 1939–1943, edited by the General Sikorski Historical Institute (London, 1961), Doc. No. 31 and Doc. No. 32, pp. 38–40 – hereafter to be referred to as *Documents on Polish–Soviet Relations*.

[3] Cf. H. Feis, *Churchill–Roosevelt–Stalin* (Rev. ed., New Jersey, 1966), p. 5 (hereafter to be referred to as Feis).

[4] Cf. T. Bor-Komorowski, *Armia Podziemna* (3rd ed., London, 1966), pp. 17–18.

1

years and in its magnitude and ferocity surpassed anything that the Poles, in their eventful and often tragic history, had had to endure.[1] But, it was also a period of great Polish military, political and diplomatic activity.

On 30 September, while the remnants of the Polish Army were still resisting the Germans in Poland, a new Polish Government was formed in Paris, under the Premiership of Gen Wladyslaw Sikorski, the old Government having been interned in Rumania. The members of the new Government had crossed into Rumania after the Red Army's entry into Poland.

In this way the continuation and constitutional legality of the highest Polish authorities – the President, Cabinet and Supreme Command – were safeguarded, and occupied Poland acquired a new leadership uncompromised by the autocratic tendencies of the pre-war regime, or by the stigma of swift military defeat.

Sikorski had, since 1908, been connected with the Polish struggle for independence.[2] In Poland he was regarded as a staunch and resolute democrat and opponent of the *Sanacja*.[3] In Switzerland, in 1936, he tried with Ignacy Paderewski to create a common opposition front to the *Sanacja*.[4] On 30 September he was commissioned by W. Raczkiewicz, the new President of Poland, to form a Polish Government in exile, in which the pre-war Opposition Parties were represented. On 7 November he was appointed the C-in-C of the Polish Armed Forces.[5] By combining these two offices – of both political and military head of the Government – Sikorski became

[1] For a comprehensive and detailed account of the German occupation policy in Poland see: C. Madajczyk, *Polityka Trzeciej Rzeszy w Okupowanej Polsce*, II, vols (Warsaw, 1970). For an account of developments in the Polish territories occupied by the U.S.S.R. and the treatment of the Poles by the Soviets see: E. Rozek, *Allied Wartime Diplomacy: A Pattern in Poland* (New York, 1958), pp. 37–50 (hereafter refered to as Rozek).

[2] During the First World War he served in Pilsudski's Legions. In the Russo–Polish war of 1920 he commanded the Fifth Army which contributed to the Polish victory on the Vistula. After the war he served as Chief of the General Staff. In 1922 he was for six months Prime Minister of Poland and later, in the years 1924–5, he was the Minister of Military Affairs. From 1926 until 1928 he served as the Commander of the Lwow Military Area. In 1928 he was suspended from active duties and devoted himself to historical writings and journalism. M. Kukiel, *General Sikorski* (London, 1970), pp. 8ff.

[3] The term *Sanacja* was used to describe the regime which ruled Poland in the years 1926–39.

[4] M. Kukiel, *op. cit.*, pp. 76ff.

[5] The Diary of Gen Sikorski's activities in the Archives of the General Sikorski Historical Institute in London (hereafter referred to as the GSHI).

the dominant figure of the Cabinet. In Poland he was regarded as the country's war-time leader.

Sikorski's Government tried to create the Polish Army in exile and the resistance movement in Poland,[1] to direct the struggle against the occupiers, and to represent the Polish cause and Polish interests abroad.

After the fall of France in June 1940 the Polish Government and the remnants of the Polish Army which had been created in France, about 17,000 men, were evacuated to Great Britain. A period of close Anglo–Polish political and military co-operation ensued which continued until the end of the war.[2] Great Britain assumed special responsibility for the fate of Poland, while the Polish Armed Forces under British Command and the Polish resistance movement rendered great services to the common cause.

2. *Russo–Polish Relations 1941–3*

Apart from being one of the most decisive events of the Second World War, the German attack on Russia, which began on 22 June 1941, opened new possibilities with regard to Russo–Polish relations, which for centuries had been unhappy and strained. The fact that both the Russians and the Poles were fighting against a common enemy made for a temporary Russo–Polish understanding. The British Government, interested in promoting harmony in the Allied Camp, played an important part in bringing about a Russo–Polish *rapprochement*.[3]

On 30 July a Soviet–Polish pact was signed in London. The treaty provided for the restoration of Russo–Polish diplomatic relations, military co-operation, the creation of the Polish Army in the U.S.S.R., and an amnesty for all Polish citizens detained in the Soviet Union. It failed to settle conclusively the issue of future boundaries between the two countries, although Moscow recognised that the Soviet–German agreements of 1939 with regard to Poland had 'lost their validity'.[4] During the negotiations leading to the conclusion of the Soviet–Polish treaty it became obvious that each side laid claim to pre-war eastern Poland. The Poles stood by their

[1] For details see pp. 80ff of this study.
[2] On this, see: J. Garlinski, *Poland, SOE and the Allies* (London, 1969).
[3] L. Woodward, *British Foreign Policy in the Second World War* (London, 1962), p. 200 – hereafter to be referred to as Woodward.
[4] For the text of this treaty see: *Documents on Polish–Soviet Relations*, vol. I, Doc. No. 106, pp. 141–2.

Riga frontiers, while the Russians, who in November 1939 had incorporated Polish territories occupied by them into the Soviet Union, considered them as now belonging to the Soviet Ukraine and Byelorussia. The large towns in these regions were Polish, especially Wilno, Lwow and Bialystok, but the majority of the population was Ukrainian and Byelorussian. Out of the total population of some 13 millions about 5 millions were Polish.[1]

Sikorski's failure to settle the frontier problem in 1941[2] left open and undecided the whole question of the future of Russo–Polish relations, especially in the event of a decisive Soviet victory; in view of the conflicting Russian and Polish claims to the disputed territories the Russo–Polish pact of 1941 was a diplomatic anomaly made possible because these areas were under German occupation.[3] This lack of Russo–Polish understanding with regard to the territorial question made co-operation between the Russians and the Poles difficult and led to a split in the Polish Cabinet.[4]

A number of important problems bedevilled Russo–Polish co-operation. First, there were arguments connected with the size, equipment and deployment of the Polish Army in Russia, which finally led to its withdrawal to the Middle East in the summer of 1942, in an atmosphere of mutual recrimination.[5] Secondly, there was the question of about 8,000 missing Polish officers, captured by the Russians in September 1939,[6] whose disappearance Stalin could not explain satisfactorily.[7] Finally, there were constant Russo–Polish disputes about the citizenship of all persons who resided in the Polish territories annexed by the Soviet Union.[8]

The main bone of contention was, however, the unresolved frontier dispute, which intensified at the beginning of 1943, when the Red Army began to regain the initiative on the Eastern Front, and its eventual return to Poland appeared likely.[9]

At the end of February 1943, the Polish Government again stated that they stood by the pre-war frontiers.[10] In reply Moscow accused

---

[1] *Documents on Polish–Soviet Relations*, vol. I, Note 67, p. 572.
[2] On this, see p. 134 of this study.
[3] Woodward, p. 201.   [4] M. Kukiel, *op. cit.*, pp. 172ff.
[5] For this, see: W. Anders, *An Army in Exile* (London, 1951); S. Kot, *Conversations with the Kremlin and Dispatches from Russia* (Oxford, 1963); M. Kukiel, *op. cit.*, pp. 182ff; and Rozek, pp. 111ff.   [6] Rozek, pp. 123ff.
[7] *Documents on Polish–Soviet Relations*, vol. I, Doc. No. 159, pp. 232ff.
[8] Rozek, pp. 105ff.   [9] Cf. Woodward, p. 203.
[10] *Documents on Polish–Soviet Relations*, vol. I, Doc. No. 294, pp. 488–9.

the Poles of refusing to recognise the 'historic rights' of the Ukrainians and Byelorussians to national unity.[1]

Further, Stalin informed the British Government that he wanted the Curzon Line,[2] with some adjustments, as a new frontier with Poland, and that Russo–Polish relations 'would depend on the character of the Polish Government'.[3] This prompted London to try to bring about, with the help of Washington,[4] a 'general settlement of the Russian frontier', in spite of 'insuperable' difficulties involved in such an undertaking.[5]

It became obvious that Russo–Polish relations were again entering a new and dangerous stage; they were approaching a breaking point.[6]

The final break occurred on 26 April 1943, soon after the German announcement of the discovery, at Katyn Woods, near Smolensk, Soviet territory occupied by the *Wehrmacht* of the mass graves of thousands of Polish officers captured by the Red Army in September 1939. This discovery was followed by Polish and German requests to the International Red Cross in Geneva for an investigation of the whole affair.[7] In response to this tactically unfortunate Polish move the Russians accused the Polish Government of co-operating with the Nazis in slandering them and of putting pressure upon them in order to gain territorial concessions. They argued that this made relations between Moscow and the Polish Government impossible.[8]

Thus a wide chasm opened between the Soviet and Polish authorities, at a time when close understanding was needed. Churchill tried to prevent this, but to no avail.[9] He was determined, however, to heal the breach between Russia and Poland, in the interests of Allied Unity.

---

[1] *Ibid.*, Doc. No. 296, pp. 501–2.

[2] For a clear exposition of the significance of the Curzon Line see: Woodward, p. 201; and *Foreign Relations of the United States, Diplomatic Papers 1943*, vol. III, *The British Commonwealth and Europe* (Washington, 1963), p. 1220, f. 15.

[3] Woodward, p. 203.

[4] The United States of America entered the war in December 1941.

[5] Woodward, p. 203.

[6] *Documents on Polish–Soviet Relations*, vol. I, Doc. Nos 299–300, pp. 504ff.

[7] For details concerning the Katyn affair, see: *Documents on Polish–Soviet Relations*, vol. I, Doc. Nos. 305–12, pp. 523–33; and J. K. Zawodny, *Death in the Forest* (London, 1971).

[8] *Documents on Polish–Soviet Relations*, vol. I, Doc. No. 313, pp. 533–4.

[9] On this, see: Woodward, pp. 203–5.

3. *The Anglo–Polish Talks in London*

In the autumn of 1943, while Bor-Komorowski and his Staff were finally trying to formulate a Home Army attitude to the Russians, high-level Anglo–Polish diplomatic talks were being held in London, on the future of Poland and on ways of ending the Russo–Polish political and territorial *impasse*.

The British Government was anxious to solve the Russo–Polish conflict – because it presented a threat both to the proper functioning of the war-time coalition and to the prospect of post-war co-operation with the U.S.S.R. – and to ensure Stalin's collaboration in the restoration of Poland. The British authorities were also anxious to convince the London Poles of the need to adopt a realistic attitude to Russia, even if that meant curtailing some of their political and territorial ambitions. Eden was very disturbed by the fact that the Poles were 'very difficult about their aspirations', which to him seemed to be 'completely unrealistic'.[1]

The Polish Government, on their part, tried to secure British support for their post-war plans and their stand against Soviet territorial demands; they felt that any suggestion of compromise, on their part, in the dispute over Poland's eastern frontiers would lose them the support of the Polish people and army.[2]

The British attitude to the Polish question was summarised by Churchill during a conversation with the Polish President in July 1943. He said that, while Britain had, undeniably, acted in defence of her own interests in declaring war on Germany, the fact remained that this action had also been one of direct defence of Poland. Great Britain's loyalty to her ally would continue unchanged and Churchill, personally, was prepared to 'take grave risks' in keeping his country's pledge.[3] But he 'had never wanted and was still unwilling to assume any obligations in regard to the Polish frontiers. Frontiers were not a 'taboo' and could be changed, perhaps by population exchange . . .'[4] He realised, however, that Great Britain was under an obligation to restore a strong and independent

---

[1] *Foreign Relations of the United States, Diplomatic Papers 1943*, Vol. III, *The British Commonwealth and Europe* (Washington, 1963). p. 14 (hereafter to be referred to as the *FRUS*).

[2] Despatch from the Prime Minister to the Government Delegate, 25–6 January 1944, Ldz. K519/44. GSHI–11.

[3] Notes on the talk between Premier Churchill and the President of the Republic held on 26 July 1943. GSHI–A.II/49/SOW/6.

[4] *Ibid.*

Poland, 'capable of playing a responsible part in post-war Europe'.[1] Further, he 'did not deny the Polish Government the right to defend the integrity of their state – he realised that this was their duty. But, for his part, he did not wish to conceal his views . . .'[2]

Churchill had earlier urged the Poles to adopt a realistic attitude to Russia because of her 'potentialities' and her 'importance'. He warned them that 'a policy which would provoke the Soviets would be harmful and dangerous' to Poland as she could not hope to exist without coming to terms with the Russians, although they were, as he put it, 'odd people' and at times it was 'difficult to understand fully their motives . . .'[3]

Briefly, then, while accepting that it was his duty to restore a strong and independent Poland, he felt that it would have to be a Poland within frontiers acceptable to the Soviet Union. He was therefore trying to persuade the Polish Government to come to terms with Moscow, even at the expense of great territorial concessions. This was to remain his position until the outbreak of the Warsaw Rising.

Churchill's approach to the Polish problem, was conditioned by his attitude to Russia: he recognised that she was of cardinal importance in the struggle against Germany. While believing that the Soviet Government was capable of being consistent to the point of inhumanity, and of pursuing its end regardless of any moral considerations, unmoved by simple compassion for suffering, he nevertheless rejected as inadmissible the idea of an Allied policy based on shocked outrage.[4] He tried to impress it upon the Poles that the Red Army was playing a crucial role in the liberation of Europe and that this must be taken into account by them all, even though Moscow was using 'ruthless methods and language not customary among friendly states'.

He was thinking about the likely direction of Russia's evolution in the future. He believed that because of the war Russia was changing much more quickly than had been anticipated by the Soviet leadership. He felt unable, however, to predict the final outcome of these changes, 'whether they would lead to more individual freedom and the progress of democracy, or, rather, lend impetus to aggresive imperialism . . .'[5] To Churchill this was the most crucial question.

[1] *Ibid.*   [2] *Ibid.*
[3] Notes on the talk between Premier Mikolajczyk and Premier Churchill held on 21 July 1943. GSHI–PRM, L46.
[4] Notes on the talk between Premier Churchill and the President of the Republic held on 26 July 1943. GSHI–A.II/49/SOW/6.   [5] *Ibid.*

His attitude to Russia was not yet a fixed one. He was mildly hopeful that, in the course of close collaboration with Stalin, for whom he had a certain liking and even admiration, he would be able to shape the future of post-war Europe.[1]

He expected the Poles to co-operate in his work for better and closer relations with the U.S.S.R., for their own and the common benefit.[2] His plan for the solution of the Polish question was simple; by advising and encouraging the Poles to make territorial concessions to the Russians he intended to bring about a *rapprochement* between the two and to persuade Stalin to allow the exiled Government to assume power in liberated Warsaw.

The British design assumed more concrete form in August 1943, when Eden came to the conclusion that 'the Poles should recognise the Curzon Line (including Lwow) as their eastern frontier and should receive as compensation Danzig, East Prussia, and the Oppeln district of Upper Silesia'.[3] In March 1943 Eden found that Roosevelt was willing, privately at least, to accept the Curzon Line as the future Russo–Polish frontier.[4] The British knew that, by agreeing to the imposition on Poland of territorial changes, they would be acting in a way contrary to the Atlantic Charter, but they felt that this was the only way of securing Anglo–Soviet collaboration after the war and of improving Polish–Soviet relations. In September 1943 therefore Eden asked the Polish Premier whether he would consider the re-shaping of the Polish Eastern frontiers as a necessary step towards a Russo–Polish *detente*. Eden advised Mikolajczyk[5] to accept the Curzon Line, extended to give Lwow to Poland, in return for East Prussia and parts of Silesia in the West. Mikolajczyk replied that 'no Polish Government abroad would be able to discuss the question of the reduction of Polish territory'.[6]

It was obvious that the Polish Government was not prepared to discuss the problem of territorial concessions to the U.S.S.R., although any improvement in Polish–Soviet relations demanded this. The Polish Cabinet believed that by refusing to accept the

---

[1] Cf. Lord Moran, *Winston Churchill, The Struggle for Survival 1940–1965* (London, 1966), pp. 190–1.
[2] Notes on the talk between Premier Churchill and the President of the Republic held on 26 July 1943, GSHI-A.11/49/SOW/6.
[3] Woodward, p. 250.   [4] *Ibid.* p. 203; and *FRUS 1943*, vol. III, p. 14.
[5] For details of changes in the Polish leadership see pp. 149ff. of this study.
[6] Report of Ambassador Raczynski on a conversation between Premier Mikolajczyk and Mr A. Eden held on 9 September 1943. GSHI-A11.

Curzon Line they were defending their country's right to existence as a national entity.[1] They were determined that Russo–Polish relations should be restored on the basis of the pre-1939 territorial arrangements.

On 5 October 1943 Mikolajczyk informed Eden that he considered the resumption of Russo–Polish diplomatic relations to be the most important and urgent issue, but was opposed to any discussions about Poland's eastern frontiers; he insisted that, on liberation the entire country should be placed under Polish jurisdiction.[2] He was also opposed to Soviet troops alone occupying territories; he asked that 'the military forces of our Anglo-Saxon allies and friends should enter Poland together with the Soviet troops'.[3] Further, he stated that his Government had to decide what the Polish resistance was to do in the event of Russian entry into Poland during the course of military operations; should the underground army be ordered to assume control of the country, or to remain underground, in view of the threat of possible Soviet repressions? Indeed, Mikolajczyk asserted that, if the Russians employed repressive measures against the underground, it would be obliged to resort to self-defence'.[4] Hence, he argued, it would be essential to conclude a Russo–Polish military understanding after the restoration of diplomatic relations between the two countries. He asked Eden to convey these views to the Russians.

Eden seemed embarrassed and dismayed by the Polish position, which he regarded as unrealistic. He maintained that the Poles could not demand the exercise of their rights in Poland without Moscow's interference while at the same time refusing to discuss territorial problems, especially in view of the well-advertised Soviet claims to some of Poland's eastern provinces. He expected the Soviet Union to adhere 'more or less' to the Curzon Line, with some corrections favourable to Poland which might allow her to retain Lwow. In exchange, the Poles were to obtain East Prussia and the valuable territories of Upper Silesia.

However, Mikolajczyk once again rejected this idea.[5] Asking for increased British supplies of military materials to the Home Army, the Polish Premier said that hitherto he had warned that army

---

[1] *Ibid.*

[2] Note on the talk between Premier Mikolajczyk and Mr A. Eden held on 5 October 1943. GSHI–PRM, L46/9.

[3] *Ibid.*   [4] *Ibid.*   [5] *Ibid.*

against a premature rising, but now they were approaching a point 'when a rising in Poland might have considerable importance from the military point of view', for, if synchronised with the Anglo–American invasion of the continent, it could interrupt for some time the lines of communication between the Eastern and Western Fronts. Nevertheless, he knew that the Poles would have to pay a 'very heavy price' for this advantage, though he considered it was worth it in view of the anticipated results. 'Such an action . . . would require, however, a detailed understanding with the Russians and, therefore, the prompt re-establishment of diplomatic relations between Poland and the Soviet Union was imperative.'[1]

Thus, Mikolajczyk was prepared to try to reach a diplomatic *rapprochement* with the Russians by offering them the prospect of military collaboration; the Home Army and its potentially large-scale anti-German military operations were to break the dangerous deadlock.

Eden welcomed the Polish plan with great interest, as it 'provided an argument which might induce Stalin to re-establish relations with Poland. This would largely depend *on the value Stalin attached to the Polish action at the rear of the German armies* . . .'[2] The Home Army's operations, then, were regarded as being of political as well as military importance.

Eden promised to explain the Polish position at the forthcoming Moscow Conference.[3] On 7 October 1943, before his departure for Moscow, he was told by the Poles that they were ready to re-establish diplomatic relations with the U.S.S.R. but that there should be no discussion of the frontier question. Further, they opposed even temporary occupation of Poland, or any other East European State by the Soviets. The Poles proposed that an Inter-Allied Commission be established to supervise the liberation of the German-occupied territories.[4]

In addition, Edward Raczynski, the Polish Ambassador, explained to Eden that the Poles 'were afraid that the Russians would set up in Poland a puppet communist state . . . If they had such a plan, the surrender of territory would not stop them from carrying it out.

---

[1] Note on the talk between Premier Mikolajczyk and Mr A. Eden held on 5 October 1943. GSHI–PRM, L46/9.
[2] *Ibid*. My italics.   [3] *Ibid*.
[4] Memorandum from the Polish Government to the Foreign Office, 7 October 1943. GSHI–PRM, L46.

Hence the Poles regarded the resumption of Polish–Soviet relations as a test of Russian intentions'.[1]

On 8 October the Polish problem which was becoming increasingly complicated, had been discussed by the British War Cabinet. At this meeting Eden suggested that at Moscow he should say that if the Poles accepted the British solution of the Russo–Polish frontier question, 'we should expect the Soviet Government to resume relations with the Poles, and to co-operate with them and with us in finding a satisfactory solution to questions concerning Polish Underground Resistance, and to the problems created by the Russian support of a rival Polish army and parties in the U.S.S.R. hostile to the Polish Government'. Eden stressed the urgency of the problems concerning the Home Army 'since, with the advance of the Russian armies, fighting might break out between the Polish guerillas and the Russians in eastern Poland'. The problem was especially urgent because the Poles were asking for more British arms for their Home Army; Eden predicted that if the British complied without consulting the Russians, 'they would say that we are equipping a force to be used against them'.[2] Eden thought that any Russian encroachment on Poland's pre-1939 frontiers would be resisted by the Home Army – for the Poles, their main army – but, on the other hand, that army might, if fully equipped, play 'a decisive part in the liberation of Poland and subsequent maintenance of order'.[3] The British War Cabinet accepted Eden's suggested proposals for the solution of the Russo–Polish problem but, in view of the refusal of the Poles to agree to the frontier question being discussed in Moscow and of the American unwillingness to consider territorial frontiers until the end of the war, no progress towards a settlement was made at the Conference.[4]

4. *The Moscow Conference*

Eden was very anxious that a solution to the Russo–Polish difficulties should be found as soon as possible,[5] for he feared that, once the

---

[1] Woodward, p. 252; see also E. Raczynski, *W Sojuszniczym Londynie* (London, 1960), p. 207 (hereafter to be referred to as Raczynski).
[2] Woodward, p. 252.
[3] *Ibid.*   [4] *Ibid.*
[5] The Rt Hon The Earl of Avon K.G., P.C., M.C., *The Eden Memoirs: The Reckoning* (London, 1965), p. 403 (hereafter to be referred to as Avon).

Red Army had established itself in Poland, British negotiating power, 'slender as it was anyway, would amount to very little'.

Therefore, during his stay in Moscow he tried to convince Cordell Hull, the American Secretary of State, of the need to make joint Anglo–American representation to the Russians on the Polish question but without much success.

On 29 October Eden and Hull told Molotov that they hoped for the restoration of Russo–Polish relations. Eden emphasised that Mikolajczyk desired good relations with Moscow, and raised the problem of sending arms to the Home Army. Molotov retorted that 'arms could only be given into safe hands and he doubted if there were any safe hands in Poland', and hinted that the question of Polish–Soviet relations was primarily the concern of those two countries.[1]

On 12 November 1943, Eden reported to Mikolajczyk that Molotov was in favour of a 'strong and independent Poland', and wanted to see relations between Poland and the U.S.S.R. re-established but had expressed the view that progress towards such a *rapprochement* was being impeded by the absence of any manifestation of Polish goodwill towards the U.S.S.R. Finally, Eden tried to convince Mikolajczyk that Moscow had no intention of setting up a Polish puppet Government. Mikolajczyk was unimpressed and remained suspicious of Soviet intentions towards Poland. He was anxious to know who would administer Poland if the Red Army should enter the country, and asked whether this had been discussed in Moscow. Eden told him that the question would be relatively simple if only the territorial question were settled.[2]

The British Government saw little chance of Mikolajczyk's Cabinet assuming power in Poland unless they agreed to the revision of their frontiers with Russia.

On 17 November 1943 Raczynski delivered a memorandum to Eden in which the Polish Government spoke of the urgency of safeguarding their rights to assume the administration of the country as soon as it was liberated from the Germans, and asked for Churchill's intervention with Stalin. Raczynski explained that the memorandum was not Mikolajczyk's 'last word'. The Polish Government could not suggest concessions affecting the future of

[1] Avon, p. 416.
[2] Report on a conversation between Premier Mikolajczyk and Mr Eden held on 12 November 1943. GSHI–PRM, L46/23.

Poland while they were in exile and without the support of the Polish Parliament; the position would be different if 'the friends of Poland were to tell her that she must accept such and such a settlement in order to safeguard the future of the country.' This settlement would have to be guaranteed by London and Washington.

Eden explained to the Poles that at the Teheran Conference it might be possible to try to break the deadlock with the Russians;[1] but nevertheless, he told Mikolajczyk that he should not expect too much from the Conference.[2] Eden also asked the Poles to allow him to mention the frontier problem at Teheran. Mikolajczyk agreed, but wished any discussion about frontiers to include the question of Polish claims in the west. '*He also wanted the Polish Government to be given a chance of expressing their views after consulting their Underground Movement*'.[3] Mikolajczyk was very anxious to see Churchill and Roosevelt before their departure for Teheran to explain his position to them. He was told, however, that such a move might be construed as an attempt to put pressure on the Russians or to prevent Churchill and Roosevelt from jeopardising Polish interests.[4]

Thus, at the end of November 1943 the Polish Government was slowly made to realise that, in order to return to Warsaw, it would have to agree to some territorial concessions. But it wished to make it clear that the acceptance of new frontier arrangements would depend on the existence of Anglo–American guarantees for Poland and on the attitude of the resistance leaders in Warsaw. Mikolajczyk felt that he and his colleagues were 'being subjected to a softening-up process, designed to induce us to make sacrifices for the sake of a compromise'.[5]

5. *The Conference at Teheran: Churchill, Roosevelt and Stalin and the Polish Question*

The Polish problem was discussed during the Teheran Conference, on 28 November and 1 December 1943 and, as a result of these talks, a tentative provisional agreement was reached, between the leaders of the Three Big Powers, as to Poland's future frontiers with the U.S.S.R. This agreement was reached without prior consultation

---

[1] Woodward, pp. 252–3; Avon, pp. 421–2; and Raczynski, p. 212.
[2] Avon, p. 422.   [3] Woodward, p. 253. My italics.
[4] *Ibid.*, p. 252.   [5] Raczynski, p. 212.

with the Polish Government, in spite of Mikolajczyk's insistence to the contrary.

The most decisive step leading to this agreement was taken on the evening of 28 November 1943, during an after-dinner talk between Churchill and Stalin. Churchill himself suggested to Stalin that they should discuss the Polish question.[1] The British were anxious to solve the Polish problem as soon as possible. A difficulty was, however, writes Eden, that the Americans were terrified of the subject because they considered it 'political dynamite' for their Presidential elections in 1944.[2] But the British calculated that failure to reach a solution at Teheran would mean further deterioration in Russo–Polish relations in six months' time, when, they assumed, the Russian army would be in Poland and the American Presidential election certainly more imminent.[3] Churchill told Stalin that the British Government was committed to the re-establishment of a strong and independent Poland but not to any specific Polish frontiers.[4] Churchill assured Stalin that he personally 'had no attachment to any specific frontiers between Poland and the Soviet Union . . .' and 'felt that the consideration of Soviet security on their western frontiers was a governing factor'.[5] He felt

> that it would be very valuable if here in Teheran the representatives of the three governments could work out some agreed understanding on the question of the Polish frontiers which could then be taken up with the Polish Government . . . he would like to see Poland move westward in some manner as soldiers at drill execute the drill 'left close' and illustrated his point with three matches representing the Soviet Union, Poland and Germany.[6]

Stalin reacted cautiously, merely agreeing 'that it would be a good idea to reach an understanding on this question', but saying that the matter required further investigation.[7] Roosevelt was absent during these exchanges.[8]

Roosevelt raised the Polish question on 1 December. In reply to

---

[1] Winston S. Churchill, *The Second World War*, vol. v, *Closing the Ring* (London, 1952), p. 319 (hereafter to be referred to as Churchill).

[2] Avon, p. 427.   [3] *Ibid.*

[4] *Foreign Relations of the United States: Diplomatic Papers, The Conference at Cairo and Teheran, 1943* (Washington, 1961), p. 512 (hereafter to be referred to as *Conference at Teheran*). For Churchill's personal account of the conference with Stalin on Poland see: Churchill, vol. v, pp. 319–20.

[5] *Conference at Teheran*, p. 512.   [6] *Ibid.*

[7] *Ibid.*   [8] Avon, p. 427.

his reference to the need for negotiations leading to the re-establishment of relations between the Polish and Soviet Governments, Stalin claimed that the Polish Government was closely connected with the Germans, and its agents in Poland were killing Soviet partisans. At the same time he pointed out that Russia's security depended on friendly relations with Poland. The Russians were in favour of Poland's reconstitution and expansion at German expense; however, they made a distinction between the Polish Government and Poland. The rift between Russia and Poland, he alleged, was the result, not of a whim, but of Polish involvement, with the Nazis, in slanderous anti-Soviet propaganda. He said that before entering into negotiations with the Poles he would like guarantees that the Polish Government would stop killing partisans, that it would urge the people to fight against the Germans, and would not indulge in intrigues.[1]

Churchill, anxious to settle the territorial question as a prelude to a general improvement in Russo–Polish relations, asked for the Soviet views 'in regard to the frontier question', and said that 'if some reasonable formula could be devised, he was prepared to take it up with the Polish Government in exile, and, without telling them that the Soviet Government would accept such a solution, would offer it to them as probably the best they could obtain'.[2] Indeed, he stated that should the Polish Government refuse to accept this formula, 'then Great Britain would be through with them and certainly would not oppose the Soviet Government under any conditions at the peace table'.[3] Poland must be 'strong and friendly to Russia'.[4] Stalin agreed that this was 'desirable' but added that the only frontier acceptable to the Soviet Government was the 1939 line.[5] Eden pointed out to him that this was the 'Ribbentrop–Molotov' line, but Stalin was unmoved[6]

Roosevelt, no doubt anxious about the Polish vote in the United States, asked whether, in Stalin's opinion, the areas Poland was to gain from Germany were equal to those to be ceded by her to Russia; Stalin, apparently little interested in such subtleties, replied that he did not know. He wanted a solution based on ethnic considerations. Roosevelt seemed satisfied with this and asked whether a transfer

---

[1] *Conference at Teheran*, pp. 597-9.
[2] *Ibid.*, p. 599. For Churchill's personal account of the conference with Stalin and Roosevelt on Poland see: Churchill, vol. v, pp. 348–1.
[3] *Conference at Teheran*, p. 599.   [4] *Ibid.*
[5] *Ibid.*   [6] *Ibid.*

of population on a voluntary basis could be arranged. Stalin said that 'such a transfer was entirely possible'.[1]

Churchill was not satisfied with such generalities and pressed for a more concrete arrangement. He proposed 'that Poland should obtain equal compensation in the west, including East Prussia and frontiers on the Oder, to compensate for the areas which would be in the Soviet Union.'[2]

Stalin said that if the Russians were given the northern part of East Prussia he would accept the Curzon Line as the frontier between the two countries. Here, discussion of the future Russo–Polish frontiers ended. It was understood that the British were going to urge Mikclajczyk to accept the Curzon Line settlement.[3] Indeed, Churchill was to play an important role in trying to bring about a Russo–Polish understanding, for 'Roosevelt was reserved about Poland to the point of being unhelpful'.[4] During the entire Conference, his behaviour on the Polish question was very strange, and even sinister. The American Presidential elections cast a shadow over his approach to the problem and he even explained his difficulties to Stalin, although without notifying the British or the Poles that he had done so.[5] Roosevelt told the Russian leader that he agreed with his solution of the Polish question but that, in view of the six to seven million-strong 'Polish' vote in the United States, as a 'practical man', he felt unable to participate in any decision on the subject in Teheran, or even the following winter.[6] Stalin said that he understood the President's position.[7] Roosevelt's contribution to discussion of the Polish problem was 'hardly calculated to restrain the Russians'.[8]

To Churchill the Polish problem was mainly a matter of honour; he wished to discharge Britain's obligations to Poland. He was also concerned to prevent the emergence of a Russian-dominated government in Warsaw. To Stalin it was a question of State security. To Roosevelt it was a question of electoral strategy – the London Poles, therefore, stood to gain little real support from him. Both Churchill and Stalin wanted a strong Poland, friendly to Russia. In 1944 both tried to create such a Poland. Churchill believed, however, that a Poland governed by Mikolajczyk could be friendly to Russia, but Stalin had doubts about this.

---

[1] *Conference at Teheran*, p. 600.
[2] *Ibid.*, p. 603.
[3] *Ibid.*, p. 604.
[4] Avon, p. 427.
[5] *Ibid.*, pp. 427–8.
[6] *Conference at Teheran*, p. 594.
[7] *Ibid.*
[8] Avon, p. 428.

The British wanted to solve the Russo–Polish question before the Red Army's entry into Poland and before preparations for the American presidential elections paralysed United States diplomacy. This paralysis had, however, begun to set in before Teheran, while Russian dilatoriness in moving towards a settlement was probably due to the confident expectation that the Russian position regarding Poland would soon be strengthened by the arrival there of the Red Army. Russia's role as Poland's liberator would entitle her to a louder voice in that country's political life; the Russians' physical presence there would allow them to ensure that this entitlement did not go unrecognised, especially as the Polish Communists were already thinking of establishing a political authority opposed to the London Government.

Finally, the decision, made at Teheran, to open the main Second Front in France ensured that Poland would be liberated by the Red Army and not by Anglo–American forces, as the London Poles had previously assumed.[1]

The diplomatic and military decisions reached in Teheran were, then, of the utmost importance for the subsequent course of events in Poland.

6. *Eden and Mikolajczyk*

In the period between the ending of the Teheran Conference and the outbreak of the insurrection in Warsaw British diplomacy tried in vain to achieve a solution of the Polish question on the lines provisionally agreed upon by the Big Three in Persia. Both Churchill and Eden played a crucial part in these efforts, but they were thwarted by Polish intransigence, Russia's profound distrust of the London Poles, and America's reluctance to become too deeply embroiled in the Russo–Polish conflict.

During the first weeks of 1944, because of Churchill's illness and his absence from England, it fell mainly to Eden to try to bring about a Russo–Polish *rapprochement*, until, at the end of January, this role was assumed directly by Churchill himself.[2]

On 17 December 1943 Eden told Raczynski that after the recent discussions with Stalin it was 'clear that there were two aspects of

---

[1] For the discussion of the military decisions taken at Teheran see: John Ehrman, *Grand Strategy*, vol. v, *August 1943–September 1944* (London, 1956), pp. 173ff.
[2] Churchill, vol. v, p. 398.

the Polish–Russian problem. The resumption of relations was one and the future status of Poland, with her frontiers, was another.'[1] He also mentioned Stalin's allegations that the Polish Government had instructed its underground 'not to co-operate with the Russian partisans' and of his 'accusation of collaboration with the Germans'. Raczynski explained to Eden

> that owing to the severe German reprisals, the Poles had recently restricted themselves to action against the most prominent and criminal Germans. On the other hand, the Russians had been dropping agents all over Poland, who by their activities brought down reprisals on the population. It was inevitable that there should be some feeling against them. There was also the danger that Russian agents might penetrate the Polish underground organisation and break it up when the Soviet armies arrived.

Nevertheless, the Ambassador was certain that 'his Government would be able to draw up a declaration refuting Stalin's allegations and proposing co-operation'. Eden approved of this course.[2]

Three days later, on 20 December, Eden saw Mikolajczyk and urged him to enter into military co-operation with the Russians. He also assured him that the despatch of military equipment to the Home Army was being delayed only by obstacles of a technical nature. The Polish Premier was sceptical, however, as to whether military co-operation could produce any significant and lasting improvements in Russo–Polish relations, as attempts to implement it must lead to a clash over the territorial issue. But he reluctantly agreed that it could be tried.[3]

The British were in favour of such co-operation between Poland and Russia as it might lead to the restoration of Russo–Polish diplomatic relations and, even if unsuccessful, might tend to strengthen Poland's position.

Eden maintained that an effort had to be made to dispel the Russo–Polish fears and he advised the Polish Government to formulate their military policies and propositions in such a way as to show Stalin that his evaluation of the situation in Poland was wrong.

Mikolajczyk saw no need for such a declaration but he agreed

[1] Avon, p. 434.
[2] *Ibid*.
[3] Report on the talk between Mikolajczyk and Eden held on 20 December 1943. GSHI–L47.

to issue it, provided that it stressed the continuity of the Polish war-effort. Eden agreed, and emphasised that 'there was no time to lose', especially as he and Churchill had gained the impression in Teheran that an understanding with the Soviets over Poland might be possible.[1] But, he told Mikolajczyk, the Soviets insisted that the Curzon Line must be the basis for the new Russo–Polish frontier, while the River Oder was to serve as Poland's post-war frontier with Germany. In addition, Poland was to obtain East Prussia and Danzig.

Mikolajczyk was opposed, however, to the proposed new Russo–Polish frontier and stressed the importance for Poland of the Wilno and Lwow regions. Eden tried to make the new solution more appealing to him by explaining that the Poles would be able to expel all the Germans from the territories acquired in the west without any demur from the Big Three.[2]

Finally, Mikolajczyk told Eden of his intention to visit Roosevelt in the middle of January 1944. Eden was very interested in this plan but asked Mikolajczyk to postpone the visit until the return to London of Churchill, who wished to see the Polish Premier. Mikolajczyk agreed to this.[3]

Two days later Eden saw Mikolajczyk again. He was anxious to be given a British appraisal of the Soviet war potential; was the U.S.S.R. exhausted by the war and running out of reserves? Eden denied this, pointing out that the Soviets had powerful resources and well-equipped, enthusiastic and ambitious armies. Indeed, he maintained that although the post-war world would not be divided into 'the spheres of influence', after the defeat of Germany the Soviet Union would, in view of its great strength, have 'tremendous influence on the decisions affecting Europe.'[4]

Mikolajczyk repeated his demand that British troops should be sent to Poland when the Red Army entered the country, but Eden rejected it on the ground that the presence of British units in Poland would not resolve all the difficulties.

With regard to the territorial issues, Eden defended the shifting of the Polish frontiers farther west and the principle of compensation at Germany's expense for Polish losses in the east. Nevertheless, he thought that it would be inadvisable for Poland to try to acquire all the ex-German territories east of the Oder, although he was

[1] *Ibid.*   [2] *Ibid.*
[3] *Ibid.*   [4] *Ibid.*

prepared to leave this matter to the discretion of the Polish Government.

Mikolajczyk was not prepared to accept such a solution. He said that his Government could not agree to a plan which was unjust, especially in view of Poland's great sufferings and sacrifices for the common cause. Eden said that the whole matter would be discussed again after Churchill's return to England.[1]

Meanwhile, the London Poles came to the conclusion that the British Government was pursuing 'a policy of appeasement' towards Russia, that its mediations in Russo–Polish affairs would be fruitless, and they were hopeful that the 'British–Soviet disagreements' would come to a climax sooner than had been expected.[2] Sustained by these hopes, the Polish Government was not in conciliatory mood. They believed that time, far from being against them, as the British thought, was on their side.

Yet there were certain indications that the Russians were ready, at that time, to negotiate.

The British received several hints that the Russians would like to 'deal directly with the Poles'. The Czechoslovak President, Eduard Benes, 'conveyed the same impression' on his return from Moscow.[3] In fact, Benes urged Mikolajczyk to reach an understanding with Russia and offered his services as an intermediary.[4]

Meanwhile, on 30 December 1943, the Poles submitted their military plans to Eden. The note stated that since the beginning of the war Poland had been engaged in 'an uncompromising life and death struggle against Germany'. The Polish people and their leaders had 'consistently refused to collaborate with the Germans in any way'. The Polish Government had instructed the Home Army to stage 'a general rising' in co-operation with the Allies. But the implementation of this instruction demanded the co-ordination of the projected insurrectionary operations with 'the strategic plans of the Allies'. The note stated most categorically that the Home Army was not murdering Communists in Poland on the order of the Polish Government. Further, the note expressed the Polish Government's readiness to begin talks with the Soviet Government on the co-ordination of the 'political and military' conduct of the

[1] Report on the talk between Mikolajczyk and Eden held on 22 December 1943. GSHI–L47. For Churchill's views on the Polish question at the time see: Churchill, vol. v, pp. 398–9.   [2] Raczynski, p. 217.   [3] Avon, p. 435.
[4] Eduard Benes, *Memoirs* (Boston, 1954), pp. 266ff.

war against Germany. Finally, it proposed that Polish military operations 'should be included in the general strategic plans of the Allies'. The detailed planning of these operations was to be undertaken jointly, 'by the representatives of the Polish, British and American General Staffs'.[1]

In effect, the Poles were proposing that the Home Army and its strategic designs should be integrated into the Anglo–American grand strategy in the war against Germany and, thus, be saved from the possibility of destruction by the approaching Russians.

On 5 January Eden communicated the text of the Polish note of 30 December to the Soviet Ambassador, for transmission to Moscow.[2]

In spite of their secret fears and reservations about Russo–Polish co-operation and their doubts about the likelihood of an understanding being reached between Mikolajczyk and Stalin, the Polish Government had, on 5 January published an official declaration expressing an unreserved wish to enter into military co-operation with the Russians. This declaration was broadcast to Poland by Mikolajczyk a day after the Red Army's entry into Poland.

Mikolajczyk said that the Polish Government expected that the U.S.S.R. would respect the rights and interests of Poland and her citizens. The Polish Government instructed the Home Army to intensify their resistance against the Germans, to avoid all conflicts with the Soviet armies entering Poland, and to enter into co-operation with the Soviet Commanders in the event of the resumption of Polish–Soviet relations.

The Premier stressed that, if a Polish–Soviet agreement such as his Government had declared itself willing to conclude had preceded the crossing of the frontier by Soviet forces, the Home Army would have been able to co-ordinate its anti-German operations with the Soviet Command. The Polish Government still considered such an agreement highly desirable.[3]

The statement was well received by pro-London circles in Poland. It was hailed as proof of the complete unanimity between the Government in London and the Polish nation. The Government Delegate, Jankowski, assured Mikolajczyk that the entire nation

---

[1] Aide-Memoire of the Polish Government to the Foreign Office, 30 December 1943. GSHI–A.11/49/SOW/6.
[2] Minutes of a talk between Romer and Eden held on 6 January 1944. GSHI–L47.
[3] Mikolajczyk's broadcast to Poland, 6 January 1944. GSHI–A.10.9/3.

supported his efforts to restore 'good neighbourly relations with Russia'. At the same time, Jankowski stressed, the Polish nation insisted most strongly on the 'inviolability' of the pre-war Russo–Polish frontier and expected the Russians to respect Poland's sovereign rights in eastern Poland. He referred to Poland's confidence that the support of her Western Allies would be forthcoming should there be any questioning of any part of her territory. For her part, faithful to her obligations, Poland would continue to fight against Germany until victory had been achieved, and peace and freedom for the rest of the world had been established.[1]

Thus, the highest authorities in the underground movement were asking Mikolajczyk to perform impossible diplomatic gymnastics; on the one hand he was asked to stand firm against Soviet territorial demands and to try to enlist Anglo–American support for this policy, while on the other he was being encouraged to reach an understanding with a Stalin who was adamantly insisting on the revision of the Russo–Polish frontier. Further, the weakness of the Home Army's position in a Warsaw still occupied by the Germans hardly justified the expression, at this time, of such an intransigent attitude on the territorial question. First, Poland had to be freed from the Germans. Only a co-operative attitude towards Russia could have brought liberation expeditiously and with minimum sacrifice. In the circumstances, co-operation without territorial concession was a chimera. The underground authorities themselves were aware that the Red Army's entry into the country without a previous understanding with the Polish Government constituted a 'grave and difficult situation' for Poland,[2] yet they seemed unable to draw the logical inference that the main route out of the 'situation' lay in persuading Mikolajczyk to reach a practical understanding with Moscow, even at the expense, if necessary, of painful territorial sacrifices.

On 7 January 1944 Stalin told Churchill that he had strong doubts as to whether it would be possible for the British to 'bring Poland to reason'.[3] Four days later, on 11 January the official Soviet reply to the Polish declaration was issued.

[1] Despatch from the Government Delegate and the Council of National Unity to the Prime Minister, 8 January 1944, Ldz. 322. GSHI–L9.
[2] *Ibid.*
[3] Woodward, p. 280; see also: From Premier J. V. Stalin to the Prime Minister, Mr Winston Churchill, 7 January 1944, No. 222 as quoted in *Correspondence*

The Russians questioned Polish claims to the pre-war eastern territories of Poland which in 1939 were incorporated into the U.S.S.R. They proposed a frontier running approximately along the Curzon Line which provided for the incorporation of the Western Ukraine and White Russia into the Soviet Union and of districts in which Polish population predominated into Poland.

They claimed that the Polish Government had proved incapable of establishing friendly relations with Moscow and of organising an active anti-German resistance. They stressed, however, the need for the establishment of friendly relations between Poland and the U.S.S.R. and unity of their people in the common struggle against Germany.[1]

The Polish Government considered the Soviet reply to be not 'completely negative'. The fact that the Soviets did not regard the 1939 frontier as unchangeable led them to believe that the reply did not 'shut the door completely to the discussion of the eastern frontier'.[2]

In Warsaw, however, the Soviet statement was received by the leaders of the resistance in a highly critical and hostile manner and evoked emphatic resolution to defend the integrity of Poland against Soviet encroachments.[3]

In view of the international and strategic situation statements of this kind could hardly produce any direct effect on the policies of the three Great Powers towards Poland, other than in convincing them that they were dealing with an unrealistic and obstinate people. Another effect was a tendency to stiffen Mikolajczyk's opposition to the acceptance of the Curzon Line. He was being subjected to two mutually opposed pressures emanating from three different sources, London, Moscow and Warsaw. Had it not been obvious before, it was now made clear that Mikolajczyk's highly placed followers in Poland were not prepared even to discuss the possible frontier changes

---

between the Chairman of the Council of Ministers of the U.S.S.R. and the Presidents of the U.S.A. and the Prime Minister of Great Britain during the Great Patriotic War of 1941–1945, two vols in one (London, 1958), vol. I, p. 182 (hereafter to be referred to as *Correspondence*).
[1] The Soviet Government declaration of 11 January 1944; *Soviet Monitor*, No. 4083 of 11.1.1944.
[2] Rozek, p. 187.
[3] Despatch from the Government Delegate and the Council of National Unity to the Prime Minister, dated 15 January 1944, received 7 February 1944, No. 490. GSHI–PRM, L9.

with Russia, let alone accept the Curzon Line as demanded by Stalin and urged by Churchill and Eden.

The British Government saw Moscow's declaration as 'not un-reasonable . . ., except for its repetition of an attack on the Polish Government.'[1] They believed that the Russians were making con-cessions and that their statement gave a degree of latitude in relation to the frontier dispute.[2] Indeed, on 11 January Eden told Miko-lajczyk that the Soviet declaration opened new possibilities for reaching an understanding between Poland and Russia, and warned him against 'returning a sharp or hostile reply'.[3] He made it clear to the Poles that it was imperative that they should reach an agree-ment with the Russians for this was the only way to ensure their return to Poland as a 'legitimate government'. Otherwise, he feared that the Soviets would establish a new government in Poland and this would create an impossible situation for all concerned.[4] The Poles thought that he was warning them that, if they refused to negotiate with the Russians, at this stage, the British Government would not be able to support them, 'but would regard itself as having discharged . . . its obligation towards Poland'.[5] Mikolajczyk was, nevertheless, not prepared to consider any proposition that suggested the Curzon Line as an equitable settlement of the frontier problem and was highly suspicious of the Soviets.[6]

After the meeting Eden informed Washington that the Poles were in a kind of 'suicide mind'.[7]

On 13 January he again tried to overcome Mikolajczyk's reluct-ance to negotiate with the Russians by a mixture of warnings and promises. He even read to him Churchill's telegram forcefully urging negotiation.[8] Churchill was convinced that the British should not support the Poles unless Mikolajczyk supported the Teheran decisions. Eden, more sympathetic towards Mikolajczyk, was in-

---

[1] Avon, pp. 435–6.
[2] The Ambassador in the United Kingdom (Winant) to the Secretary of State, 11 January 1944. *FRUS 1944*, vol. III, p. 1224.
[3] Raczynski, p. 220.
[4] Record of a talk between Mikolajczyk and Eden, 11 January 1944. GSHI–PRM, L47.
[5] Raczynski, p. 220.
[6] Record of a talk between Mikolajczyk and Eden, 11 January 1944. GSHI–PRM, L47.
[7] The Ambassador in the United Kingdom (Winant) to the Secretary of State, 11 January 1944. *FRUS 1944*, vol. III, p. 1224.
[8] Raczynski, p. 221; and Woodward, p. 279.

clined to believe that 'the real aim of the Russians was to set up a
Polish Government which would give them the control of the Polish
territory up to the German frontier'.[1] Nevertheless, Eden continued
his efforts to solve the Russo–Polish dispute.

On 13 January he discussed with Mikolajczyk the Polish reply
to the recent Soviet statement; as a result of this talk an Anglo–
Polish agreement was reached as to its text, and the reply was handed
in next day by Eden to the Soviet Ambassador, Gusev.[2]

It stressed that the determined anti-German struggle waged by
the Polish nation under the direction of their Government provided
a 'complete answer' to Soviet accusations. While the Polish Government could not recognise unilateral decisions which had or might
take place in Poland, they were striving for a Polish–Soviet agreement which would be acceptable to both sides, and were willing to
discuss with Moscow the solution of 'all outstanding questions'.[3]

When handling the note to Gusev, Eden explained that the Polish
Government was prepared to discuss the territorial settlement with
the U.S.S.R., although it 'could not be expected to accept the
Curzon Line before negotiations started'. Eden 'asked Gusev to
tell his Government that they should not reject this offer', which he
believed 'was sincerely meant and which at last offered a chance of
negotiations leading to a settlement of differences which were acutely
embarrassing to us all'.[4] But the Soviet Ambassador was not
receptive.[5]

On 15 January the American Government instructed Averell
Harriman, their Ambassador in Moscow, to ask the Russians to
consider favourably the Polish offer of discussions in the interests
of 'general international co-operation' and of the 'common war
effort'. The Ambassador was told to express to the Russians the
American Government's willingness to extend its 'good offices' for
the initiation of the Russo–Polish discussions, leading to resumption
of diplomatic relations between Poland and the U.S.S.R.[6]

On 17 January 1944, the Soviet Government replied to the latest

[1] Woodward, pp. 279–80.
[2] Raczynski, p. 221; and Avon, p. 436.
[3] The Declaration of the Polish Government of 13 January 1944. GSHI–PRM,
L47.
[4] Avon, p. 436.
[5] The Ambassador in the United Kingdom (Winant) to the Secretary of State
19 January 1944. *FRUS 1944*, vol. III, p. 1227.
[6] The Secretary of State to the Ambassador in the Soviet Union (Harriman),
15 January 1944. *FRUS 1944*, vol. III, p. 1228.

Polish declaration, which they regarded as a refusal to accept the Curzon Line. Further, they rejected the offer of negotiations arguing, that they could not negotiate with a Government with which 'diplomatic relations had been severed', because of its 'active participation in the hostile, anti-Soviet, slanderous campaign . . . in connection with the murders at Katyn'.

Moscow considered the Polish note as yet another proof that the present Polish Government did not wish to establish friendly relations with Russia.[1]

To Eden, this reply 'was like a blow in the face'.[2] All his efforts had been in vain;[3] the Russians were not prepared to negotiate with the existing Polish Government. On 18 January Molotov told Harriman that Moscow could neither deal, nor establish permanent friendly relations with the Polish Government because it 'contained Fascist elements'. The Russians wanted 'a new government of "honest" men, untainted by Fascism and well disposed towards the Soviet Union'.[4] They were prepared to accept Mikolajczyk as the Premier of a reconstituted Polish Government, but insisted that the resumption of Russo–Polish diplomatic relations depended upon the acceptance by the Poles of the Curzon Line.[5]

If Mikolajczyk wished to reach agreement with Stalin, then, he had to comply with two conditions, acceptance of the Curzon Line and the reconstruction of his Cabinet. It was clear that the Russians fundamentally distrusted Mikolajczyk's Government 'because of their knowledge of the hostile attitude toward the Soviet Union of all its members' which was 'freely and openly expressed in London'. They were convinced that no lasting and fruitful relationship could be established with it.[6] Indeed, the Russians had such contempt for the Polish Government that they could not believe it to be capable of organising 'an underground movement of any substance'. They believed that the underground would, in any case, be 'used to establish the Polish Government in power rather than

[1] The Declaration of the Soviet Government of 17 January 1944. GSHI–PRM, L47.
[2] Avon, p. 436.
[3] The Ambassador to the United Kingdom (Winant) to the Secretary of State, 19 January 1944. *FRUS 1944*, vol. III, p. 1227.
[4] The Ambassador in the Soviet Union (Harriman) to the Secretary of State, 18 January 1944. *FRUS 1944*, vol. III, p. 1230.
[5] *Ibid.*, p. 1231.
[6] The Ambassador in the Soviet Union (Harriman) to the Secretary of State, 21 January 1944. *FRUS 1944*, vol. III, p. 1232.

to fight against the Germans'.[1] Moscow, then, considered the Home Army as potentially an anti-Soviet rather than an anti-German force and saw no pressing military reasons for establishing co-operation with it. This evaluation of the Home Army undoubtedly influenced the Soviet attitude to it in the months to come.

Briefly, the chances of achieving a Russo–Polish understanding acceptable both to Mikolajczyk and to Stalin were very slight. There are indications, however, that the situation was not utterly hopeless; on 21 January 1944 Harriman reported to Washington that, failing the construction of a new Government in London, led by Miko-lajczyk and accepting the Curzon Line, the Soviet Government would support an entirely new administration in Poland; Washington should try to effect a reconstituted Polish Government in London. In his opinion, as yet there was no indication that Stalin wished to establish Communist government in Poland; indeed there was 'some indication to the contrary'.[2]

It fell to Churchill to try to explore this possibility and to attempt to achieve a Russo–Polish understanding – as he put it, 'to bring the Poles to reason'.[3] He addressed himself to this task with no great relish, but with determination and a sense of urgency.[4] In his talks with Mikolajczyk he was often blunt and heated.

7. *Churchill and Mikolajczyk*

On 20 January 1944 Churchill personally outlined his plans for Poland to Mikolajczyk.[5] He asked him to agree 'not only in principle but with enthusiasm' to the Curzon Line and to accept compensation in East Prussia, Danzig, Pomerania, up to the Oder line, and in Upper Silesia. He was aware that this would be very hard for the Poles but,

> as a friend of their country, he was convinced that this was the best they could hope for. Personally he thought it offered a fair solution. Poland would obtain valuable territory . . . It would place Poland in the position of rendering great service to the future of Europe; they would be the guardians of Europe against Germany on the east and that would

[1] *Ibid.*   [2] *Ibid.*, p. 1233.
[3] Woodward, p. 280.   [4] Avon, p. 437.
[5] Agreed record of conversation between the Polish Prime Minister, the Polish Minister for Foreign Affairs and the Prime Minister, the Secretary of State and Permanent Under-Secretary of State for Foreign Affairs held on 20 January 1944. GSHI–PRM, L47.

ensure a friendly Russia. Moreover, the territory which they would then possess would make it possible for Poland to live as a strong and independent State.

As to whether the Polish move to the west would lead to future conflict with Germany, 'his answer would be that the United Nations would see to it that all unwanted Germans would be removed from the territory and transferred to Poland, and that Germany herself would be disarmed and mutilated to an extent that would render it impossible for her to commit any further aggression against Poland.'

He warned the Poles that it was 'unthinkable', 'useless to imagine' that Great Britain would "go to war with the Soviet Union over the Polish eastern frontier, and the United States would certainly never do so'.

He also warned Mikolajczyk that although he was now saying these things privately 'he would not hesitate if necessary to repeat them in public'.[1]

Mikolajczyk stood firmly by his own formula for the solution of the Russo–Polish conflict: first, the resumption of diplomatic relations and then negotiations on territorial issues. He said that the Polish Government 'regarded the question of frontiers as open for discussion', but the problem was, nevertheless, 'very difficult not only from a legal point of view but also from a practical point of view: the territorial question must be reserved for decision by the Polish people. To accept in advance the other party's point of view was to exclude all idea of negotiation.' The problem must be seen as a revision of the Riga Treaty, as only that Treaty validly governed the Polish frontiers. He was prepared to accept the revised Riga Line as the new Russo–Polish frontier, but not the Curzon Line. He argued that the enormous transfer of population which would be involved rendered the settlement contemplated a most radical one; the less Poland's frontiers, eastern and western, were modified, the smaller would be the scale of resulting migration, with all the attendant sufferings and difficulties for the population affected. However, that difficulty might be reduced if Poland's future could be assured by 'political and other guarantees'.[2]

Churchill promised that if an agreement could be reached it

---

[1] Agreed record of conversation between the Polish Prime Minister, the Polish Minister for Foreign Affairs and the Prime Minister, the Secretary of State and Permanent Under-Secretary of State for Foreign Affairs held on 20 January 1944. GSHI–PRM, L47.

[2] *Ibid.*

would be defended by the three Great Powers. While recognising that these frontier changes would certainly involve large-scale population transfer he felt that 'they offered the best hope for Poland'. He reminded the Polish leaders that they were not the masters of their own country and its destiny, and that they and their nation must accommodate themselves to the new solution as being the only way out of their dilemma. Russia's war-sacrifices had earned her a say in the matter. Indeed, Britain alone could not have saved Poland; Russia had made this possible. He suggested that the westward move should be presented to the Polish nation at large not as a surrender but as an act of service in that it would defend Europe against 'German eastward expansion'.

Churchill reminded Mikolajczyk of present realities. There was, after all, 'not much room for negotiation'. The Russian armies were advancing and if a settlement were not reached the situation might become impossible, with the power of decision finally transferred to Russian hands alone.

For these reasons he asked Mikolajczyk to authorise him to inform Stalin of his readiness to negotiate on the basis of the Curzon Line and compensations in the west. If Mikolajczyk agreed, Churchill promised 'to protest strongly against the Soviet tendency to call in question the authority of the Polish Government recognised by His Majesty's Government'.

Churchill repeated his warning that, without a settlement, 'Poland would be exposed to Russian wrath . . .'[1]

For his part, Mikolajczyk said that, while appreciating the strength of Churchill's arguments and recognising the inevitability of frontier changes, he felt compelled to point out his own difficulties. 'His position would be impossible unless he could tell the Polish nation that Poland would emerge from the war undiminished.' In his opinion the solution suggested demanded many painful sacrifices from Poland, not only territorial but also economic. He still preferred that negotiations with the Russians should be started on the basis of the pre-war frontier, particularly in view of the difficulties involved in the cession of Wilno and Lwow.[2]

Churchill replied that the British Government had opposed the awarding of Wilno to Poland at the last peace settlement, and although Lwow might be a Polish city, it was surrounded by country that was not mainly Polish.[3]

[1] *Ibid.*   [2] *Ibid.*   [3] *Ibid.*

The Polish Premier then referred to the Soviet 'apparent desire to interfere in Polish internal affairs', which, to him, indicated a Russian wish to make Poland eventually part of the U.S.S.R. Churchill maintained that such a possibility 'would be an argument for reaching a settlement now: if the matter were delayed that might be indeed the ultimate result . . .'[1]

Changing his ground, Mikolajczyk at this stage asked whether the solution of the Polish–Soviet problem might not be more usefully initiated by agreement on military co-operation between the Red Army and the Polish underground. He referred also to the question of supplying arms to the resistance, in view of the projected anti-German rising. In spite of Polish reminders of the urgent need for these arms, supplies had been 'practically suspended for several months'. Churchill said he would certainly 'urge the question of Soviet co-operation with the Home Army' and 'promised to do what might be possible to supply arms' to Bor-Komorowski's forces.[2]

From these exchanges between Churchill and Mikolajczyk it transpired that Churchill's idea of post-war Poland was that of a non-Communist country acceptable to Moscow, a permanent bastion in the way of German expansion to the east. The fact that Poland's western gains would be Germany's losses would tend to inch his new Poland toward closer association with Russia. 'Looked at in one way', writes Professor Feis,

> Poland was being invited to be a protector of the peace and staunch cooperator in preventing any further assertion of German will . . . Looked at in the reverse way, the Poles were to be bound to remain in association with the Soviet Union whether they liked it or not, because Germany, if and as it ever recovered, would feel injured by both. Poland would never again be able, as it had between the two wars, to try to stand as a neutral between Germany and the Soviet Union, disliking and fearing them both, and ready to conspire against either of them.[3]

This was the deeper sense and meaning of Churchill's proposals. To the London Poles, however, the prospect of a Poland dependent

---

[1] Agreed record of conversation between the Polish Prime Minister, the Polish Minister for Foreign Affairs and the Prime Minister, the Secretary of State and Permanent Under-Secretary of State for Foreign Affairs held on 20 January 1944. GSHI–PRM, L47.

[2] *Ibid.*　　　　　　　　　　　　　　　　[3] Feis, p. 288.

upon Moscow for protection and survival was an anathema hard to reconcile with their conception of Polish independence, dignity and honour. Their vision was of a post-war Poland linked to and protected by the West, free from too great a dependence on Moscow. The gulf was great between these two conceptions and it was Churchill's task to try to convert the Poles to his solution as the only realistic proposition open to them. By agreeing to accept the Curzon Line as their new frontier with the U.S.S.R. they were to end, once and for all, their long-standing territorial feud with Moscow. The cession of Wilno and Lwow – two old centres of Polish culture and learning in the eastern provinces – was to be the price they had to pay for a lasting *rapprochement* with Russia and a safeguard against a new Molotov–Ribbentrop Pact. Had Mikolejczyk made such a move at this time it might have provided the basis for a non-Communist post-war Poland, at least for a time.

Mikolajczyk discussed Churchill's plans with his Cabinet on 20 January and decided that before replying to Churchill he would have to consult both the underground leaders in Warsaw and the Americans.[1] It was also decided to submit a formal memorandum to the British Government, concerning its guarantees for new solutions. These moves indicated that, unwilling to agree on his own responsibility to Churchill's urgent request that he should negotiate with Stalin on the basis of the Curzon Line, Mikolajczyk had decided to play for time, in spite of the facts that the Red Army was already in Poland and Bor-Komorowski was mustering his troops for their great battle against the Germans. On 23 January Raczynski handed to Eden a letter formulating Polish demands and 'requests for assurances':[2]

The Poles wished to know, in particular, whether the British could guarantee that the Polish authorities would take over the administration of Poland when she was liberated from the Germans; that the Polish and Allied contingents would participate in the occupation of Poland; and, that the Polish territories would be evacuated as soon as hostilities were over?

Further, they wished to know whether they could expect British and, if possible, American guarantees of the territorial integrity and political sovereignity of Poland and, assurances that none of the Three Big Powers would claim the right to establish bases in Poland? The Poles also wanted guarantees that the transfer of the ex-German

[1] Rozek, p. 196.   [2] Raczynski, p. 229.

territories to Poland would be permanent, that all Germans would be removed from Poland and, finally, asked the British Government to protect and help to repatriate all Polish citizens residing in the U.S.S.R., or territories under the Soviet control?[1]

The British reply to these demands was reserved: the British Government would be able to answer the Polish questions only after consultation with other governments and when agreement between Poland and the Soviet Union was reached.[2]

A few days later Mikolajczyk submitted basically similar questions to President Roosevelt.[3] Roosevelt's reply was non-committal and evasive: although be guardedly advised the Poles to reach an understanding with Moscow 'without delay', he did not press them to accept the Curzon Line.[4] Because of the seriousness of the situation it might be held that he was doing the Poles great disservice by not advising them more strongly to negotiate with the Russians on the basis of the Curzon Line, although he was urged to do so by his own Ambassador in Moscow.[5] It would seem that, again, the approaching presidential elections were dictating his anxiety to leave such unpleasant and politically inconvenient problems to Churchill. Mikolajczyk was of this opinion, and informed Jankowski accordingly.[6] Similarly, he faithfully reported to Warsaw Churchill's views and proposals, as communicated to him on 20 January, and invited the opinions and comments of the underground leaders. He asked them to advise him whether he should accept the Curzon Line as the basis for negotiations with the U.S.S.R., bearing in mind that Great Britain and the United States were not going to fight for the Polish eastern frontiers and that it was possible that a pro-Soviet Government would be established in Warsaw if he refused to talk to the Russians at all.[7] Warsaw's reply was, as usual,

---

[1] Memorandum from the Polish Government to the Foreign Office, 23 January 1944. GSHI-PRM, L47.
[2] Letter from the Foreign Secretary to the Polish Ambassador, 1 February 1944. GSHI–PRM, L47.
[3] Memorandum from the Polish Government to President Roosevelt, 23 January 1944. GSHI–PRM, L47.
[4] The United States Government's reply to the Polish Government's Memorandum of 23 January 1944, dated 2 February 1944. GSHI–PRM, L47.
[5] The Ambassador in the Soviet Union (Harriman) to the Secretary of State, 11 January 1944. *FRUS 1944*, vol. III, p. 1224.
[6] Despatch from the Prime Minister to the Government Delegate, 8 February 1944. GSHI–PRM, L47.
[7] Despatch from the Prime Minister to the Government Delegate, 25–6 January 1944, Ldz. K591/44. GSHI–L11.

couched in most intransigent terms. If Mikolajczyk was inclined to give consideration to the idea of negotiating on the basis of the Curzon Line, the leaders in Warsaw were not.[1]

Meanwhile, Churchill told Stalin about his talks with Mikolajczyk and the questions which the Polish Government had submitted to the British. He informed Stalin that he had advised the Polish Government to accept the new frontier proposals, which they 'were very far from rejecting'. He mentioned that they were 'deeply concerned about the relations between the Polish underground and the advancing Soviet forces, it being understood that their prime desire was to assist in driving out the Germans'.[2] Finally, he stressed the need for good relations 'between whatever forces can speak for Poland and the Soviet Union'. He warned: 'The creation in Warsaw of another Polish Government . . . together with disturbances in Poland, would raise an issue in Great Britain and the United States detrimental to the close accord between the three Great Powers upon which the future of the world depends.'[3]

On 2 February Stalin told Sir Archibald Clark Kerr, the British Ambassador in Moscow, that he required, from Mikolajczyk's Cabinet, a statement that they definitely accepted the Curzon Line, and that he required the reconstruction of the Polish Government before Russo–Polish relations could be resumed. He was critical of the Polish Government's direction of the underground movement; any underground opposition to the Russians would result in the Home Army being attacked and disarmed, while it would benefit from co-operation with the Red Army. On the other hand, Stalin said there was no need for the Poles to feel anxious about their position when the Red Army occupied Poland west of the Curzon Line. The Polish Government would be allowed to return and set up the broad-based kind of government they envisaged.[4]

Stalin's reply to Churchill's communication was on similar lines, but categorically insisted on the incorporation of part of East Prussia, including Königsberg, into the U.S.S.R. He also reminded

---

[1] Despatch from the Government Delegate and the Council of National Unity to the Prime Minister, dated 15 February 1944, received 9 March 1944, Ldz. K1930/44. GSHI–PRM, L48/96.
[2] Message from Mr Churchill to Marshal Stalin, 1 February 1944. No. 235. *Correspondence*, vol. I, pp. 193–4.
[3] *Ibid.*, p. 195.
[4] Woodward, pp. 280–1.

Churchill that as early as May 1943 he had written to him saying that 'the composition of the Polish Government could be improved' and that he 'would work towards that end'. He stated that if the Polish Government recognised the Curzon Line and agreed to its own reconstruction, an agreement on Russo–Polish military co-operation would present 'no difficulty'[1].

After receiving this telegram the British believed that a settlement was now more feasible.[2] On 6 February Churchill saw Mikolajczyk again, to review the situation and discuss recent communications from Moscow. During this meeting Churchill once again urged the Poles to adopt a realistic attitude to the Soviet demands. He stated that there were three courses of action open to him:

1. To make an agreement in which all parties joined.
2. To make an Anglo–Russian agreement, in which he would endeavour to settle the frontier problem and to procure humane treatment for the Poles.
3. To do nothing, while the Russian steam-roller moved over Poland, a Communist Government was set up in Warsaw and the present Polish Government was left powerless to do anything but make its protests to the world at large.[3]

Mikolajczyk replied that he was 'not at all anxious to be left out of the agreement. He had already gone so far as to accept negotiations on all questions, including changes of frontiers during the war, and had issued orders to the underground movement to enter into friendly contact with the Russians even though no agreement should be reached.' He could not accept the Curzon Line and give away Wilno and Lwow.

At this stage Churchill became heated, saying that 'in that case he must look at the matter from the British point of view and make his own agreement with Stalin'. He thought, and would say in Parliament, that the Polish Government had no grounds for complaint. He was blunt with the Poles to the point of rudeness. Referring to the 'many wrong turns' Poland had taken in her history, he direly warned that 'a refusal now might be the most fatal and disastrous of all'.

Mikolajczyk remained unmoved. He said that while appearances

[1] From Premier J. V. Stalin to the Prime Minister Mr Winston Churchill, 4 February 1944, No. 236. *Correspondence*, vol. I, pp. 196–7.
[2] Woodward, p. 281.
[3] Record of a meeting held at Chequers on Sunday 6 February 1944 at 3 p.m. between Premier Churchill and Premier Mikolajczyk. GSHI–PRM, L47.

might suggest that only the frontier line was in question, he was sure that, in truth, his Government was 'defending the independence of Poland itself'. At this, Churchill countered that the Polish Government did not possess the power necessary for such defence, but Mikolejczyk continued to defend his position. He said that he had to respect the opinions of people in Poland who were determined to 'maintain Poland's territorial integrity'.[1] Churchill said that the situation was, then, hopeless; agreement on such a basis was impossible and a Soviet-dominated Poland would emerge.

The Polish Premier produced a telegram from Poland, informing London about the establishment in Warsaw, by the Communists, of a 'National Council'[2] in opposition to the Polish underground movement. He considered this move to be a clear indication of real Soviet intentions towards Poland. He feared that, before her army crossed the Curzon Line, Russia intended to establish a 'Committee of National Liberation', composed of pro-Soviet Polish elements recruited from among Poles living in the U.S.S.R. and the U.S.A. and, if possible, also in Britain. He believed that after the Red Army had crossed the Curzon Line this 'National Council' would become the Government of Poland. Churchill agreed that such a danger existed and would be intensified if agreement between Poland and Soviet Russia was not reached.

Nothing that was said during this talk altered Mikolajczyk's position; he was willing to enter into discussions on all outstanding questions, but, in his opinion, the acceptance of the Curzon Line as the basis of such discussions 'could only undermine the Polish Government's authority with the Polish nation and also disrupt the latter's unique solidarity'. Instead, he suggested that a solution to the territorial problem might perhaps be found 'on the basis of a demarcation line within which the Polish administration would be set up immediately after the liberation of the territory from the German occupation. The fixing of the Polish–Soviet frontier would [then] be left over to be decided after the conclusion of hostilities.'

Churchill asked that the Polish Government would carefully consider all that had been said. Finally, he promised that for the next three months the supply of arms to the Home Army would be trebled.[3]

---

[1] *Ibid.*   [2] For details see pp. 106ff. of this study.
[3] Record of a meeting held at Chequers on Sunday 6 February at 3 p.m., between Premier Churchill and Premier Mikolajczyk. GSHI–PRM, L47.

Once again, agreement on a joint Anglo–Polish approach to the territorial question had not been reached.

On 15 February 1944, the Polish Government formally informed the British authorities that they would not re-open negotiations with the Russians on the basis of the Curzon Line.

The Poles suggested, however, that a line of demarcation, running east of Wilno and Lwow should be established immediately. The territories west of this line were to be administered by the Polish authorities, those east of it by the Red Army assisted by the Allied representatives. They objected to Stalin's intention of incorporating Königsberg into the U.S.S.R. instead of into Poland, and stated that the changes in the composition of the Polish highest authorities could not be dictated by a foreign power.[1]

Polish refusal to accept the Curzon Line appears to have been finally clinched by Mikolajczyk's fears that acceptance might cause his supporters in Poland and abroad to reject his leadership. He feared that, if he accepted the Curzon Line or even smaller territorial changes in the east, the opposition abroad might brand him and his Cabinet as traitors and stage a mutiny in the army.[2] He also feared that his acquiescence in Russian territorial demands might lead to the 'eventual collapse' of the underground movement in Poland with all the attendant consequences. At the same time, he also knew the situation demanded that he should express a certain willingness to negotiate with the Russians and to make concessions; he feared that a flat refusal to negotiate frontier revisions might lead to the repudiation of his Government by London and Washington.[3] Hence his proposal to Churchill that the territorial issue should be settled, for the time being, on the basis of the demarcation line, leaving Wilno and Lwow under Polish administration. Further, he felt that the Russians were not being honest with him; if they genuinely intended to honour their promise to recognise his Government if he accepted the Curzon Line it would be simple for them, he reasoned, to bring his Government into negotiations as they had 'all the trump cards'.[4] He suspected that the Russians had planned

---

[1] Memorandum from the Polish Government to Premier Churchill, 15 February 1944. GSHI–PRM, L47.

[2] Despatch from the Prime Minister to the Government Delegate, 25–6 January 1944, Ldz. K.519/44. GSHI–PRM, L11.

[3] *Ibid.*

[4] Record of a meeting held at Chequers on Sunday 6 February at 3 p.m. between Premier Churchill and Premier Mikolajczyk. GSHI–PRM, L47.

Polish refusal of their terms in advance as a preliminary step towards 'the Sovietisation not only of Poland, but of entire Europe'.[1]

On 16 February 1944 Churchill again employed all his eloquence in trying to persuade the Poles to accept the Curzon Line as a *sine qua non* of wider understanding and co-operation between Poland and Russia. Again, he failed. He presented his case for Polish concessions in sombre but realistic terms. His arguments might well have been, for Mikolajczyk, a lesson in *Realpolitik*.

Churchill asked Mikolajczyk whether he would like him to inform Stalin that no progress could be made; after all, this might be an easier course for Britain. The Russians were already advancing rapidly and might soon set up a well-supported puppet government in Poland, followed by a manipulated plebiscite. Churchill agreed that if Polish fears that the Russians were untrustworthy proved justified it would be a bad prospect for the world 'but worst of all for the Poles'.

Churchill went so far as to say that he 'had heard talk of a second Munich. No Pole should say this because the Poles had participated in the pillage of Czechoslovakia.'[2] He added that he 'felt quite differently towards our foe Germany and towards Russia, without whose armies there would have been no means of recreating the Polish State'.[3] He returned, then, to his original point, that 'there must be some *modus vivendi*'. If, because of the Polish Government's inability to accept a final frontier agreement now, their suggestion of a temporary demarcation line were to be taken up, that line would still be based only on the Curzon Line. Churchill tried to persuade the Poles that the Russians would, in fact, keep their pledges to them.

He also stressed that tactically this was the best time for talks with the Russians: the Second Front was in preparation and Russian occupation of Poland as yet incomplete. His 'heart bled' for Poland. The Russian advance was a 'brutal fact' which 'could not be overlooked', and could no more be stopped than the tide from coming in.[4] Later, returning in more optimistic vein to the subject of Russia, Churchill said there were no grounds for supposing that Russia would repeat the German desire for domination of Europe. After the war, with strong British and American forces, there were

---

[1] Despatch from the Prime Minister to the Government Delegate, 25–6 January 1944, Ldz. K.519/44. GSHI–PRM, L11.

[2] Record of a meeting held at No. 10 Downing Street between Premier Churchill and Premier Mikolajczyk, 16 February 1944. GSHI–PRM, L47.

[3] *Ibid.*   [4] *Ibid.*

'good hopes of . . . a [world] peace of thirty or forty years which might then prove much more lasting'.

Although Mikolajczyk was silent during the greater part of the meeting, he did say 'that he hoped that Great Britain would live up to her reputation of protection of the weak', and complained that his Government had 'no practical guarantee in return for their concessions'.[1]

During these talks Churchill tried several times to impress it upon the Poles that they must not expect more from Britain than she could offer. They must come to terms with the immutable facts of history, strategy and geography and settle for friendly co-existence with Russia, harsh though she might be, if they wished to avoid the emergence of Communist leadership in Poland. Such co-existence could, he was sure, only be achieved by taking the risks and making the sacrifices he was urging on them. By accepting Stalin's assurances and reaching a *modus vivendi* with Russia Poland had everything to gain and little to lose. In any case, the only way of proving the true nature of Stalin's intentions was by trying to work with him. The only other alternatives for the London Poles would be to wait for a third world war or to fade slowly into obscurity. Churchill himself had no desire to see a Communist government in Poland but could do nothing to avoid this without Polish co-operation. Neither did he want a break with Russia over Poland. For all these reasons he repeatedly urged the Poles, often in a hectoring manner, to accept the Curzon Line settlement as the most advantageous in the circumstances.

However, his arguments met with little response. While recognising that territorial changes were inevitable, Mikolajczyk still wished to limit their extent. He could not bring himself to renounce Poland's rights to Wilno and Lwow, which for centuries had been the two main pillars of the Polish State in the east and for which Poles had fought in the years 1918 to 1920; he felt that relinquishing them would have amounted to high treason.

Despite this grave disappointment Churchill decided to approach Stalin directly once again on the Polish issue. The text of his message was discussed with the Poles and Mikolajczyk approved it.[2]

After his failure to make Mikolajczyk accept the Curzon Line,

---

[1] Record of a meeting held at No. 10 Downing Street between Premier Churchill and Premier Mikolajczyk, 16 February 1944. GSHI–PRM; L47.
[2] Woodward, pp. 280–1.

Churchill now changed his tactics, and began trying to persuade Stalin to accept a compromise solution, that is, to allow the Polish Government to postpone their formal acceptance of the new frontier with Russia until the end of the war, after their return to Warsaw. Such a solution would give the Russians *de facto* control over the territories east of the Curzon Line and free the Poles from the unpleasant task of formally recognising this Line immediately. This modified position was the result of Churchill's fear that, if Mikolajczyk did accept the Curzon Line while hostilities were still in progress, the Polish Government might be repudiated by a large section of its followers in Poland and abroad, this might, in turn, lead to the emergence of a Communist-dominated administration in Warsaw.

On 27 February the new suggestions were embodied in a telegram in which Churchill told Stalin that the Polish Government was ready to declare that the pre-war Russo–Polish frontier was no longer realistic and that it was prepared to discuss with Moscow new Polish frontiers. But as the western compensations Poland was to receive could not be publicly or precisely stated the Poles could not immediately declare publicly their willingness to cede territory to Russia, as this would have a one-sided appearance and would lead to disaffection among large numbers of their supporters at home and abroad. Therefore, the final and formal settlement could only be made after the war, when the Polish Government had returned to Poland and had been allowed to consult the Polish people.[1]

Churchill told Stalin that the Poles were anxious to administer Wilno and Lwow, but that he had explained to them that the Russians would not accept this. He wanted to assure them, nevertheless, that they would be allowed to administer 'at least all Poland west of the Curzon Line'.

He also said that the Polish Government assured him that they had at no time given instructions to their underground movement to attack Soviet partisans and that they were most anxious to establish with the Red Army military co-operation, which, he re-iterated, he considered to be of 'the highest significance and importance'.

As for the composition of the Polish Government, the Poles were determined to see that, once Russo–Polish relations were

---

[1] Message from Mr Winston Churchill to Marshal Stalin, 27 February 1944, No. 243. *Correspondence*, vol. I, p. 201.

re-established, it would be composed of 'none but the persons fully determined to co-operate with the Soviet Union'.[1]

The British Ambassador in Moscow had instructions to tell the Russians that this message had been drafted in close consultation with Mikolajczyk, and that Russian rejection of the offer 'would have a serious effect on British and American opinion'.[2]

As on previous occasions, Churchill sent a copy of his message to Roosevelt,[3] who telegraphed to Stalin that he supported this plan for a tentative settlement and hoped that Stalin would accept it. He also said that it was now most important to ensure that the Red Army would be assisted by the Poles during its advance through Poland.[4]

Stalin received Churchill's communication in 'a harsh and unfriendly way'.[5] On 28 February he told the British Ambassador 'that he had little hope of a settlement on the basis of the Prime Minister's letter'. Further, he 'did not think that the Poles really wanted a settlement. He asked only for the Curzon Line and the reconstruction of the Polish Government. He would not agree that the Polish Government could not now accept the Curzon Line, and that the reconstruction of their Government should await their return to Warsaw.'[6] He was adamant in his demands, unwilling to make the situation easier for Mikolajczyk or Churchill.

Both Stalin and Mikolajczyk were placing the British Government in an extremely difficult position; the obstinacy of each left the mediator with little scope for manoeuvre and made British hopes of a 'fair' solution impossible to realise. Churchill considered the Soviet territorial claims to be just but was deeply reluctant to abandon the Poles to their own fate because of their refusal to accept them immediately and entirely.

Stalin formally replied to Churchill and Roosevelt on 3 March: 'that the time is not yet ripe for a solution of the problem of Soviet–

---

[1] Message from Mr Winston Churchill to Marshal Stalin, 27 February 1944, No. 243. *Correspondence*, vol. I, pp. 202–4.

[2] Woodward, p. 284; see also: The British Prime Minister (Churchill) to President Roosevelt, 21 February 1944. *FRUS 1944*, vol. III, pp. 1263–4.

[3] The British Prime Minister (Churchill) to President Roosevelt, 20 February 1944. *FRUS 1944*, vol. III, pp. 1259ff.

[4] President Roosevelt to the Chairman of the Council of People's Commissars of the Soviet Union (Stalin), received by Stalin on 28 February 1944. *FRUS 1944*, vol. III, p. 1264.

[5] Woodward, p. 285.   [6] *Ibid.*

Polish relations.'[1] This sounded ominous and sinister. If the time was 'not yet ripe' what, then, was Stalin waiting for? For Mikolajczyk's acceptance of his demands or, rather, for the Red Army to penetrate Poland to such an extent that he would become the real master of that country, in a position to decide the form and content of the Polish Government? On 3 March Stalin also told Harriman that the Poles were 'fooling' the British and that 'he did not believe Churchill would be able to accomplish anything . . . Either Mikolajczyk's Government would change or another Government would emerge in Poland.' Yet he 'didn't know how the situation would work out, circumstances would show'.[2] These remarks suggest that Stalin may still have been prepared to recognise Mikolajczyk's Cabinet, provided that it was reconstructed and was willing to accept the Curzon Line; that his attitude to Poland would be governed by 'circumstances' as they developed, rather than by some master-plan inexorably aimed at the establishment of a Communist regime in Warsaw.

In London, Stalin's reply was badly received. Eden considered it 'cavalier as well as dusty' and was worried by its wider implications. He wondered, anxiously, whether the Soviet regime would 'ever co-operate with the West? . . .'[3] Furthermore, he believed that the British Government 'could not leave matters at this stage'. Having persuaded the Poles to make concessions it was obliged to protect them against Russian intransigence. The War Cabinet agreed with this and another communication was sent to Moscow.[4] In it, Churchill pointed out that his own recent proposals would have given the Russians *de facto* control of the territories east of the Curzon Line 'with the assent of the Poles . . ., and with the blessing of your Western Allies at the general settlement'. 'Force can achieve much', Churchill continued,

> but force supported by the good will of the world can achieve more. I earnestly hope that you will not close the door finally to a working arrangement with the Poles which will help the common cause during the war and give you all you require at the peace. If nothing can be arranged and you are unable to have any relations with the Polish Government which we shall continue to recognise as the Government

[1] From Premier J. V. Stalin to the Prime Minister, Mr W. Churchill, 3 March 1944, No. 249. *Correspondence*, vol. I, p. 207.
[2] The Ambassador in the Soviet Union (Harriman) to the Secretary of State, 3 March 1944. *FRUS 1944*, vol. III, p. 1265.
[3] Avon, p. 439.   [4] Woodward, p. 285.

of the ally for whom we have declared the war upon Hitler, I should
be very sorry indeed.[1]

Nevertheless, the British war leader assured Stalin that he would
earnestly try to prevent an Anglo–Soviet rift over Poland, as all his
hopes for the future of the world were 'based upon the friendship
and co-operation of the Western democracies and Soviet Russia'.[2]

The British Ambassador in Moscow was instructed to tell Stalin
that the British Government would have to explain to the Poles
'the general sense of the Russian answer'.

> The answer might become public, and cause great disappointment in
> Great Britain and the United States. The Prime Minister would also
> have to make a statement in Parliament. Furthermore the instructions
> sent to the Polish Underground Movement had anticipated a friendly
> settlement. If fighting now broke out between the Underground Move-
> ment and the Russian forces, the position would be even worse.[3]

The British could not renounce their recognition of Mikolajczyk's
Government, 'and a divergence of policy in the matter between the
U.S.S.R. and the two Western Powers would affect the operations
which all three were about to undertake'. The Ambassador was told
to emphasise the importance of these considerations, but was cautioned to say nothing which might be interpreted as a threat or as
evidence of a change of policy towards Moscow, the British were
following a line of approach which seemed to them most likely
to keep open the channels of communication between Churchill
and Stalin and least likely to damage the personal relations between
the two leaders. In addition, Churchill suggested that 'the worst
difficulties would be avoided if, without making any formal agreement and resuming relations with the Poles, the Soviet Government
observed the spirit of our proposals'.[4]

Briefly, then, Churchill was appealing to Stalin, in the name of
present and future co-operation between East and West, to reach some
modus vivendi with the Poles, while hinting that a failure to do so
might affect the preparations for the opening of the Second Front.

On 16 March, Stalin sent a telegram to London complaining that
his latest communications about Poland had been leaked to the
British Press. He considered this 'a violation of secrecy' and said

---

[1] Message from Mr Churchill to Marshal Stalin, 7 March 1944, No. 250.
Correspondence, vol. I, p. 208.
[2] *Ibid.*   [3] Woodward, p. 286.   [4] *Ibid.*

that such leakages made it difficult for him to speak his mind freely.[1] On the same day Churchill assured Stalin that he was not responsible for the leakages. Further, he reminded Stalin that very soon he would have to make a statement about Poland in the House of Commons. He would have to inform the House that attempts to bring the Soviet and Polish Governments together had failed, that Britain would continue to recognise the Polish Government, that the British view was that all questions of territorial change must now await the post-war peace conference and that in the meantime Britain would not recognise any territorial changes imposed by force.[2]

A week later, on 23 March Stalin said that both Churchill's messages and the Ambassador's statement 'bristle with threats' which he considered to be inappropriate between allies and harmful to mutual co-operation. He accused Churchill of breaking the agreement reached in Teheran in regard to the future Polish frontiers, even saying that, if Churchill had persevered in the position he had adopted at Teheran 'the conflict with the Polish émigré Government could have been settled'. For his part, he could not depart from the Curzon Line; in spite of Churchill's post-Teheran reference to his Curzon Line policy as one 'of force', he still believed it to be the only legitimate settlement.[3] He was also offended by Churchill's suggestion that the solution of the Russo–Polish territorial problem ought to be postponed until the armistice conference was convened. Finally, he told Churchill that he would regard the proposed statement to the House of Commons as 'an unjust and an unfriendly act'. Nevertheless, he too hoped that the Anglo–Soviet breakdown on the Polish question would not affect Anglo–Soviet co-operation – which he was anxious to preserve – in other spheres.[4]

The telegram trenchantly showed that, far from producing any of the desired results, British intervention in the Russo–Polish dispute had led only to deterioration in Anglo–Soviet relations, expressed in mutual recriminations between London and Moscow. Churchill himself had possibly unwittingly sown the seeds of failure at Teheran, where he had, in effect, deprived himself of room

[1] From Premier J. V. Stalin to the Prime Minister, Mr W. Churchill, 16 March 1944, No. 254. *Correspondence*, vol. I, p. 210.
[2] Message from Mr Churchill to Marshal Stalin, 21 March 1944, No. 256. *Correspondence*, vol. I, pp. 211–12.
[3] From Premier J. V. Stalin to the Prime Minister Mr W. Churchill, 23 March 1944, No. 257. *Correspondence*, vol. I, p. 212.
[4] *Ibid.*, p. 213.

for future manoeuvre by not only unconditionally agreeing to but indeed suggesting the Curzon Line as the basis for settlement. He had done this without first consulting Mikolajczyk; his mistake really lay in underestimating the tenacity and passion with which the Polish Premier was to resist a settlement of this kind.

Churchill decided to delay sending an answer to the Russian telegram until he had consulted Roosevelt.[1]

Churchill now told his colleagues, perhaps not entirely consistently, that there had been no firm agreement at Teheran about the Curzon Line. This view was disputed by the Foreign Office, where the view was that Stalin could indeed say with reason that Britain was committed in principle to the Line 'as part of a general agreement'.[2]

The War Cabinet decided that reply should be made in the name of the British Government, and not personally in Churchill's name. It was to say that Churchill had not repudiated the Teheran agreement, which he had advised the Poles to accept as being a fair and reasonable settlement. His earlier communications to Moscow had suggested a 'working arrangement' to overcome the difficulty presented by Polish refusal to agree publicly to the Curzon Line without settlement of other issues concerning Poland's future which could not be settled at the present. The British Government still considered such working agreements to be necessary in the interests of Russo–Polish military co-operation.[3] Moreover, if the Russians were unwilling to discuss the Polish question further the British Government would have to withdraw their mediation and announce their failure, without wishing to 'insult or discredit' their Soviet ally.[4]

Churchill sent a copy of this draft telegram to Roosevelt, saying that he 'believed the Soviet bark to be worse than their bite', and that, out of a desire to avoid separating themselves from their Western Allies, the Russians might 'be careful, about Poland' even if they gave no actual assurances. He also suggested that Roosevelt should now see Mikolajczyk in Washington.[5] On 5 April Roosevelt communicated his agreement with the terms of the message.[6]

On 9 April Churchill told Mikolajczyk that he had interrupted his negotiations with the Soviets on Poland because he had felt that an understanding was out of reach, that further discussion would lead nowhere and would only poison the situation.[1] He advised Mikolajczyk to go to Washington to present his case to the Americans. Nevertheless he told the Polish Premier that he himself stood firmly by the Curzon Line settlement with concomitant compensation to Poland in the west, and advised him to dismiss Gen Sosnkowski immediately. The latter should appreciate that his person must stand in the way of Polish interests and should spontaneously resign from his post. However, Mikolajczyk rejected this suggestion. He argued that although, if necessary, Sosnkowski would spontaneously resign, it was not necessary because, apart from Soviet objections to him, the way of agreement was blocked by other Russian conditions, quite unacceptable to the Polish Government.

He then told Churchill of recent Soviet overtures regarding co-operation between the Red Army and the Home Army in the Volhynia district. It should be realised that he was unaware, at this stage, of the real state of affairs in Volhynia, that the negotiations between the Russian and Polish commanders had been interrupted before they were completed.[2]

Churchill believed that any contact established between the Home Army and Soviet forces should be fully utilised to give the lie to Russian accusations of Home Army collaboration with the Germans and its alleged wish to fight against Russia. As for the possibility of Russian reprisals against the Home Army he regarded this as an unlikely development, in view of the importance to Russia of Anglo-Saxon opinion.

Mikolajczyk then asserted that the establishment of partial Russo–Polish military co-operation provided a fresh opportunity for joint Anglo–American intervention, in Moscow, to end the deadlock between Russia and Poland; moreover, he regarded this as a good moment to send Anglo–American missions to Warsaw and Volhynia. Churchill could not agree. He believed that the Russians would see such missions as those of spies, sent to 'ascertain on the spot whether the Soviets were murdering the Poles'.[3] Consequently, such a move would inflame rather than improve relations with Moscow.

Mikolajczyk reported that, in some Polish quarters, the Russians had been offering to settle the conflict on the following terms:

---

[1] Record of a conversation between Mikolajczyk and Churchill, 9 April 1944. GSHI–PRM, L48.
[2] For details see p. 190ff of this study. [3] *Ibid.*

Russian recognition of the 1939 frontier as a goodwill gesture to-wards Poland (that such a concession should have been offered, or, if so, offered with any sincerity, would seem, at the very least, to be highly inconsistent with the official Soviet position at, and before this time); the Polish Government's recognition of Berling's army;[1] the dismissal of the C-in-C, Sosnkowski, and the reconstruction of the Cabinet; finally, the conclusion of an agreement on these terms without the knowledge of London or Washington.

Mikolajczyk interpreted the Russian overtures he had reported in a sinister light. In his view, Stalin wanted to create a favourable political atmosphere for turning Poland into a Russian satellite, and Berling's army was to be an instrument in this aim. He repeated his information that the Soviets were planning to set up a new Polish Government in Lublin after crossing the Curzon Line.[2]

Churchill assured Mikolajczyk that neither England nor America would ever allow Poland to lose her independence and become a satellite State. London would not recognise a Polish Government set up arbitrarily by the Soviets. Finally, he promised to review and give an answer on the question of British help to the Home Army, about which Mikolajczyk repeated earlier complaints, this time more strongly; since October 1943 supplies had come almost to a standstill; out of 301 planned flights to Poland during the period October 1943 to March 1944 only 28 had been made and, during the last two months of that period, only two. The military result was that during this crucial period the resistance was short, not only of arms, but also of money and wireless equipment.[3] It is impossible to say whether this reduction in British supply-flights to Poland was due primarily to technical causes, as Churchill alleged on a number of occasions, or to political considerations, or to both. It should be repeated, however, that on 5 October 1943 Eden had told the War Cabinet that the question of supplying the Home Army with arms was difficult, as such action, undertaken without consultation with the Russians, might antagonise them. At the same time, a well-equipped Home Army would be useful in helping to liberate Poland and subsequently maintaining order there.[4] Therefore, it can be said that the problem of British help to the Home Army

---

[1] For details see p. 105 of this study.
[2] Record of a conversation between Mikolajczyk and Churchill, 9 April 1944. GSHI–PRM, L48.
[3] *Ibid.*   [4] Woodward, p. 251ff.

was conditioned by three basic considerations: a desire not to antagonise the Russians; a desire to make of the Home Army a strong force and mainstay of public order (given the state of Russo–Polish relations, the fulfilment of both of these desires was hardly possible); finally, there were undoubtedly genuine technical difficulties arising out of the geographical distances involved.

The British interpretation of events in Volhynia was that the Poles 'were still nervous, but hoped that similar contacts might be made elsewhere'.[1] Hence, Eden favoured postponing the reply to Stalin's telegram and the proposed Parliamentary statement until the situation had clarified itself. He also believed that the opening of the Second Front would reinforce British influence on Soviet policy.[2] Churchill wished to avoid an argument with the Russians because he was 'anxious to save as many Poles as possible from being murdered.'[3] He decided, for the time being, to 'relapse into moody silence so far as Stalin is concerned'.[4] In April and May 1944 no messages on Poland were exchanged by Churchill and Stalin.[5]

At the end of April Churchill again encouraged Mikolajczyk to go to America and present his case to Roosevelt. He emphasised that the President was anxious not to lose the Polish vote in the next presidential elections but he warned Mikolajczyk against expecting any concrete results from his visit. It should, however, strengthen the prestige of the Polish Government and its Premier and improve their international standing.

Regarding Volhynia, Churchill quoted Molotov's description of the Russo–Polish military contacts established there as 'small, insignificant incidents'.[6]

Mikolajczyk commented on the recent increase in British supply-drops to Poland. Churchill promised that the drops would continue as planned.

It was also arranged that Churchill would meet the newly-arrived representatives of the underground movement, Z. Berezowski, a leading member of the National Democratic Party, and Gen S. Tatar ('Tabor'), the deputy Chief of Staff of the Home Army.[7]

The meeting took place on 25 April 1944. Berezowski told Churchill about the continuous and unyielding Polish resistance to the Germans, in spite of cruel reprisals. He said that the Poles trusted

---

[1] *Ibid.*, p. 288.   [2] *Ibid.*   [3] *Ibid.*, p. 291.   [4] *Ibid.*   [5] *Ibid.*, p. 288.
[6] Note on a conversation between Mikolajczyk and Churchill held on 23 April 1944. GSHI–PRM, L48.   [7] *Ibid.*

Great Britain and her Prime Minister and counted on his staunch and firm support in ensuring Poland's real independence and the integrity of her frontiers. Churchill said that while he was willing to assist Poland in regaining her independence he could not vouch for the integrity of her frontiers; he reaffirmed his support for the Curzon Line, surrendering Wilno and Lwow to Russia and compensating Poland in the West. Berezowski responded with an emphatic re-statement of Poland's determination to keep Wilno and Lwow, and if necessary to fight for them. Churchill answered 'in a grave, . . . even . . . gloomy, manner: "Obviously, a decision to resist, regardless of the consequences, is the privilege of every nation, and it cannot be denied even to the weakest . . ." '[1] Finally, at Churchill's request, Gen Tatar gave a general outline of the organisation, aims and potentialities of the Home Army.[2]

At the end of May Churchill made a statement in the House of Commons in which he outlined his policy towards Poland and tried to remove Russian suspicions concerning his motives. He paid tribute to the Polish forces in Poland and on other fronts, restated the disinterested motives behind Britain's mediation in the Russo–Polish dispute and emphasised the importance, to Europe and to Allied harmony, of eventual understanding between the two nations. In this statement he said his impression was that 'things are not so bad as they may appear on the surface between Russia and Poland'.[3] This tentative optimism was probably based on a hopeful assessment of events in Volhynia and the establishment, in London, of unofficial diplomatic contacts between the Polish and Russian Governments.[4]

The Polish Government still thought that their continuing control of the Home Army was a weapon strong enough to allow them to resist Russian pressure because the Russians valued the collaboration of the Polish forces. Recent Russian diplomatic moves in London possibly strengthened them in this view.[5] On 23 May V. Lebedev, the Russian Ambassador to Allied Governments established in London, had taken the initiative in calling a secret meeting with S. Grabski, Chairman of the Polish National Council in London.

[1] Note on a conversation between Churchill and Mikolajczyk and the delegation of the Polish underground movement held on 25 April 1944. GSHI–PRM, L48.
[2] *Ibid.*
[3] Parliamentary Debates 5th Series, House of Commons, vol. 400, cols 778–9.
[4] Woodward, p. 288.   [5] *Ibid.*

The meeting was followed up on 31 May when Grabski suggested a Polish delegation, led by Mikolajczyk might visit Moscow, 'to conclude a treaty supplementing the Soviet–Polish agreement of July 1941, and settling the question of collaboration between the Polish Underground organisation and the Soviet forces'.[1] Post-war relations and the frontier question would also be discussed, and diplomatic relations would be resumed when the treaty had been concluded.[2] The Russians had also made less direct overtures in London; at the request of the Russians, the Czechoslovak President, Dr E. Benes, had visited Mikolajczyk to communicate Soviet views on 'certain questions which the [Russians] felt it difficult to raise with the Poles'. The Russians sincerely desired an agreement, and while recognising that the composition of the Polish Government was a Polish affair, they objected to the presence in the London establishment of Gen Sosnkowski, the Polish C-in-C, Mr Kot, the Minister of Information and Gen Kukiel, the Minister of National Defence.[3]

On 31 May Churchill again tried to convince Mikolajczyk that it was absolutely necessary for the Polish Government to come to terms with Stalin and with the Polish forces in Russia.[4] In his reply, Mikolajczyk began by stating that neither he nor his Government wished to prolong the quarrel with Russia unnecessarily. The Poles had no 'intrinsic hatred' of Russia, but feared and would resist subservience to her.[5] Neither had the Poles in the West any desire to be 'cut adrift' from the Poles in Russia; on the contrary, it was the Russians themselves who were continually trying to split the two groups.[6] Mikolajczyk said he could distinguish clear phases in the development of Russian policy towards Poland. First, hoping to break the Polish spirit altogether, the Russians had concentrated on the frontier question; the second phase had been characterised by Russian attempts to create 'disarray' in the Polish Government and to dictate its composition; now, having been thwarted by strong British resistance to all attempts to thus harm the Polish Government, the Russians had embarked on the third phase, which consisted of attempts to undermine 'the Polish people, politicians, parties and soldiers', who had so far presented a united front.[7]

[1] *Ibid.*, p. 289.   [2] *Ibid.*   [3] *Ibid.*
[4] Record of a meeting held at No. 10 Downing Street on Wednesday 31 May 1944 between Premier Churchill and Premier Mikolajczyk. GSHI–PRM, L48.
[5] *Ibid.*   [6] *Ibid.*   [7] *Ibid.*

If the third phase could be survived, Mikolajczyk was optimistic about the advent of a fourth, more hopeful, phase ending in the resumption of Polish–Soviet relations. But if the third phase were to be survived the British Government would have to continue to support the Polish Goverment as strongly as before, and would have to appear to do so.[1]

Mikolajczyk was satisfied, then, that his policy of intransigent resistance to the Russian claims was not a sterile one, given continued Anglo–American support and the backing of the Polish nation and army, but one that would finally lead to Russo–Polish *rapprochement* on terms he considered to be favourable.

Churchill assured him that he had never given Stalin 'the slightest grounds for thinking that he was weakening in his support' for the London Poles, and that he had no intention of changing his attitude, but he again reminded the Polish Premier of the need for the Poles to 'help themselves and . . . help him to help them' by generally displaying, in spite of all provocations, a desire to reach agreement with Moscow. His own desire to strengthen Mikolajczyk's position had dictated his suggestion to Roosevelt that Mikolajczyk should be invited to America. Churchill felt that this would be an important visit. Equally important was the need for Mikolajczyk to practise the 'utmost discretion' while in America, because of the forthcoming presidential elections. However, he advised Mikolajczyk to give Roosevelt an account of the military situation and the plans and potential of the Home Army. The President might then feel inclined to advise Stalin that Russo–Polish military co-ordination would be useful to Russia.[2]

Recognising the American President's special difficulties, Churchill had, then, suggested a renewed invitation to Mikolajczyk as offering to Roosevelt an opportunity to help clear the path towards a Russo–Polish understanding without placing him in an embarrassing position. While Churchill was mildly optimistic about the outcome of the visit, Mikolajczyk was more intensely hopeful that it might help to secure stronger American suport for his cause and thus strengthen his position vis-à-vis Russia.[3]

[1] Record of a meeting held at No. 10 Downing Street on Wednesday 31 May 1944 between Premier Churchill and Premier Mikolajczyk. GSHI–PRM, L48.
[2] *Ibid.*
[3] Letter from the Polish Premier to President Roosevelt dated 25 March 1944. GSHI–PRM, L48.

Further, when, before his departure, Lebedev requested an interview with him, Mikolajczyk refused, preferring 'to see Roosevelt first'.[1]

8. *Mikolajczyk and Roosevelt*

The Polish Premier, with Gen 'Tabor', arrived in Washington on 6 June 1944, the day of the Anglo–American landings in Normandy.[2]

Roosevelt's interest in the Polish question was not as great as Mikolajczyk had hoped. In the middle of May he had told Harriman to tell Stalin 'that he could not take an active interest in the Polish question until after the election; that the Curzon Line, with some adjustments, seemed to him a sound basis for settlement though he remained puzzled about Lwow; that he had put off Mikolajczyk's visit as long as he could . . . and that he intended to tell him that he must get rid of those elements around him which would not co-operate with the Soviet Union if he wished a settlement.'[3]

Further, Roosevelt '. . . hoped that Soviet statements about the Poles would avoid further controversy and would stress the affirmative side of Soviet intentions – friendship and independence for the Poles and freedom of religion – so that arguments over the question should not be aroused during the election campaign.'[4]

Harriman delivered this message to Molotov on 3 June, adding that Roosevelt was firm in his 'determination to carry out the understanding reached at Moscow and Teheran for solidarity in Soviet–American relations and that no minor difficulties would affect this determination to work out agreements on all questions'. However, Harriman told Molotov that the President hoped that Moscow would find it 'possible to work out their Polish relations in such a way that all Poles could unite to fight wholeheartedly the common enemy'.[5]

Some days later, Harriman saw Stalin himself and repeated to him personally the President's message. The Soviet leader 'appeared pleased' about Roosevelt's attitude and 'appreciated' his position.[6] He promised to keep Washington informed 'of any important

---

[1] Stanislaw Mikolajczyk, *The Pattern of Soviet Domination* (London, 1948), p. 71 – hereafter to be referred to as Mikolajczyk.
[2] *Ibid.*, p. 64.   [3] Feis, p. 300.   [4] *Ibid.*
[5] The Ambassador in the Soviet Union (Harriman) to the Secretary of State, 7 June 1944 *FRUS 1944*, vol. III, p. 1276.
[6] *Ibid.*, 12 June 1944, *FRUS 1944*, vol. III, p. 1282.

developments in Soviet–Polish relations'.[1] Harriman described this meeting as the first friendly talk he had had with Stalin about Poland. He gained the impression that the Marshal 'saw a solution in the making which would be acceptable all around'.[2]

This conversation took place on 11 June,[3] five days after Mikolajczyk's arrival in Washington. Stalin had good reason for feeling pleased; Harriman's contributions to the talks clearly indicated that Roosevelt still considered the Polish question to be a minor issue, important to him only insofar as it might affect his elections, rather than an intrinsically important problem facing the Grand Alliance. Stalin could now feel sure that there was no question of a strong and determined Anglo–American pressure on behalf of the London Poles. It appeared that Churchill, and especially Mikolajczyk, were to be disappointed in their hopes of Roosevelt.

Mikolajczyk was only partly aware of this. He still hoped that frank, personal exchanges with Roosevelt would encourage the President to support his Government and its policy towards the U.S.S.R. Since the autumn of 1943 he had been trying, in vain, to see Roosevelt.[4]

While in Washington he had a number of meetings with Roosevelt, but they were not very fruitful. The President was 'reassuring but nimble in his avoidance of obligations'.[5] He assured Mikolajczyk that he could rely on 'the moral support' of Washington in his efforts to reach an understanding with Moscow.[6] He explained that he had, at Teheran, given Stalin the reasons why he could not join any 'detailed discussion' on Poland, and suggested to Mikolajczyk that 'he might be able to be of further assistance later on'. Mikolajczyk said he understood Roosevelt's position and had no wish to embarrass him.[7] Expressing the hope that Mikolajczyk would, at least, be able to devise ways to full military co-operation between Polish and Soviet forces, Roosevelt suggested that he might be able to give supplies and funds to the Home Army, to help in its resistance to the Germans.

---

[1] The Ambassador in the Soviet Union (Harriman) to the Secretary of State, 12 June 1944, *FRUS 1944*, vol. III, p. 1282.
[2] *Ibid.*, p. 1283.   [3] *Ibid.*, p. 1282.   [4] Rozek, p. 213
[5] Feis, p. 373.
[6] Memorandum by the Secretary of State to President Roosevelt, 14 June 1944. *FRUS 1944*, vol. III, p. 1283.
[7] The Secretary of State to the Ambassador in the Soviet Union (Harriman) 17 June 1944. *FRUS 1944*, vol. III, p. 1288.

When, suggesting that it would be a good idea for the Polish Government to make plans to return to Poland as soon as possible, the President said that the success of such plans could only be assured if Mikolajczyk dismissed the persons to whom Stalin objected, Mikolajczyk disagreed, 'stating that it would be misunderstood, particularly since one of them is the President of the Republic'.[1]

The President said he felt sure that Sovietisation of Poland was not Stalin's aim. He urged Mikolajczyk to trust in Stalin's good intentions.[2]

Saying that it might be useful for Mikolajczyk to go to Moscow for personal talks with Stalin, the President mentioned that, although he felt unable to suggest this plan directly, he might agree to 'intimate' to Stalin that Mikolajczyk was amenable to it. Without committing himself to the idea of such a meeting, Mikolajczyk said it might be useful, if no 'prior conditions' were imposed.[3]

Regarding the territorial question, Roosevelt expressed the view that, if other matters could be settled, Stalin 'would be reasonable' about it.[4] Mikolajczyk reported that, again referring to Teheran, the President said: 'Neither Stalin nor I proposed the Curzon Line as the frontier between Poland and the Soviet Union. It was Churchill who suggested it, and obviously Stalin immediately picked it up and accepted it.'[5] From this Mikolajczyk deduced that Roosevelt was 'opposed to the Curzon Line' and he informed Jankowski accordingly.[6]

Roosevelt also told Mikolajczyk that he, too, believed that territorial changes should not be settled until the end of the war and undertook, then, to support Poland's retention of Lwow, Tarnopol and the oil areas of eastern Galicia and her acquisition of Königsberg as well as the rest of East Prussia and Silesia.[7] He

---

[1] *Ibid.*   [2] *Ibid.*, p. 1289.
[3] That is, that Russia should not make such talks dependent on the acceptance by Poland of Soviet territorial demands and changes in the Polish Government; that Washington should not threaten to dissociate itself from Polish affairs if such talks fail. Roosevelt assured Mikolajczyk that there was no danger of this. Despatch from the Prime Minister to the Government Delegate, 21 June 1944, .No. 135, Ldz. K.3443/44, in the Archives of the Polish Underground Study Trust in London, hereafter referred to as the APUST, File MSW50; see also: The Secretary of State to the Ambassador in the Soviet Union (Harriman), 17 June 1944. *FRUS 1944*, vol. III, p. 1289.
[4] *Ibid.*, p. 1289.   [5] Rozek, p. 221.
[6] Despatch from the Prime Minister to the Government Delegate, 21 June 1944, No. 135, Ldz. K.3443/44. APUST, File MSW50.
[7] Avon, p. 464; see also Mikolajczyk p. 66 and Woodward, p. 289.

'urged Mikolajczyk to make every effort possible now to reach a mutually satisfactory solution with the Soviets'.[1]

Roosevelt said that, in general, he had considerable influence on Stalin and that he would be able to get more from him than Churchill could.[2] However, it was obvious that he was not prepared to become too involved in the Russo–Polish dispute, particularly at the time of the presidential elections. He left Mikolajczyk with the impression that, in his view, provided that the Poles reconstructed their Government and were willing to co-operate militarily with the Red Army, acceptance of the Curzon Line need not be an essential prerequisite of reaching a settlement.[3] Thus, he encouraged false hopes in Mikolajczyk's mind and indirectly strengthened his determination to resist the Soviet territorial demands, although the President himself had agreed, at Teheran, to accept the Curzon Line as the new Russo–Polish frontier.[4] In a sense, therefore, Roosevelt here aggravated the Russo–Polish situation. Complete sincerity on his part was called for at this stage as the most recent Russian statements now made it obvious that only Polish acceptance of the Curzon Line would make settlement possible. In general, Russo–Polish relations were becoming a vicious circle of claims and counter-claims, proposals and counter-proposals, and Roosevelt, in spite of his great authority and power, was doing very little to 'bring the Poles to their senses' and reconcile them to the inevitability of the Curzon settlement.

Meanwhile, Poland was moving towards the tragedy of the Warsaw Rising, which was to cost her her capital and lead to the virtual destruction of one of the greatest centres of the European resistance movement. Today it seems clear that this tragedy could only have been avoided if, before the outbreak of the rising, there had been close Russo–Polish liaison. Poland was to pay a heavy price for the exiled authorities' miscalculations and false hopes, in which, they were encouraged by Roosevelt.[5] While in America Mikolajczyk

---

[1] The Secretary of State to the Ambassador in the Soviet Union (Harriman), 17 June 1944. *FRUS 1944*, vol. III, p. 1289.

[2] Despatch from the Prime Minister to the Government Delegate, 21 June 1944, No. 135, Ldz. K.3443/44. APUST, File MSW50.

[3] Memorandum by the Under Secretary of State (Stettinius) to the Secretary of State. *FRUS 1944*, vol. III, pp. 1280–1.

[4] For details see pp. 15–16 of this study.

[5] Despatch from the Prime Minister to the Government Delegate, 21 June 1944, No. 135, Ldz. K.3443/44. APUST, File MSW50.

had estimated that the Russians were now realising the strength of the Home Army and were therefore more inclined to enter into agreement with the Government which controlled it, despite that Government's refusal to accept the Curzon Line prior to negotiations.[1]

In reality, however, the Home Army was a very weak instrument and Mikolajczyk was well aware of this; the possibility of American help with equipment and money was touched on in the Washington discussions, though no practical decisions on the question were reached. In Washington Gen Tatar told the combined Chiefs of Staff that the Home Army was about a quarter of a million strong but had enough weapons for only about 32,000 men. He said that, in consequence, unless it received more arms from the West it would be incapable of undertaking any large-scale operations against the Germans[2] who, although exhausted and weakened after three years in Russia, were still an opponent to be reckoned with.[3] He predicted that, during their retreat, the Germans would defend the line of the Vistula.[4] In view of this realistic assessment of the Home Army's potentialities it should have been obvious that, if it were to conduct successful large-scale anti-German operations, there had to be close co-operation with the Red Army and substantial help, in the form of supplies, from the West. Secondly, without material assistance from the West the Home Army's *immediate* military usefulness to the Russians would be limited; it represented a possible reservoir of manpower, rather than a strong fighting force as such. This was overlooked by Mikolajczyk, who was unduly impressed by the tactical Russo–Polish arrangement in Volhynia.

Mikolajczyk's visit to Washington produced a certain amount of confused thinking in Polish circles, and no concrete results. One direct result was Roosevelt's telegram to Stalin assuring him that 'no specific plan or proposal in any way affecting Polish–Soviet relations was drawn up' during the recent talks, and asking him in guarded terms to invite Mikolajczyk to Moscow.[5] Stalin's reply was disappointing. He said that because of Mikolajczyk's continued

[1] Memorandum of the Acting Secretary of State to President Roosevelt, 6 June 1944. *FRUS 1944*, vol. III, p. 1274.

[2] Leon Mitkiewicz, 'Powstanie Warszawskie', *Zeszyty Historyczne*, No. 1/1962, p. 134.

[3] *Ibid.*, p. 132.   [4] *Ibid.*, p. 133.

[5] The Secretary of State to the Ambassador in the Soviet Union (Harriman), 17 June 1944. *FRUS 1944*, vol. III, p. 1284.

refusal to change his Cabinet or accept the Curzon Line he was not prepared to invite him to Moscow.[1]

9. *Mikolajczyk's Visit to Moscow*

On his return to London Mikolajczyk informed Warsaw and the British of the outcome of his talks in Washington, which had greatly encouraged him.[2] Indeed, on 21 June he told Jankowski that his visit to Washington was a significant step towards a solution of the Russo–Polish *impasse*, 'an important manifestation of the American attitude to Poland and her Government and a proof of the significance attached by the Americans to . . . [the Polish] question'.[3] He mentioned Roosevelt's belief in his own influence with Stalin and assured his followers in Poland that the President was opposed to the Curzon Line. He also told them that Roosevelt had encouraged him to visit Moscow and to reconstruct his Government. 'In general', he wrote, 'the Americans would like to see the restoration of Polish–Soviet relations, the postponement of the solution of the disputed issues and the establishment of a military and administrative *modus vivendi*, in the hope that the development of practical co-operation will, as a matter of course, facilitate the solution of the disputed problem'.[4]

But Eden 'thought the President – not for the first time – was dangerously vague and optimistic'.[5] On 22 June Churchill himself told the Poles that they 'should not harbour illusions'.[6]

Mikolajczyk was optimistic about his chances of reaching a favourable agreement with the Russians, not only because of his satisfaction with his visit to Washington, but also because he was, at the time, conducting with the Russians secret unofficial talks which at first were friendly and promising. Between 20 June and 23 June he saw Lebedev three times and discussed with him the possibility of re-establishing relations between their two Governments.[7]

During their first meeting Mikolajczyk asked Lebedev what should be done to re-establish diplomatic relations. Lebedev had no

---

[1] To the President Mr F. Roosevelt from Premier J. V. Stalin, 24 June 1944, No. 206. *Correspondence*, vol. 2, p. 148.
[2] Cf. Avon, p. 464.
[3] Despatch from the Prime Minister to the Government Delegate, 21 June 1944, No. 135, Ldz. K.3443/44. APUST, File MSW 50.
[4] *Ibid.*   [5] Woodward, p. 289; see also: Avon, p. 464.
[6] Raczynski, p. 269.   [7] Raczynski, pp. 267ff.

instructions but said that Stalin wanted an agreement with a Polish Government friendly to Russia; if the Polish Government were re-constituted, Stalin and Mikolajczyk could then easily settle their problems in 'direct negotiations'. Mikolajczyk rejected the idea of a change of President as out of the question and said that the question of Cabinet changes was, in any case, Poland's internal problem. First, he said, they must agree on 'the principles of collaboration' and then he would modify the Cabinet accordingly so that 'the agreed obligations could be carried out loyally and exactly'. These principles were: (*a*) resumption of normal diplomatic relations; (*b*) a common plan of action for the Polish and Soviet forces; (*c*) co-operation between the Polish home authorities in their administrative capacity with the Soviet military authorities entering Poland; (*d*) possible changes of frontier to be postponed until the end of the war.[1]

Lebedev said there would probably be no difficulties over administration. They should keep secret Moscow's replies to these four Polish points, which he expected to be favourable. Then, having made changes in his Cabinet, Mikolajczyk would go to Moscow as Premier in the new Government and while he was there the decisions concerning the four points would be announced.[2]

At the next meeting, on 22 June, Lebedev was 'equally forthcoming'[3] but asked for amplification of the proposal that the problem of the Polish–Soviet frontier should be postponed until the end of the war. Mikolajczyk explained that his Government had not the constitutional power to make any agreement which would change Poland's frontiers, but was willing to discuss the problem of frontiers together with all other future territorial problems. It was important, now, he said, to establish a demarcation line, with Polish administration to the west of it; this would lead to 'maximum war effort' among the Polish nation and would leave under Polish administration the areas mainly populated by Poles.[4] However, for ethnic reasons, the demarcation line would not be acceptable as the basis of any future frontier. Here, Lebedev emphasised Russian insistence on the Curzon Line but Mikolajczyk argued that this would deprive Poland of 'half of its territory and . . . 11 millions of its population

[1] The Chargé to the Polish Government in Exile (Schoenfeld) to the Secretary of State, 9 July 1944. *FRUS 1944*, vol. III, p. 1293.
[2] *Ibid.*, p. 1294.   [3] Raczynski, p. 268.
[4] The Chargé to the Polish Government in Exile (Schoenfeld) to the Secretary of State, 9 July 1944. *FRUS 1944*, vol. II, p. 1294.

including at least 5 million Poles'. It was therefore unacceptable and would 'make a friendly Russo–Polish co-operation afterwards impossible'.

The next day Lebedev categorically informed Mikolajczyk that the Soviet position was still that the Russo–Polish frontier must run along the Curzon Line, but that Polish administration to the west of it would be established as soon as the Red Army crossed it. Mikolajczyk refused to consider any discussion of revision of the pre-war frontiers without knowing what would happen to Poland's western and northern frontiers.[1]

Lebedev said that the Russian position was that the resumption of diplomatic relations depended on fulfilling the following conditions: the dismissal of Raczkiewicz, Sosnkowski, Kukiel and Kot from the Polish Government;[2] the inclusion of representatives of Poles from London, the U.S.S.R., the U.S.A. and the Communist-sponsored underground movement in Poland in the reconstituted Cabinet; condemnation by the new Cabinet of its predecessor for 'its mistake in the Katyn affair'[3] and acceptance of the Curzon Line as the new frontier.

Mikolajczyk refused to accept these conditions and the talks came to an end.[4]

Russo–Polish relations had once again reached a dangerous deadlock. This coincided with the opening of the Red Army's summer offensive on the Eastern Front, which, at the end of July, was to bring its units to the very gates of Warsaw and precipitate the outbreak of the insurrection in the Polish capital. After the breakdown of his talks with Lebedev, and at the start of the offensive, Mikolajczyk believed that the Soviet Government would now 'renew its efforts to develop pro-Soviet support among different Polish elements' and that if these efforts failed Moscow would again try to reach agreement with the London Government.[5] He also thought that Anglo–American victories in Europe might strengthen the role of the United States within the Grand Alliance and, thus,

---

[1] The Chargé to the Polish Government in Exile (Schoenfeld) to the Secretary of State, 9 July 1944. *FRUS 1944*, vol. II, pp. 1294–5.
[2] The President of the Republic, the C-in-C, the Minister of National Defence and Minister of Information respectively.
[3] For details see p. 5 of this study.
[4] The Chargé to the Polish Government in Exile (Schoenfeld) to the Secretary of State, 9 July 1944. *FRUS 1944*, vol. III, p. 1296.
[5] *Ibid.*

help Mikolajczyk himself in any new negotiations with Stalin. Yet he was worried that, in view of the Soviet offensive, delay in reaching a Russo–Polish settlement might lead to the creation of a Communist administration in Poland.[1]

The day Russo–Polish negotiations in London were broken off – 23 June 1944 – the Union of Polish Patriots in the U.S.S.R. formally denounced Mikolajczyk's Cabinet by declaring that only the Communist-sponsored National Council of Poland, established in Warsaw on 1 January 1944, represented the interests and aspirations of the Polish nation.[2] The Union announced that the National Council was paving the way to the creation of 'a Provisional National Government' and the establishment of an 'independent, free, strong and democratic Poland'.[3] This Government would liberate Poland and ensure her international co-operation with all the free countries of the world. The Union of Polish Patriots placed itself and its armed forces at the disposal of the National Council of Poland.[4] Thus, a fusion between the Communist-inspired groups in the U.S.S.R. and in Poland was established. Stalin had received a delegation of the National Council of Poland, had recognised it as representing the Polish nation and had agreed to establish official relations with it after the creation of its executive organ as early as 22 May – that is, a month before the London talks between Mikolajczyk and Lebedev. He also decided to provide the Communist-sponsored Polish resistance movement with weapons, uniforms and medical supplies.[5] Thus foundations were laid for the creation of the Polish Committee of National Liberation at the end of July 1944, and the consolidation of Communist-controlled resistance in Poland.

The situation of the London Poles was thus becoming desperate and a decisive confrontation with the Russians and Polish Communists was fast approaching. At this stage it appeared that only a visit by Mikolajczyk to Moscow and direct Russo–Polish negotiations resulting in an understanding could retrieve the situation

---

[1] Despatch from the Prime Minister to the Government Delegate, 21 June 1944, No. 135, Ldz. K.3443/44. APUST, File MSW 50.

[2] For a discussion of events leading to the creation of the National Council of Poland see pp. 106ff. of this study.

[3] *Wolna Polska*, No. 24(65), 1 July 1944.

[4] *Ibid.*

[5] Jerry Pawlowicz, *Strategia Frontu Narodowego PPR. III. 1943–VII, 1944* (Warsaw, 1965), pp. 169–70.

and lead to the establishment of a united anti-German front in Poland; otherwise, the emergence of a new Polish administration capable of satisfying Stalin's demands seemed both inevitable and imminent, once the Red Army had crossed the Curzon Line.

On 29 June Mikolajczyk saw Eden and discussed recent diplomatic developments with him. They were both worried about the abrupt ending of the Russo–Polish negotiations and 'the sudden toughening of the Soviet attitude' to the Polish Government.[1]

Eden, trying to find a way out of the dilemma, advised Mikolajczyk to reorganise his Cabinet.[2] The Polish Premier was still prevaricating, however. At the beginning of July he urged Jankowski to intensify the Home Army's operations against the Germans and assume administration, in the name of the exiled Government, in the areas the Home Army liberated.[3] He intended to stress the significance of the force under his control and thereby make Stalin more willing to reach an understanding with him as the representative and leader of a viable, powerful anti-German movement in Poland. In this way, the diplomatic *impasse* in Russo–Polish relations was again affecting the military operations of the Home Army.

At the same time Mikolajczyk decided to visit Moscow for 'a personal discussion with Stalin' and asked Churchill and Eden to arrange this.[4] On 20 July Churchill wrote to Stalin: '. . . With respect to Poland I have avoided saying anything because I trust in you to make comradeship with the underground movement if it really strikes hard and true against the Germans. Should Mikolajczyk ask to come to see you I hope you will consent.'[5]

The same day J. C. Dunn, the Director of the Office of European Affairs at the State Department, told his superiors that as the Red Army had crossed the Curzon Line 'it is possible that new developments in the Polish–Soviet dispute will arise at any time'.[6] To him it was clear that there was 'virtually no hope of any resumption of diplomatic relations between the Polish Government-in-exile and the Soviet Government'. On the contrary, he expected Moscow to

[1] Raczynski, p. 270; and Avon, p. 465.

[2] Raczynski, p. 270.

[3] Despatch from the Prime Minister to the Government Delegate, 4 July 1944, Ldz. 1784/6 jn./44. GSHI–PAM, 11.

[4] Woodward, p. 298.

[5] Message from Mr Churchill to Marshal Stalin, 20 July 1944, No. 299. *Correspondence*, vol. I, p. 241.

[6] Memorandum by the Director of the Office of European Affairs (Dunn) to the Secretary of State, 20 July 1944. *FRUS 1944*, vol. III, p. 1296.

recognise the National Council of Poland 'as the provisional representative of the Polish people'. 'Should this . . . development take place . . . the situation which the British and ourselves have sought to avoid will be created.' London and Washington would be

> dealing with and recognising . . . the present Polish Government . . . while the Soviet Union would be dealing with and supporting . . . a rival organisation. The split between British–American policy . . . and Soviet policy . . . in regard to Poland would be complete. The obvious danger of civil war is very real, with one side (and probably the losing one) fighting with at least moral support from the United States and Great Britain, while the other was being actively supported by the Soviet Union. Furthermore, . . . the recognition by the Soviet Government of a rival Polish organisation would impose a severe strain on the unity of the Allies since throughout the world such a rival government would be regarded as a Soviet puppet . . .[1]

This analysis of the situation was borne out by future events. Ensuing developments fully revealed the complete failure of the attempts of Anglo–American diplomacy to solve the Polish question during the previous eight months. On 23 July Stalin told Churchill that the advances of the Red Army presented him with 'the practical problem of administration on Polish territory'. The Soviets did not intend to establish 'their own administration' on Polish soil, for this would amount to interference in 'Poland's internal affairs'. Instead, they decided to approach the recently-established Polish Committee of National Liberation which intended to set up 'an administration on Polish territory' because they had found no other forces in Poland capable of administering the country.[2] Stalin continued:

> The so-called underground organisations led by the Polish Government in London have turned out to be ephemeral and lacking in influence. As to the Polish Committee, I cannot consider it a Polish Government, but it may be that later on it will constitute the *core* of a Provisional Government made up of democratic forces. As for Mikolejczyk, I shall certainly not refuse to see him. It would be better, however, if he were to approach the Polish National Committee, who are favourably disposed towards him.[3]

[1] *Ibid.*, p. 1297.
[2] From Premier J. V. Stalin to the Prime Minister, Mr Churchill, 23 July 1944, No. 301. *Correspondence*, vol. I, p. 242.
[3] *Ibid.*

Thus, from the Russian point of view, the situation was becoming 'ripe' for the solution of the Polish problem.

On 21 July the Polish Committee of National Liberation was established and, in Moscow, a few days later – on 27 July – an agreement was signed between this committee and the Soviet Government in regard to the administration of the liberated territories in Poland and the conduct of the resistance against the Germans.[1] From this moment onwards there were two rival Polish Governments in existence, one in Lublin, supported by the Polish Communists and their sympathisers and backed by the Soviet Union, and another in London, supported by the Underground State in Poland and backed by Great Britain and the United States. On 25 July Mikolajczyk submitted a note to Eden stating that the Committee was a body of usurpers. The note also stated '. . . with the consent of the Soviet Government facts have been accomplished on Polish territory, undisputed by the Soviet Union and indicating its intention to impose on the Polish people an illegal administration which has nothing in common with the will of the nation'. 'Such moves, . . . constitute an attempt against the independence of Poland.' The note demanded an immediate British *démarche*, in Moscow against the formation of the Committee of National Liberation and the restatement of British support for the exiled Government.[2]

Meanwhile, after 'some hesitation' and consultations with Churchill, Mikolajczyk decided to go to Moscow to see Stalin and 'to meet the National Committee'; in Churchill's opinion the Poles who were collaborating with the Russians were 'neither quislings nor communists'.[3] On the same day the British leader informed Stalin that Mikolajczyk would leave for Moscow the next day.[4]

Two days later Churchill telegraphed Stalin again informing him that Mikolajczyk was on his way to Russia. He assured Moscow that the Polish Premier was 'most anxious' to promote the unity of all Poles along the lines agreed between Russia, Britain and

---

[1] For details see p. 229 of this study.
[2] Memorandum from the Polish Government to the Foreign Office, 24 July 1944. GSHI-A.11.49/SOW/6.
[3] Woodward, p. 299.
[4] Message from Mr Churchill to Marshal Stalin, 25 July 1944, No. 303. *Correspondence*, vol. I, p. 244.

America.[1] He also warned Stalin that it would be 'a disaster' if the Western democracies recognised one body of Poles as the governing executive, and the Russians another. This could have serious repercussions on their co-operation in wider spheres.[2]

His intention was clear; he wished to bring about fusion between the Poles supported by Stalin and the Poles supported by himself and Roosevelt, and thus save Poland from the spectre of civil war and ensure the unity of the Grand Alliance. He had adjusted his earlier hopes to present realities and now realised that the Polish Communists would have to be represented in the new Government, although he still hoped that this would be headed by Mikolajczyk.

On 28 July Roosevelt told Moscow that he hoped very much that Mikolajczyk and Stalin could reach an agreement 'to the best advantage of our common effort'.[3] Mikolajczyk was then on his way to Moscow and Warsaw was preparing for her insurrection.

On 26 July Mikolajczyk sent a telegram to Jankowski authorising him to order the insurrection on his own initiative.[4] Before he left London, at about 6 p.m. on 26 July he received from Jankowski and Bor-Komorowski the news that they were ready to open their battle for Warsaw at any moment.[5] This news must have encouraged Mikolajczyk greatly; a successful insurrection in the capital, instigated and executed by his supporters, seemed bound to strengthen his hand in the negotiations with Stalin and the Committee of National Liberation. Before his departure he informed Churchill and Eden that the Home Army Command had ordered a state of readiness for the general insurrection in Poland as from 25 July.[6]

On the way to Moscow Mikolajczyk had talks in Cairo with Tomasz Arciszewski, a leading Polish socialist and Dr Jozef Retinger, one of Mikolajczyk's emissaries in Poland.[7] They were on their way to London from Warsaw. Arciszewski told him that it was necessary

---

[1] Message from Mr Churchill to Marshal Stalin, 27 July 1944, No. 305. *Correspondence*, vol. I, p. 245.

[2] *Ibid.*

[3] For Marshal Stalin from President Roosevelt, 28 July 1944, No. 215. *Correspondence*, vol. II, p. 153.

[4] For details see p. 231 of this study.

[5] A. Pomian, 'Rosja, komunisci a powstanie w swietle dokumentow', transcript of Pomian's broadcast on the Radio Free Europe, 26 July 1944. APUST.

[6] Record of a meeting between Mikolajczyk and Eden held on 25 July 1944 at 11.00 a.m. GSHI–Talks–MSZ Amb. E. Raczynski collection No. 32.

[7] For detailed discussion of Dr Retinger's mission to Poland see: Z. S. Siemaszko, 'Retinger w Polsce w 1944 r', *Zeszyty Historyczne*, No. 12 (1967), pp. 56ff.

to reach an agreement with Russia, in spite of the formation of the Committee of National Liberation and the agreement between this body and Stalin.[1] It seems that on hearing about this agreement Mikolajczyk was reluctant to continue his journey but, prompted by telegrams from Churchill and Roosevelt, finally decided to see Stalin after all.[2]

He intended, during his talks with the Soviet leaders, to clarify the state of Russo–Polish relations and to ascertain whether it was still possible to reach an agreement with Stalin 'guaranteeing the independence of the Polish State and safeguarding the home country against the consequences of unco-ordinated military operations'. He hoped that whatever the outcome of these talks might be he would be able to convince world opinion that he had 'exhausted all means of achieving an understanding'.[3] He was sure that Churchill would continue to recognise the Polish Government 'whatever the results of the conversations', and hoped that Roosevelt would do the same.[4]

Thus, Mikolajczyk's visit to Moscow was to be 'the final attempt to reach an understanding between Poland and the Soviets'.[5] Before learning of the Moscow–Lublin agreement of 27 July he had hoped that his visit to Moscow might prevent the emergence of a Communist administration in Poland; after learning of the agreement he thought that he might be able to persuade Stalin to disown the Committee of National Liberation or 'to clarify the situation finally'.[6] Yet, although at this stage he greatly wished to reach an agreement with the Soviets, he still did not have his Cabinet's formal authorisation to agree to 'territorial or other [political] changes'.[7] Indeed, he was still determined to see that Poland should not emerge from his talks with Stalin territorially reduced; she was to retain Wilno and Lwow. Personally, however, he was willing to cede to Russia the predominantly Ukrainian areas of pre-war Poland as a maximum concession. He wanted to reach a temporary administrative and

[1] W. Pobog-Malinowski, *op. cit.*, p. 604.
[2] Mikolajczyk, p. 178.
[3] Despatch from the Minister for Foreign Affairs to the President of the Republic, 28 July 1944. GSHI–A/11/49/SOW/8. [4] *Ibid.*
[5] Despatch from the Minister of National Defence to the C-in-C, 27 July 1944, Ldz. 6077. APUST.
[6] Despatch from the Minister of National Defence to the C-in-C, 24 July 1944, Ldz. 5938. GSHI–Kol.17/2–f.1/4.
[7] General Kukiel's Note. 'What the Premier is taking /to Moscow/, 26 July /1944/.' GSHI–A.XII.3/90–2.

military agreement which would put under Polish administration as much of the territory east of the River Bug – roughly speaking, the Curzon Line – as possible.

He also wanted to reach an agreement with Stalin about holding general elections in Poland as soon as possible after her liberation.[1]

Thus, the concessions Mikolajczyk intended to make to the Russians were small, in comparison with the Russian demands; in view of this the chances of Russo–Polish agreement were not very great. The London Poles were still reluctant to make the concessions necessary for reaching an understanding with Moscow. Kukiel, the Minister of National Defence, believed that if the Committee of National Liberation proved able to achieve 'better frontiers' with the U.S.S.R. it should be allowed to do so and Mikolajczyk's Government should then remain abroad, its brief limited to the protection of Polish interests in London and Washington.[2] This, he said, would be preferable to 'a bad compromise'. The Polish Foreign Minister, Romer, agreed with this opinion.[3] They seemed to forget, however, that the imminence of the planned Warsaw insurrection, which was intended to give control of the capital to the London Poles, left no time for making the re-alignments implicit in such a solution.

On 30 July 1944 Mikolajczyk arrived in Moscow,[4] where he was told by the British Ambassador that compliance with the following points might help him to reach an agreement with Stalin:

1. The remodelling of the Polish Government so as to exclude certain elements believed here to be reactionary and anti-Soviet.

2. The acceptance of the Curzon Line as a basis for negotiations.

3. Some kind of withdrawal from the suggestion that the killing at Katyn was done by the Russians . . .

4. Some kind of a working arrangement with the Polish Committee of National Liberation.[5]

The Polish Premier refused to consider these suggestions as he was not prepared 'to capitulate to the Russians',[6] but he 'was disturbed to discover that the British were on the Soviet side in these

---

[1] *Ibid.*

[2] General Kukiel's Note. 'I have told Min. Romer on 26.VII.', 27 July 1944. GSHI–A.XII, 3/90–2.

[3] *Ibid.*   [4] Mikolajczyk, p. 78.

[5] Rozek, p. 233. See also Adam Pragier, *Czas Przeszly Dokonany* (London, 1966), pp. 737–8.

[6] General Kukiel's oral evidence; see also Despatch from the Minister of National Defence to the C-in-C, 27 July 1944, Ldz. 6077. APUST.

issues'.[1] Once again, therefore, he was adopting an unrealistic attitude to Russia, especially in view of the preparations in the Polish capital. Only a prompt Russo–Polish agreement might have ensured the military co-operation in the Warsaw area which could have saved Poland from catastrophe. Yet once again he was deluding himself that diplomatic and military considerations might make the Russians more amenable to the idea of abandoning some of their conditions.

On 31 July Mikolajczyk saw Molotov.[2] He told him that in spite of the suspension of Russo–Polish relations his Government, which was directing the anti-German struggle in Poland, had worked out concrete plans for establishing military co-operation between the Home Army and the Soviet forces during the decisive stage of the fighting there. These plans had been submitted to the British and the Americans with the request 'that they should be communicated to the Soviet authorities'. Mikolajczyk further stated that in practice Russo–Polish military co-operation had 'long since been established . . . in accordance with the instructions issued by the Polish Government to the Home Army'.

Molotov said that Soviet information on the matter did not corroborate this.

The Polish Premier also said that before his departure from London he had discussed with Gen Tatar 'the measures to be taken in connection with the outbreak of a general rising in the Warsaw area . . .' Molotov was not impressed and remarked that the Red Army units were now only 10 kilometers from Warsaw, implying, probably, that Red Army occupation of Warsaw was, in any event, imminent.[3]

In Mikolajczyk's opinion, however, military co-operation was to open the way to wider political and diplomatic understanding.[4]

On 3 August Mikolajczyk saw Stalin for the first time.[5] By this time Warsaw was already fighting and the premature outbreak of the insurrection had reduced him to the role of a perplexed and pliant client begging for Russian help for the stricken city.[6] Thus, the out-

---

[1] Rozek, p. 233.

[2] Record of a talk between Mikolajczyk and Molotov held on 31 July 1944 at 9.00–9.30 p.m. GSHI–PRM–Z–4.

[3] *Ibid.*   [4] *Ibid.*

[5] Record of a conversation between Premier Mikolajczyk and Marshal Stalin held at the Kremlin, on 3 August 1944. GSHI–PRM–Z–4.

[6] *Ibid*; see also record of a conversation between Premier Mikolajczyk and

break of the ill-timed insurrection in the Polish capital weakened
rather than strengthened his position during the negotiations with
Stalin. The Home Army Generals' mistake obliterated all his hopes
and expectations that their operations might help him to achieve an
understanding with the Russians.

Meanwhile, the Polish authorities in London were trying to arrange
for Britain help for Warsaw. On 27 July Raczynski told Eden that
insurrection in Warsaw was imminent and passed on to him Bor-
Komorowski's requests for air support as soon as the fighting broke
out.[1] These comprised requests for: '1. The despatch of the Polish
parachute brigade to Warsaw; 2. The bombing by the R.A.F. of
German airfields around the capital; 3. The despatch of Mustang
or Spitfire squadrons to airfields under Home Army control.'
Raczynski also requested 'the issue of warning through the B.B.C.
to the Germans to prevent their denying combatant rights to the
Home Army'.[2] He 'also drew attention to reports that the Soviet
forces approaching Warsaw were disarming Home Army units and
arresting their officers, and [he] requested British protection against
such acts'.[3]

On 28 July the British informed Raczynski:

> that, quite apart from the difficulties of co-ordinating such action with
> the Soviet Government, whose forces are operating against the Germans
> in Polish territory, operational considerations preclude us from meeting
> the three requests you made for assisting the Rising in Warsaw . . .
>
> . . . Therefore, there is nothing that His Majesty's Government can do
> in this connection.[4]

Thus, diplomatically no preparations had been made for the
Warsaw Rising. As Eden put it: 'It was set off by the local Polish
commander without consultation with us and without co-ordination
with the Soviet forces advancing on the city . . .'[5]

Finally, before the outbreak of the insurrection the British failed

Marshal Stalin held at the Kremlin, on 9 August 1944. GSHI–PRM–Z–4;
and Telegram from Premier Mikolajczyk to Marshal Stalin, 13 August 1944.
GSHI–Amb. R. P. Londyn, A.XIII.73/7.

[1] Record of a conversation between Ambassador Raczynski and Minister Eden
27 July 1944. GSHI–Talks–MSZ, Collection No. 33.

[2] *Ibid.*, Appendix 2.

[3] Record of a conversation between Ambassador Raczynski and Minister Eden,
27 July 1944. GSHI–Talks–MSZ, Collection No. 33.

[4] Letter from O. G. Sargent to Polish Ambassador, 28 July 1944, No. C.9937/8/G.
GSHI–Talks–MSZ, Collection No. 33.

[5] Avon, p. 427.

to pass on to the Russians the information received from Poland,[1] that it was imminent.[2] The Russians learned about the possibility for the first time from Mikolajczyk, at about 9 p.m. on 31 July;[3] that is, about three hours after Bor-Komorowski had given the order for the insurrection to begin. Within less than twenty-four hours Warsaw became a battlefield.

Mikolajczyk's visit to Moscow was long overdue; he should have settled the political and territorial problems with Stalin, even at the expense of great sacrifices, before encouraging the underground leaders to act.

[1] Record of a conversation between Ambassador Raczynski and Minister Eden 27 July 1944, Appendix 2. GSHI–Talks–MSZ, Collection No. 33.

[2] The Ambassador in the Soviet Union (Harriman) to the Secretary of State, 10 September 1944. *FRUS 1944*, vol. III, p. 1396; see also The Ambassador in the Soviet Union (Harriman) to the Secretary of State, 11 August 1944. *FRUS 1944*, vol. III, p. 1312.

[3] Record of a talk between Mikolajczyk and Molotov held on 31 July 1944 at 9.00–9.30 p.m. GSHI–PRM–Z–4.

2

The Genesis of the Polish Resistance Movement

The first steps towards the formation of the Polish resistance movement, the nucleus of the future Home Army and the Polish Underground State whose leaders were primarily responsible for the outbreak of the Warsaw Rising in August 1944, were taken in Warsaw in the last days of September 1939.[1] On 27 September Lt-Gen J. Rommel, the Commander of the Polish troops defending Warsaw, empowered Maj-Gen M. Tokarzewski to create an underground military organisation, the Victory for Poland Service – *Sluzba Zwyciestwu Polski*, SZP.[2]

General Tokarzewski was a professional soldier and had been a staunch follower of Marshal Pilsudski. He had, however, certain long-established contacts with the leaders of the Polish Socialist and Peasant Parties.[3] Tokarzewski was a serving army General with certain political ambitions, in itself a quite common phenomenon among Polish pre-war military leaders.

During the First World War he served in Pilsudski's Legions and took part in the Russo–Polish War of 1920.[4] In the last days of the campaign of September 1939 Gen Tokarzewski served as Gen Rommel's representative on the Defence of Warsaw Council, a civic advisory body attached to Gen Rommel's Staff.[5] Many leading Polish politicians and civic leaders were also on this Council; some of them were to take part in the creation of the resistance movement. Tokarzewski used these contacts and his familiarity with Polish

---

[1] For details see: The Affidavit of Lt-Gen Michal Tokarzewski, in the Archives of the Polish Underground Study Trust in London (APUST); Janina Karasiowna, 'Pierwsze Polrocze Armii Podziemnej', *Niepodleglosc* (London, 1948) pp. 265ff, and Zygmunt Zaremba, *Wojna i Konspiracja* (London, 1957), pp. 81–2.

[2] Juliusz Rommel, *Za Honor i Ojczyzne* (Warsaw, 1958), p. 359.

[3] Isaac Deutscher, *The Tragedy of Polish Communism Between the Wars* (London, undated), p. 17, and Stefan Korbonski, *Fighting Warsaw* (London, 1956), p. 23, and Jan Rzepecki, *Wspomnienia i Przyczynki Historyczne* (Warsaw, 1956) p. 192.

[4] Jerzy Kirchmayer, *Powstanie Warszawskie* (Warsaw, 1959) p. 12, fn. 1.

[5] Tokarzewski's Affidavit, APUST.

political life to improve his position as the leader of the underground movement.

He maintains that on 26 September 1939, he told Gen Rommel that he was ready to assume full responsibility for 'organisation of armed resistance against the occupying powers and preparation of the country's moral and physical readiness to begin open warfare when conditions are favourable'.[1] Hence, even at this exploratory and embryonic stage of the movement's existence its leader was convinced that his task was twofold; first, to organise a force capable of staging day-to-day resistance to the aggressors, and secondly, to prepare his organisation and the country for the launching of large-scale insurrectionary operations – open warfare – at the most opportune moment of the war.

In February 1940, the main task of the resistance was more explicitly defined as the preparation in Poland of 'armed insurrection at the rear of the occupying army at the moment of entry into the country of the Polish Regular Forces'.[2] From the outset, therefore, the leaders of the movement tried to envisage and prepare a general plan of resistance activities in Poland. This plan, as formulated in February 1940, embraced intelligence, sabotage and subversion activities, the carrying out of reprisals against enemy military and civil personnel and, finally, the launching of a national insurrection.[3]

In accordance with this plan, the period of 'armed resistance' which was to precede the outbreak of 'open warfare' was merely the prelude to an overall national uprising. In brief, almost from the day of the underground movement's inception its leaders were acting on the assumption that preparations for and launching of a national rising at the most crucial moment of the war for Poland should be their paramount task and guiding consideration. In the years to come they were to be most reluctant to abandon or compromise this idea. Indeed, to some extent, at least the subsequent history of the Polish resistance movement might be regarded as a series of endeavours on the part of its leaders to realise this policy in action. The realisation of this policy was attempted in the summer of 1944 when the German troops were retreating from pre-war eastern and central Poland under the pressure of the advancing Soviet armies.

[1] Tokarzewski's Affidavit, APUST.
[2] The Statute of the Association for Armed Struggle – *Zwiazek Walki Zbrojnej*, ZWZ, APUST.
[3] *Ibid.*

Tokarzewski was convinced that the movement also had another task. In his own words, the SZP had to 'ensure the continuity of the State, maintain the honour and morale of the nation and, on this basis, continue the struggle against the Germans and certainly also the Bolsheviks . . .'[1] The General's statement implies that he intended to establish an underground force capable of assuming wider than purely military functions and responsibilities; the movement was expected to serve as the centre of a clandestine political and administrative authority on a national scale. To realise these far-reaching aims, Tokarzewski appealed for help and support to those sections of the defeated army which had managed to avoid destruction and capture, and to the leaders of the main pre-war Opposition parties – the Polish Socialist, Peasant, National Democratic and Labour Parties. He intended that the army should provide the resistance with trained and experienced military cadres, while the opposition was to furnish the political and social base.

His appeal met with a favourable response in both military and political quarters. A number of senior army officers put themselves at his disposal and were used by him to form the nucleus of the High Command of the underground army. In this way close links were established between the pre-1939 army, especially its professional Officer Corps, and the resistance movement. The underground army was, throughout its existence, commanded and officered mainly by the members of the Polish pre-war military establishment. From the military point of view, there was little of the amateur about the High Command and top echelons of the conspiratorial army.[2] These officers brought with them into the resistance ideas, attitudes, traditions and professional doctrines and standards acquired during their service in the pre-war army.[3] This was to have consequences in the future.[4]

As for the politicians, M. Niedzialkowski, a leading member of the Polish Socialist Party, M. Rataj, the leader of the Peasant Party, and L. Nowodworski, the Dean of the Warsaw Bar and a prominent member of the National Democratic Party, agreed on behalf of their respective Parties to lend their support to Tokarzewski's venture.

[1] Tokarzewski's Affidavit, APUST.
[2] Cf. Hans von Krannhals, *Der Warschauer Aufstand 1944* (Frankfurt, 1962) p. 112.
[3] For a discussion of the pre-war Polish army's strategic and tactical doctrines see: Eugeniusz Kozlowski, *Wojsko Polskie 1936–39* (Warsaw, 1964) pp. 301ff.
[4] Jerzy Kirchmayer, *Powstanie Warszawskie* (Warsaw, 1959) pp. 434–5.

This led to the formation of a Supreme Political Council attached to the SZP. This Council was to advise the Commander of the underground army on political and social problems and was to try to secure popular support for it.[1] So began a period of close cooperation between the secret army and the parties of the pre-war Opposition, eventually leading to the formation and development of the Polish Underground State – *Panstwa Podziemnego* – and its political, administrative and military organs. This close association between the pre-war opposition and the military organisation was of paramount importance for the future of the movement. The Opposition provided the secret army with its political and social cachet. It should be emphasised that the Polish Socialist, Peasant, National Democratic and Labour Parties between them represented the greater part of the politically articulate and organised section of the nation.[2]

Before embarking upon a more detailed discussion of the motives which prompted Tokarzewski, who had been a faithful follower of Pilsudski, to seek the support of the Opposition for his plans, it might be of some interest to examine briefly at this stage the roles which the army – the Officer Corps – and the Opposition had played in Polish pre-war political and social life. These two bodies between them provided the movement with a high proportion of its political and military leadership. By the time war broke out in 1939 the Polish Officer Corps was 18,668-strong[3] and recruited mainly from the intelligentsia, the middle class, the landed gentry and the more prosperous sections of the peasantry.[4] Its upper echelons were composed primarily of Pilsudski's ex-Legionnaires; 65 per cent of all divisional and brigade Commanders had served during the First World War in Pilsudski's Legions.[5] As to the professional qualities of the inter-war Officer Corps, it is generally agreed that junior officers and field Commanders were well trained and highly competent while the majority of high-ranking officers and generals were inadequately versed in the art of modern warfare.[6] This was mainly a result of the shortcomings in the system of higher military education and training, and of undue reliance on practical rather than theoretical knowledge among senior Commanders. Only 903 pre-war officers

[1] Tokarzewski's Affidavit, APUST.
[2] Cf. Hugh Seton-Watson, *The East European Revolution* (London, 1956) p. 38.
[3] Eugeniusz Kozlowski, *op. cit.*, p. 77.
[4] Jan Rzepecki, *op. cit.*, p. 175 and Eugeniusz Kozlowski, *op. cit.*, p. 75.
[5] Joseph Rothschild, *Pilsudski's Coup D'Etat* (New York, 1966) p. 192.
[6] Eugeniusz Kozlowski, *op. cit.*, p. 76.

were graduates of the Staff College.[1] Pilsudski himself regarded the High Command as the weakest point in the army.[2] The aptness of his judgement was shown in the outcome of the 1939 campaign, during which the Polish High Command failed dismally, while field Commanders displayed exceptional tactical skill.[3] The army had been brought up on the Pilsudski legend and inculcated with his political ideology. The majority of its officers were on the whole deeply attached to the Marshal's memory and his highly nationalistic and romantic ideas, which were treated in the army with the utmost reverence. Pilsudski was considered by many Poles, especially soldiers, to be Poland's redeemer, the embodiment of the Polish insurrectionary tradition. The Pilsudski legend rested mainly on his exploits and the services, real and imaginary, which he had rendered to the cause of Polish independence in the years 1914–20. His political ideology was strongly permeated by romanticism, insurrectionary traditions and a belief in the greatness of Poland.[4]

The insurrectionary traditions were to a large degree sustained by what J. Talmon describes as 'the Polish religion of nationalism', with its strong messianic and romantic tendencies.[5] They also stressed national independence, self-sacrifice and hostility towards the use of compromise in politics.[6]

There were in Poland, especially after the defeat of the 1863 rising against Russia, strong opponents of the insurrectionary traditions and the ideas and values associated with them. They pointed out that every rising had ended in defeat and had led to severe reprisals and repressions. They claimed that the risings had weakened the nation by decimating its most dynamic and courageous elements and by economically impoverishing it. They attacked

the entire revolutionary tradition in Poland, declaring that the besetting sin of the old Poland had been the *Liberum Veto* and that the vice of the present was the *Liberum Conspiro*, by which any Pole could in the name of his fatherland consider himself at liberty to enter into revolutionary

---

[1] *Ibid.*, p. 76.

[2] Hans Roos, *A History of Modern Poland* (London, 1966) p. 167.

[3] *Ibid.*, p. 164.

[4] Isaac Deutscher, *Stalin: a political biography* (London, 1961) p. 89; A. Bromke, *Poland's Politics: Idealism vs. Realism* (Cambridge, Mass., 1967), pp. 25–42.

[5] J. L. Talmon, *Political Messianism. The Romantic Phase* (London, 1960), pp. 267–8.

[6] Feliks Gross, *The Seizure of Political Power* (New York, 1958), p. 343.

activity and thus bring ruin and disaster to his country, when in fact the country needed economic and social reconstruction.[1]

But, by the outbreak of the First World War, neo-romanticism had reappeared in Polish political life.[2] From his early years Pilsudski believed that Poland could regain her independence only by armed action supported from abroad.[3] He believed that each Polish generation 'must demonstrate with blood that Poland is alive and that she is not reconciled to foreign bondage'.[4] Hence, he taught his followers and soldiers to cling to such martial virtues as discipline, honour, heroism and readiness to sacrifice self. He also taught them to attach great importance to moral as well as physical and material strength. He argued that 'the art of overcoming obstacles is the art of not regarding them as such'.[5]

These highly romantic ideas profoundly influenced Pilsudski's ex-Legionnaires, many of whom occupied high positions in the pre-war army and, subsequently in the resistance. They considered the army to be the repository of Polish insurrectionary traditions and values. They were also influenced by Pilsudski's belief that Russia was the chief enemy of Poland.[6] In addition, the Marshal's successes in the years 1914–20 encouraged them in the belief that pre-war Poland was a great power.[7] The Pilsudski cult continued almost undiminished among the senior officers of the underground army.[8] Further, the army, or rather its Officer Corps, was influenced by Pilsudski's dislike of parliamentary government and party politics as such. 'He [Pilsudski] was obsessed with the idea of Poland's unity and greatness, and could not endure either to be out of power himself or to watch the disputes of parliamentary parties, which seemed to him no more than sordid wrangles.'[9] In practice this attitude led Pilsudski and his successors to involve many officers in contemporary political conflicts. In consequence, 'the army began to enter into the political life of the nation, became ubiquitous,

---

[1] R. F. Leslie, *Reform and Insurrection in Russian Poland 1856–1865* (London, 1963) p. 245.
[2] Feliks Gross, *op. cit.*, p. 33.
[3] Adam Bromke, *op. cit.*, p. 23.
[4] *Ibid.*, p. 26.
[5] Jozef Pilsudski, *Pisma Wybrane* (London, 1943) p. 92.
[6] *Ibid.*, p. 189.
[7] Adam Bromke, *op. cit.*, pp. 37–8.
[8] 'Jozef Pilsudski', *Insurekcja*, No. 5/1941; and Jan Rzepecki, *op. cit.*, pp. 210ff.
[9] Hugh Seton-Watson, *op. cit.*, p. 47.

became a burden to society, began to turn the society against itself'.[1]
This increasing militarisation was taking place despite the fact that,
officially at least, the army was allegedly 'apolitical' and ready to
serve and defend the overall national interests. In brief, in the period
1926 to 1939 the army was often an obedient instrument[2] in the
hands of the ruling regime, which was noted for its growing partiality
for more conservative and reactionary groups and interests in
Poland.[3] The authority of this regime rested on the strength of the
army and the legends connected with the struggle for independence.[4]

This close association of the army with the '*Sanacja*' regime and
its ideology tended to produce an ambivalent and suspicious
attitude among the rank and file of the Opposition. The soldiers
and the politicians differed profoundly in their respective views of
Pilsudski's role in Polish national life. To the soldiers he appeared
primarily as Poland's 'redeemer' and a victorious C-in-C, an object
of inspiration and veneration. The politicians saw him as a rival and
a dictator who for thirteen years debarred them from political
power and influence, and who discriminated ruthlessly against their
followers.[5]

Even after the shattering events of September 1939 the politicians
of the Opposition were apprehensive about the soldiers' real intentions towards them. They feared a repetition, in the long run, of
the events of May 1926, when, supported by large sections of the
army, Pilsudski had established his dictatorial *regime*. At the same
time they feared that, in the short run, the soldiers would attempt
to militarise or dominate the movement unduly.[6] The soldiers, for
their part, accustomed to the privileged status which they had
acquired under the *Sanacja*, were extremely unwilling to submit
themselves to political control.[7] These mutual fears and suspicions,

---

[1] Stefan Grot-Rowecki, *Duch wojska narodowego* (Warsaw, 1942), as quoted in
Jan Rzepecki, *op. cit.*, pp. 177–8.
[2] Jan Rzepecki, *op. cit.*, p. 176.
[3] Hugh Seton-Watson, *Eastern Europe Between the Wars, 1918–1941* (Cambridge,
1945) p. 163.
[4] Cf. Isaac Deutscher, *The Tragedy of Polish Communism Between the Wars*
(London, undated) pp. 15–16.
[5] Hugh Seton-Watson, *Eastern Europe Between the Wars, 1918–1941* (Cambridge,
1945) p. 163.
[6] Stefan Korbonski, *op. cit.*, p. 24 and p. 39.
[7] Cf. Tokarzewski's Affidavit, APUST.

as we shall see, greatly affected the course of the future development of 'Underground Poland'.[1]

It could hardly be claimed that, as a body, the pre-war Opposition was a force striving for the establishment of democracy and parliamentary rule in Poland. The Opposition possessed neither a common allegiance to democratic principles, nor a common approach to the economic and social problems which faced inter-war Poland.[2] All the main component parties of the Opposition – the National Democratic Party, the Polish Socialist Party, the Labour Party and the Peasant Party – represented different political, social and economic traditions and interests in a nation which had for so long and until so recently been denied the unifying experience of common statehood and normal political development. In general, in the period 1926–39, the Opposition as a body lacked the unity of purpose and sense of direction which might have transformed it into a potent force striving for the establishment of democracy and social justice in Poland. At the same time, however, all the parties forming the pre-war official Opposition were closely attached to the idea of Polish statehood and independence, and were antagonistic to the *Sanacja* regime and its policies. These common characteristics made co-operation possible in the formation of the underground.

In appealing to the leaders of the Opposition for their assistance and support in the creation of the resistance, Tokarzewski was prompted by the following general considerations. First, he wished to dissociate his venture from the public stigma and odium attached to the *Sanacja* and its leading political and military personalities, whom at that time the majority of the people considered almost entirely responsible for the humiliating defeat which Poland had suffered in September 1939.[3] The General was convinced that, partly because of his former association with the pre-war regime, without the Opposition's explicit approval of his plans they would not gain

[1] The term 'Underground Poland' – *Polska Podziemna* – was often used in occupied Poland by its supporters to describe the political and military resistance loyal to the Government-in-exile.

[2] Indeed, it was only in the closing years of the Second World War, to some extent under the direct challenge of communism, that serious attempts were made by the leaders of the pre-war Opposition to formulate a common political, social and economic programme. For details, see pp. 122ff of this study.

[3] Komisja Historyczna Polskiego Sztabu Glownego w Londynie, *Polskie Sily Zbrojne w Drugiej Wojnie Swiatowej*, vol. III, *Armja Krajowa* (London, 1950), p. 50, hereafter referred to as *Polskie Sily Zbrojne*; and Antoni Chrusciel ('Monter'), *Powstanie Warszawskie* (London, 1948), p. 4.

the popular support which was essential for the creation of a large-scale movement. Secondly, in view of the complete destruction of the organs and apparatus of State, Tokarzewski intended to use the Opposition's extensive organisational framework (as yet almost intact), personnel and contacts as the potential foundations of the underground organisation.[1] Thirdly, it appears that as early as the last days of September 1939 Tokarzewski had anticipated, or was even informed of, efforts to form abroad a new Polish Government in which the pre-war Opposition would be represented.[2] Finally, he intended to establish between the conspiratorial army and the Opposition an organic unity which would serve as the political and social base of the underground movement. Nevertheless, he wished to subordinate the politicians to the overall control of the commander of the military organisation.[3]

For their part, the politicians were prepared to collaborate with Tokarzewski and further his designs because, on the whole, they were convinced that 'the war did not end with the defeats in Warsaw and Poland'.[4] They were conscious that Poland was a member of the anti-German coalition and had a part to play, however small, in the unfolding drama.[5] As we shall see, this conviction was in essence maintained throughout the war. The fact that the struggle in Poland was to assume conspiratorial forms seemed to them, in view of Poland's historical experiences, natural and acceptable.[6] In any case, it should be stressed that a large measure of co-operation between the Opposition and the Army had already existed, in embryonic form, during the German siege of Warsaw. Hence, the politicians' decision to lend their support to the SZP was but a continuation of their earlier resolve to take part in the defence of the Polish capital, in September 1939.[7] Indeed, the climate created during the defence of Warsaw defined the initial character of the conspiracy and left a lasting imprint on the entire period of underground struggle.[8] Moreover, the politicians seemed aware that the

[1] Tokarzewski's Affidavit, APUST.
[2] Cf. *Polskie Sily Zbrojne, op. cit.*, p. 50.
[3] Report No. 2 of the Commander of Area D, No. 1, 6 January 1940 (Appendix C and D), APUST, and Stanislaw Dolega-Modrzewski, *Polskie Panstwo .Podziemne* (London, 1959), pp. 22ff.
[4] Zygmunt Zaremba, *op. cit.*, p. 63.   [5] *Ibid.*, p. 99.
[6] Stefan Korbonski, *op. cit.*, p. 11, and Zygmunt Zaremba, *op. cit.*, p. 63.
[7] Zygmunt Zaremba, *op. cit.*, pp. 99–100.
[8] Cf. Jerzy Kirchmayer, *Powstanie Warszawskie* (Warsaw, 1959), pp. 431–3, and Zygmunt Zaremba, *op. cit.*, p. 88.

nation as such did not feel defeated but, rather, *frustrated* by the fact that the speedy collapse of the regular Polish resistance had prevented the country from taking part in the armed struggle against the Germans.[1] The people did not abandon the hope that final victory would fall to the Allies and to Poland. On the contrary, they believed that it was their duty to stage a general resistance to the aggressors.[2] Undoubtedly, the politicians were convinced that they had to channel and provide organisational outlets for these popular sentiments.[3]

Towards the end of 1939 the Commander of the secret army formulated, with the politicians, the general aims of the movement and the principles on which their mutual co-operation was to be based. The general aims of the movement were embodied in the Statute of the SZP and the Ideological Declaration of its Supreme Political Council. The Statute expressed the aims of the organisation in the following terms:

(a) To undertake a decisive and unrelenting struggle against the invader in every field of his activity in Poland and to continue this struggle with all the means at the movement's disposal until the day of the liberation of Poland within her pre-war boundaries.
(b) To re-organise the Polish army.
(c) To create the nucleus of a temporary national authority in Poland.

The Statute included repeated exhortations 'to continue an unrelenting struggle against the invader with the help of the Allies, who will undoubtedly assist Poland in her struggle'. Yet it stated that, without independent Polish effort, 'no-one can save us or restore Poland'. The Statute also stressed that the main aim of the movement was the restoration of an independent Poland 'without which our families and their property, our towns and national wealth and our lives . . . are meaningless'.[4]

The aims expressed in the Statute were corroborated and augmented in the Ideological Declaration of the Supreme Political Council. The Declaration stated:

[1] Cf. Kazimierz Iranek-Osmecki, 'Zarys Rozwoju Armii Krajowej', *Niepodleglosc*, vol. 1, (London, 1948), p. 249. [2] *Ibid*.
[3] There was a spontaneous outburst of conspiratorial activity in Poland in the first few months of the German occupation. *Vide* the Report of the Commander of the SZP to Gen Sikorski, 7 December 1939, APUST, and Report No. 17 of the Commander of the ZWZ in the German Zone of Occupation to the Supreme Commander of the ZWZ, 15 April 1940, APUST.
[4] The Statute of the SZP, APUST.

1. The struggle, for the independence of Poland, against the Germans and Russians continues. It will continue until our final victory is achieved. Every Pole has the duty . . . to take part in this struggle. One of the conditions of its success and the efficacious use of all our forces is the uniformity of its leadership over the entire territory of Poland. Subordination to the leadership and loyal co-operation with it are the least we expect today from every citizen.
2. We are fighting, not only for Poland, but also for free men in a free Europe. [. . .] Our enemies are all totalitarian ideologies, and, today, in the first place, hitlerism and bolshevism.
3. Free Poland will be genuinely democratic . . .
4. Free Poland must become so strong that she will become an effective prop to the Western-cultured Slavonic countries and other small nations situated between Germany and Russia.
5. . . . The structural foundations of the Polish State and its social and economic system will be decided by the Parliament, assembled on a wide democratic basis immediately after the restoration of independence.[1]

In these two documents, behind all the twentieth-century concerns and anxieties, we seem to hear echoes of the voice of eighteenth- and nineteenth-century insurrection. It is important to remember that the general aims of the leaders of the movement played a very influential part in moulding its later history; in fact, we shall meet them again in discussing the indirect causes of the Warsaw Rising itself.

With regard to the Declaration's references to long-term plans for the establishment of a parliamentary democracy in post-war Poland, the question of whether these aims would have been realisable, in the form of viable and long-lasting institutions, under any post-war circumstances would seem to be a controversial one, in view of the political attitudes of some National Democrats and the past traditions of the Army. Yet, this attachment to democracy was one of the main tenets of the movement. Indeed, it is alleged that the activities of Tokarzewski were at that time inspired by a vision of a future democratic Poland in which the proletarian and peasant masses would be expected to play a dominant part in the affairs of the State.[2] Tokarzewski himself stated that he wished to embrace all Polish political groups, including the remnants of the *Sanacja*, within the framework of the resistance, provided that they were

[1] Report No. 2 of the Commander of Area 1, 6 January 1940 (Appendix E), APUST.
[2] *Polskie Sily Zbrojne, op. cit.*, p. 50, and Tokarzewski's Affidavit, APUST.

ready to subordinate themselves to the policies formulated by the Polish Socialist, Peasant and National Democratic Parties.[1] The problem of the movement's attitude to the Polish communists as yet hardly arose. The Communists, their Party disbanded on Stalin's orders in 1938,[2] did not at that time display any noticeable signs of organised activity on a national scale. Their reappearance in Polish political life was to take place, in a significant manner, in the winter of 1941–2.

Apart from these efforts to clarify, with the political leaders, the general aims on which the movement was to be based, during the last months of 1939 Tokarzewski attempted to extend the scope of authority of the SZP to establish a network radiating from Warsaw to other areas of Poland, and to make contact with the Polish Government in exile, which was formed in Paris, under the Premiership of Gen Wladyslaw Sikorski, on 30 September 1939.

Tokarzewski's repeated efforts[3] to establish direct contact with the Government in Paris were unsuccessful at first because the Prime Minister, Gen Sikorski, was suspicious of Tokarzewski's association with the *Sanacja*[4] and uncertain about his claims as to the real strength of his organisation,[5] and was reluctant to grant official recognition either to the General as head of the resistance or to the SZP itself.[6] This attitude towards Tokarzewski was consistent with Sikorski's pre-war opposition to the *Sanacja* and his distrust of its leading personalities.

While, in Warsaw, the resistance movement was already in the process of formation on a national scale, in Paris Sikorski and his newly-formed 'Government of National Unity' initiated their own

[1] Tokarzewski's Affidavit, APUST.

[2] For details see: M. K. Dziewanowski, *The Communist Party of Poland: An Outline of History* (Cambridge, Mass., 1959), pp. 139–54, and Isaac Deutscher, *The Tragedy of Polish Communism Between the Wars* (London, undated), pp. 29–34.

[3] For details see: Halina Karasiowna, *op. cit.*, pp. 270–1.

[4] Gen Tokarzewski claims that his transfer to a less important position was to some extent engineered by the National Democrats, who resented his former association with the *Sanacja* and his left-wing sympathies. Cf. Gen Tokarzewski's Affidavit, APUST.

[5] The situation in Poland at that time was confused and there existed a number of other conspiratorial groups which aspired to leading status. Cf. Report No. 17 of the Commander of the ZWZ in the German Zone of Occupation to the Supreme Commander of the ZWZ, 15 April 1940, APUST.

[6] Cf. Wladyslaw Pobog-Malinowski, *Najnowsza Historia Polityczna Polski*, vol. 3 (London, 1960), p. 123.

plans for the creation of an underground force in Poland. On 13 November 1939, Gen Sikorski appointed a Ministerial Committee for Home Affairs, under the chairmanship of Gen Kazimierz Sosnkowski. This was to deal with all home and resistance affairs and problems.[1] In the years 1911 to 1920 Sosnkowski had been one of the closest collaborators of Jozef Pilsudski. During the critical stage of the Russo–Polish War of 1920 he had served as the Deputy Minister of Military Affairs. After the War he continued to serve in the Army. In 1926, during Pilsudski's *coup d'état*, he tried to commit suicide, and from this time his relations with Pilsudski and the regime deteriorated. In September 1939 he was appointed Minister of War Economy but he refused to accept this nomination, which he considered meaningless under the circumstances, and served instead as an army Group Commander.[2]

In addition to the Ministerial Committee for Home Affairs Gen Sikorski established an official underground organisation, the Association for Armed Struggle – *Zwiazek Walki Zbrojnej*, ZWZ – which, commanded and directed from Paris, was to assume responsibility for the conduct of all resistance activities in Poland. Gen Sosnkowski was appointed as the Supreme Commander of the ZWZ and was to exercise his duties from Paris. He was to act under the direct control of the C-in-C and Prime Minister, Gen Sikorski.

A Statue of the Government-sponsored movement introduced a division between the purely political, or social, and the military aspects of the underground activities in Poland. This distinction was made more conspicuous by the fact that the political and social work of the resistance was to be financed from the general Government budget, while the expenses of military activities were to be met out of the Armed Forces budget. The activities of the ZWZ were to cover the whole of Poland, both the German and Soviet Zones of Occupation. The whole territory of Poland was divided into six areas, which were to be commanded directly from Paris.[3] In January 1940, however, the command structure was simplified; the Commander of the Warsaw District was appointed Commander of the under-

---

[1] The Statute of the Association for Armed Struggle, APUST.

[2] Kazimierz Sosnkowski, *Materialy Historyczne* (London, 1966), pp. xvii–xviii.

[3] The Statute of the Association for Armed Struggle, APUST and Instruction No. 1 of the Supreme Commander of the ZWZ to the Commander of Area No. 1, 4 December 1939, APUST.

ground organisation in the German Zone of Occupation, while the Commander of the Lwow area was given similar powers in the Russian Zone. Col Stefan Grot-Rowecki, who since the middle of October 1939 had been Chief of Staff to Gen Tokarzewski, was appointed the military Commander of the Warsaw area and consequently of the entire German Zone.[1] Col Grot-Rowecki, a grandson of the insurrectionist of 1863, was a professional soldier who had, during the September campaign, commanded a motorised brigade. Like many other high-ranking officers he had, during the First World War, served in Pilsudski's Legions and he took part in the Russo–Polish War of 1920. Despite his personal admiration for Pilsudski he did not take part in the 1926 *coup d'état*. He regarded himself primarily as a soldier and tried to avoid political involvements.[2]

Under the plan to simplify the command-structure Tokarzewski himself was ordered to go to Lwow to assume command of the underground in the Soviet Zone.[3] The appointment of two high-ranking Commanders of the SZP to responsible posts in the new organisation signified that it was to be based on the framework of the earlier movement. Furthermore, all other resistance forces were to acknowledge the authority of and merge with the ZWZ.[4] These steps, initiated and undertaken by Sikorski, were designed to ensure for himself and his Government full and undisputed control over the resistance forces in Poland. These decisions, dated 4 December 1939, reached Warsaw by special courier on 1 January 1940.

There was a significant difference between Sikorski's approach to the organisation of resistance work in Poland and that of Tokarzewski. The former wished to split the movement into two spheres, military and political, both directly subordinate to his Government, whereas Tokarzewski wished to establish an organic unity between the military and political parts of the movement under a Supreme Commander in Warsaw. In Poland Sikorski's decisions and plans were accepted, though with some misgivings and even bitterness. The Government was accused of undoing rather than consolidating

---

[1] Instruction No. 2 of the Supreme Commander of the ZWZ to the Commander of Area No. 1, 16 January 1940, APUST.
[2] General Grot-Rowecki's Papers, APUST.
[3] Instruction No. 2 of the Supreme Commander of the ZWZ to the Commander of Area No. 1, 16 January 1940, APUST.
[4] The Statute of the ZWZ, APUST.

the progress already made towards the establishment of a unified resistance force in Poland.[1] Nevertheless, a direct link had now been established between the resistance movement in Poland and the exiled Government. This connection was to continue throughout the movement's history; it led to the emergence of the Polish Underground State and of the Home Army (*Armia Krajowa* – AK), which together represented the Government's interests and authority in occupied Poland. The link between the Government and the underground organisation had serious repercussions for the future of the resistance movement and of Poland herself. From now on the émigré Government's policies, activities and standing among Poland's allies affected the fortunes of the resistance in Poland, and vice versa. Indeed, as will be seen in later chapters, in one sense the Warsaw Rising may be regarded as an attempt by leaders of the underground movement to help this Government to overcome the *impasse* in Russo–Polish relations which existed from April 1943 and which reached a dangerous climax in the midsummer of 1944. From the outset one of the essential aims of the resistance was to assist the exiled Government in restoring an independent Poland. This aim was to be furthered, it was intended, by the staging of a large-scale insurrection in the closing stages of the war. All the main efforts of the resistance were to be directed towards preparation for a rising and the organisation of cadres for the future administrative organs of the State. This demanded the achievement of national unity and close co-operation between the Government and the resistance.

[1] S. Korbonski, *op. cit.*, pp. 39–41, and Z. Zaremba, *op. cit.*, pp. 103–4.

3

Attempts to Unify the Polish Resistance Movement

1. *Attempts to Unite the Resistance in Poland*

The Association for Armed Struggle (ZWZ) was formed in January 1940 as the nucleus of the future Home Army. It was hoped that its leaders, as the representatives of the Polish Government, would be able to bring under their control and consolidate all resistance forces in the country, so creating a fully representative national movement which would shape and follow policies reflecting Sikorski's strategic and political plans.[1] The exercise of control on this scale would also be of considerable value at the end of the war, in helping the pro-London leaders to emerge as the undisputed leaders of Poland, as it would ease their assumption of power at the political and administrative helm of the nation. The existence of a single military underground organisation would be a safeguard against the dangers of ill-co-ordinated action against the Germans and civil strife after, or even during the war. It would mean more efficient utilisation of the resources of resistance and the creation of a force capable, during the final stages of the war, of launching the nation-wide insurrection which was to be the crowning achievement of the Polish underground.

For these reasons, in establishing the Association the exiled authorities categorically stated that, thenceforth, only one military underground organisation should exist in Poland; the military elements of other organisations were told to place themselves at the disposal of the ZWZ.[2] In 1942 Sikorski decided to re-name the ZWZ the Home Army (*Armia Krajowa* – AK) to emphasise the fact that it was an integral part of the Polish Armed Forces loyal to the exiled Government.[3]

[1] Instruction No. 1 of the Supreme Commander of the ZWZ to the Commander of Area No. 1, 4 December 1939, APUST.
[2] Instruction No. 2 of the Supreme Commander of the ZWZ to the Commander of Area No. 1, 16 January 1940, APUST.
[3] The C-in-C's order renaming the ZWZ the Home Army, 14 February 1942, Ldz. 627, APUST.

Between 1939 and 1944 repeated efforts were made to create a unified and centrally-directed underground army in Poland and the order calling upon other military organisations to subordinate themselves to the Home Army was re-issued on a number of occasions.[1] These attempts were, however, only partially successful.[2] Despite its considerable, though often qualified, popularity, the pro-London movement failed to bring all resistance forces under its control. This failure had grave repercussions; it led to a bitter struggle for power between rival resistance groups during the last years of the war. Some of the political and ideological aspects and causes of the Warsaw Rising may be traced to this internal conflict.

There were many reasons for the failure to consolidate resistance forces. In part, it was due to the internal dissension which plagued the London movement until the middle of 1943.[3] The tension and mistrust between the Generals and the politicians,[4] the fundamental lack of understanding between the National Democrats on the one hand and the Peasant and Socialist Parties on the other[5] and the strained relations which existed, from time to time, between the exiled Government and the underground leaders in Poland[6] all tended to divert the attention of the pro-London leaders and to detract from their authority in the country, thus hampering their plans for absorbing other military groups into the Home Army. The primary cause of this failure was, however, the existence in the country of extreme political and military resistance organisations of both left and right; the Communist-controlled People's Army (*Armia Ludowa* – AL) and the ultra-nationalist near-fascist National Armed Forces (*Narodowe Sily Zbrojne* – NSZ). These groups differed so widely from the pro-London movement as regards their

---

[1] For details see *Polskie Sily Zbrojne, op. cit.,* pp. 128ff.

[2] Cf. *Ibid.,* p. 126.

[3] Despatch from the Government Delegate to the Prime Minister, received in London 29 September 1943, No. 166, Ldz. K5353/43; GSHI–L9.

[4] Report of emissary 'Antoni', 4 April 1941, Ldz. 1820/Tj/41, APUST. *Polskie Sily Zbrojne, op. cit.,* p. 132; Zygmunt Zaremba, *op. cit.,* pp. 161ff, and Stefan Korbonski, *W. Imieniu Rzeczypospolitej* . . . (2nd ed., London, 1964) pp. 39ff.

[5] Organisational Report of the Commander of the Home Army, No. 118, Ldz. 4121/42, APUST; Special Report of the Commander of the Home Army to the C-in-C, 22 May 1944, Ldz. 549/GNW/44, APUST; and Zygmunt Zaremba, *op. cit.,* pp. 99–100.

[6] Cf. Despatch from the Prime Minister to the Government Delegate, 3 February 1943, Ldz. 157/XXII/43, GSHI–File 105; and Despatch from the Government Delegate to the Prime Minister, dated 31 July 1943, received 9 September 1943, No. 165, Ldz. K5212/43, GSHI–L9.

political and ideological aims that they could not be brought under its control. As early as February 1943 this was clearly recognised by Sikorski, who stated emphatically that there was no room for communists and fascists within the London camp, as their inclusion would have altered its essential character.[1] Sikorski's ideal Poland was to be a liberal, parliamentary democracy, with a primarily capitalist economy, closely allied to Great Britain and the United States.[2] Hence, there was, he felt, no place for the left- or right-wing forces dedicated to more radical, even eventually revolutionary settlements of Poland's problems and, in the case of the communists, to the idea of drastic reorientation of Poland's foreign policy through the establishment of close ties with the U.S.S.R.[3] The existence, then, of the AL and NSZ and their respective political centres rendered the achievement of national unity and harmony in war-time Poland impossible and led to a struggle for power and national supremacy in post-war Poland between the AK and AL during the closing stages of the German occupation.

The establishment of the AL and NSZ in the years 1942–4 initiated a process of polarisation of political and social forces in Poland. In the summer of 1943 the Communists began a concerted effort to capture the allegiances of the left-wing elements,[4] including the Marxists, the left-wing Socialists and the Peasants, while the NSZ embarked on a similar campaign with regard to the right-wing elements.[5] The London camp was at the centre of the political spectrum. Under the impact of these developments the internal differences within the pro-London movement began to lose their earlier significance and by the end of 1943 the movement's internal consolidation was practically complete.[6]

During the months immediately preceding the Warsaw Rising the existence of the AL and the NSZ, outside the authority of the London camp, precluded the formulation of a common policy relating to the departing Germans and advancing Russians. In the summer of 1944 the three groups each pursued distinct and different

---

[1] Despatch from the Prime Minister to the Government Delegate, 3 February 1943, Ldz. 157/XXII/43, GSHI–File 105.
[2] *Ibid.*   [3] *Ibid.*
[4] Cf. Jerzy Pawlowicz, *Strategia Frontu Narodowego PPR; III. 1943–VII. 1944* (Warsaw, 1965), pp. 42ff.
[5] Z. Stypulkowski, *W Zawierusze, Dziejowej: Wsponienia 1939–1945* (London, 1951), p. 128.
[6] Zygmunt Zaremba, *op. cit.*, pp. 193ff.

policies and tactics. The leaders of the Home Army had designed a policy of military action against the Germans and political opposition to the Russians and the Polish Communists, in the hope that, with Western help, they would be able to secure undisputed power for the exiled Government;[1] the Communists were fighting the Germans and, with the help of the Russians, were installing their own administrative organs in the territories already liberated, thereby opposing the political aims of the London camp;[2] the NSZ was spreading confusion and fomenting civil strife in Poland by concentrating its main efforts on the struggle against both the Communists and the left-wing elements within the pro-London movement, which was regarded by the NSZ as a pro-Russian organisation.[3] The NSZ intended to liquidate as many as possible of their political opponents, in an attempt to weaken the forces which, in their opinion, were ready to collaborate with the Russians.[4] The NSZ's long-term plans for Poland appear to have been connected with their anticipation of a new conflict in Poland between the U.S.S.R. and the Anglo–Saxon powers.

2. *The People's Army*

The Communist-controlled resistance came into existence in January 1942, when the Polish Workers' Party (*Polska Partia Robotnicza –* PPR) was created in Warsaw, with the approval and help of Moscow.[5]

The first leaders were Marceli Nowotko and Pawel Finder – ex-members of the old Communist Party of Poland which had been disbanded by the Comintern in 1938 – who were parachuted into Poland in December 1941, with instructions to establish contact with Communist organisations in the country and use them as a basis in creating a new Polish Marxist-Leninist Party. Nowotko and Finder were members of a special 'Initiative Group' assembled

[1] For details see pp. 164ff of this study.
[2] For details see pp. 106ff of this study.
[3] Special Report of the Commander of the Home Army to the C-in-C, 22 May 1944, Ldz. 549/GNW/44, APUST; Despatch from the Prime Minister to the President of the Republic, 29 July 1944, No. 2129, GSHI–PRM–Z–4; Despatch from the Prime Minister to the Government Delegate and the Commander of the Home Army, 31 July 1944, No. 6206, Ldz. 2147/2/tjn/44.
[4] Letter from T. Salski, the representative of the NSZ in London, to the C-in-C, 28 August 1944, GSHI–A.XII, 1/4.
[5] Antoni Przygonski (ed.), *Polski Ruch Robotniczy: w okresie wojny i okupacji hitlerowskiej: wrzesien 1939–styczen 1945* (Warsaw, 1964), pp. 155–6, hereafter referred to as *Polski Ruch Robotniczy*.

and trained at the Comintern School at Pushkino, near Moscow, in the second half of 1941, in preparation for work in Poland.[1]

One of the main tasks of the 'Initiative Group' was the formulation of a programme for the new party. The Soviet leaders suggested that the PPR manifesto should be guided by five considerations. These were: the need to take into account the war-time alliance between socialist forces and the bourgeois democracies, in planning the strategy and tactics of the international workers' movement; the essential aim of all Communist parties in occupied Europe to establish broad anti-German national fronts consisting of the left-wing, peasant and bourgeois democratic parties; the need for the new party to be free of the sectarian tendencies which had plagued the old Polish Communist Party; the desirability of communist participation in the government of liberated, democratic Poland; and finally, the long-term requirement that communists should strive for eventual social revolution in the country. Until the time for this arrived the Party should concentrate on demands for the democratisation of Polish political, social and economic life by pressing for the establishment of an eight-hour working day, land reform and equality for national minorities.[2]

The first party manifesto, drafted in Russia, reflected some of these considerations. It called for the creation of a national front 'for the struggle for free and independent Poland'. The Party pledged itself to promote national unity and disclaimed any desire to compete with other parties which were 'honestly fighting' for national liberation. The party insisted that the post-war system in Poland must be free from fascism and social and economic exploitation, must give land to the peasants and provide work and social services for the workers and the intelligentsia. It called for the unity of the working class, which the Party hoped to place firmly in the vanguard of the struggle for national liberation, and promised help to the proletariat in the task of freeing itself from 'the yoke of capitalism'. The Party was, however, to possess a very broad social base, as its ranks were to be open to 'all honest workers, peasants and intelligentsia' who might wish to join them, regardless of previous party affiliations.[3]

[1] M. Malinowski, 'Ksztaltowanie sie zalozen programowych polskiego ruchu komunistycznego w latach 1939–1942', *Z Pola Walki*, *IV*, No. 4 (1961), p. 40.
[2] *Ibid.*, pp. 40–2.
[3] *Ksztaltowanie sie Podstaw Programowych Polskiej Partii Robotniczej w Latach*

Although close links existed between the PPR and the Comintern, the Party was at pains to stress that, officially at least, it was not a member of the Comintern.[1]

At this stage the PPR was prepared to co-operate with Sikorski's Government as it represented Polish interests abroad and organised the Armed Forces. The Party was ready to collaborate with the Government's plenipotentiaries in Warsaw in establishing a common anti-German front,[2] probably hoping by this means to enter the mainstream of national political life as the representative of radical and progressive forces in the country. The PPR was preparing, therefore, to assume the role of champion of national liberation and social progress in Poland, preparing to pursue a policy which might make it attractive to patriots and radicals alike.[3]

In the military field the Party intended to assist in the preparation of a national anti-German insurrection and help the Red Army by organising guerilla warfare, so opening a 'second front' in Poland.[4] The PPR's desire to shape its military strategy in the light of the demands of the struggle on the eastern front later became one of the main sources of conflict between the communists and pro-London forces in Poland. Initially, however, this conflict was of little practical importance as the PPR devoted the first year of its existence mainly to its own organisation and the creation of its military detachments, the People's Guards (*Gwardia Ludowa* – GL), which in 1944 became the People's Army.[5] In June 1942 the Party allegedly had 4,000 members and had recruited 3,000 men to its military detachments.[6] By the end of 1942 the PPR's military activities comprised intelligence and sabotage work and the preparations for armed insurrection.[7]

From its inception, its political and propaganda activities gave rise to deep concern among the pro-London circles, who accused the

---

1942–45 (*wybor materialow i dokumentow*) (Warsaw, 1958), pp. 11–15 (hereafter referred to as *Ksztaltowanie*).

[1] *Ibid.*, p. 28.   [2] *Ibid.*, pp. 32–3.

[3] Cf. Report No. 140 of the Commander of the Home Army to the C-in-C, 19 October 1942, Ldz. 4140/tjn/42, APUST.

[4] *Ksztaltowanie*, p. 15.

[5] Czeslaw Madajczyk, 'Wazna Decyzja', *Najnowsze Dzieje Polski*, vol. IV (Warsaw, 1960), p. 6.

[6] Nowotko's Despatch to Comrade G. M. Dymitrov, No. 1, 9 July 1942, 'Depesze KC PPR Do Georgi Dymitrowa', *Z Pola Walki*, IV, No. 4 (1961), p. 174.

[7] Report No. 140 of the Commander of the Home Army to the C-in-C, 19 October 1942, Ldz. 4140/tjn/42, APUST.

party of preparing plans for a communist take-over at the end of the war, of attempting to discredit the Government-sponsored resistance by claiming that only the PPR was actively engaged in fighting the Germans, of calling upon the people to launch immediate, and therefore premature armed action against the Germans, of undermining public faith in the Western Powers and the London authorities, and, finally, of fomenting class-struggle and inspiring revolutionary sentiments.[1] In the opinion of Grot-Rowecki the PPR's propaganda was proving effective, especially among what he described as the less politically conscious elements. The Communist appeals for the launching of immediate armed struggle against the Germans were well-received among the young people, who were impatient to fight and were finding it irksome to wait for the Home Army's signal for universal insurrection.[2] The timing of the large-scale anti-German operations was becoming the main bone of contention between the pro-London and pro-Communist forces. The Home Army planned to stage its main military effort during the moment of German collapse, while the PPR was demanding the immediate intensification of anti-German operations, to assist the Red Army. After the collapse of France the pro-London authorities, especially their leaders abroad, were prepared to stage only 'limited warfare',[3] in spite of the demands of their own supporters for more drastic anti-German measures. They feared that premature intensification of the struggle would only lead to unnecessary losses and frustrate their long-term plans.[4] However, in the second half of 1942 Grot-Rowecki came to the conclusion that because of the German terror the policy of limiting the Home Army operations was becoming untenable and was helping the Communists win more followers. In August 1942 he reported to London that the Germans' use of the principle of collective responsibility and mass terror as

---

[1] Report No. 140 of the Commander of the Home Army to the C-in-C, 19 October 1942, Ldz. 4140/tjn/42, APUST.

[2] *Ibid.*, and Report on the situation of K. [the Communists], 20 November 1943, Ldz. 6581/tjn/43, APUST.

[3] Despatch from the C-in-C to the Commander of the ZWZ, 18 June 1940, Ldz. 3814/40, APUST; and Order for the Commander of the ZWZ, 14 February 1941, Ldz. 525/41, APUST.

[4] Despatch from the Deputy Prime Minister to the Commander of the Home Army, 25 December 1942, Ldz. 5522/42, APUST., and Despatch from the Deputy Prime Minister and Minister of National Defence to the Government Delegate and the Commander of the Home Army, 8 January 1943, Ldz. 5522/44 APUST.

means of subduing the nation was causing heavy losses. This was happening despite Polish efforts to avoid heavy German reprisals by limiting active armed resistance to a bare minimum for the time being while concentrating, instead, on sabotage and intelligence work. In view of this policy the more active and impatient individuals were joining Communist resistance groups. Moreover, the Home Commander feared that the present defensive attitude might adversely affect the offensive spirit of his troops during the insurrection. Hence, he proposed to the Government in London that from September 1942 he should be allowed to intensify armed resistance and even, in the territories of eastern Poland, initiate guerilla warfare. He was anxious to ensure that, under the impact of growing German terror and the attractive Communist resistance policy, the initiative should not pass from his hands.[1]

At the end of 1942 his determination to intensify operations was further strengthened when the Germans started to expel Polish peasants from the Lublin and Zamosc districts and replace them with Germans brought from Rumania. The expulsion of the Poles was associated with the worst kind of atrocities and excesses, which led to mass escapes of young people to the woods.[2] In consultation with the Government Delegate, Grot-Rowecki ordered his troops in that region to retaliate by attacking German lines of communication, burning the evacuated farms and killing domestic animals.[3] The Warsaw leaders were, however, ordered by the Government to limit retaliatory operations to a bare minimum, not to extend them beyond the areas affected by the expulsion and at all costs to prevent the outbreak of general insurrection. They were told to resist the demands of the masses for more drastic measures.[4] This order inspired a number of articles in the London-controlled underground press, designed to cool the general ardour for more active

---

[1] Despatch from the Commander of the Home Army to the C-in-C, 1 August 1942, Ldz. 3085, APUST.
[2] Despatch from the Commander of the Home Army to the C-in-C, dated 23 December received 24 December 1942, Ldz. 5521, APUST.
[3] Organisational Report of the Commander of the Home Army, No. 190, 1 March 1943, Ldz. 5277/43, APUST.
[4] Despatch from the Deputy Prime Minister to the Commander of the Home Army, 25 December 1942, Ldz. 5522/42, APUST, and Despatch from the Deputy Prime Minister and Minister of National Defence to the Government Delegate and the Commander of the Home Army, 8 January 1943, Ldz. 5522/43, APUST.

and determined anti-German resistance;[1] the Government had consistently said that the Home Army was to act on a large scale only at the end of the war.[2]

In February 1943 the Germans stopped the expulsions.[3] Thus, the first large-scale Home Army operations met with a success which tended to indicate that determined Polish opposition could exercise a restraining influence on German terror. The Communists exploited this success in accusing the Home Army of undue caution and passivity. They argued that terror must be countered in kind.[4]

Thus, relations between the pro-London forces and the PPR were becoming more tense. At first, the growing rivalry between them found expression primarily in a propaganda battle. Early in 1942 Grot-Rowecki ordered the creation, in the Home Army's Propaganda and Information Bureau, of a unit which was to specialise in anti-Communist propaganda.[5]

Nevertheless, at the end of 1942 the PPR decided to approach the pro-London leaders with the suggestion that all resistance forces in Poland should be consolidated.[6] This decision coincided with a change of leadership in the PPR. In November 1942 Marceli Now-otko, the secretary of the central committee of the PPR, was assassinated on the instigation of Boleslaw Malojec, one of the founders of the party.[7] In December 1942 Pawel Finder became the head of the party.[8] Finder empowered Wladyslaw Gomulka, a member of the new Party secretariat, to start negotiations with the Government's Delegate, Prof Jan Piekalkiewicz.[9] The Professor, a member of the Peasant Party, was apparently well-disposed towards an understanding between the London camp and 'the entire left' and may have considered co-operation with the PPR a practical possibility.[10] However, the outcome of the negotiations between

[1] 'Z Bronia U Nogi', *Biuletyn Informacyjny*, 11 February 1943, No. 6 (161); and 'Akcja Zbrojna? Tak–Lecz Ograniczona!', *Biuletyn Informacyjny*, 3 April 1943, No. 13 (168), APUST.
[2] Despatch from the Deputy Prime Minister to the Commander of the Home Army, 25 December 1942, Ldz. 5522/42, APUST.
[3] Organisational Report of the Commander of the Home Army, No. 190, 1 March 1943, Ldz. 5277/43, APUST.   [4] *Ksztaltowanie*, p. 124.
[5] Organisational Report of the Commander of the Home Army, No. 118, 1 March 1943, Ldz. 4121/42, APUST.
[6] Czeslaw Madajczyk, *op. cit.*, p. 7.
[7] *Polski Ruch Robotniczy*, p. 205.   [8] *Ibid.*
[9] *Ibid.*, p. 263, and Czeslaw Madajczyk, *op. cit.*, p. 13.
[10] Maria Turlejska, *O Wojnie i Podziemiu* (Warsaw, 1959), p. 120, and Czeslaw Madajczyk, *op. cit.*, p. 11.

Piekalkiewicz and the PPR depended to a large extent on the attitude of Grot-Rowecki who, although a military Commander, exercised considerable influence over the purely political affairs of the London movement.[1]

During his talks with Piekalkiewicz, Gomulka was to be guided by the resolutions of the Central Committee of the PPR, adopted in January 1943, which stated that, in view of the recent Allied victories, the problem of staging national insurrections in occupied countries had become a pressing one, but that preparations for an insurrection would demand the creation of a broad national front and the intensification of guerilla warfare as an army-tempering prelude to insurrection itself. The PPR envisaged that the insurrection would be the last, decisive stage of the guerilla warfare. The Party believed that merely to provide the underground units with untested weapons and theoretical training was not sufficient preparation for the insurrection.[2]

Grot-Rowecki also believed that the insurrection should be preceded by a period of more intensified diversionary operations, to give the Home Army a chance to gain combat experience and test its command structure.[3] In April 1943 he told London that he had begun intensifying his own diversionary and armed operations and was resorting to counter-terror against the Germans. He reported that his operations were successful and had so far led to no German reprisals, but stressed that he did not intend to 'overstep the limit'. His operations were not to be allowed to escalate into general insurrection. More significantly, his plans differed from those of the PPR in that he had no desire to shape his strategy primarily in terms of what would be most useful to the Red Army. He informed his C-in-C that because of the Russo–Polish dispute he had diminished operations against the *Wehrmacht* and 'especially [those] against the communication lines leading to the East', was concentrating his efforts on German security and administrative organs and intended to continue with this policy.[4] Thus, the differences in attitude to Russia were preventing the development of fruitful co-

[1] Letter from Colonel Janusz Bokszczanin ('Sek') to the author of this study, 19 April 1965 (hereafter referred to as Bokszczanin's letter).
[2] *Ksztaltowanie*, pp. 66–81.
[3] Despatch from the Commander of the Home Army to the C-in-C, 1 August 1942, Ldz. 3085, APUST.
[4] Despatch from the Commander of the Home Army to the C-in-C, dated 29 April, decoded 5 May 1943, Ldz. 2312, APUST.

operation between the Home Army and the PPR and were bound to affect the negotiations between the two.

On 15 January 1943, as a prelude to the negotiations the PPR sent to the Government's Delegate an open letter which was published a fortnight later in the PPR's main press organ, *The Tribune of Freedom* (*Trybuna Wolnosci*), in the hope that this would force the pro-London authorities to enter into negotiations. The letter criticised the pro-London forces' strategy and tactics and called for immediate armed operations against the Germans. It again stressed the need for the creation of a national front in Poland, especially in view of the mounting German terror and repressions, and asserted that only a policy of concerted, determined resistance could save the Polish nation from mass extermination. It drew attention to the plight of the Jewish community in Poland and suggested that the same fate might await the other Poles unless they were prepared to strengthen their resistance. It warned against the possibility of fratricidal strife in Poland and invited the pro-London circles to clarify their attitude towards the U.S.S.R. It stated that national concord and consolidation of all patriotic forces in the struggle against the Germans would hasten the day of liberation and of the creation of an independent and progressive Poland. Finally, it said that the realisation of these aims would depend to a large extent on the attitude of the Polish Government and its representatives in Warsaw.[1] Clearly, the PPR was fully aware that at this stage, with only about 8,000 members, it was in no position to create a strong and viable resistance movement without the help of the London camp.[2]

The letter remained unanswered. Yet, shortly after its publication negotiations between the PPR and the London leaders were opened. Gomulka, for the PPR, stated that his Party wished to enter into military and political co-operation with the London camp.[3] The military collaboration was to be based on the following conditions: intensification of the armed resistance, the attachment of People's Guard representatives to Home Army Headquarters and territorial Staffs and retention by the Communist units of their own organisational structure. In regard to political co-operation the PPR

---

[1] *Ksztaltowanie*, pp. 82–92.
[2] Despatch from Finder to Dymitrov, 12 January 1943, No. 10, 'Depesze KC PPR Do Georgi Dymitrowa', *Z Pola Walki*, IV, No. 4 (1961), p. 178.
[3] *Polski Ruch Robotniczy*, p. 263.

put forward the following proposals: that the PPR should be given the right to share with other parties in making political decisions, the extent of their influence being commensurate with their strength in the country; that wider understanding should be established between all Polish parties with the exception of the *Sanacja* and National Radical Movement; finally, that a new Government should be created in Poland which could, in time, replace the Cabinet in London. This Government should direct the launching of the insurrection and organise the elections to the constituent assembly, after the liberation.[1] The PPR stated that it was well-disposed to the Government in London but had reservations about its composition and its social and political tendencies. In the view of the PPR the exiled Government acted as a necessary representative of Polish interests abroad, but should not be allowed to assume power automatically when it returned to Warsaw. Therefore, Gomulka stated, a new Government should be established, within the country, in which some members of Sikorski's Cabinet, including the General himself, should be allowed to serve.

Gomulka described his Party as an independent Marxist-Leninist working-class organisation, without affiliation to the Comintern, striving for national independence and the transformation of the existing social system by constitutional means. The PPR was well-disposed to the Soviet Union, supported the Russo–Polish treaty of July 1941 and believed that the question of the Soviet–Polish frontier was open to discussion and could be solved on a basis of national self-determination. The Party stated that the rejection, by the London authorities, of its offer of collaboration would be tantamount to giving it 'a free hand' in respect of its future plans and actions. At the same time, the Party expressed readiness, should its present proposals for closer collaboration prove unacceptable to the London leaders, to enter into more limited co-operation with the London camp, for example in regard to the co-ordination of day-to-day resistance activities.[2]

Almost simultaneously the PPR published its political and ideological programme, 'What We Are Fighting For', which was to guide its activities in the period immediately after the war. The programme called for free and democratic elections to the constituent assembly

---

[1] *Ibid.*, pp. 263–4; see also Czeslaw Madajczyk, *op. cit.*, p. 15, and Maria Turlejska, *op. cit.*, pp. 125–6.
[2] Maria Turlejska, *op. cit.*, pp. 126–7.

which would, in turn, elect the new president and government and enact the new constitution. The constitution should guarantee basic human freedoms to all citizens, should embrace plans for the nationalisation of banks and large-scale industrial undertakings and for far-reaching land reform, involving the expropriation without compensation of large estates – all holdings over fifty hectares – and the re-distribution of the land among small-holders and agricultural workers. The State was to guarantee to everyone the right to work, was to prepare a grand plan of economic reconstruction, industrialisation, agricultural improvement and solution of the housing problem. Economic planning was to be introduced and the social services were to be extended to provide free secondary and higher education and a health service.[1]

The PPR's declarations revealed that the Party was very anxious to secure a place in those highest agencies of the underground movement which might eventually become the new Government of Poland and was, as a prelude to this, determined to cast itself in the twin rôles of champion of national liberation and of social progress. Its negotiations with the London camp were conducted under very unfavourable circumstances, as they coincided with a deterioration in Russo–Polish diplomatic relations and the arrest by the Germans of Professor Piekalkiewicz.[2] His successor, Jan Stanislaw Jankowski, was more right-wing than his predecessor; he was a member of the Christian Labour Party but was less politically-minded than the Professor. He was primarily a good administrator and a bureaucrat, rather than a far-sighted politician able to see the possible advantages of co-operation with the PPR.[3]

Further, Grot-Rowecki suspected that the PPR's declared readiness to collaborate with his forces was mainly a Communist stratagem to secure PPR infiltration into Home Army ranks, and also that it represented a ploy to gain public recognition as a leading Polish force in the struggle for liberation.[4] He believed that the Communists wanted this recognition because it might help them to legalise their Party after the war and would make it possible for them to offer more effective collaboration to the Russians if and

[1] *Ksztaltowanie*, pp. 93–6.   [2] Cf. *Polski Ruch Robotniczy*, p. 265.
[3] Julian Kulski, *Zarzad Miejski Warszawy 1939–44* (Warsaw, 1964), pp. 38–9, and Karol Popiel, *Na Mogilach Przyjaciol* (London, 1966), p. 36 and p. 42.
[4] Despatch from the Commander of the Home Army to the C-in-C, 14 March 1943, No. 370, APUST, and Organisational Report of the Commander of the Home Army, No. 190, 1 March 1943, Ldz. 5277/43, APUST.

when the latter entered Poland.[1] In his opinion, the possibility of co-operation with the Communists should be considered only if the PPR first declared publicly that it was not a member of the Comintern, that it was unreservedly loyal to the Government and that it recognised the integrity of the pre-war Russo–Polish frontier.[2]

Against a background of suspicion, scepticism and rapid deterioration in Russo–Polish diplomatic relations, the chances of establishing an understanding between the PPR and the London camp were very slender. Relations between Russia and Poland were finally severed on 26 April 1943.[3] Three days later, on 28 April Jankowski replied to the PPR's offer of collaboration. It strongly reflected Grot-Rowecki's attitude and demands. The Government's Delegate stated that further talks with the PPR would be fruitless unless the party was prepared to fulfil the following conditions: first, a pledge of absolute loyalty to the pro-London leadership; secondly, a declaration of complete independence of foreign authorities and of readiness to defend the country against aggression from any quarter; finally, a recognition of the inviolability of Poland's pre-war frontiers.[4] Thus, the pro-London leaders were insisting on what amounted to an undertaking, from the PPR, to fight against Russia if necessary. Predictably, the Party found this unacceptable. In 1943 no Communist could have agreed to such a demand. This would have amounted to an acknowledgement of the doctrine of two enemies, which the PPR was combating in the name of Russo–Polish co-operation. Similarly, the PPR could not recognise the integrity of the pre-war Russo–Polish frontier, the revision of which Stalin regarded as a *sine qua non* of *rapprochement* between the two countries. Finally, the PPR refused to cut itself off from, or reject the 'ideological authority' of, 'the international communist movement', so admitting, by implication, that its ties with the Comintern were not as tenuous as it had suggested in its official declarations, and that its activities were to a large extent guided by Moscow.[5]

The London leaders' reply clearly showed that they were not prepared to collaborate with a party which was pro-Russian in its attitudes and policies. Indeed, only public renunciation by the

---

[1] *Ibid.*
[2] Report from the Commander of the Home Army, No. 202, Part B, 22 June 1943, Ldz. 5555/43, APUST.
[3] For details see p. 5 of this study. [4] Maria Turlejska, *op. cit.*, pp. 132–3.
[5] *Polski Ruch Robotniczy*, p. 266.

PPR of its pro-Russian sympathies could have opened the way to the co-operation which that party had suggested. The negotiations were broken off, although it is claimed that unofficial contact between the Government Delegate's office and the PPR was maintained until the outbreak of the Warsaw insurrection.[1] After this failure to reach an understanding with the London movement as a body the PPR made several efforts to reach agreement with its left wing, the Peasant and Socialist Parties.[2] Following the rebuff received from Jankowski and Grot-Rowecki, in the summer of 1943 the PPR started to discuss the formation of 'a democratic national front' in Poland as a direct rival and challenge to the pro-London movement.[3] This marked the beginning, in Poland, of a struggle for power between the pro-London and pro-Moscow factions.

The pro-London authorities made a serious political mistake in refusing to come to an understanding with the Communists which might well have allowed them to influence the PPR's policies, or might at least have prevented the Communists from creating a rival national authority. Further, collaboration between the pro-London movement and the PPR would probably have tended to make the Communists more independent of Moscow by reducing their sense of isolation and their feelings of bitterness towards other parties and by encouraging those among their followers whom even the Home Commander described as 'Polish elements' (i.e., conventional patriots).[4] Finally, co-operation with the PPR might have led to the establishment of the Russo–Polish military co-operation which was so sadly lacking in the summer of 1944.

The pro-London leaders probably thought that the example of their public rejection of the PPR would be echoed among the population as a whole and would thus condemn the Party to isolation and impotence. But the pro-London hierarchy soon realised that this was not what was happening. In August 1943, Gen Bor-Komorowski, Grot-Rowecki's successor, told London that, although the PPR's hostility to the Government and its representatives had led to some 'spontaneous liquidation of Communists' in the provinces, among some groups of the radical intelligentsia prone to revolutionary ideas pro-communist tendencies were growing, in the expectation that the

[1] Andrzej Korbonski, Politics of Socialist Agriculture in Poland 1945–60 (New York and London, 1965), p. 56f. 79.
[2] Cf. Jerzy Pawlowicz, *op. cit.*, p. 22ff.   [3] *Polski Ruch Robotniczy*, pp. 376–7
[4] Report from the Commander of the Home Army concerning the situation of K. [the Communists], 20 November 1943, Ldz. 6581/Tjn/43, APUST.

U.S.S.R. would play a decisive part in the transformation of post-war Europe.[1] Jankowski, too, noted that communist activity in Poland was increasing. In his opinion there were two reasons for this: the successes of the Red Army, and the growth of the German terror. The Red Army victories were bringing about a change in the attitude of many Poles to the Soviet Union. They encouraged the hope that the war would soon end and persuaded many that the country would be occupied by the Russians, who would become influential not only in Poland, but throughout Eastern Europe. These predictions frightened certain sections of the bourgeoisie and intelligentsia, but among others they inspired a readiness for compromise with the U.S.S.R., or a feeling of resignation to the inevitable.[2]

The mounting German terror, coupled with the growing Polish belief that the war would soon end, was giving rise to a general demand for the intensification of underground operations against the Nazis; the intensification of German reprisal-action against the population was, therefore, acting upon Polish morale in a way exactly the reverse of that intended by the occupiers. The Communists, who from the outset had been propagating the idea of intensification and expansion of sabotage and guerrilla activities, were profiting from this situation. Their slogan, 'The Red Army is doing its job – we must do ours', was gaining currency.[3] The Government Delegate said that the position of the pro-London circles was becoming more difficult because officially they could not counteract propaganda of this kind, especially as the British and American politicians were full of praise for the Red Army; he complained that their pro-Soviet statements, probably made for 'political reasons', were reaching the Polish public and there causing 'acute disorientation'.[4]

All these developments were tending to make the communists more acceptable to the Polish masses. Indeed, Jankowski believed that even in the event of the outcome of the war being favourable to the London camp, the PPR would be highly influential among the

---

[1] Report No. 198 – Special Report concerning K. [the Communists'] activities in the period 16 March to 17 May 1943, dated 27 August 1943, APUST.
[2] Report from the Government Delegate concerning the Communist activities in Poland in the period November 1942 to February 1943, dated 24 July 1943, Ldz. 3728, APUST.
[3] *Ibid.*
[4] *Ibid.*

Polish youth and the working class and this would affect 'social relations' in post-war Poland.[1]

Thus, both Jankowski and Bor-Komorowski were aware that the Communists were gaining ground in Poland and that the Polish masses were becoming more radical. In November 1943 Bor-Komorowski told London that the PPR was strong enough to initiate a premature insurrection in Poland.[2] Such a turn of events would have been catastrophic for the London leaders, who based their entire strategy on the assumption that they would be able to control the timing and the course of the insurrection. The General also believed that the PPR might be dangerous to the pro-London movement during the insurrection. Hence, in October 1943 he was already maintaining that one of the tasks of the insurrection would be to suppress anarchy, which might be fomented by the Communists among the impoverished and war-demoralised masses who might all too easily accept the PPR's leadership. Bor-Komorowski believed that, during the rising, the PPR would try to establish a 'People's Government', thus attempting to spread disunity among the insurgents. He expected that the Communists, 'cynically using attractive patriotic and radical slogans', would be able to attract the support of the radical left-wing elements.[3] He feared that, immediately after Germany's defeat, Poland might be faced with the danger of civil war. He argued that the PPR was bent on staging a social revolution leading to the creation of a pro-Soviet Government. Hence, he urged that the pro-London leaders must be prepared for a struggle against the PPR.[4] He asserted that the insurrection must be accompanied by the Government Delegate's seizure of *de facto* power over the entire area affected by the Home Army's operations, and advocated the creation by the civil authorities of a special security corps to maintain law and order in the liberated territories. He also advocated the proclamation, by the highest Polish authorities,

[1] Report from the Government Delegate concerning the Communist activities in Poland in the period November 1942 to February 1943, dated 24 July 1943, Ldz. 3728, APUST.

[2] Report from the Commander of the Home Army concerning the situation of K. [the Communists], 20 November 1943, Ldz. 6581/Tjn/43, APUST.

[3] Paper delivered by the Commander of the Home Army to the Home Political Representation, 14 October 1943. Report from the Commander of the Home Army, No. 221, 14 October 1943, Ldz. 3269/44, APUST.

[4] Despatch from the Commander of the Home Army to the C-in-C dated 14 October decoded in London 6 November 1943, Ldz. 6112/O.S./Tjn/43, GSHI–A.XII.3/89.

of a political and social manifesto guaranteeing the introduction of social, economic and constitutional reforms justly demanded and expected by the people. This manifesto should serve as the political and ideological 'banner' of the Home Army, its antidote to the PPR programme.[1] Finally, Bor-Komorowski asked for the prompt despatch to Poland of all Polish troops serving abroad and a few Anglo–American divisions, to deal with the 'anarchy' and to maintain 'security'.[2]

Bor-Komorowski's preoccupation, in October 1943, with the problems of possible internal 'anarchy' suggests that the insurrection, as he at that time envisaged it, although primarily to be aimed against the Germans, was intended also to frustrate the anticipated attempts by the PPR to gain political power in the country. Thus, the absence of an understanding with the PPR was seriously affecting and complicating the Home Army's insurrectionary plans. Simultaneously, the relations between the London camp and the Communists deteriorated even further when, in September 1943, Bor-Komorowski instructed his troops to 'combat brigandry'.[3] This the PPR interpreted as an order to quash its activities rather than to free the country from the bandits who were at that time a serious problem.[4] Bor-Komorowski's order was, indeed, ambiguously expressed.[5] He told his subordinates 'to combat brigandry' as the activities of bandits 'of various origins' were 'harmful to our interests and plans'. His troops were to 'liquidate the leaders and agitators', not 'entire bands'. The operations were to be organised and executed in extreme secrecy and only when success could be assured.[6] The order was phrased in such a way that it could have applied equally to ordinary criminals or to Communist resistance groups; the PPR's existence was not officially recognised by the pro-London forces. Bor-Komo-

[1] Paper delivered by the Commander of the Home Army to the Home Political Representation, 14 October 1943. Report from the Commander of the Home Army, No. 221, 14 October 1943, Ldz. 3269/44, APUST.

[2] Despatch from the Commander of the Home Army to the C-in-C, dated 14 October decoded in London 6 November 1943, Ldz. 6112/O.S./Tjn/43, GSHI–A.XII.3/99.

[3] Organisational Report of the Commander of the Home Army, No. 220, 31 August 1943, Ldz. 3214/44, APUST; and Despatch from the Commander of the Home Army to the C-in-C, No. 1747, dated 14 October received 20 October 1943, Ldz. 5726, APUST.

[4] *Polski Ruch Robotniczy*, pp. 300–1.

[5] Cf. Jan Rzepecki, *op. cit.*, p. 259.

[6] The Order of the Commander of the Home Army, No. 116, 15 September 1943, APUST.

rowski himself informed his superiors in England that his intention was to free the country from 'the plundering, or *subversive* brigand elements'.[1] The Communists obtained the text of this order, which they published in their press and transmitted to Moscow;[2] the affair was heatedly discussed by Stalin in Teheran.[3] The publication of the order caused considerable disquiet among the pro-London circles. This compelled Bor-Komorowski to explain to his C-in-C that his real intention had been to combat brigandry as such, not to foment 'fratricidal struggle'. He claimed that only the NSZ was 'liquidating' Communists, but admitted that his own order had provided the PPR with an opportunity to discredit the Home Army.[4]

In April 1944 Bor-Komorowski ordered his troops to adopt 'a negative but unaggressive attitude' to the Communist units.[5] In July 1944 this order was repeated in a more categorical form – at all costs, the Home Army was to avoid conflict with the Communists.[6] Clearly, the General wished to repair the harm done by his unfortunate order of September 1943. The Communists also stated that they would refrain from fratricidal struggle.[7] In January 1944 Gomulka told Moscow that the Home Army Generals were disclaiming any part in the killing of Communist guerrillas. He claimed, however, that they were tacitly leaving this task to the NSZ.[8] It is indeed surprising that, far from clearly dissociating themselves from the NSZ, the Home Army leaders made several partially successful attempts to incorporate this organisation into their ranks, thus creating the unfortunate impression that they were prepared to tolerate the activities of the semi-fascists. It was not until July 1944 that the pro-London leaders finally decided to condemn the NSZ, which by this time was murdering, not only Communists, but also

[1] Organisational Report of the Commander of the Home Army, No. 220, 31 August 1943, Ldz. 3214/44, APUST.

[2] Despatch from the Commander of the Home Army to the C-in-C, No. 87/WK (67) 19 January 1944, Ldz. 927, APUST.

[3] For details see p. 15 of this study.

[4] Despatch from the Commander of the Home Army to the C-in-C, No. 87/WK (67), 19 January 1944, Ldz. 927, APUST.

[5] Operational Order from the Commander of the Home Army to the Commander of the Bialystok Area, 14 April 1944, Ldz. 634/III, Appendix 2 to Report No. 243 from the Commander of the Home Army to the C-in-C, 14 July 1944, Ldz. 6302/44, APUST.

[6] Order of the Commander of the Home Army, 'Attitude to the Soviets', Appendix 3 to Report No. 243 from the Commander of the Home Army to the C-in-C, 14 July 1944, Ldz. 6302/44, APUST.

[7] *Polski Ruch Robotniczy*, p. 302.　　　　　　[8] *Ksztaltowanie*, p. 212.

left-wing members of the London movement.[1] During the war, Bor-Komorowski argued that he was anxious to secure an understanding with the NSZ for military reasons.[2] After the war he admitted that the political consequences of NSZ activities had been very harmful.[3]

Meanwhile, in October 1943 the PPR started to prepare for the establishment in Warsaw, in co-operation with other parties if possible, of the National Council of Poland (*Krajowa Rada Narodowa* – KRN) which would organise 'a democratic national front' and act as a rival to the pro-London authorities. The task of making these preparations fell to Gomulka, who became Secretary-General of the Party in November, after Finder had been arrested by the Germans.[4] In the same month the PPR produced a more comprehensive version of its March programme, including a number of important additions to its previous resolutions. The November declaration stated that the establishment of a democratic system in post-war Poland could not be entrusted to the London Government, as its authority rested upon the provisions of Pilsudski's 'undemocratic, illegal' Constitution of 1935.[5] Instead, the Party suggested that the task should be entrusted to a Provisional Government, to be formed, at some unspecified date, by 'the anti-fascist national front'.[6] This Government would supervise free elections to the National Assembly, which in turn would elect the President, the Government, and enact a new Constitution. The Provisional Government would also organise a 'People's Militia' to combat anarchy and speculation, create a democratic army recruited from among the officers and soldiers who had distinguished themselves in the struggle for national liberation, and introduce democratic freedoms.[7] It would also introduce far-reaching social and economic reforms, as outlined in the March programme but with a number of significant changes in regard to the solution of the agrarian question.[8] Both private and church estates were to be expropriated and redistributed. The Party stated that it would approve the seizure of estates by

---

[1] For details see p. 87 of this study.
[2] Despatch from the Commander of the Home Army to the C-in-C, No. 469 and No. 469/3, 15 March 1944, APUST, and Special Report of the Commander of the Home Army, 22 May 1944, Ldz. 549/GNW/44, APUST.
[3] Tadeusz Bor-Komorowski, *Armia Podziemna* (3rd ed., London, 1966), p. 168.
[4] Jerzy Pawlowicz, *op. cit.*, pp. 19ff.   [5] *Ksztaltowanie*, pp. 140–69.
[6] *Ibid.*, p. 144.   [7] *Ibid.*, pp. 146–7.
[8] For details see pp. 95–6 of this study.

the peasants and agricultural workers during the take-over period. Finally, the party insisted that the test of the truly democratic nature of any political movement must be the request for expropriation of landed estates without compensation.[1] By these provisions the PPR was making a determined bid for the support of the peasants who formed the majority of the nation. The Party re-stated its views with regard to the revision of the Polish frontiers, and suggested that post-war Poland should, because of her geographical position, act as 'a bridge between the East and the West'.[2] She should continue to co-operate with her war-time allies, Great Britain, the U.S.S.R., and the United States. A Russo–Polish understanding would strengthen Poland's defences, economic potential and position in Europe.[3]

The PPR warned that the supporters of the pre-war *Sanacja* were well-entrenched in the military and administrative organs of the London camp and were pursuing a policy hostile to the Soviet Union. The PPR accused the political parties supporting the London Government of siding with these elements.[4] The November declaration claimed that the PPR was determined to cultivate the best traditions of all Polish left-wing parties, including those of the Peasant and Socialist Parties.[5]

In November and December 1943 Gomulka tried unsuccessfully to reach an agreement, with the Peasant and Socialist Parties, which might lead to their participation in the creation of the 'democratic national front'.[6] Yet at least one Peasant Party provincial leader, S. Banczyk, advocated that his Party should co-operate with the PPR. He made this proposal to his Party leaders after Gomulka had stated that the PPR had no intention of forcibly introducing communism into the country. Gomulka had also argued that the West was not interested in the fate of Poland and that the Peasant Party should therefore realise that the country would find herself in the Soviet sphere of influence. Consequently, if the Peasant Party continued to support the London Government it could not participate in the future Government of Poland. Banczyk's suggestion was rejected by his Party leaders.[7]

The PPR's attempts to create the 'democratic national front' in Poland followed the establishment in Moscow, in March 1943, of the communist-inspired Union of Polish Patriots (*Zwiazku Patriotow*

---

[1] *Ksztaltowanie*, pp. 163–4.   [2] *Ibid.*, p. 143.
[3] *Ibid.*, pp. 145–6.   [4] *Ibid.*, pp. 154–7.   [5] *Ibid.*, pp. 167–9.
[6] Jerzy Pawlowicz, *op. cit.*, p. 52ff.   [7] Andrzej Korbonski, *op. cit.*, p. 59.

Polskich – ZPP), ostensibly to unite and organise the one and a half million Poles in Russia for the struggle against the Germans regardless of their political affiliations;[1] in reality, the ZPP was intended to form the nucleus of the future Government of Poland. In June 1943 – shortly after the suspension of Russo–Polish diplomatic relations – the ZPP pledged itself to help Poland to liberate herself from Nazi domination, to create in the U.S.S.R. Polish military formations which were to fight on the Eastern Front, to strive for the restoration of parliamentary democracy and, finally, to strengthen the ties between Poland and her 'natural ally', the Soviet Union.[2] The ZPP would work for the revision of Poland's post-war frontiers; in the west they were to be extended to the river Oder and in the east limited to the mainly Polish-inhabited territories. With regard to social and economic questions, the ZPP promised to introduce land-reform, to guarantee the right of everyone to work, and to free the nation from exploitation by monopolistic and financial interests.[3] The ZPP's manifesto made no reference to the establishment in post-war Poland of a communist, or even socialist, system

At the end of 1943, when it had become clear that Poland would be liberated by the Red Army, the ZPP started to prepare plans for the assumption of power in the country by trying to establish in Moscow a Polish National Committee, which would assume the role of Provisional Polish Government; its creation was intended to stop the London Government from returning to Warsaw.[4]

The ZPP's plans were not co-ordinated with those of the PPR, or even discussed with the communists in Poland, because of a break-down in radio contact with Warsaw, which lasted from November 1943 until January 1944.[5] Moreover, certain elements within the ZPP, especially those connected with its military formations, under Gen Z. Berling, were ready to exclude the PPR from their plans for assuming power after the entry of the Red Army into the country. They favoured the establishment of a strong non-party Government in Poland, backed by the Polish Army formed in the U.S.S.R. In reality, therefore, they wanted to create a left-wing military dictatorship and were obviously not prepared, at this stage, to share power with the PPR. These plans were at variance with the official policy of

---

[1] On this, see: *Polski Ruch Robotniczy*, pp. 359ff, and Fryderyk Zbiniewicz, *Armia Polska w ZSSR* (Warsaw, 1963), pp. 13ff.

[2] *Ksztaltowanie*, pp. 449–56.   [3] *Ibid.*

[4] Fryderyk Zbiniewicz, *op. cit.*, pp. 169–70.   [5] *Ksztaltowanie*, p. 545.

the ZPP, which promised to restore parliamentary democracy, and they were hotly debated by the Communist activists in Russia, some of whom regarded them as dangerous and opportunist, as their realisation would once again have made the Army the chief arbiter in Polish political life.[1] The existence of these plans reveals the very deep divisions within the ZPP and shows that the question of the Union's co-operation with the PPR was far from settled.

The disputes within the ZPP led to the creation in Moscow, in January 1944, of the Central Bureau of Polish Communists in the U.S.S.R. (*Centralne Biuro Komunistow Polskich* – CBKP) which assumed political control over all activities of the ZPP, including those of its armed forces, and was to act as the link between the ZPP and the Soviet authorities and the PPR.[2]

While the ZPP was trying to settle its internal problems and was preparing the creation of the Polish National Committee in Moscow, the PPR established in Warsaw, on 31 December 1943, the National Council of Poland (*Krajowa Rada Narodowa* – KRN). When, in January 1944, the ZPP was told of the creation of the National Council, its members abandoned their own plans for establishing a National Committee in Moscow.[3] The PPR leaders had decided to set up the KRN, in spite of the refusal of the Peasant and Socialist Parties to serve on it, in the hope that many of the left-wing rank-and-file members of these parties might be willing to support the Council and its activities.[4] The absence of official co-operation from the Peasant and Socialist Parties meant, however, that the KRN was a Communist-dominated body with a narrow political base.

The KRN declared itself to be 'the factual political representation of the Polish nation' for the duration of the war. It renounced the London Government, the 1935 Constitution, and advocated a return to the provisions of the 1921 Constitution as the fundamental laws of the country. Yet it conceded 'the need for the existence abroad' of a body which would represent Polish interests to the Allied powers.[5] The KRN claimed for itself the power to issue binding decrees until such time as the proper legislative body was established. The executive power was vested in its presidium, headed by Boleslaw Bierut, a leading member of the PPR. In the provinces the KRN was to be represented by a network of provincial councils. The KRN pledged itself to unite and mobilise the

---

[1] Fryderyk Zbiniewicz, *op. cit.*, pp. 149ff.   [2] *Ibid.*, pp. 176–7.
[3] *Ibid.*, p. 172.   [4] *Ksztaltowanie*, p. 216.   [5] *Ibid.*

entire nation and its resources for the struggle against the Germans. It renamed its People's Guards the People's Army, under Gen Michal Zymierski, and rather extravagantly declared itself to be in command of all Polish armed forces fighting against the Germans.[1] It announced that, at the appropriate moment, it would establish a Provisional Government capable of assuming power in the country, and would introduce far-reaching social reforms: land reform and the nationalisation of the main branches of the national economy – the key industries, coal-mines, banking and transport. The KRN stated that it would work for the return to Poland of all those Polish territories in the west and north which had been forcibly Germanised, for the solution, on the basis of self-determination, of the Russo–Polish territorial dispute, and, finally would make friendly co-operation with Soviet Union the cornerstone of Polish foreign policy.[2]

The formation of the KRN constituted a warning to the London camp that unless it changed its attitude to the U.S.S.R. Stalin might refuse to negotiate with it and might decide to recognise the Council as the new Polish national authority. In January 1944 Gomulka explained to the CBKP in Mosow that the PPR had decided to establish the KRN because the political parties supporting the London Government intended to exclude other parties from representation in the government of the nation, and also because the PPR believed that conditions existing in the country favoured such a move.[3] In his opinion, although other parties, or their leaderships, refused to co-operate with the PPR growing radicalism and increasing disenchantment with the London Government among the followers of these parties and the popular masses might make it possible to recruit many new converts to the KRN. He argued that Polish political life was dominated by two factors: the German terror and the attitude to the U.S.S.R. In view of the German atrocities all Poles, even those opposed to the Soviet system, were looking to the Red Army for deliverance. Thus, the German terror was affecting the attitude of the people and making them more amenable to the forces advocating Russo–Polish *rapprochement*. More important, the PPR wished to suggest to the Allies that the nation did not support

---

[1] *Deklaracja KRN. Protokol pierwszego plenarnego posiedzenia KRN*, wyd. Biura Prezydialnego KRN (Warsaw, 1947), pp. 38–9.

[2] *Ibid.*, pp. 30–6; and *Ksztaltowanie*, pp. 470–1.

[3] *Ksztaltowanie*, p. 205ff.

the policies pursued by the London Government, particularly the attitude of that Government to the U.S.S.R. and the question of military co-operation with the Red Army. Gomulka told the CBKP that his Party had created the KRN with the intention of entrusting to it the task of establishing the provisional government even though it was difficult to predict when this government would finally be formed. In his opinion, this would largely depend on the Party's ability to develop a powerful People's Army and the extent of popular support for the KRN. He argued that the creation of a strong People's Army depended on the supply of arms, cadres and money from Russia. He complained that the AL units were practically without arms and that the PPR was short of well-trained activists and of money. The KRN decided to appeal to the Allies for arms. Gomulka considered that the Home Army was better armed and financed than the AL, a disparity which might be dangerous for the PPR in its 'struggle for power'.[1] Gomulka also complained that even the purely military usefulness of the anti-German operations of the AL was not fully appreciated in Moscow.

He told his colleagues that the PPR believed the entry of the Red Army would greatly facilitate its political plans, and assured them that, in spite of enormous difficulties, his Party was becoming a decisive force in Poland. Yet he warned the CBKP that 'the reaction' – the London camp – intended to offer armed opposition to the formation of a pro-Soviet Government in Poland, in the hope that such action might prompt Great Britain and the United States to intervene on their behalf; but preparation by the London camp for action of this kind would require intensification of their anti-Soviet and anti-PPR campaign.[2] Gomulka's shrewd prediction was soon fulfilled; some of the political aspects of the Warsaw Rising may be traced to the anti-Soviet and anti-PPR campaign launched by the pro-London leaders in the summer of 1944.

The creation of the KRN met with a storm of protest and condemnation among pro-London elements; it was described as an act of 'treason' against 'the Polish Nation and State', perpetrated by 'a foreign communist agency' which paraded in national colours and fraudulently exploited 'patriotic and national slogans'. The PPR was accused of 'threatening the vital interests of the nation', weakening national unity and 'spreading chaos and strife' at a decisive moment of the war. The KRN and the Command of the AL were described as

[1] *Ksztaltowanie*, p. 218.　　　　　　　　　　[2] *Ibid.*, pp. 214–15.

'insignificant institutions' representing 'minority forces', and created primarily to impress observers abroad. The pro-London hierarchy appealed to the nation to disregard the KRN and remain loyal to the orders of the Polish Government and its representatives at home.[1]

The creation of the KRN led to the intensification of the Home Army's anti-Communist propaganda, which was designed to brand the KRN and PPR as Soviet agencies, while avoiding polemical discussion of their social programmes.[2]

The Polish Communists in Russia also reacted to the creation of the KRN with certain misgivings as they felt that its social and political base was too narrow.[3] The CBKP suggested that the PPR should try to create a wide national front embracing the Peasant and Socialist Parties. To make this possible, they advised that the PPR should broaden and liberalise its political and social programme.[4] In reply, Gomulka pointed out to the CBKP that *the main bone of contention between the PPR and other parties was the attitude to the U.S.S.R. and the question of revision of the eastern frontiers, rather than their respective approaches to social and economic problems.*
He complained: 'If in Poland the Brotherhood of St. Anthony favoured the revision of Poland's eastern frontiers, the forces of reaction [the London Camp] would brand it also as the agent of Moscow, paid to deliver the Polish nation into Stalinist slavery'.[5]

He maintained that the PPR's repeated attempts to reach an understanding with the democratic parties supporting the exiled Government had failed, not because of the sectarian tendencies within his party, but because the leaders of the pro-London parties were anti-Soviet and anti-Communist in their attitudes and in their refusal even to contemplate frontier changes in the east. He complained that in Poland the class-struggle was intensifying, despite German occupation, and was assuming the proportions of 'a small-

[1] Declaration of the political and social organisations in Poland supporting the Polish Government in London, dated 9 January, received 19 February 1944. Ldz. 1333/Tjn.44. GSHI–PRM, L48; and Order of the Commander of the Home Army, 12 January 1944, GSHI, File 121/44.

[2] Cf. Tadeusz Bor-Komorowski, *op. cit.*, pp. 164–5; Aleksander Skarzynski, 'Niektore aspekty dzialalnosci BIP-u Komendy Glownej AK', *Wojskowy Przeglad Historyczny*, No. 3/1961, p. 67; and W. Gomulka, *W walce o demokracje ludowa*, 2 vols (Warsaw, 1947), vol. I, pp. 58–61.

[3] Jerzy Pawlowicz, *op. cit.*, pp. 190–1.

[4] Jerzy Pawlowicz, *Z dziejow konspiracyjnej KRN 1943–1944* (Warsaw, 1961), p. 185.

[5] Jerzy Pawlowicz, *op. cit.*, p. 186.

scale civil war', instigated by 'the Polish reaction', which felt threatened by the Soviet Union.[1] His party's aim was 'to unify the entire nation' under its own leadership. Its leaders made repeated efforts to reach an understanding with the Peasant and Socialist Parties and even some sections of the National Democrat Party.[2] These attempts were not very fruitful, although during the first half of 1944 Gomulka was able to secure the support of some left-wing Socialists for the KRN.[3] At this time he devoted his attention chiefly to establishing complete agreement between the PPR and the Polish Communists in the U.S.S.R., and to obtaining Stalin's backing for the KRN; in March 1944 he sent a delegation to Moscow to explain the policies of the PPR and KRN to the CBKP and the Soviet authorities, to request their support for the KRN and to ask for material help for the People's Army. The delegation was also to clarify Poland's international position, establishing liaison between the KRN and allied Governments, and was to put forward the view that the KRN, rather than the London Government, expressed the true interests of the Polish nation.[4]

The first part of the delegation left Warsaw on 16 March, arriving in Moscow on 16 May. It was headed by Edward Osobka-Morawski, deputy-chairman of the KRN, and Col Marian Spychalski, a member of the Central Committee of the PPR. On 22 May Stalin received the first part of the delegation together with the representatives of the ZPP. He stated that he was prepared to recognise the KRN as representative of the Polish nation and to enter into official relations with it once it had established an executive organ. The latter would be of use to him in his negotiations with Churchill and Roosevelt, who were urging him to recognise the London Government, which he had no intention of recognising in its existing form. It was agreed that the hard core of the new Polish Government should be recruited from the KRN and its supporters and certain unnamed politicians then in Poland. These were to head the main Ministries and command the Army. He agreed to supply the People's Army with war-

[1] Jerzy Pawlowicz, *Strategia Frontu Narodowego PPR: III. 1943–VII. 1944* (Warsaw, 1965), pp. 192–3.
[2] Marian Spychalski, 'Informacja przedstawiciela KC PPR na zebraniu komunistow polskich w Moskwie 8 czerwca 1944r', *Z Pola Walki*, No. 4/1961, p. 193.
[3] Jerzy Pawlowicz, *Z dziejow konspiracyjnej KRN 1943–1944* (Warsaw, 1961), pp. 51ff.
[4] Jerzy Pawlowicz, *Strategia Frontu Narodowego PPR: III.1943 – VII.1944* (Warsaw, 1965), p. 169.

materials,[1] and the Polish Partisan Staff created a few days earlier was entrusted with the task of delivering them.[2]

On 23 May the ZPP recognised the KRN as the leading centre of the struggle for national liberation.[3] On 15 July, Stalin pressed the delegation to create an executive body, to be known as 'the Committee of National Liberation'.[4] On the same day Edward Osobka-Morawski, chairman of the KRN delegation, and Wanda Wasilewska, head of the ZPP, sent a letter to Stalin on behalf of the KRN, stating that 'the situation is ripe for the creation of the Polish Provisional Government and further delay might lead to serious complications'.[5] Otherwise

> the entry of the Red Army into Poland will immediately be represented by hostile elements in Poland and abroad as signifying the beginning of 'Russian occupation'. The creation of the Provisional Government would undermine the basis of the clandestine administration of the émigré Government in Poland and its military organisation and accelerate the disintegration of the reactionary camp at home and abroad . . .
>
> The establishment of the Provisional Government would allow the restoration of relations between the Soviet Union and Poland on the basis of inter-State agreements. The most urgent problem is the acceptance by the Provisional Government of the Curzon Line as the basis for the establishment of frontiers between Poland and the U.S.S.R., and also as a demarcation line between the Soviet and Polish administrations. The establishment of Soviet administration west of the Curzon Line . . . might weaken the position of democratic camp and undermine the Polish nation's trust in the Soviet Union.
>
> The establishment of the Provisional Government would allow the unification under one command of the Polish armed forces in Poland and the U.S.S.R., which is absolutely necessary in order to avoid serious complications and disharmony.

The letter pointed out that, once established, the Provisional Government could proceed to general mobilisation into the KRN-controlled army. The writers suggested that the Provisional Government should be formed around the KRN with the initial addition of the representatives of the ZPP and later of the representatives of 'other democratic organisations at home and abroad'.[6] Apparently, the possibility that at some stage the London Poles might be represented in the Provisional Government was still not ruled out.

[1] *Ibid.*, pp. 169–70.
[2] Fryderyk Zbiniewicz, *op. cit.*, p. 305.
[3] *Ibid.*, pp. 308–10.
[4] Jerzy Pawlowicz, *op. cit.*, p. 171.
[5] *Ibid.*, p. 261.
[6] *Ibid.*, pp. 261–2.

On 17 July Stalin agreed to 'the immediate formation of the Committee of National Liberation'.[1] His choice of this style rather than
'Provisional Government', favoured by Osobka-Morawski and
Wasilewska, possibly showed that he was still willing to reach an
understanding with the London Government if they would recognise
the Curzon Line as the new Russo–Polish frontier and reconstruct
their Cabinet. His choice of terms also possibly reflected a wish to
avoid a clash with London and Washington at a time when they
not only still recognised the London Government as the Government of Poland, but were pressing Moscow to do the same. Nevertheless, with the Red Army about to enter central Poland Moscow's
role in the Russo–Polish dispute was becoming of crucial importance,
while the influence of London and Washington was declining;
clearly the entire country would soon be in Stalin's hands and he
intended to exploit the Russian presence in Poland to his own and
the KRN's advantage. Only the strongest pressure from Churchill
and Roosevelt and very skilful diplomacy on the part of the London
Poles might have prevented the emergence of a Communist-dominated Government in Warsaw.[2]

On 19 July the Soviet leader told the delegates of the KRN and
ZPP that a Polish executive organ must be created as soon as possible,
and reproached them for their procrastination. He informed them
that as soon as the executive had been established he would conclude
an agreement with it regarding the demarcation line between the
Soviet and Polish administrations.[3] Stalin also insisted that the
KRN must announce that it was assuming control of the ZPP and
the Polish Army in the U.S.S.R. Such a move on the part of the KRN
was intended, no doubt, to provide a precedent for placing other
Polish bodies under its control. In Stalin's opinion the situation was
now ripe for the adoption of such methods, as the Red Army was on
the point of entering Poland and in his view the KRN was gaining
popularity in the country and abroad.[4] On the following day – 20
July – the KRN passed a resolution by which it assumed control
of the ZPP and the Polish troops in the U.S.S.R. Simultaneously, in
consultation with the Soviet authorities, the Polish delegates decided
that the KRN's executive body would assume the title of Polish

---

[1] Jerzy Pawlowicz, *op. cit.*, pp. 262–3.
[2] For discussion of the diplomatic background to the Warsaw Rising see Chapter
1 of this study.
[3] Jerzy Pawlowicz, *op. cit.*, pp. 263–4.   [4] *Ibid.*, pp. 176–7.

Committee of National Liberation, *Polski Komitet Wyzwolenia Narodowego* – PKWN. Its formation was announced on 21 July.[1]

Meanwhile, the PPR leaders in Warsaw were still striving for an understanding with democratic elements within the London Camp. On 1 July 1944 – that is, three weeks before the formation of the PKWN and a month before the outbreak of the Warsaw insurrection – the Party once again publicly called upon the Peasant and Socialist Parties to join the PPR in forming a broad national front. The Party stressed that the creation of such a front was a most important task, in view of the situation which was then facing the country. The Party implied that, while opposing the London Government and its plenipotentiaries in Poland, the PPR accepted Mikolajczyk, its Prime Minister, as the potential popular leader of the reconstructed Cabinet. The PPR was willing to recognise that Mikolajczyk was striving for an understanding with the Soviets, but argued that the presence of reactionary elements in his Government was making his task impossible. The PPR insisted that the interests of Poland demanded that the official Polish attitude to the U.S.S.R. should change. Hence, the PPR appealed to the Peasant and Socialist Parties to contribute to the restoration of Russo–Polish relations by striving for the reconstruction of the London Government – even, if necessary, by 'unconstitutional' means – and by freeing the Home Army of its reactionary generals. The PPR pointed out that it was not hostile to the Home Army as such, but only to its reactionary leadership.[2] This appeal seems to suggest that some at least of the PPR leaders continued to the very end their efforts to reach some kind of *modus vivendi* with the London camp and, further, that the Party believed that it was vital to establish in Poland, initially at least, a coalition Government representative of the main democratic political forces. The creation of such a front would have frustrated the pro-London leaders' plans for staging their anti-Soviet and anti-Communist campaign, and, hence, would have freed the country from the danger of civil war, would have helped to achieve the Russo–Polish military co-operation vital for the pursuance of the struggle against the Germans and would probably have improved the Polish position vis-à-vis the Russians. It would also, of course, have improved the standing of the PPR and its leadership as the main architects of national understanding and unity.

This conciliatory appeal remained unanswered; a few days before

[1] *Ibid.*, pp. 264–5.   [2] *Ksztaltowanie*, pp. 255–66.

the outbreak of the Warsaw insurrection the leaders of the PPR had no choice but to leave Warsaw for Lublin, where the PKWN was being formed. For there, in their estimation, the question of power was now to be decided. Only a skeleton leadership was left in Warsaw,[1] which suggests that Gomulka and his lieutenants did not have a large-scale Communist-sponsored or inspired insurrection in mind.[2] At this stage, it is claimed, the PPR had about 20,000 members. Its hard core comprised the ex-members of the old Polish Communist Party. Considerable numbers of the PPR's members were recruited from the left-wing sections of the Peasant and Socialist Parties. The majority of its members consisted of those who had become politically active during the occupation.[3] The People's Army, it is claimed, was about 50,000–60,000-strong.[4] It was still much weaker than the Home Army.[5] The Polish Army returning from Russia had about 107,000 men of whom 65,000 served in its combat formations and were ready for action.[6] The degree of popular support for the KRN and PKWN, in July 1944 cannot be ascertained. In 1957 Gomulka himself admitted that in this crucial period the PPR and the KRN were not supported by the majority of the nation.[7] Thus, despite a shift to the left in public opinion and a considerable degree of popular dissatisfaction with the pro-London leadership, the PPR had failed, during the years 1942 to 1944, to secure the support of the majority of the nation for itself and its programme. The PPR's pro-Soviet attitude was, no doubt, one of the main reasons why it was unattractive to the Polish people. Anti-Russian feeling in Poland was strong and hampered the PPR's attempts to 'win the masses over' to 'the idea of a Polish–Soviet alliance'.[8] This anti-Russian feeling was deeply rooted in the history of Russo–Polish relations.[9] Feeling against Russia was further strengthened by the Soviet territorial demands, and was exploited by the London camp's propaganda.[10] The pro-London leaders' aim was, with the

---

[1] Antoni Przygonski, *Z Problematyki Powstania Warszawskiego* (Warsaw, 1964), pp. 37–8.

[2] Cf. *Ibid.*, pp. 47ff.

[3] Jerzy Pawlowicz, *op. cit.*, pp. 256–66.   [4] *Ibid.*, p. 243.

[5] For details see pp. 115–16ff of this chapter.

[6] Fryderyk Zbiniewicz, *op. cit.*, p. 324.

[7] *Trybuna Luda*, No. 14, 15 January 1957.

[8] Jerzy Pawlowicz, *op. cit.*, p. 198.

[9] Edward J. Rozek, *Allied Wartime Diplomacy: A Pattern in Poland* (New York, 1958), pp. 395–6.

[10] Tadeusz Bor-Komorowski, *op. cit.*, pp. 164–5.

help of the Western Powers, to re-establish a Poland free of any dependence on Russia or Germany. But in 1944 this aim was unrealistic and the logic of the situation demanded that it be renounced.

3. *The Home Army*

Although there are no reliable statistics as to the exact strength of the Home Army we know that it was undoubtedly by far the largest resistance force in the country. Estimates of its strength vary considerably.[1] In all probability, in the summer of 1944 the Home Army's strength amounted to a few hundred thousand men which, given the prevailing conditions, represented a great achievement, even though most of them were unarmed.[2] Its operational potential was limited by the acute shortage of arms rather than the number of men at its disposal. In June 1944, the Polish General Staff in London estimated that Bor-Komorowski had arms for only 32,000 men, which meant that only a small minority of his men could take part in the fighting.[3] In practice, therefore, the vast majority of the Home Army soldiers had no weapons at all.

In Warsaw, shortly before the insurrection, the Home Army was about 50,700-strong, including 4,300 women;[4] the fact that the force was particularly strong in the capital had considerable effect on Bor-Komorowski's decision to start the insurrection in that city.[5] Again, however, the troops in Warsaw were lamentably short of arms. Adam Borkiewicz estimated in 1957 that on 1 August 1944 the Home Army in Warsaw had, in theory, sufficient weapons for only one-sixth of its soldiers.[6] Aleksander Skarzynski estimated in 1964 that the Home Army had enough weapons for only 3,500 men; as its fighting units were about 35,000-strong, he claims that, in theory,

---

[1] For details see: Leon Mitkiewicz, 'Powstanie Warszawskie', *Zeszyty Historyczne*, No. 1/1962, pp. 113ff; *Polskie Sily Zbrojne, op. cit.*, p. 119; Tadeusz Bor-Komorowski, *op. cit.*, p. 135; Memorandum from the C-in-C to the Prime Minister, 22 October 1943, Ldz. 1420/Op. tjn, GSHI–A.XII/3/89; and Witold Babinski, *Przyczynki Historyczne* (London, 1967), p. 377.

[2] Cf. Stanislaw Kopanski, *Wspomnienia Wojenne 1939–1946* (London, 1961), p. 297; and Jan Ciechanowski, *Powstanie Warszawskie* (London, 1971), pp. 58–60.

[3] Leon Mitkiewicz, *op. cit.*, p. 134, and Witold Babinski, *op. cit.*, p. 377.

[4] Aleksander Skarzynski, *Polityczne Przyczyny Powstania Warszawskiego* (Warsaw, 1964), p. 338, and Adam Borkiewicz, *Powstanie Warszawskie 1944: zarys dzialan natury wojskowej* (Warsaw, 1957), p. 30.

[5] For further discussion of this point see pp. 257ff of this study.

[6] Adam Borkiewicz, *op. cit.*, p. 36.

only one soldier in ten could be armed.[1] The shortage of arms was one of the force's main problems and greatly reduced operational capabilities. In January 1944 the Polish C-in-C told the British authorities that the Home Army's equipment was inadequate for its requirements, especially with regard to automatic weapons; he asked for increased deliveries of necessary supplies to Poland.[2] In Warsaw itself, the shortage of weapons decisively affected the outcome of the initial attack launched in the late afternoon of 1 August 1944.[3]

From the functional point of view the Home Army soldiers, all volunteers, were divided into three basic categories. The first and most important, though relatively small, group, consisted of full-time members of the force – in Bor-Komorowski's words, 'professional conspirators' – who formed the hard core of the organisation and had to lead a completely clandestine existence 'under false identity, with forged documents and labour permits'.[4] Naturally enough, all Home Army senior officers belonged to this group. The full-time members of the force received no payment, other than relatively small monthly allowances to cover their living expenses. The allowances were calculated in dollars, although paid in Polish war-time currency, and ranged from 6 to 18 dollars a month, according to rank. Occasionally, these allowances were supplemented by additional payments to cover the periodic price increases or fluctuations in dollar exchange rates.[5] In general, the payments were calculated in such a way as to provide for basic necessities only, even though the organisation was never really short of funds, for it was believed that the members of the force should not be 'spoiled' by receiving too much money. However, this policy often meant considerable material hardship for 'full-time conspirators'.[6]

The second category of Home Army soldiers consisted of those who had served in its partisan units. 'They lived mainly in the forests, wore uniforms and fought the Germans openly'.[7] Until the beginning of 1944 this group was also relatively small; at the end of August

---

[1] Aleksander Skarzynski, *op. cit.*, p. 343.
[2] Aide-memoire from the C-in-C to Maj-Gen C. McV. Gubbins, D.S.O., M.C., 6 January 1944, GSHI–A.XII/3/89.
[3] Cf. Adam Borkiewicz, *op. cit.*, p. 99.
[4] Tadeusz Bor-Komorowski, *op. cit.*, p. 136.
[5] *Polskie Sily Zbrojne, op. cit.*, p. 347.
[6] Jan Rzepecki, *op. cit.*, p. 202.
[7] Tadeusz Bor-Komorowski, *op. cit.*, p. 136.

1943 the Home Army had about 40 partisan units in the field, their strength varying from 30 to 100 men.[1] It is claimed that in the second half of 1943 only about 2,000 to 2,800 Home Army soldiers were serving in the partisan units.[2]

The third and largest category consisted of part-time resistance members, leading, as it were 'double lives'. Their Commander described them thus:

> In ordinary everyday existence they differed in no way whatsoever from any other man in the street. They worked in offices and factories, on railways, in agriculture, etc; every one of them was, nevertheless, in touch with his direct superior in the organisation, from whom he got orders and tasks to fulfil connected with espionage (Intelligence), sabotage, or diversion, to be performed where he had opportunity through his employment. Often a whole group was used as a team for some major task, in which case they had to be trained together. But the object in view was always the ultimate task . . . the general insurrection. After action, such a group was scheduled to return to 'normal' life.[3]

The overwhelming majority of Home Army soldiers belonged to this group and were recruited, organised and trained with the planned insurrection in view.[4] They received no payment for their services to the organisation.[5]

Politically and socially, the Home Army represented a cross-section of the community. Its members were recruited from all social classes and all political parties, with the exception of the PPR.[6] Many of its units had originally been para-military organisations of the National Democrat, Peasant, Socialist and Labour Parties, subscribing to divergent and even mutually opposed social and political ideals. The right of each party to continue to propagate its own ideals among the units it had 'contributed', even after the merger, perpetuated the political differences existing within the ranks of the force. In May 1944 Gen Bor-Komorowski admitted that it was impossible to reduce these differences and transform the Home Army into an 'apolitical' military organisation. The General also

[1] *Polskie Siły Zbrojne, op. cit.*, p. 524.
[2] Colonel Juszczakiewicz's oral evidence. See also Jerzy Kitchmayer, *Powstanie Warszawskie* (Warsaw, 1959), p. 27.
[3] Tadeusz Bor-Komorowski, *op. cit.*, p. 136.   [4] *Ibid.*, p. 135.
[5] Colonel Juszczakiewicz's oral evidence.
[6] Special report from the Commander of the Home Army, dated 25 May received in London 5 June 1944, Ldz. 549/GNW/44, APUST. See also Tadeusz Bor-Komorowski, *op. cit.*, p. 46.

complained of the marked discrepancies between the political and social views of his officers and those of the rank and file; he asserted that the officers, too conservative in outlook, were out of touch with the far more progressive ideas of their men and of society at large. He was fully aware that many of his soldiers distrusted the political and social leanings of their commanders, suspecting that they might, after liberation, try once again to make Poland a military dictatorship.[1] Thus, the Home Army lacked ideological cohesion.[2] In the summer of 1944, anxious to remedy this, Bor-Komorowski decided on a campaign to spread more democratic and progressive ideas among his right-wing officers and men. Further, the General felt some apprehension about the attitude of his troops towards the approaching Red Army. Certain that they would readily and energetically fight against the Germans, he could not with similar confidence predict their behaviour in the event of a clash with the Russians. This, he felt, would be 'much less popular' among them; the more left-wing of his units might become unreliable, a prey to divided loyalties.[3] Fears of this kind influenced Bor-Komorowski's determination to fight resolutely against the Germans in the summer of 1944; the unambiguous and universal popularity of such a struggle would strengthen the loyalty and unity of his troops.

He was similarly prompted repeatedly to press the Government to announce plans for radical post-war reforms.[4] It is, perhaps, surprising that such requests should be made by a military Commander rather than by the civil authority. The members of the Civil authority of the underground were hampered even in the discussion of such questions by their political and ideological differences. The underground state was a coalition of very diverse and mutually incompatible political forces held together only by the need to preserve the semblance of national unity in the face of foreign aggression and a communist 'menace'. All its pronouncements were the result of compromise between the conservative-orientated National Democrats, the right-wing Socialists and the moderate Peasant and Labour Parties.[5] Consequently, they were often

---

[1] Special report from the Commander of the Home Army, dated 25 May received in London 5 June 1944, Ldz. 549/GNW/44, APUST.

[2] Jan Rzepecki, *op. cit.*, p. 267.

[3] Special report from the Commander of the Home Army, dated 25 May received in London 5 June 1944, Ldz. 549/GNW/44, APUST.

[4] For details see p. 218 of this study.

[5] Jan Rzepecki, *op. cit.*, p. 271.

expressed in terms which were disappointingly mild and vague to the increasingly radical masses. The general's concern to see the introduction of reforms was also due, in part, to their responsibility for the political as well as the military state of their troops, the result, in turn, of the existence in Poland of two underground organisations, military and civil, each directly responsible to the Polish authorities in London.[1] This division was intended to strengthen the exiled Government's authority over the underground by preventing the emergence in Warsaw of a unified civil and military command which, it was felt, might, in time, become a serious rival to the Cabinet abroad.[2] But it meant, in practice, that although the military Commander was expected to act in close consultation with the Government Delegate,[3] the secret army was never subordinated to the civil resistance authorities.[4] This system had functioned adequately under Gen Sikorski, in whose person had been combined the offices of Premier and C-in-C of all Polish troops, and who had thus been in a position to issue binding and authoritative directives to both branches of the underground.[5] But, after his death in July 1943, these offices were separately assigned and, in consequence, this unity of command was disrupted, especially as relations between the new Premier, Stanislaw Mikolajczyk, and the C-in-C, Gen Kazimierz Sosnkowski, were from the outset far from cordial, mainly because of their differences in regard to the Polish attitude to the U.S.S.R.[6] In theory, the C-in-C could not issue the Home Army with binding operational directives without first consulting the Cabinet.[7] In practice he could – and Sosnkowski often did – try to inspire the Home Commander to disregard the Government's directives, without actually ordering him to do so.[8] Further, these differences between the Premier and the C-in-C tended not only to diminish the Government's authority and prestige among the resistance leaders in Warsaw but even encouraged the latter to formulate and pursue

---

[1] *Ibid.*, p. 264.
[2] Cf. Eugeniusz Duraczynski, *Stosunki w Kierownictwie Podziemia Londynskiego 1939–1943* (Warsaw, 1966), p. 27; Wladyslaw Pobog-Malinowski, *op. cit.*, p. 214.
[3] Despatch from the C-in-C to the Commander of the ZWZ, 18 June 1940, APUST.
[4] Cf. Eugeniusz Duraczynski, *op. cit.*, p. 191.
[5] For details see pp. 80–3 of this study.
[6] Cf. Jan Rzepecki, *op. cit.*, p. 257.
[7] Witold Babinski, *op. cit.*, p. 374.
[8] For details see pp. 181ff of this study.

their own policies and solutions, without discussing them with their superiors abroad.[1] The leaders in Warsaw were encouraged in this by their conviction that the exiled authorities were often out of touch with conditions in Poland and were thus not in a position to issue realistic and timely directives.[2] In general, the pro-London leaders, both abroad and in Warsaw, had to formulate policies and make decisions under exceptional and difficult conditions. The Cabinet in London, while in a position to assess realistically Poland's diplomatic position, was remote from the people and events in Poland, and this tended to lower its standing in the country. The authority of any government exiled from the country it claims to govern and represent is bound to be questioned, particularly if the period of exile is prolonged. Its chief problem is to maintain the manifest allegiance of the people it claims to represent. The inability of the Polish Cabinet to communicate directly with the people in Poland made it very dependent upon the leaders in Warsaw, who were obviously in a better position to judge the mood of the people than their superiors abroad.[3] The Cabinet knew only as much about the internal situation as the resistance authorities were willing and able to tell them, in relatively short reports. The Warsaw authorities could not themselves communicate freely with the masses for reasons of security.[4] Consequently, the Cabinet's appreciation of the internal scene was far from perfect. Inevitably, it was coloured by the opinions of the leaders in Warsaw, a bias, which, under the circumstances, the exiled Cabinet was hardly in a position to question.

Such a situation was highly dangerous, tending to transfer the initiative into the hands of the leaders in Warsaw, who, although better informed on internal problems, in their turn lacked first-hand knowledge and experience of international affairs. Too remotely situated to be able to form for themselves a picture of Poland's diplomatic position, they had to rely for this on second-hand sources, mainly reports from London.[5] Consequently, they often made unrealistic representations, expecting their Government to

[1] Cf. 'Wypowiedz Gen T. Pelczynskiego na 2-gim zebraniu relacyjnym w inst. Jozefa Pilsudskiego w Londynie z 17/X/1950'. APUST.

[2] Colonel K. Iranek-Osmecki's oral evidence.

[3] Cf. Adam Pragier, *Czas Przeszly Dokonnany* (London, 1966), p. 717.

[4] Cf. Special Report from the Commander of the Home Army, May 22, 1944, Ldz. 549/GNW/44, APUST.

[5] Kazimierz Baginski, ' "Proces Szesnastu" w Moskwie', *Zeszyty Historyczne*, No. 4 (1963), pp. 75–6.

accomplish more in the diplomatic realm than was feasible with the slender means at its disposal.[1] This was highly dangerous and unfortunate for all concerned; the Cabinet in London could hardly ignore these demands, anxious as it was to maintain close rapport with its followers in Poland.[2] Thus, the conditions under which the pro-London leaders had to act made them poor guides of Poland's destinies; the exiled authorities lacked a clear understanding of the internal scene, while the underground leadership had only a partial appreciation of the international situation. These limitations were bound to be reflected in decisions and could not be eliminated.

The two main channels of communication between London and Warsaw were the wireless and couriers which, given the conditions under which they had to operate, allowed only limited exchange of ideas and information.[3] Many attempts were made to improve liaison between London and Warsaw by establishing special institutions intended to serve as channels of authority and information. The Government Delegate and his Staff, or *Delegatura*, acted as the highest representative in the country of the exiled Government, and a link between the Cabinet and the political parties which supported it at home. It was the Government Delegate's function to inform the parties about the Government policies and pass their suggestions and comments to London. It was also his task to co-ordinate the activities of the resistance, especially of its civil branch, and to prepare the necessary administrative machinery for the assumption of power after the liberation. The *Delegatura* was the highest pro-London civil authority in Poland.[4] In July 1944 the Government Delegate became the Deputy Premier of the exiled Government and, with two other ministers, served on an underground Home Council of Ministers.[5] These appointments were designed to strengthen the

---

[1] For details see pp. 21ff of this study.

[2] Cf. Adam Pragier, *op. cit.*, p. 717.

[3] For a detailed description of the Home Army's communications network see: *Polskie Sily Zbrojne, op. cit.*, pp. 215–62. For a more personal account of the methods used and difficulties encountered in maintaining radio contact between the Government Delegate and representatives of political parties in Warsaw and Polish authorities in London see: Stefan Korbonski, *W Imieniu Rzeczypospolitej* . . . (2nd ed., London, 1964), especially chapters II, IV, VII, XV and XVIII. For a critical discussion of the organisation and functioning of the Polish military radio communications network shortly before the Warsaw Rising see: Z. S. Siemaszko, 'Lacznosc Radiowa Sztabu N. W. w Okresie Powstania Warszawskiego', *Zeszyty Historyczne*, No. 6 (1964).

[4] The Decree of the President of the Republic, 26 April 1944, APUST.

[5] Record of the Cabinet Meeting No. 40, 26 July 1944, APUST.

links between the Cabinet and the resistance and to satisfy the desire of the top resistance leaders to play a greater part in the affairs of the London camp.[1] The Delegate acted in close co-operation with the Political Consultative Committee – *Polityczny Komitet Porozumiewawczy*, or PKP – which was the deliberative and consultative organ of the resistance.[2] There is little doubt that the parties forming the PKP – the National Democratic, Peasant, Socialist and Labour Parties – represented between them the vast majority of the politically organised part of the nation, although it is impossible to assess their numerical strength in occupied Poland. In May 1944 the Peasant Party was the strongest political force in central Poland; apparently, its rank-and-file members were far more radical in their attitudes and aspirations than their leaders. The National Democrats, the traditional representatives of the Polish middle class and richer peasantry, were the only organised political force in western Poland, a region which had always been one of their traditional strongholds. The Socialist Party, though weakened by an internal split, had a considerable following among the urban working class. The Labour Party was the weakest member of the PKP, where it tried to occupy a central position between the conservative National Democrats and the more left-wing Peasant and Socialist Parties.[3]

In August 1943 the four parties decided to enter into closer co-operation, at least until such time as free elections could be held. They announced that during the period between the end of the war and the holding of these elections they would jointly govern the country as the representatives of the main political forces. The four parties also outlined the common programme which was to guide their war-time and post-liberation activities. They pledged themselves to support the exiled Government and to collaborate with the Government Delegate and the Home Commander in promoting harmonious co-operation between the civil and military branches of the resistance. The main object of this war-time co-operation was the preparation of the projected insurrection. The parties also explained their position with regard to Poland's foreign and internal policies. They stated that Polish diplomacy should try to promote close co-operation between Poland and her Western allies and to secure 'her

[1] Cf. Andrzej Korbonski, *op. cit.*, p. 42.
[2] Cf. Stefan Korbonski, *op. cit.*, pp. 38–40.
[3] Special Report from the Commander of the Home Army, 22 May 1944, Ldz. 549/GNW/44, APUST.

sovereign rights and territorial integrity', especially the 'absolute' inviolability of the pre-war Russo–Polish frontier. Further, it was in their view important that Poland should try to counter the growing Soviet influence on Allied diplomacy by stressing the dangers inherent in 'Russo-Communist totalitarianism', and that she should secure wide access to the Baltic at Germany's expense and receive from that country suitable indemnities.[1] In the view of the PKP the remaining objectives of Polish diplomacy should be the establishment of a central and east European federation of states and the equitable settlement of the problem of national minorities in Poland.

With regard to social and economic arrangements, the parties stated that immediately after the liberation the Government would issue a number of decrees ensuring civic freedoms and establishing economic, social and cultural self-government. It would give proper recognition to human labour as the highest social value and the foundation of the economic welfare and development of the country, and would provide for the establishment of state control, which would be exercised in collaboration with local authorities over all enterprises previously owned by Germans, and any others which had become ownerless. All public utilities would be taken over by local authorities. The Government would initiate land-reform involving the redistribution of arable land in such a way as to ensure the creation of the largest possible number of efficient, viable one-family farms, together capable of providing the nation with adequate food supplies. All land ear-marked for land-reform would be placed under government control at the time of the liberation. Finally, the Government would formulate a plan of economic reconstruction, organise the repatriation of Polish citizens from Germany and Russia, and end unemployment.[2]

The social and economic programme of the four parties represented a compromise between the conservative-orientated National Democrats and the more left-wing Peasant and Socialist Parties; hence its vagueness and absence of detail, especially with regard to the proposed land-reform. The question of compensations and maximum size of large holdings was left unresolved. Similarly, the questions of labour relations and unemployment were dealt with in a most perfunctory manner; there was no suggestion of any practical

---

[1] Declaration of the political agreement between the four political parties forming the Polish Home Political Representation, *Rzeczypospolita Polska*, No. 15, 20 August 1943, APSUT.   [2] *Ibid.*

means by which they might be resolved. Nevertheless, the four parties recognised the need for and publicly declared themselves in favour of the social and economic reconstruction of the country.

This powerful four-party coalition was designed to prevent the emergence, after the expulsion of the Germans, of a power-vacuum which might be exploited to establish a Government not approved by the four parties, such as a military dictatorship or communist-inspired Cabinet. The four parties combined to try to ensure that post-war Poland would be fashioned by themselves.

Their intransigent attitude towards Russia showed their inability to realise that, after Stalingrad, that country was fast becoming the dominant power in eastern and central Europe; they were unable to assess Poland's position in post-Stalingrad Europe realistically or to understand that the achievement of a *modus vivendi* with Stalin was essential for Poland. Indeed, the main difference between the four parties and the PPR was in the realm of foreign affairs. The London camp intended to build post-war Poland in close co-operation with Great Britain and the United States, while the PPR looked to the U.S.S.R. At the same time, both sides agreed that some social and economic changes were inevitable. There is little doubt that, had the London Poles agreed to change their attitude to Russia, the PPR would have been more than ready to co-operate with them, at least temporarily, in regard to military, social and economic problems.

In March 1944 the PKP was finally transformed into a Council of National Unity – *Rada Jednosci Narodowej*, or RJN – which assumed the role of quasi-parliament of the pro-London movement.[1] The RJN, under the chairmanship of Kazimierz Puzak ('Bazyli'), one of the leaders of the Socialist Party,[2] was established in response to the creation in Warsaw, in January 1944, of the Communist-inspired KRN. The RJN, the *Delegatura* and the Command of the Home Army were the highest authorities of the pro-London resistance movement. In July 1944 the Government Delegate, the Home Commander and the Chairman of the RJN, representing between them the administrative, military and deliberative organs of the pro-London resistance, became its highest executive body.[3]

---

[1] Although the decree creating the Council of National Unity was dated 9 January 1944, the Council was constituted on 12 March 1944. Despatch from the Commander of the Home Army to the C-in-C, 23 January 1944, Ldz. 616, APUST.

[2] Zygmunt Zaremba, *op. cit.*, p. 200.

[3] Despatch from the Government Delegate to the Prime Minister, No. 74,

In March 1944 the RJN issued its political and ideological programme under the title 'What the Polish nation is fighting for'. To a large extent, the manifesto repeated the 1943 declaration of the four parties, but it included a number of more specific proposals on social, economic and territorial questions. Post-war Poland was to be a parliamentary democracy with strong executive authority. The first freely-elected post-war parliament was to democratise the pre-war Pilsudski Constitution. The army was to become a truly apolitical body dominated by democratic ideals. In the west, Poland's frontiers were to be extended to embrace East Prussia, Danzig, Western Pomerania and Silesia. In the east they were to remain unchanged. In the international sphere Poland was to seek close co-operation with Great Britain, the United States, France and Turkey. Friendly relations with the U.S.S.R. were to be developed, but on two conditions: the recognition by Moscow of the validity of the pre-war Russo–Polish frontier and Russia's non-intervention in Poland's internal affairs. Poland was to sponsor the idea of a federation of states in central and south-eastern Europe, to prevent the domination of this area by any single state.

With regard to socio-economic problems, the declaration promised the introduction of a planned economy into Poland. The state would protect the economic and social interests of the masses. This was to be achieved by extending property ownership, state control of the economy, and an improved and justly distributed national income. The state would have the right to nationalise public utilities, transport, key industries and banking, where it was in the public interest. The post-war Parliament was to decide whether the former owners of nationalised concerns and estates were to be compensated or not. Anxious for the support of the peasants, the authors of the declaration promised far-reaching land-reform; as soon as hostilities were over, the state would requisition all privately-owned estates over fifty hectares. The confiscated land would be used to create small one-family farms of eight to fifteen hectares. Existing smallholdings would be expanded to that norm and all forests would be nationalised. In addition, the state would provide funds for the improvement of transport facilities, construction works, electrification, the creation of agricultural co-operatives and the development of vocational education and training. Those unable to find employment in agri-

dated 12 July 1944, received in London 21 July 1944, Ldz. K.4775/44, GSHI–L9.

culture would be given vocational training and directed to work in other sectors of the economy. Thus the pre-war problems of rural poverty and overpopulation would be attacked. Further, the declaration promised full employment and the provision of health, education and social security services by the state.[1]

Like the 1943 programme of the four parties the RJN's declaration was, in its socio-economic aspects, the result of an uneasy compromise between the parties concerned. The National Democrats regarded some of its provisions as too radical: the Peasant and Socialist Parties criticised them as not far-reaching enough. The Socialists favoured outright nationalisation of the key industries[2] and the Peasant Party maintained that its aim was the expropriation without compensation of all private and church estates of over fifty hectares.[3] The National Democrats, on the other hand, had serious misgivings about the proposed land-reform.[4] They advocated full compensation to landowners, opposed limiting the permitted size of estates to fifty hectares and insisted that only inefficient estates should be broken up. They wished the agrarian question to be solved by the consolidation and enlargement of existing farms and state provision of financial aid to agriculture.[5] Neither the National Democrats nor the Labour Party favoured the idea of competing with the PPR on its own ground by espousing the cause of radical social change. They tended to believe that more support was to be gained by emphasising the differences, rather than manufacturing similarities between the Communists and themselves.[6] These differences on social and economic problems again revealed a wide gulf between the National Democrats and the Socialist and Peasant Parties. The existence of differences so wide and deep indicated the possibility of a split within the RJN, which was kept together primarily by fear of the PPR. In May 1944 Bor-Komorowski himself reported to London that the members of the RJN lacked a 'common political

---

[1] The Declaration of the Council of National Unity, 15 March 1944 – 'What the Polish Nation is fighting for.' APUST.
[2] Situational Report from the Commander of the Home Army, No. 8, 10 May 1944, APUST.
[3] Jerzy Pawlowicz, *Strategia Frontu Narodowego III. 1943–VII. 1944*, p. 142.
[4] Special Report from the Commander of the Home Army dated 22 May received 5 June 1944, Ldz. 549/GNW/44, APUST.
[5] Czeslaw Madajczyk, *Sprawa Reformy Rolnej w Polsce 1939–1944* (Warsaw, 1961), p. 53.
[6] Andrzej Korbonski, *op. cit.*, pp. 49–50.

line'.[1] In March of that year this lack of genuine agreement had already prompted the Chief of the Information and Propaganda Department of the Home Army, Col Jan Rzepecki ('Sedzia'), to advocate to Bor-Komorowski the creation of a united Peasant-Socialist Front as an answer to the PPR's political and ideological 'offensive'.[2] Other parties could, if they wished, support this popular Front; if not, they should be abandoned to their own fate. Rzepecki argued that only the creation of such a Front would allow the London camp to maintain its leadership over the increasingly radical masses. In Rzepecki's opinion, the masses generally were demanding the abolition of large-scale private property and of all class and individual economic, social and political privileges. Rzepecki also suggested that the Home Army cadres should be purged of die-hard conservative and reactionary elements.[3]

Clearly, then, the Home Army leaders were aware that the people were restive, and demanding more far-reaching reforms than those promised by the RJN. Indeed, Rzepecki's representations to Bor-Komorowski were an indirect attack on and critique of the socio-economic aspects of the RJN's declaration. Further, they were an attempt to free the London camp from the conservative tendencies and policies of the National Democrats. However, Bor-Komorowski rejected Rzepecki's suggestions and to have accepted them would have amounted to an internal revolution within the London camp.[4]

But the absence of radicalism and dynamism among the top echelons of the London camp was reducing its attractiveness to the growing left-wing elements of the population, thus providing the PPR with fertile ground for propaganda. At the end of May 1944, Bor-Komorowski was fully aware that the RJN had failed to isolate the PPR by 'consolidating' all Polish political groups.[5] This failure, coupled with the entry of the Red Army into Poland, confronted the leaders of the London camp with a dangerous and explosive situation. They tried to prevent the PPR from gaining ground and to maintain the loyalty of the masses by increasing their anti-German operations.[6]

[1] Special Report from the Commander of the Home Army dated 22 May, received 5 June 1944, Ldz. 549/GNW/44, APUST.
[2] Jan Rzepecki, *op. cit.*, p. 275.
[3] *Ibid.*, pp. 275–7.   [4] *Ibid.*, p. 277.
[5] Special Report from the Commander of the Home Army dated 22 May, received 5 June 1944, Ldz. 549/GNW/44, APUST.
[6] Situational Report No. 243 from the Commander of the Home Army to the C-in-C, dated 14 July, received in London 8 August 1944, Ldz. 6302/44. APUST.

They regarded as their supreme task the preparation of an anti-German insurrection, to be launched at the most crucial moment.

Yet their attitude to Russia, a country which, after June 1941, was a member of the Grand Alliance, also deeply influenced their strategy and tactics. Indeed, the formulation of their attitude to Russia led to a prolonged dialogue between the pro-London leaders in Poland and abroad. This dialogue continued almost uninterrupted from the day of Hitler's attack on Russia to the outbreak of the Warsaw Rising and even to the very end of the existence of the Polish underground. It formed the conceptual background against which the decision to launch the insurrection in Warsaw was taken.

4

The Polish Grand Strategy, 1941–1943

1. *The General Background*

In the autumn of 1943 another direct Russo–Polish confrontation seemed imminent. The Red Army was on the offensive; by the first days of October 1943 they stood on the White Russian sector of the Eastern Front, less than sixty miles from Poland's pre-war frontier.[1] Their entry into the country could not be long delayed. It would occur during an acute political impasse between Poland and Russia, as diplomatic relations between the two countries had been suspended and the future of Eastern Poland – or, to the Russians, the Western Ukraine and White Russia – was disputed.

At this time Russia's political and military standing within the Grand Alliance was at its highest. The Soviets' victories at Stalingrad and Kursk unambiguously revealed to the world their military and political prowess. It opened before them new vistas in eastern and central Europe; it marked the beginning of their advance towards Berlin, the very heart of Germany. After Stalingrad Russia was no longer fighting for her survival but was harvesting the strategic and political fruits of this victory. In brief, she was fast becoming one of the most formidable world powers, a power whose continued participation in the conflict was essential for the final Allied victory in Europe. The Soviet Union still bore the main burden of the land-war against Germany, whose energies for war were far from being spent. The Western Allies were as yet only preparing their main invasion of Europe and the battle for Germany was an event to come. Furthermore, Russia's co-operation in the campaign against Japan and her active participation in the post-war settlement was greatly desired by Roosevelt and Churchill.[2] The chances of a lasting peace depended on close collaboration between the three big powers following the conclusion of hostilities.

---

[1] Count Edward Raczynski, *In Allied London* (London, 1962) p. 168.
[2] Woodward, pp. xxxviiff.

Meanwhile, Poland lay prostrate and exhausted by four years of German exploitation and oppression. In all these circumstances a Russo–Polish detente appeared to be essential if the reconstruction of the Polish State was to take place and the conflict between the two countries to be averted. In spite of this the leaders of the pro-London Poles, both in Warsaw and abroad, seemed to feel that their cause would prevail only against the background of a defeated Germany and a Russia seriously weakened, or at least persuaded, with the help of the Western Allies, to accept the leaders of the London camp as the rulers of post-war Poland. Here they were faced with a dilemma; they greatly desired the defeat of Germany, without which Poland's survival as a nation would be doubtful, yet they feared that in the moment of victory they might be faced with a triumphant and demanding Russia. It was in this frame of mind that, on 13 October 1943, the Polish C-in-C expressed the opinion that the situation which faced Poland was catastrophic and that only with the help of 'divine providence' could the impending disaster be averted.[1]

In theory, at least three courses were open to the Polish leaders. First, they might try to appease Russia by meeting her political and territorial demands, or at least strive for a compromise solution of the Russo–Polish crisis. Secondly, they could try to oppose Russia, regardless of the possible consequences, in the hope that Great Britain and America would feel compelled to champion their aspirations in Poland – but by adopting this course they would be endangering Allied unity. Finally, they might go through the motions of reaching an understanding with Russia while in reality resisting her, in the belief that rivalry between the Great Powers would sooner or later reassert itself, leading to a conflict between East and West which would favour their designs for Poland. They thought that their underground forces would be an important instrument of their policy towards the U.S.S.R. They had finally to decide whether the resistance was to treat the approaching Red Army as friend or foe.

They had also to decide what part, if any, the Home Army was to play in the imminent Russo–German battles in Poland. Their answer to this question was implied, to some degree at least, in their policies towards Germany, and earlier orders issued to the underground. It must be remembered that the chief *raison d'être* of the

---

[1] Leon Mitkiewicz, 'Powstanie Warszawskie', *Zeszyty Historyczne*, No. 1/1962, p. 127.

underground movement was, apart from the pursuit of the day-to-day resistance to the Germans, to rise against them during the last stages of their rule in Poland, to expel them, and then to institute in the country an administration loyal to the exiled Government. To this end the underground forces were organised, trained and husbanded. It was intended that seizure of political power for the London Government at the end of hostilities would constitute the crowning of their military success and the culmination of their struggle against the Germans.[1] Moreover, a refusal to engage the *Wehrmacht* during its retreat from Poland might compromise their anti-German record in the opinion of the public at home and abroad. In short, it might strengthen the position of the Communists who would then be able to claim that they were the only force in Poland prepared to fight against the Germans and assist in the work of liberation. These questions had to be faced and answered, or at least examined, as all previous plans for an anti-German rising in Poland had generally presupposed that in the last analysis it would be possible to co-ordinate it with the Anglo–American strategy in Europe. Before the autumn of 1943 it was expected in pro-London quarters, that Poland would be liberated by British and American rather than Russian forces. Now it was clear that the Red Army would be the first to enter Poland.[2]

Because of this a number of other pertinent questions had to be answered. Should the Home Army fight against the Germans in co-operation, at least in the operational sense, with the Soviet High Command, regardless of the state of Russo–Polish diplomatic relations, in the hope that a common struggle would lead to some *modus vivendi* in the future, or should it rather continue its fight independently of the Russians? If they were to act independently of the Soviets a decision had to be made in regard to the secret army's *modus operandi*. Here, there were four basic possibilities. The Home Army might emphasise its independent status – that is, its loyalty to the exiled Government – by assuming the role of a sovereign host to the Red Army. It might put itself under the Soviet command and accept all Russian demands. Its units might attempt to return underground after fighting the Germans and await further developments and orders. Finally, they might disband after firing the last shot against the Germans. Moreover, if the Home Army was to act independently of the Russians, was the area of its operations to cover,

[1] Cf. T. Bor-Komorowski, *The Secret Army* (London, 1950) pp. 172–3.
[2] T. Bor-Komorowski, *op. cit.*, pp. 173–4.

or exclude, the disputed territories – the eastern provinces of inter-war Poland? In a military sense the projected uprising in these regions would be directed against the Germans. In political terms, however, these operations, to be undertaken without the cognisance of the Soviet authorities, would be directed against the U.S.S.R., in that they would facilitate the establishment of an administration loyal to the exiled Government in these disputed territories. Thus, operations in these areas would tend to heighten rather than relax the existing tension and might result in an armed clash between the Home Army and the Soviet Security forces. More important, they might compromise the achievement of a Russo–Polish *rapprochement*. Another question was, would an independent Polish action command the support of the Western Allies, and, if so, support of what kind and strength? Finally, if the avoidance of a possible Russo–Polish conflict with all its consequences for the population was, after all, to be a primary consideration – and if it should be plainly impossible to reach a prior agreement with the Russians – would it not be advisable to disband the secret army before the Soviet entry into Poland, leaving the entire field to the Polish Communists? This final solution would certainly mean the end of the resistance loyal to the exiled Government; hence, it was never fully examined.

The situation demanded clear and far-reaching decisions which had to be taken in consultation with Poland's allies.[1]

2. *The First Dialogue*

Although the new situation was more urgent, ways and means of coping with it had already been discussed by Sikorski and Grot-Rowecki in their protracted wireless dialogue over the preceding two years. This dialogue is worthy of detailed examination; it went far beyond military or indeed strategic considerations, although it was chiefly concerned with the operational plans for the Home Army and its attitude towards the Russians, if they, and not the Western Allies should liberate Poland. It dealt with the very essence of the Polish grand strategy, internal and international politics.

In accordance with the C-in-C's instructions, as late as March 1942 – despite the fact that Russo-Polish diplomatic relations had been re-established in July 1941 – the secret army was under strict

[1] Despatch from the Commander of the Home Army to the C-in-C, 27 October 1943, Ldz. 6004/tjn.Sp/43, APUST.

orders to resist the Soviets, if they tried to enter Poland without the prior consent of the Polish Government. At the same time the Home Army was to continue its struggle against the Germans.[1]

In retrospect these orders provide a glaring example of the Polish High Command's gross overestimation of their own strength and potentialities and underestimation of the resilience and power of the Germans, their real opponents, and the Russians, in their view a potential enemy.

The orders to resist the Soviets were countermanded by Sikorski in March 1942,[2] after his visit to Moscow, where in December 1941 he had signed with Stalin a 'Declaration of Friendship and Mutual Assistance' for the duration of the common struggle.[3] Under the terms of the new directives the Home Army was to refrain from precipitating hostilities towards the Russians on their entry into the country, as this, 'at least in the eyes of the Western Democracies, would be tantamount to solidarity with the Germans, which would be calamitous for Poland'.[4] This departure, Sikorski explained, was made possible by the conclusion of political and military treaties with Stalin, after the German attack on the U.S.S.R.

Further, he insisted that in the event of a decisive Soviet victory in the East, which in his view, at this stage of the war, seemed a remote possibility, the 'reconstruction of the State' and its attributes could only proceed with Soviet goodwill and help from the Western Allies.[5] This solution of the Russo–Polish problem was to be achieved by diplomatic rather than military means and was to be subject to Anglo–American arbitration. Nevertheless, according to the C-in-C's dispositions the Russians were, on arrival, to be met by strong and well organised Home Army forces, especially in the eastern provinces of Poland, which in 1939 had been occupied by and annexed to the Soviet Union.[6] The secret army's presence in these regions was intended to stress their links with Poland and emphasise

---

[1] Despatch from the Chief of the General Staff to the Commander of the Association for Armed Struggle, 20 November 1941, Ldz. 3853, APUST.

[2] Despatch from the C-in-C to the Commander of the Home Army, 4 March 1942, Ldz. 608/42, APUST and the C-in-C's 'Personal and Secret Instruction to the Home Commander', 8 March 1942, Ldz. IIII/42, APUST.

[3] *Documents on Polish–Soviet Relations*, Doc. No. 161, p. 246.

[4] Despatch from the C-in-C to the Commander of the Home Army, 4 March 1942, Ldz. 608/42. APUST.

[5] The C-in-C's 'Personal and Secret Instruction to the Home Commander', 8 March 1942, Ldz. IIII/42, APUST.

[6] *Ibid.*

Polish claims to them. There is little doubt that this order was prompted largely by political considerations arising out of the failure to settle conclusively the post-war status of these areas during the negotiations leading to the Russo–Polish *rapprochement* of 1941.

At the moment of the collapse of the Eastern Front, Sikorski ordered the Home Army was to stage a rising against the Germans, disarm them, assume security duties in the liberated territories and enable the civil administration appointed by the Government's Delegate to function. If the Russians were unwilling to recognise the Polish authorities they would have to assume full responsibility for their actions before the 'entire world'. Finally, Sikorski told Grot-Rowecki that he should not count too much at this stage of the war on support for the rising from the Polish air and airborne forces, then stationed in England.[1] Sikorski's subsequent instructions to the Home Army attempted to clarify, develop and justify these orders of March 1942, and in essence they reflected three broad suppositions which conditioned and governed his entire policy towards Russia: first, that the maintenance of good relations with the Soviet Union was essential for Poland's survival as an independent national entity; secondly, that Poland's territorial integrity was to be defended in the face of Russian demands, primarily by political means; finally, that Poland's attitude to the Russians must take into account their standing within the Grand Alliance.[2]

In retrospect, the first two aims – the maintenance of good relations with the U.S.S.R. on the one hand, and the defence of Poland's territorial interests on the other – were clearly incompatible. Incompatibility of aims was, indeed, the main weakness of Sikorski's approach to Russia. In December 1941 Stalin had already made it plain to him that the revision of the Russo–Polish frontiers was one of his main tasks and in his opinion a prerequisite of good relations between the two countries. Sikorski refused, however, even to discuss territorial issues with Stalin.[3] Failure to resolve this problem conclusively in 1941 was to cast a bleak shadow on Russo–Polish relations up to the outbreak of the Warsaw Rising in August 1944.

[1] The C-in-C's 'Personal and Secret Instruction to the Home Commander', 8 March 1942, Ldz. IIII/42, APUST.
[2] Cf. Despatch from the C-in-C to the Commander of the Home Army, 28 November 1942, Ldz. 5060/Tj/42, APUST.
[3] For details see: *Documents on Polish–Soviet Relations*, vol. I, Doc. No. 160, pp. 244ff, and Edward J. Rozek, *Allied Wartime Diplomacy, A pattern in Poland* (New York, 1958), pp. 94–5.

Sikorski's dispositions of March 1942 were received in the Home Army Headquarters with strong misgivings and criticisms.[1] Grot-Rowecki favoured the adoption of a different policy regarding Russia. He duly submitted his own analysis of the situation, and conclusions based on it, to the C-in-C in the summer and early autumn of 1942.[2] They reflected his deep mistrust of and hostility towards Russia. 'For formal reasons I include Russia among the Allied countries', he wrote. 'In reality I maintain that she will adopt a clearly hostile attitude towards us when her strength allows, and will conceal this attitude when she is too exhausted.'[3] He was convinced that 'Russia is and will be our enemy', an enemy opposed to the very idea of Poland's independence – and that the history of Russo–Polish relations bore witness to this. The Soviet–Polish pact of July 1941 was, in his opinion, a temporary and makeshift arrangement imposed on the two sides by Hitler's attack on Moscow.[4] At the same time, like Sikorski, he did not anticipate, any spectacular Soviet victories, at this juncture, in view of the heavy losses inflicted on the Soviets by the Germans. This opinion was tempered by his belief that 'the threat of the Russians' entry into Poland in the final phases of the war has not altogether disappeared'.[5] He argued that the C-in-C's order forbidding him to resist the Russians on their entry into the country should apply only if they won a decisive victory in the East and if there was no Soviet animosity towards the Home Army. His attention was mainly devoted to the question of how best to use the conspiratorial army in the 'final reckoning with Russia', the outcome of which would he believed decide the future of Poland.[6] He suggested to Sikorski that if the Russians defeated the *Wehrmacht* and entered Poland close on the heels of the retreating Germans, so becoming a dominant influence in Eastern Europe, the idea of an anti-German rising should be abandoned.[7] If this happened, he argued, the Home Army would have 'neither opportunity nor cause' to rise against the Germans.[8] There would be no time to deploy the underground forces for the seizure of the country before the arrival of the Soviets, or to organise the resistance

---

[1] Cf. *Polskie Sily Zbrojne, op. cit.*, p. 545.

[2] This commentary is contained in two reports from the Home Commander to the C-in-C: Report No. 132, 22 June 1942, received in London 6 October 1942, Ldz. 4132 APUST hereafter referred to as Report No. 132 and Report No. 154, 8 September 1942 respectively.

[3] Report No. 154.   [4] Report No. 132.   [5] Report No. 154.
[6] Report No. 132.   [7] *Ibid.*   [8] *Ibid.*

against them should they become hostile to the London forces. He claimed that under such conditions the German occupation would be superseded by the Russian; nevertheless, the civil organs of the secret state should try, even though without military support, to assume administrative control of the country. Under these circumstances the Polish Armed Forces fighting in the West should not return home. The conspiratorial army should remain underground, to 'emerge into the open' only when the exiled Government had received 'adequate guarantees' from the U.S.S.R. and the Western Powers that the former would not impede the 'restoration of independent Poland' within the pre-war frontiers. Russia's refusal to give these guarantees should, he insisted, be interpreted as conclusive proof of her traditional opposition to 'Poland's Independence'. 'In this event the military organisation at home will not come out of hiding', he wrote. 'The Army organised abroad will become the centre of an independent Polish force. . . . The struggle for independence will enter into a phase of conflict with Russia, the new occupying power, a main enemy.'[1]

Grot-Rowecki considered the conclusion of a 'reinsurance treaty' with the U.S.S.R., guaranteed by the British and American Governments, to be a *sine qua non* of possible Russo–Polish military co-operation in the task of the country's liberation. Further, he believed that some sort of military resistance to the Russians, at least of a defensive nature, should be seriously considered if they entered Poland without a prior agreement with the Polish Government, even though he was ready to admit that the solution of the Russo–Polish problem should be sought on the political rather than military plane.[2] That he was thinking in these terms is borne out by another proposal of his, by which, if it should be found possible to stage the rising while the Soviet troops were still some distance from the Polish borders, and the Home Army was subsequently, in the initial stages of the 'post-rising' reorganisation, unable to resist the Russians on the whole territory of Poland, his forces were to retreat to a prearranged area, possibly Pomerania on the Baltic coast. There he would maintain contact with the Polish forces abroad, and organise a 'defensive redoubt' which might become the 'Piedmont of future Poland'.[3] Within the confines of this 'redoubt' the Home Army was to await the Russian guarantees and prepare for the worst. The

---

[1] Report No. 132.   [2] Report No. 154.   [3] Report No. 132.

units unable to reach the 'redoubt' were in time to disperse and emerge into the open.

Meanwhile, the Western Powers would have to decide whether to support Russia or Poland, as represented by the London Government. Grot-Rowecki considered Western support essential if the Polish question was to be solved on the lines advocated by the exiled Government and its followers. A Western decision to support Russia, he pointed out, would make 'our chances for the immediate future very slender'. Yet he insisted that even then the idea of a last stand against the Soviets should not be abandoned 'even if a hopeless struggle will await us', in view of 'our responsibility to future generations'.[1]

Turning to more pressing considerations, Grot-Rowecki decided, in doubt as to the exact shape in which the 'Russian threat' would present itself – he considered the answer to this question would be provided by future developments – to concentrate his efforts exclusively on 'the preparation for the struggle against the Germans'. This decision was prompted by his reluctance to confuse his subordinates, at this stage, with possibly distorted hypotheses regarding the future behaviour of Russia.[2]

The Home Commander was, in his political thinking, pledged to the doctrine of two enemies, in accordance with which both Germany and Russia were seen as Poland's traditional enemies, and it was expected that support for Poland, if any, would come from the West. These notions conditioned and coloured his analysis of the situation facing his troops and country. The Home Army's rising, under ideal conditions – Germany defeated by the Anglo–American forces and the U.S.S.R. seriously weakened – was to assume an anti-German and anti-Russian character, if the Soviets tried to impinge on Poland's territorial and political rights. In the event of a decisive Soviet victory in the East and speedy occupation of the country by the Red Army, Grot-Rowecki felt that the Home Army should refrain from fighting the Germans, remain underground and await further developments. If the secret army proved able, after all, to stage its anti-German rising it was to retreat to a 'defensive redoubt' and wait. The Polish Army serving under British command should remain abroad and also wait. The question of what these Polish forces were to be waiting for is not fully answered. Were they to wait only for 'adequate guarantees' from the U.S.S.R., a chance to stage

[1] *Ibid.*   [2] Report No. 154.

a hopeless battle, or a conflict among the victors, which might determine the shape of peace to come?[1]

Grot-Rowecki's suggestions of resisting the Russians were contrary to the spirit and letter of the C-in-C's directives sent to him in March 1942.[2] In November 1942 these suggestions were firmly rejected by Sikorski, who told Warsaw that it would be 'sheer madness' to try to resist the Red Army's entry into Poland in pursuit of the Germans and that attempts to conceal the underground army from the Russians – who were 'well-informed' about its existence – 'would lead to an open clash between the Soviets and the Home Army', a clash which would provide the Communists with an opportunity to spread among the allies 'distorted views' about the forces loyal to the exiled Government. To avoid such possibilities the C-in-C ordered Grot-Rowecki to take steps in preparation for the Home Army's mobilisation and emergence into the open before the Russian authorities. The secret army was to assume the role of sovereign host to the Soviets – to quote Sikorski, 'to manifest its sovereign status and emphasise its positive attitude to Soviet Russia'. Sikorski told Grot-Rowecki that he was 'preparing for this in the international field, for that is where a decision of a political nature will settle our frontiers'.[3] The C-in-C believed that in the last analysis the fate of Poland would be decided by 'the actual balance of power at a given moment' between the Great Powers. He expected 'that this will be favourable to Poland'. He was still hopeful that with British and American support he would be able to reach a *modus vivendi* with Stalin.

Finally, Sikorski warned his subordinate that the underground must maintain 'a totally united front', as disunity could be used by the communists to further their own solution of the Polish problem.[4] The C-in-C's orders were clear and unambiguous. The Home Army was to treat the Russians as allies, refrain from any hostilities towards them and reveal its organisational framework to them, while at the same time stressing its loyalty to the exiled Government. All military operations were to be directed against the Germans; the secret army was to rise against them at the moment of the collapse.[5]

---

[1] Cf. Jan Rzepecki, 'W Sprawie Decyzji Podjecia Walki w Warszawie', *Wojskowy Przeglad Historyczny*, No. 2 (7), Warsaw 1958, pp. 296ff.

[2] See p. 133 of this study.

[3] Despatch from the C-in-C to the Commander of the Home Army 28 November 1942, Ldz. 5060/Tj/42 APUST.

[4] *Ibid.*   [5] Cf. *Polskie Sily Zbrojne, op. cit.*, p. 545.

In January 1943 the Home Commander informed London that he would carry out this order, if strong and victorious Russian armies were to enter Poland.[1] This did not prevent him, however, from entertaining serious doubts about the wisdom of Sikorski's directives and entire approach to Russia. He repeated to his superior his belief that 'Russia is our enemy number two', and that 'the Russians, once they enter Poland, will leave her only when faced with force'.[2]

At this point Grot-Rowecki introduced a number of new military, political and even social considerations into his dialogue with the C-in-C. He suggested to Sikorski that the beginning of the rising should be co-ordinated with the pace of Soviet advance into Poland rather than, as was previously planned, with the state of morale and battle-worthiness of the *Wehrmacht*. This change of emphasis was motivated by his intention to start the rising before the arrival of the Russians, in order that the Home Army should precede the Russians in the liberation of Poland.[3] He was convinced that the projected rising should take place consecutively, zone by zone, as the Russo–German Front rolled across the Polish plains.[4] This new stratagem would, he hoped, reduce the interval between the beginning of the Home Army's operations in a particular region and the arrival there of the Soviet troops and hence would tend to increase the chances of success in these undertakings.[5] *Thus, instead of a general insurrection occurring simultaneously throughout that part of Poland covered by secret army garrisons, Grot-Rowecki proposed a number of regional, or localised, uprisings, starting in the east and then extending to other parts of the country.*

To ensure success he begged Sikorski to arrange for the Polish paratroopers, then stationed in Great Britain to be sent to Poland. Their arrival, he claimed, would be of military and political significance; they would strengthen the underground troops and serve

---

[1] Despatch No. 60 from the Commander of the Home Army to the C-in-C, 12 January 1943, Ldz, 247/tjn/43 APUST (hereafter referred to as Despatch No. 60).

[2] *Ibid.*   [3] *Ibid.*

[4] This idea was further clarified by Grot-Rowecki and submitted by him for the C-in-C's approval at the end of February 1943. The first zone was to cover the Wilno and Lwow regions, the second the rest of the eastern provi.. :es, as far as the line of the rivers Bug and San; roughly, the first two zones were to include all the disputed territories. The further zones were to extend to the rest of the country. Despatch (c.300/I) from the Commander of the Home Army to the C-in-C, 28 February 1943, Ldz. 950, APUST.

[5] Despatch No. 60.

as a symbol of close co-operation between Poland and the Western Powers while tending to restrain the Russians from 'acts of disloyalty to us'.[1]

With regard to the political aspects of the problem he again asked his Government to try to achieve the necessary territorial guarantees; he suggested that as a preliminary token of Russia's goodwill towards Poland Soviet partisan units operating in Poland might be placed under his command.[2]

He also claimed that the orders received could be implemented only under conditions of 'disciplined public opinion' at home. It would be essential to encourage the nation to receive the Russians with friendliness tempered with caution. He felt that it would be a mistake to put the nation entirely off its guard, as this might lead to its 'psychological capitulation' to the Russians; he repeated that if they should break their pledges to the exiled Government they would automatically become the enemies of Poland.[3] In his view the achievement of a high degree of national unity would also involve the solution of general social problems, as well as a reassessment of policy towards the Ukrainans and White Russians, who constituted the majority of the population in the eastern provinces of pre-war Poland. Otherwise he prophesied that both the national minorities and the social problems could be used by the Soviets as levers to further their own designs in Poland. They might assume the role of protectors of the Ukrainians and White Russians in the eastern provinces, and act as the sole champions of social progress in the country. To avoid this he asked the Government to issue a declaration guaranteeing the national minorities full rights of citizenship with cultural autonomy, and to inaugurate a programme of far-reaching post-war social and economic reforms. He insisted that half-measures and vague promises would not be enough to secure national concord, without which the rising might end in dismal failure.[4] The Home Commander wished to act not only as a resolute military leader, ready to defend the territorial and political integrity of Poland, but also as the advocate of political and social progress.[5] In this respect he was transcending his purely military functions and duties, and was becoming a political figure.

The dialogue continued; the tempo of the exchange of communica-

---

[1] Despatch No. 60.   [2] *Ibid.*   [3] *Ibid.*   [4] *Ibid.*
[5] Report of the Commander of the Home Army to the C-in-C. No. 169, 4 December 1942. Ldz. 270/tj/43, APUST.

tions between London and Warsaw was increasing. Sikorski replied to Grot-Rowecki's January dispatch at the beginning of February 1943:

> I fully understand the attitude of the Homeland towards the Russian problem . . . On the other hand you must realise that Poland cannot afford to conduct a war on two fronts, neither now nor in the future, and that an understanding with Russia is essential.[1]

He said that he was striving for a closer *rapprochement* with the U.S.S.R., 'without compromising Polish political and territorial aspirations'. He expressed the sanguine hope that Russia's hostile attitude to the London Poles would 'undergo a radical change, under . . . pressure from Roosevelt and Churchill'.[2] However, if attempts to achieve this reorientation of Russian policy should fail, Sikorski expected that in Washington and London, such a failure would be interpreted as proof that 'it is impossible for a democracy to reach an understanding with totalitarian Russia. In this respect our relations with Soviet Russia are in the nature of a test.' He alleged that among the governing circles in Great Britain and America there was increasing realisation of the danger of possible 'Sovietisation' of Europe: the idea that the Soviets should be forestalled in Central and Eastern Europe was growing. Upon this he based the hope that Anglo–American forces would reach Poland before the Russians. If, in the event, the Russians should enter the country first, his earlier orders to the Home Army were to be put into operation. It was to rise against the Germans and co-operate with the Russians, in the way outlined in earlier dispatches. The C-in-C assured Warsaw that he would be able to derive 'political advantage' from Russo–Polish military co-operation. In the event of Soviet disloyalty the Home Army Command was to 'demand Anglo-Saxon intervention'.[3] An important aim of the rising was to be 'the forestalling of the Russians' in liberating the country. This was to be achieved by a policy of accomplished facts – the seizure of political and administrative power in Poland by the resistance, especially in Wilno and Lwow. He reserved for himself the right to give the orders for the rising. In connection with the problems of internal policy raised by Grot-Rowecki, Sikorski informed him that these were the subject of Cabinet deliberations, the result of which would

---

[1] Despatch from the C-in-C to the Commander of the Home Army, 6 February 1943, Ldz. 247/43, APUST.
[2] *Ibid.*   [3] *Ibid.*

be communicated to the military leaders via the normal political channels – the office of the Government's Delegate.[1] In a communication to the Delegate, Sikorski, as Prime Minister, described the concept of the rising as an opportunity for social or nationalist revolution as potentially highly dangerous, or even fatal, for the country. He feared that such a revolution might give the U.S.S.R. an opportunity to interfere in Poland's internal affairs.[2] The Premier apparently wanted to stand above party politics and act as an impartial arbiter of the national interest. Consequently, for better or worse, the problem of the proposals made in military quarters for the social reconstruction of post-war Poland was conveniently shelved.[3]

This matter being temporarily closed, in his next communication Grot-Rowecki dealt mainly with military issues.[4] He repeated his earlier suggestion for a series of localised consecutive uprisings in the event of Russian entry in pursuit of the retreating *Wehrmacht*, and suggested that he, and not the C-in-C, should be responsible for ordering the insurrections in the eastern provinces of pre-war Poland. He went on to inform London that the uprisings in these regions would certainly fail without Allied support; 'Without this help even our most unsparing efforts will be too weak to produce results.'[5] This admission reveals the weakness of the Home Army's position in these areas. Grot-Rowecki went on to say that the attitude of the underground towards the Red Army should be based on a Russo–Polish agreement which would define the conditions of military and civil co-operation. If such an agreement proved impossible he demanded that his troops should be provided with a detailed Instruction defining the behaviour they were to adopt towards the Russians, especially in the eastern regions.

He dispatched his own draft of an Instruction to the Eastern Commands of the underground army. This said that all their available units were to rise against the retreating Germans and assume the role of sovereign hosts to the advancing Russians. More precisely as much territory as possible was to be liberated by Polish efforts,

[1] Despatch from the C-in-C to the Commander of the Home Army, 6 February 1943, Ldz. 247/43, APUST.

[2] The Prime Minister's Instruction to the Government's Delegate, 11 February 1943, GSHI, File 105.

[3] The High Command of the Home Army returned to this question on the very eve of the Warsaw Rising.

[4] Despatch from the Commander of the Home Army (c.300/I-8) to the C-in-C, 26 February 1943, Ldz. 950, APUST (hereafter referred to as Despatch No. 300).

[5] *Ibid.*

authority over it assumed 'in the name of the Republic' in co-operation with the civil organs of the resistance.

A special effort was to be made to capture large towns, influential in their regions and Home Army garrisons were to be established there. To facilitate their success the proposed operations were to coincide with the complete 'disorganisation' of the Germans, which was expected to occur not more than twenty-four hours before the withdrawal of the German rearguards from a particular town or region, and occupation of it by the Red Army.[1] These operations were to be directed only against the German rearguards delaying the advance of the Soviet offensive. It is evident, therefore, that they would be of only limited military usefulness to the Red Army and that their success would depend on this progress of the Russian forces, as well as on perfect timing and resolute Polish leadership. The Commanders on the spot were to be responsible for issuing the final battle-orders to their troops.[2]

Thus Grot-Rowecki envisaged a number of local uprisings against the Germans, aimed at the seizure of territory from them. In fact this type of operation was put into practice by Bor-Komorowski in July 1944 and culminated in the outbreak of the Warsaw Rising itself.

Politically, the operations suggested by Grot-Rowecki would testify to the Home Army's determination to fight against the Germans and emphasise Polish claims to the eastern provinces of pre-war Poland. But in view of Soviet counterclaims to these areas these operations might easily turn into an open clash with the Russians, who looked upon the eastern regions of Poland as part of the U.S.S.R. It is clear, therefore, that these operations, while to be directed militarily against the Germans, were, in a political sense, to be directed against the Russians too. In Grot-Rowecki's view the Home Army was to stage an armed political demonstration which would both engage the Germans in open combat after long years of underground struggle and confront the Russians with accomplished facts regardless of the consequences.

Paradoxically, the success of this demonstration would depend largely not only upon the Red Army's ability to defeat the Germans, but also on their willingness to come to the rescue of the Poles, if their uprising should be badly timed. At the end of March 1943 the C-in-C approved Grot-Rowecki's plan for the eastern provinces,

[1] Despatch No. 300.   [2] *Ibid.*

with the proviso, however that he would himself be responsible for issuing the order putting it into effect. Further, he told Grot-Rowecki that, should the 'Russian attitude to us become clearly hostile', it would be advisable 'to reveal [in the eastern regions] only the civil administration and to withdraw the Home Army units into the interior of the country to save them from destruction'. The C-in-C warned Warsaw not to expect help from the West, in the shape of airborne units or even supplies, during the actual fighting as it would be very difficult to co-ordinate supporting operations with the tempo of events. He drew Grot-Rowecki's attention to the fact that the staging of the struggle zone by zone in the immediate German rear 'might lead to Nazi reprisals in the interior of the country'.[1]

In his last dispatch of June 1943 the C-in-C ordered the Home Commander to use his forces sparingly because he thought that they would be 'irreplaceable in the final phases [of the struggle] and in the period of post-war reconstruction'.[2]

For his part, and at the same time – June 1943 – Grot-Rowecki was urging Sikorski to revise his policy regarding the U.S.S.R. and to allow the Home Army to adopt a clearly hostile – in his word, 'defensive' – attitude to the Russians who, he insisted, had in any case been considered as 'enemy number two' for the last three years, in pro-London circles in Poland.[3] Political considerations, he wrote, might prompt the Government to try to reach an understanding with Russia, even without real hope of immediate success. But in his opinion it was impossible to vary the attitude to the Soviets according to 'political fluctuations' and to 'regard Russia once as an enemy, then as a fully-fledged ally, and finally as a more or less suspect party to a fight in the common cause'. A choice must be made, he demanded: 'Either the Russians are our enemies or our allies.'[4] To him the choice was obvious, as he believed that a strong Russia was, by definition, Poland's enemy and should be treated as such. He estimated that Russia must at that time be strong, or even 'exceptionally strong', because she was refusing either to have relations with the

[1] Despatch from the C-in-C to the Commander of the Home Army, 24 March 1943, Ldz. 950/43, APUST.
[2] Despatch from the C-in-C to the Commander of the Home Army, 25 June 1943, Ldz. 3179/43, APUST.
[3] Despatch from the Commander of the Home Army (500/I-6) to the C-in-C, 15–22 June 1943, Ldz. 2993/43, APUST (hereafter referred to as Despatch No. 500/I-6).
[4] *Ibid.*

Polish Government or to recognise its political and territorial demands. This indicated that she wished ultimately to 'swallow' Poland.[1] He argued that it was wrong even to pretend that the Russians were Poland's allies, especially at this stage of the war. The attitude which he prescribed could be changed in the future, if Russia should become more amenable to the London Government. In short, Grot-Rowecki once more rejected the very idea of a compromise solution of the Russo–Polish dispute. Instead, he advocated the adoption of a 'defensive attitude' to the Soviets, and preparations should be made to resist the Red Army on its entry into Poland. The following anti-Soviet military operations were envisaged by the General: first, sabotage activities in the eastern provinces; secondly delaying Red Army advances by destroying lines of communication as far as the line of the Vistula and San; thirdly, staging pitched battles against Soviet forces in areas where even minimal opportunities existed; finally, in the areas where such opportunities did not present themselves the Home Army units should remain underground, ready to act against the Russians at a suitable moment on the orders of the C-in-C.[2]

When suggesting resistance to the Russians Grot-Rowecki seemed fully aware that the necessary preparations would not easily escape Soviet notice and could result in further inflammation of Russo–Polish relations; yet he was not greatly perturbed by such a contingency, convinced as he was that a strong Russia would be determined to solve the Polish question in a manner favourable to herself, and would always be in a position to find justification or pretext for this. He was also convinced that the adoption of a 'defensive attitude' to the Soviets by the Polish underground would certainly, if reluctantly, be sanctioned by the Western Powers.[3]

This counsel was couched in brave, though hardly expedient, terms. It was indeed the voice of despairing and impassioned Polish nationalism, which could not come to terms with the idea of Russia's victory in the East. To Grot-Rowecki the Russo–German conflict was, in essence, a bitter and protracted struggle between Poland's two mortal enemies. The emergence of both in an exhausted and weakened condition was the essential background to the establishment of his ideal Poland, with the help of Western Allies, who would then become the undisputed victors and arbiters in Europe. It seems that he hoped for a repetition of the events of 1917 and 1918, when

[1] *Ibid.*   [2] *Ibid.*   [3] *Ibid.*

both Russia and Germany were defeated and faced with internal upheavals. This situation had made it possible for the newly-emergent Poland to take her place in Europe as a fully independent power, following a policy of non-alignment in regard to her two mighty neighbours. The recurrence of such circumstances at the end of the Second World War would no doubt have allowed the followers of the London camp to satisfy their ambitions and aspirations for and in Poland.

The adoption of Grot-Rowecki's plan would have signified a complete departure from Sikorski's policy regarding Russia, and would tend to turn the Home Army into a quite openly anti-Soviet as well as anti-German force. It is hard to imagine what Grot-Rowecki wished to achieve by throwing the Home Army into a battle against the Red Army, apart from displaying its readiness to defend the symbolic rights of a defeated state. Here, a question arises: was he contemplating some heroic but, for all practical purposes, meaningless gesture? Alternatively, was he really hoping that he would delay the advance of the victorious Soviets long enough to enable the Western Allies to occupy at least a part of Poland? Was he hoping that Polish opposition to the Soviets would prompt the Western Allies to intervene in the conflict on the side of Poland, as represented by the exiled Government? Or was his proposal to resist the Soviets just an empty pose? It is probable that a heroic though forlorn gesture was intended. This supposition is supported by his earlier plan to establish a 'defensive redoubt' on the Baltic, where a 'hopeless' battle against the Red Army was to be staged. It is doubtful whether such a policy would have been acceptable to Great Britain and America as, during the years 1941–5, these two Powers wished to maintain good and close relations with the U.S.S.R., and considered as their allies only those forces which were willing to fight unreservedly against Hitler; by fighting both the Germans and the Russians the Home Army would be putting itself in an ambiguous position.

The very fact that plans to oppose and resist the Russians were seriously contemplated and discussed by Grot-Rowecki, despite Sikorski's repeated and well-argued warnings to the contrary, tends to create an impression that in regard to these problems the Home Commander lacked a sense of political and military realism and was addicted to highly dangerous propositions of doubtful political value.

At this time diplomatic relations between the U.S.S.R. and Poland were already broken, and there was no sign of improvement in spite of British attempts at mediation between the two parties.[1]

These diplomatic developments, coupled with the Home Army leaders' firm belief that the Russians were responsible for the Katyn massacre, undoubtedly tended to confirm Polish antagonism to the Soviets and influence the Home Army's plans for the reception of the Russians on Polish soil.[2] The Home Army's antagonism was further encouraged by the fact that it was shared by the *political* leaders of the resistance in Warsaw. The politicians in Warsaw also subscribed to the doctrine of two enemies; they believed that a lasting understanding with a strong Russia would be impossible and were opposed to the very idea of a Russo–Polish compromise on territorial issues.[3]

Grot-Rowecki's June despatch remained unanswered. At the beginning of July 1943 the first dialogue between Warsaw and London, concerning the Home Army's attitude to the Soviets, was brought to an abrupt end by dramatic and tragic events. On 30 June 1943 Grot-Rowecki was arrested in Warsaw by the Gestapo; he was later shot on Himmler's orders during the Warsaw Rising. A few days later, on 5 July 1943, Sikorski was killed in an air-crash off the coast of Gibraltar. In this way, within the space of less than a week, Poland lost her war-time leader, who combined the offices of Prime Minister and C-in-C, and the Commander of her secret army.

Because of this double tragedy the dialogue ended inconclusively. To the last, Sikorski refused to revise his instructions ordering the Home Army to treat the Russians as allies and to co-operate with them.[4] Grot-Rowecki, for his part, remained unconvinced, to the day of his arrest, of the wisdom of these instructions. He urged the adoption of a less conciliatory stand.[5] Sikorski wished to prevent an open, armed Russo–Polish conflict; in accordance with his dispositions the opposition to the Russians, if any, was to be of a political, not military, nature.[6] Grot-Rowecki was dissatisfied with the role which his superior assigned to his forces with regard to the

---

[1] For this, see p. 5 of this study.

[2] T. Bor-Komorowski, *op. cit.*, pp. 126ff.

[3] A memorandum from the Government's Delegate to the Prime Minister, 10 January 1944, Ldz. 110/44, GSHI, Kr.I (1943–4).

[4] The C-in-C 'Personal and Secret Instruction to the Home Commander', 8 March 1942, Ldz. 1111/42. APUST.

[5] Despatch No. 500/I–6.   [6] Despatch 5060.

Russians, and advocated the need for armed resistance.[1] In their dialogue their respective positions were repeatedly defined and clarified. Reason was on Sikorski's side, while Grot-Rowecki represented narrow patriotism and rampant nationalism. To the end, the two Generals found it impossible to reconcile their views.

Further, Grot-Rowecki's contributions to this dialogue with his Prime Minister and C-in-C suggest that he saw his role not only as that of the mere executor of policies dictated to him from London, but also as that of their critic and re-modeller. During his term of office, the High Command of the secret army was becoming a policy-making body which often stood in contradiction to directives decided upon in London. This tendency was to survive Grot-Rowecki's arrest, and become more noticeable at the end of 1943 when Sikorski's firm generalship was lacking and the new Home Commander was able not only to recommend his own policies but to obtain the Cabinet's approval for them. Sikorski's death was a great loss for Poland, as it marked the beginning of the disintegration of the command-structure and compromised the unity of purpose.

This dialogue between Sikorski and Grot-Rowecki was important, as many of the ideas which emerged from it were later incorporated into the plans for the Home Army's operations in 1944.

Soon, a new dialogue was to develop between London and Warsaw, once more attempting, this time finally, to define the Home Army's attitude to the Soviets. The dialogue continued while the Red Army was advancing through Poland and, for the purpose of this study, ended during the Warsaw Rising itself.

[1] Despatch No. 500/I-6.

5

The 'Tempest' Plan

1. *The Changes in London and Warsaw*

In July 1943 the President of Poland appointed Stanislaw Miko-lajczyk as the new Prime Minister of Poland, and General Kazimierz Sosnkowski as Commander-in-Chief.[1]

Mikolajczyk was one of the leaders of the Peasant Party, and during the period 1941–3 served in Sikorski's Cabinet as Deputy Prime Minister and Minister of the Interior. In this capacity he was responsible for the political side of the resistance movement in Poland. It was expected that the new Premier would follow his predecessor's policy towards Moscow.

> Mikolajczyk was anxious to reach a compromise with Russia which would allow our Government and Army to return to Polish soil . . . He . . . believed that he could play the part of a leader inside Poland with the support of the peasant masses . . . He believed that Poland's policy could be established on the basis of solidarity between the Eastern and Western Allies . . .[2]

Sosnkowski, whose nomination was opposed by Mikolajczyk and accepted by the British Government with some reluctance because of his anti-Russian views, was unlike the Premier in both personality and opinions.[3] For many years he was intimately linked with

---

[1] Under the terms of the 1935 Constitution, the President was personally charged with the duty of appointing and dismissing the C-in-C, who was directly responsible to him, and not to the Government, for the discharge of his military duties and the conduct of war. If put into practice, this would mean that the conduct of the war would be controlled by the military, and not political, leaders. This anomaly was overcome, in May 1942, when a Presidential decree made the Cabinet responsible for the over-all conduct of the war, thereby establishing a large measure of political control over military affairs. In practice, this meant that the C-in-C could not issue important orders to the Army without the Cabinet's approval. Nevertheless, day-to-day control of the Army rested in the hands of the C-in-C. Cf. Wladyslaw Pobog-Malinowski, *Najnowsza Historia Polityczna Polski 1864–1945*, vol. 3 (London, 1960) pp. 315ff.

[2] Count Edward Raczynski, *op. cit.*, p. 154.

[3] Cf. *Ibid.*, p. 151.

Pilsudski and his ideology, which tended to make him *persona non grata* in the eyes of Polish left-wing political parties. In July 1941 he resigned from Sikorski's Cabinet, in which he had held the post of Secretary of State responsible for Home military affairs, in protest against the signing of the pact with Russia, which he regarded as detrimental to Polish interest in that it failed to commit the Russians to recognition of the Riga Line as their post-war frontier with Poland. Sosnkowski believed that a more unconciliatory Polish stand during the negotiations leading to conclusion of the pact would have brought better results for Poland.[1] He was to advocate a similar course during Mikolajczyk's attempts to arrange a *modus vivendi* with Stalin in 1944. He believed that his position as C-in-C entitled him to play an active part in political life.[2] As a result, his relations with Mikolajczyk were strained and unhappy and this was to affect the course of events in Poland.[3]

During the first days of July 1943 Sosnkowski appointed General Tadeusz Bor-Komorowski as Grot-Rowecki's successor. Bor-Komorowski was a pre-war cavalry officer of aristocratic origin, who veered, in his political sympathies, towards the National Democrats. The General had served in the clandestine army since 1939, and from 1941 had acted as its Deputy Commander. His Chief of Staff was General Tadeusz Pelczynski ('Grzegorz') who had occupied this post since 1941. Pelczynski served in Pilsudski's legions during the First World War, and, in the inter-war period, was for a number of years closely connected with the *Sanacja* as the head of military intelligence – the Second Bureau of the General Staff. Among high-ranking Home Army officers in Warsaw there was a certain amount of opposition to Bor-Komorowski's appointment, apparently because of his right-wing connections. Col Jan Rzepecki ('Sedzia'), head of the Information and Propaganda Department of the Home Army High Command, formally registered his opposition to Bor-Komorowski's appointment by informing Pelczynski that he considered it 'highly undesirable' that a person of Bor-Komorowski's political views should command the Home Army at a time when a move to the left was taking place in the general climate of opinion. Rzepecki went so far as to ask Pelczynski directly whether it were

[1] S. Sosabowski, *Najkrotsza Droga* (London, 1957), pp. viiiff.
[2] Cf. Stanislaw Kopanski, *Wspomnienia Wojenne 1939–1946* (London, 1962), p. 292.
[3] Cf. *Ibid.*, pp. 300–1.

not possible to secure 'the appointment of someone else, or alternatively to persuade Komorowski to resign'. Pelczynski refused to interfere with Bor-Komorowski's appointment, while admitting that it might be necessary to 'prop up' the Commander by 'helping' him to take the right decisions.[1] Some members of Bor-Komorowski's Staff would seem to have believed it their duty to influence his decisions in the direction they considered desirable, in addition to discharging their more conventional functions of chief advisers and executors of his orders.

In fact, there were other possible objections, of a more professional nature, to Bor-Komorowski's appointment; these were not mentioned by Rzepecki. The General lacked higher military training – he was not a graduate of Staff College, which traditionally provided the Army with its high-ranking Commanders – and had no experience of high command. Apart from his two years as the Deputy Commander of the secret army there was nothing in his training or career to suggest that he was qualified to hold so elevated and responsible a post during such difficult times.

2. *The Government's and C-in-C's Instruction of 27 October 1943*

Throughout October 1943 the émigré leaders in London – the Cabinet and the C-in-C – were deliberating and formulating new political and military directives for the underground in Poland which they hoped would finally determine its policy and strategy during the approaching German defeat.

On 5 October 1943, Sosnkowski informed Bor-Komorowski of these high-level deliberations and told him that on their conclusion he would be given his military dispositions.[2] Meanwhile, the C-in-C furnished the Home Commander with his own confidential analysis of the political and military situation which in his opinion was facing Poland, and communicated to him his personal views concerning the attitude of the secret army towards the Soviets. These opinions are important because they reveal Sosnkowski's position and suggest the way in which he hoped to influence the Government and his subordinates in Warsaw.

The C-in-C argued that the secret army should regard the Russians

---

[1] Jan Rzepecki, *Wspomnienia i Przyczynki Historyczne* (Warsaw, 1956), pp. 257ff.
[2] Despatch from the C-in-C to the Commander of the Home Army, 5 October 1943, Ldz. 5371/tjn/43, APUST.

as enemies unless the latter were willing to satisfy a number of Polish political conditions; first, recognition of the Riga Line as their post-war frontier with Poland – a territorial arrangement which he thought the Western Allies ought to guarantee; secondly, agreement that the representatives of the exiled Government should administer the liberated territories; thirdly agreement to stationing mixed Allied commissions in Poland; finally, demobilisation or transfer to Polish control of the Moscow-sponsored Polish military units recently formed in the U.S.S.R.[1] Further Sosnkowski insisted that should the Red Army enter the country before the reopening of Russo–Polish relations on the basis suggested above, the Polish Government should make a number of diplomatic representations to the Western Allies stating that the presence of the Russians in Poland should not 'infringe upon our rights of sovereignty' in the country, and proclaiming that 'should Russia revert to her practices of 1939–1940, acts of self-defence . . . must, in advance, be considered as justified'. In addition, the Government should demand that the Western Powers safeguard 'the lives, rights and property of our citizens' and press them to state that 'they do not recognise territorial changes arising out of military operations'.[2]

Sosnkowski thus made it patently clear that he considered the conclusion of a political *rapprochement* with the Soviet Union, without in the least compromising of Polish interests and ambitions, to be an essential prerequisite of Russo–Polish military co-operation.[3] The C-in-C emphatically rejected the idea of unqualified military co-operation between the Soviet and Polish forces in the task of liberating Poland.[4] It did not occur to him that it was just such military co-operation that might open the way for subsequent political accommodation.

Indeed, it seems that he deliberately set out to heighten, rather than reduce, Russo–Polish tension, by insisting that the exiled Government should call upon the Western Allies to intervene directly in Russo–Polish affairs, and publicly proclaim that measures would be taken against the Russians if they tried to re-annex the Eastern territories or took steps to suppress the underground.

[1] Despatch from the C-in-C to the Commander of the Home Army 5 October 1943, Ldz. 5371/tjn/43, APUST.
[2] Despatch from the C-in-C to the Commander of the Home Army, 21 October 1943, Ldz. 6029/43, APUST. Hereafter referred to as Despatch 6029.
[3] For Grot-Rowecki's views on this subject, see pp. 135–46 of this study.
[4] Despatch 6029.

(Under such circumstances this was to assume an inimical stand towards the Soviet authorities and to act independently of them.)

He wrote, 'In regard to the character, extent and timing of armed action at Home, we ought to maintain complete independence and freedom of decision, as England and America are doing in regard to the problem of the opening of the Second Front.'[1] An anti-German rising might be launched in Poland, he stated, but only if and when it appeared to be in the interests of the exiled Government, bearing in mind the 'colossal sacrifices' it would entail for the population.[2] In his view this freedom of decision to launch the rising in Poland was of such great political importance that it should only be renounced 'in return for binding Allied guarantees in regard to our territorial questions'.[3]

With the territorial question in mind, Sosnkowski told Warsaw that the British press was urging the Polish Government to spare no efforts in trying to restore diplomatic relations with Moscow, and to accept the Curzon Line as the basis of their frontier with the U.S.S.R. In return for concessions in the east, Poland would receive compensations in the west at Germany's expense. The C-in-C alleged that this solution of the territorial dispute between the two countries was favoured by significant sections of Anglo–American public opinion.

Sosnkowski rightly predicted that Great Britain and America would try to improve their relations with the U.S.S.R., in the interests of the successful continuation of the war and conclusion of a harmonious peace settlement.[4] The desire of the Western Powers, for closer relations with Moscow appeared to him to be a natural development, though possibly a dangerous one for Poland. He was haunted by the spectre of a second Munich, this time over Poland; indeed, he said that in spite of the best Anglo–American intentions towards Poland she might soon find herself in a similar position to that of Czechoslovakia in 1938.[5] The General feared that the Polish question might be solved by the Great Powers alone, without regard to Polish interests as represented by the exiled Government. Such a possibility must, in his opinion, be resisted; Polish policy should aim at the hardening of the Anglo–American attitude towards Russia, and the uncompromising defence of the Polish position.[6] He was anxious that the Polish Government should adopt an

[1] *Ibid.*   [2] *Ibid.*   [3] *Ibid.*
[4] *Ibid.*   [5] *Ibid.*   [6] *Ibid.*

intransigent attitude to all forces which might urge on it a compromise solution of the Russo–Polish dispute, even if this involved the
splitting of Allied unity and a conflict between East and West.
Indeed, he felt that agreement between the Great Powers was as yet
not a foregone conclusion; he observed that in some western circles
there was growing suspicion of Soviet long-term intentions.[1] His
unconciliatory attitude remained despite the prospect of a communist regime being established in Warsaw; he envisaged this
might result from failure to reach an agreement with Moscow. On the
contrary, he suggested that the establishment of a 'Red Government'
in Poland might be advantageous to the London Poles as it would
tend to heighten the Western suspicion of Russia, and possibly ease
'the struggle against Bolshevism in the Homeland', presumably by
bringing the conflict out into the open. In any case, he believed that
the formation of a Soviet-sponsored administration would be a
function of Russia's military prowess, rather than of the state of
Russo–Polish diplomatic relations.[2]

In fact he said, in February 1944, that

> our cause will win completely only when Germany and Russia have
> weakened themselves to such an extent that final victory will fall into
> the hands of the Anglo-Saxon Powers, who will occupy the German and
> Polish territories. The present predicament is caused by the fact that
> these Powers under-estimate their strength; they are, as it were, tired of
> war and . . . allow Russia too much scope for manoeuvre in Europe,
> especially that part of the continent with which our fate is linked. This
> . . . is, so it seems, the cause of Poland's drama . . .[3]

In Sosnkowski's opinion Moscow was aiming at the 'Sovietisation'
of Poland' within the frontiers defined by Stalin.

Yet he thought it possible that sooner or later Great Britain would
be compelled to resist 'Russian imperialism'. The questions were,
when would this happen, and would the London camp be able to
survive the difficult transition period? He suggested that the war
might last much longer than expected and envisaged the possibility
of many as yet unforeseen changes during its course.[4] The tenor of
these pronouncements was quite clear; they testified to Sosnkowski's
adherence to the doctrine of two enemies. This doctrine provided

[1] Despatch 6029.   [2] *Ibid.*
[3] Despatch from the C-in-C to the Commander of the Home Army, 12 February
1944, Ldz. 1217/tj/44, APUST.
[4] *Ibid.*

him with his political bearings, and inspired his communications with Bor-Komorowski.

Apart from his attempts to act as political as well as military mentor to the Home Army leaders in Warsaw, the C-in-C wished to assume a similar role in regard to his own Government in London.[1]

The General was trying to reconstruct the existing Cabinet by introducing into it, apparently in the name of national unity, followers of the pre-war regime and extreme right-wing nationalists, who were sympathetic to his views and opinions. In this manner, the Army, as personified in and represented by its Supreme Commander, was becoming an active factor in émigré politics. Sosnkowski was not to be satisfied with the role of non-political servant and highest military adviser to his Government. This was to have serious consequences in the future.

Nevertheless, at the end of October 1943 a large measure of agreement on the policy to be pursued by the resistance movement in Poland was, for the time being, achieved between the Prime Minister and the C-in-C. On 1 November 1943 the Cabinet's and C-in-C's Instruction to the Underground dated 27 October 1943 was dispatched to Poland.[2] It contained political and military directives to the leaders of the secret State. The tone of this Instruction suggests that Sosnkowski was one of its main authors.[3] In its treatment of the Russian problem it represented a drastic departure from the dispositions which Sikorski had sent to Warsaw during the years 1942–3. In this respect it tended to resemble the views of the first Commander of the Home Army, General Grot-Rowecki.[4] This seemed to indicate that it would be favourably received in the High Command of the conspiratorial army, which was staffed by Grot-Rowecki's former close collaborators. Yet this was not to be the case.

The Instruction stated that the Government might, at some future date, order the underground in Poland to 'intensify the armed operations against the Germans'. These operations might assume the form of a 'rising' or, alternatively, that of an 'intensified sabotage-

---

[1] Despatch 6029.

[2] The Government's and the C-in-C's Instruction of 27 October 1943, Ldz. 5989/43, APUST. Hereafter referred to as the Government's Instruction.

[3] Cf. Andrzej Pomian-Dowmuntt, *Powstanie Warszawskie* (London, 1946), p. 34.

[4] Sikorski's and Grot-Rowecki's views on the Russo–Polish problems are discussed on pp. 133–48 of this study.

subversion activity'.[1] The question which of these two forms of operation would be adopted was to be decided by the general strategic and political situation in Europe. The Instruction stated that a rising was to be launched in the event of either of two possible contingencies – if it were possible to obtain Allied approval of an assistance for it, in which case it would be co-ordinated with Allied strategy on the continent of Europe, or, alternatively, in the event of a total German defeat and the collapse of the German military machine in the East. In the latter case the rising was to be undertaken even if it proved impossible to secure Anglo–American help for the insurgents in Poland. In both instances, however, the actual order for the rising was to be given by the Government, in the first instance after consultation with the Allies, and in the second on the recommendation of the underground authorities, who were charged with the duty of appraising the military situation and the state of German morale on the Eastern Front.[2] Hence, the Cabinet and the C-in-C in London were to be primarily responsible for the issuing of final marching orders to the Home Army in Poland. The role of the underground leaders, in this respect, was severely restricted and clearly defined; they were to act merely in an advisory capacity, and were not authorised to start large-scale anti-German operations on their own responsibility. Delegation of authority on this issue was not as yet intended or envisaged.

The rising was to aim first at the liberation of as much Polish territory as possible from the Germans. This would then serve as a base for the restitution in the country of 'Polish state sovereignty' and 'reconstruction of the [regular] Armed Forces at Home', secondly, at the delivery of a blow against the Germans, in their rear, at the 'most critical moment for them' and thirdly, at the 'protection of Poland from final destruction during the Germans' systematic withdrawal from the East'.[3] From the 'political point of view' the rising was to prove Poland's determination to continue her struggle against the Germans to the bitter end, to restore Poland's sovereignty on her territories at the moment of German collapse, and finally to make a substantial, though costly, contribution to the 'common Allied victory'.[4]

In his 'commentaries' on the Instruction, sent to Warsaw in December 1943, Sosnkowski emphasised to Bor-Komorowski that

---

[1] The Government's Instruction.   [2] *Ibid.*   [3] *Ibid.*   [4] *Ibid.*

the first plan of action it outlined was based on the assumption 'that the rising in Poland will be closely co-ordinated with the operations of the Anglo–Saxons on the continent of Europe', though he added that, so far, the Government had failed to secure any binding decision or promise from the British or Americans in this matter. Sosnkowski ascribed the reluctance of the British and American Governments to pledge themselves to support the rising in Poland to geographical and political causes. Nevertheless, the C-in-C still hoped that it might be possible to secure this support.[1] He further believed that there were 'reasons to expect the possible collapse of the German resistance in the near future, which might result in a rising, even without external help'. Bor-Komorowski and his insurgents would then have to rely entirely on their own strength and resources for 'a certain period of time'. Nevertheless, even if this did happen, the Polish Government would try to obtain Western assistance.[2]

Thus, Anglo–American help for the rising was considered by the Polish leaders in London to be an important condition of its success. They were, however, in a quandary, because they were unable to tell their subordinates in Poland in what form, if any, such help would materialise. Thus, those parts of the Instruction referring to the possibility of a rising in Poland were couched in somewhat vague terms. This lack of precision, to some extent unavoidable in war-time conditions, was largely caused, it appears, by the reluctance of the Polish leaders in England to admit, in their plans for the rising, the possibility that it might prove necessary to launch it, if at all, in co-operation with the Red Army rather than the Anglo–American forces operating in Europe.

The motives which prompted the Polish leaders to secure Anglo–American assistance for the rising were both political and military. This was made clear by Mikolajczyk, who stated in October 1943 that in the event of an Anglo–American undertaking to supply the Home Army with arms and send to Poland even small airborne detachments, the Home Army should be ordered to start the rising, during the *Wehrmacht's* retreat from Russia, and that the rising should assume an anti-Soviet as well as anti-German character. Then, Mikolajczyk argued, '. . . the Home Army would resist a Soviet invasion, while the presence of the allied troops would

---

[1] Despatch from the C-in-C to the Commander of the Home Army, 2 December 1943, Ldz. 6761/43, APUST. Hereafter referred to as Despatch 6761.
[2] Despatch 6761.

perform a political role of halting the invasion'.[1] In short, the rising, assisted by the Anglo–Saxons, was intended not only to make the London Poles the masters of the political situation on the Vistula, but also to prevent the Russians from setting foot on Polish soil. This impression is strengthened by Mikolajczyk's apparent reluctance, at this stage, to commit the Home Army to staging a rising without Anglo–American support.[2]

Moreover, according to the Instruction the following conditions were to accompany a rising undertaken in 'close co-operation' with the Western Allies; the stabilisation of the Russo–German Front beyond the Polish frontiers long enough to enable the Allies to penetrate sufficiently far into Europe for them to help the insurgents with air-support and troops; the fulfilment of Western promises to support the Home Army with necessary arms and equipment; the landing in Poland of Allied liaison officers and of the Polish Parachute Brigade (then stationed in Great Britain); the direction, in co-operation with the British and American authorities, of support operations by the Polish Government either from Polish soil or Allied-occupied territory on the Continent; finally, Allied assistance for the Polish Government in the task of reaching an understanding with the Soviets, should this not already have been concluded.[3]

Sosnkowski shared the Prime Minister's misgivings concerning the staging of the rising without sufficient help from the West, with one reservation; he maintained that 'acts of despair are sometimes unavoidable in the lives of nations in view of the common feelings of the population, the political symbolism of such acts and their moral significance for posterity'.[4]

He made this reservation while fully aware that an unsupported rising might well become a 'desperate attack', marking the end of the Home Army's struggle and the beginning of 'wholesale slaughter of the population' by the Germans, should their troops be retreating from Poland in good order. He was also aware that, notwithstanding the real nature of Polish intentions, such a rising might well assist the Soviets in their occupation of the country. He begged the Government, therefore, to consider seriously the 'symbolism and significance

---

[1] The records of a meeting called by the President of the Republic on 1 October 1943, APUST.
[2] *Ibid.*
[3] The Government's Instruction.
[4] The C-in-C's letter to the Prime Minister 22 October 1943, Ldz. 1420/op. tjn., APUST.

of an act of despair' before committing the resistance movement to it.[1] The C-in-C was not entirely opposed then, to the idea of a desperate Home Army venture in defence of his romantic conception of national integrity, even though he realised that it might end tragically and would not produce any immediate tangible results; he was fully aware that it might end in national disaster but he was prompted by considerations of an emotional rather than rational nature. This approach to the question suggests a certain ideological similarity between Sosnkowski and Grot-Rowecki, who had also tried to justify the staging of a desperate battle in terms of its alleged 'significance for posterity'.[2]

However, the Government contemplated staging a rising only in co-operation with the Anglo–American plans for the invasion of Europe, or alternatively in the case of the virtual collapse and disintegration of the German military machine. The rising was to realise well-defined political and military objectives. It was to free the country from the Germans and be instrumental in winning political power in Poland for the exiled Government; it was to make the restoration of Polish sovereignty an accomplished fact. It was to manifest the resourcefulness, strength and viability of the pro-London forces in Poland and thus augment their prestige at home and abroad. The Instruction stated that if it were impossible to coordinate the rising with Anglo–American strategy in Europe, and if the German front were to collapse without the disintegration of its rear, the Government would call on the resistance to stage an 'intensified sabotage-diversionary action against the Germans'. This action was to assume a 'politically demonstrative and protective character only'.[3] For its part, the Government was to try to secure from the Western Allies the necessary supplies for this purpose.[4] The Instruction failed to specify in greater detail what objectives this operation was to achieve, or what was meant by 'politically demonstrative and protective character'. We may safely assume, however, that a Home Army engagement with the Germans was to serve as a manifestation of Home Army loyalty to the Western Allies and the exiled Government, and would also be a way of trying to protect the population of the country from Nazi reprisals

[1] *Ibid.*
[2] For Grot-Rowecki's views on this matter see p. 137 of this study.
[3] The Government's Instruction.
[4] *Ibid.*

during the German retreat from Poland. In comparison with a rising it was to be an operation of limited extent and ambition.

The second part of the Instruction dealt with the behaviour and attitude of the underground movement to the Russians, should they enter Poland before her 'complete or partial liberation', presumably by the Home Army and Anglo–American forces.[1] To provide for this eventuality two alternative courses of action, depending on the state of Russo–Polish relations, were outlined by the authors of the Instruction; neither of them, however, envisaged the staging of a rising under such conditions. Instead, both alternatives involved the staging by the Home Army of intensified sabotage-diversionary operations against the retreating Germans – as described in the first part of the Instruction – while at the same time it was stressed that the Home Army was neither to present itself to the Russian authorities nor to co-operate with them during the initial stages of their stay in Poland. The first of the two plans was to be adopted if Russo–Polish relations were restored before the Red Army's entry into Poland. In this event, the Home Army was to fight against the Germans in the territories occupied by them, while remaining underground in the regions held by the Soviets until the exiled Government assumed political power. This assumption of power was to be achieved when the administrative organs of the secret State emerged into the open and the Government, returned to Poland accompanied by representatives of the British and American authorities. After the Government's return, Russo–Polish military co-operation was to be established.[2] Hence, Soviet recognition of the London Government as the sovereign authority in Poland was to be the essential prerequisite of Russo–Polish military co-operation. The decision to conceal the Home Army from the Soviets until the London Government's arrival seems to have been intended as a possible source of bargaining-power during negotiations with Moscow. In the event of Soviet attempts to suppress the movement – arrests and reprisals – 'unavoidable acts of self-defence' were to be undertaken.[3]

Further, if, in spite of the re-establishment of diplomatic relations between the two countries, the Russians should still decide to incorporate the eastern territories into the U.S.S.R., the Polish Government would protest against this move and demand allied 'intervention' to restore the pre-1939 frontiers.[4] The exact character

[1] The Government's Instruction.   [2] *Ibid.*   [3] *Ibid.*   [4] *Ibid.*

of such 'intervention' was not discussed. All these provisions reflected a great mistrust of Soviet intentions on the part of the London Poles.

The second plan was to be put into operation if the problem of Russo–Polish relations remained unresolved at the time of the Soviet entry into Poland. Under such conditions the Home Army should act behind the German lines and remain underground in the Russian-held areas until further orders from the Government. The political organs of the resistance were also to remain underground. Meanwhile, the Government would 'protest to the Allies against the violation of Polish sovereignty . . . and announce . . . that the Homeland will not co-operate with the Soviets'.[1] The Government would also 'issue a warning that in the event of the arrest of the representatives of the underground movement and reprisals against Polish citizens, the secret organisations will resort to self-defensive actions'.[2] In practice the adoption of this policy would amount to a virtual declaration of war against Russia; at the end of August 1943 Mikolajczyk remarked that, if the Russians did enter Poland without a prior understanding with the London Government, and if they then began to adopt a hostile attitude towards the resistance, the Government would proclaim 'a state of war with Russia'.[3] This would have been an act of despairing folly which, as Sikorski had earlier suggested, might have resulted in the complete abandonment of Poland by her allies, and unnecessary bloodshed.[4]

The decision to conceal the Home Army from the Russians was also a dangerous proposition, as the existence of a secret military organisation in the immediate Soviet rear while Russo–German hostilities were still in progress might have seriously provoked the Russians. It could hardly be expected that they would tolerate the existence of such an organisation, or that they would adopt an attitude of neutrality towards it. It seems certain, therefore, especially in view of the 'self-defence' clause in the Instruction, that concealment of the Home Army from the Russians would have led to an open Russo–Polish clash, with all its tragic consequences. It could have resulted only in further aggravation of the Polish problem, rather than a solution.

[1] The Government's Instruction.   [2] *Ibid.*
[3] The records of a meeting held by the President of the Republic on 28 August 1943, APUST.
[4] For Sikorski's view on this issue see p. 138 of this study.

Moreover, the Instruction contained a contradiction of which its authors appeared unaware; the 'intensified sabotage-subversion action' was intended to be a political demonstration,[1] yet if the Red Army entered Poland it was to be carried out in conditions of almost complete anonymity, as on the arrival of the Soviets in a particular area or locality troops involved in anti-German operations were expected to revert to a clandestine existence. In fact, the émigré leaders were demanding that the Home Army should perform a political act while insisting that the agents of that act should not disclose their identity. Anonymity would have considerably reduced the political impact of the demonstration, as the demonstrators' return underground on the arrival of the Russians would leave the entire field to the Communists, who would be able to claim full credit for all anti-German operations in Poland. In any case, the implementation of such an operation would demand a great measure of self-discipline from the insurgent troops, who were expected to participate in an open clash with the Germans, only to revert once more to clandestine existence.

It would have been more logical, once the decision to intensify the struggle against the Germans had been made, to issue an order calling upon the Home Army to co-operate with the Russians, while insisting on its political independence. This was not done because the Government and the C-in-C had no intention of assisting the Russians during their passage through Poland, and because they wished to maintain their undisputed control over the Home Army until the very moment of a final reckoning with Stalin. Only a few weeks later – in December 1943 – the C-in-C was urging Bor-Komorowski to make provision for the creation of the nucleus of an anti-Soviet resistance movement, especially in the eastern territories around Wilno and Lwow.[2]

A different plan of action was urged by General Kukiel, Polish Minister of National Defence in London, who insisted that the Home Army should concentrate its efforts on the seizure of Warsaw and the establishment there of an administration loyal to the émigré authorities, before the Russians occupied the city and attempted to install a Communist-sponsored Government.[3] Kukiel's plan was simple; instead of the whole country, Warsaw alone was to rise, performing

---

[1] For details, see pp. 159–61 of this study.   [2] Despatch 6761.
[3] The records of a meeting held by the President of the Republic on 25 October 1943, APUST.

the tasks previously assigned to the whole of Poland. This policy was, in fact, adopted by General Bor-Komorowski at the end of July 1944, and put into operation on 1 August.

However, in October 1943 Kukiel's proposal was ignored in the Government's directives. Although it was a bold and dangerous proposal it was, on purely logical grounds, more consistent with the Government's plan of staging a political demonstration in Poland. The adoption of Kukiel's suggestion at this early stage would have given Bor-Komorowski ample time and opportunity to examine and prepare for the problem with which he was to be confronted less than a year later, or even to abandon it after realising the enormity of the risks and dangers involved.

The third part of the Instruction dealt with the movement's response to a Russo–German collusion, and stated that, if this should take place, the resistance was to curtail its activities and await further orders.[1] In general, four main criticisms might be levelled against the Instruction. First, the directives were unrealistic because they tended to treat the most probable eventuality – the Soviet entry into Poland while diplomatic relations remained suspended – only as one of a number of possibilities, and devoted most of their attention to the staging of a rising in co-operation with the Western Allies, instead of concentrating on the most likely issue. In consequence, the Instruction created the impression that the émigré leaders thought that their country would be liberated by the Anglo–American, rather than Soviet forces, though they knew that the main Allied invasion of Europe could not be expected earlier than spring 1944, and that the Red Army already stood close to Poland's pre-war frontiers. Hence it appears that they under-estimated Soviet military potentialities and strength.

Secondly, the attitude towards the Russians which the Instruction prescribed for the Home Army would put the force into a hopeless and tragic position by exposing it to Soviet as well as German hostility.

Thirdly, while committing the underground forces to the policy of intensified struggle against the Germans, the Instruction failed to specify what assistance, if any, they could rely upon during the fighting.

Finally, the Instruction omitted to say what attitude the resistance was to adopt towards the Polish Communists, who would redouble their activities during the Russo–German fighting in Poland.

[1] The Government's Instruction.

The Instruction was too hypothetical and lacking in precision to serve as the basis for staging of large-scale military operations which were to realise far-reaching political aims; it could hardly provide the underground with the overall guidance which it would need in the months to follow, during which the fate and character of post-war Poland would be decided.

At this stage the leaders in London felt unable to provide the movement with more detailed instructions.

3. *The Order of the Commander of the Home Army of 20 November 1943*

Given its nature, it is not surprising that the Instruction was, on the whole, badly received in Warsaw by the leaders of the resistance who expected from the Cabinet more specific and realistic directives.[1] Two of its points were welcome: the Warsaw leaders shared the Cabinet's determination to intensify the struggle against the Germans because they feared that failure to engage the Nazis in a more decisive manner might be interpreted at home and abroad as tacit siding with the Germans, which would lead to the abandonment of the movement by the Western Allies, and mass desertions from its ranks to the Communist-sponsored organisations; secondly, they were pleased that the Government was trying to obtain help from the West for their forces.[2]

They were dissatisfied with the relatively passive role which the Cabinet wished to assign to the movement during the approaching Russo–Polish confrontation, and independently decided to disregard their superiors' decision on this issue. Bor-Komorowski told the Cabinet of this development in his communication to Sosnkowski, dated 26 November 1943, and received in London during the first days of January 1944, by which time the Russians were already on territory which before the war had been Polish. He wrote:

> I have issued an order . . . instructing all commanders and units which will take part in the fighting against the retreating Germans to reveal their presence to the Russians. *Their task . . . will be to manifest . . . the existence of Poland.* My order is in disagreement with the Government's Instruction. I see no reason to create a vacuum on Polish soil arising out of the absence of any action in the face of the Russians by the force

[1] Cf. *Polskie Siły Zbrojne, op. cit.*, p. 555.
[2] Cf. T. Bor-Komorowski, *op. cit.*, pp. 180ff.

representing Poland and her legal authorities. Otherwise all our actions [against the Germans] would be credited to the elements standing at Soviet disposal. My opinion is shared by the Government's Delegate and Home Political Representative. The concealment . . . of our mass organisation under the Soviet occupation would be impossible. In practice, I will limit the number of the commands and units which will reveal their existence to an indispensable minimum. The remainder I will try to safeguard by formal demobilisation. In case of . . . Russian occupation, I am preparing in the utmost secrecy the skeleton network of a new clandestine organisation which will stand at your [Sosnkow- ski's] disposal . . . It will take the form of a separate network uncon- nected . . . with the Home Army . . . [which is] to a large extent known to the groups in Soviet service.[1]

A number of points emerge from this communication. The under- ground authorities were prepared to act independently of the Govern- ment, if the Cabinet's decisions were unacceptable to them. This meant that from this moment onwards there were to be two separate high policy-making bodies within the London Camp, one in Warsaw and another in London, making co-ordination difficult. They had decided to revert finally to the attitude to the Russians advocated by Sikorski since March 1942, while at the same time, in deciding to create a nucleus of anti-Russian resistance outside the Home Army network, assuming a posture of defensive readiness against the Russians, as urged by Grot-Rowecki and Sosnkowski. The Home authorities' decision to disclose certain units of the Home Army to the Soviets might be regarded as an attempt to reconcile and integrate these two divergent attitudes. In reality, however, their decision represented a partial qualified acceptance of the essential features of each of these two attitudes – on the one hand, to act as a host to the Russians, on the other to prepare resistance against them. Nevertheless, it might be held that these two policies were irreconcil- able and thus the attempt to fuse them into one in reality meant a departure from both and the emergence of a third.[2] Bor-Komorow- ski's decision represented the acceptance by the Home Army High Command of the principle of limited co-operation with the Soviets. As the General put it: 'We had to show our good will towards those whom the Western Powers called their "great friends and allies in

[1] Despatch from the Commander of the Home Army to the C-in-C 26 November 1943, Ldz. 2100, APUST. My italics.
[2] For Sikorski's and Grot-Rowecki's views on this subject see pp. 133ff of this chapter. For Sosnkowski's opinions see pp. 151ff of this chapter.

the East".'[1] This co-operation was to be, however, more apparent than real.[2]

The anti-German operations and the partial disclosure of the Home Army to the Russians were intended to fill the administrative vacuum in Poland which would exist at the end of the war. The Home Army was to represent the 'existence of Poland' to the Soviets. Thus the Home Army was identified with Poland herself. The Russians would be compelled either to accept the pro-London resistance as a part of sovereign authority in Poland, or to suppress it in full view of world public opinion. The Home Army leaders hoped that Soviet hostility to the organisation might result in Anglo–American protests and intervention on the side of the pro-London circles.[3] In addition, by staging large-scale operations against the Nazis they wished to prevent the Communists from assuming the leadership of the anti-German resistance forces in the country.[4] Here they acted on the assumption that the Communists would try to instigate a rising the moment the Red Army entered central Poland and that they would be joined by many Home Army soldiers if these were denied action in their own ranks.[5] The political intent of Bor-Komorowski's orders was clear: '*By giving the Soviets minimal military help we are creating political difficulties for them.*'[6] In this way the Home Army would win political power in Poland for the pro-London elements, or at the very least would create obstacles for the Communists in their bid for power; the operations of the Home Army were in the military sense to be directed against the Germans, in the political sense against the Russians and the Communists.

The Home Commander believed, when drafting his order, that 'the only chance of gaining anything was a constant demonstration of our will to fight Germany to the last, sparing no effort, in the teeth of every adversity'.[7] From this grim determination to fight, it appears that, in general, to Bor-Komorowski activity offered the only possibility of success, however slender, and that passivity was associated, in his mind, with inevitable defeat.[8] This belief

[1] T. Bor-Komorowski, *op. cit.*, p. 180.
[2] Report No. 243 from the Commander of the Home Army to the C-in-C, 14 July 1944, Ldz. 6302/44, APUST.
[3] Report No. 243 from the Commander of the Home Army to the C-in-C, 14 July 1944, Ldz. 6302/44, APUST.
[4] *Ibid.*   [5] *Ibid.*   [6] *Ibid.* My italics.
[7] T. Bor-Komorowski, *op. cit.*, p. 180.
[8] Report No. 243 from the Commander of the Home Army to the C-in-C, 14 July 1944, Ldz. 6302/44, APUST.

meant that the top echelons of the conspiratorial army were to sin, if at all, on the side of the commission rather than omission; they would not let pass any opportunity of throwing their troops into battle.

These battles were to take the form of either a 'general and simultaneous rising' in central Poland and covering actions in the east – the aims of such a national rising were to be identical with those laid down in the Government's Instruction – or 'intensified diversionary activity', which received the code name 'Burza', – 'Tempest'.[1] The state of the German military machine, especially on the Eastern Front was to determine which of these alternatives was to be adopted; the national rising, if decided upon, would be undertaken at the moment of German military collapse, whereas 'Burza' would be launched during the German retreat from Poland, should the staging of a national rising prove impracticable.

The military aims of 'Burza' were defined as follows: to manifest the Home Army's will to fight against the Germans, even under unfavourable conditions – i.e. German superiority – and to protect the population from Nazi attempts to destroy it during their retreat from the East. Operation 'Burza' was to consist of resolute Home Army attacks upon the 'German rearguards', or the 'rear units of the rearguards', and strong subversion in the whole territory of Poland aimed especially at the German communication lines.[2] With regard to the deployment of the Home Army two methods were to be followed. In eastern Poland – the disputed areas – all units and resources were to be used. The operation was to start in the east and then move westward as the Russo–German Front advanced through Poland; and on no account were the Home Army forces to withdraw from the disputed areas – Sikorski had recommended this in the event of further deterioration of Russo–Polish relations.[3] The decision to include the eastern regions in the 'Burza' plan seems illogical in view of the fact that, as Grot-Rowecki had pointed out, the Home Army units in these areas were too weak to undertake any effective operations without substantial external help.[4] In central Poland all partisan and first-line units were to be deployed, together

[1] The Order of the Commander of the Home Army, 20 November 1943, Ldz. 2100, APUST.
[2] The Order of the Commander of the Home Army, 20 November 1943, Ldz. 2100. APUST.
[3] For details on this subject see p. 144 of this chapter.
[4] Cf. p. 142 of this chapter.

with the 'necessary number of armed insurrectionary [second-line] platoons'.

The order to begin Operation 'Burza' was to be issued by Bor-Komorowski himself, during the 'general German retreat', by means of a 'special radio signal' on reception of which all regional commanders were to start operations in their commands. If the signal were not received regional commanders of all ranks were to commence operations on their own initiative at the moment when the German retreat from their respective areas began.[1] In essence, 'Burza' was to consist of a number of consecutive uprisings initiated in each area when the German retreat began, rather than a synchronised operation beginning in all areas of Poland simultaneously. Thus the plan for 'Burza' meant in reality a return to Grot-Rowecki's ideas as embodied in his recommendations to Sikorski in the Winter of 1943.[2]

Bor-Komorowski ordered the adoption of the following attitude towards the Russians during Home Army operations:

1. The Soviet partisan units operating on our soil should be given full operational freedom in regard to their anti-German activities. From now on you must avoid friction with the Soviet units. Those of our own units which have already been involved in disputes with the Soviet units . . . should be transferred to other regions. [. . .]
2. You should counteract the tendency among the population of the eastern territories to flee to the west in the face of the Russian danger . . . as this would be tantamount to the relinquishing of the Polish claims to these territories.
3. In regard . . . to the Russian regular army, act as a host . . . A Russian Commander should be met by a Polish Commander, with a battle against the Germans to his credit, and therefore every right to act as a host. [. . .] The local Polish Commander together with . . . a representative of the civil administrative authorities should report to the Russian Commander and act in accordance with his wishes, bearing in mind:
(a) that his separation from the Polish high authorities is temporary, and that they, and not the Russians, remain his proper superiors and that the character and extent of the Soviet authority [in Poland] should be defined for the Polish citizens by the legal authorities of the Republic;
(b) that all attempts to incorporate Polish units into the Russian Army or the Berling Units are violations and should be resolutely resisted . . .[3]

[1] The Order of the Commander of the Home Army, 20 November 1943, Ldz. 2100, APUST.   [2] Cf. p. 139 of this study.
[3] The Order of the Commander of the Home Army, 20 November 1943, Ldz. 2100, APUST.

In accordance with this order all military operations were to be directed against the Germans; in no event, unless in self-defence, was armed action against the Soviets to be contemplated.[1]

The tasks of units taking part in the 'Burza' operation were to end with the arrival of the Red Army in a particular area or locality. Co-operation with the Soviet units during the actual fighting was not to be undertaken hastily, in view of the absence of Russo–Polish diplomatic relations. The Commanders were asked to carry out their tasks, if possible, independently of the Red Army.[2] This insistence on the independent character of the 'Burza' operations meant that the Home Army was not to attempt operational co-ordination with the Russians before the fighting began and that the actual demands of the battlefield were to regulate the extent of tactical co-operation while the fighting was in progress.

The success of 'Burza' was to depend on Polish courage, resolution and, above all, on the infallible timing of the operations, as the premature engagement of the Germans, especially under the conditions of mobile warfare, would, if coupled with Soviet inability to assist the Home Army, turn the attack into a dismal and costly fiasco. In theory the best time to begin 'Burza' operations in any particular region would be during the last hours of the German retreat from there, and shortly before the arrival of the Red Army. Correct appraisal of the situation and front-line developments would demand efficient intelligence and communication systems.

In a sense, the 'Burza' plan was simple, but its execution involved many hazards and dangers. To eliminate these risks the establishment of at least tactical Russo–Polish co-operation, before 'Burza's' execution, would have been advisable, in the interests of military success, regardless of the inflamed state of diplomatic relations between Russia and Poland. Such contact was not established, presumably because it would have reduced the political impact of 'Burza'. Indeed, any attempts which were made to establish Russo–Polish military co-operation occurred either during the progress of the actual fighting or after its conclusion.

Initially, large towns were excluded from the 'Burza' plan; fighting in large towns was considered only in connection with a 'general and simultaneous rising'. This decision was dictated by the

---

[1] *Ibid.*
[2] The Order of the Commander of the Home Army, 23 March 1944, No. 144/ III/KSZ, Ldz. 6302/44, APUST.

desire to spare the urban population unnecessary suffering and losses.[1] At the beginning of July 1944 this decision was counter-manded by Bor-Komorowski, who ordered his troops to occupy large towns before the arrival of the Russians, as he had finally realised that the capture of the large centres of national life would be essential if the force was to assume the role of hosts to the Russians.[2] The Home Army Staff realised that the role could not be fulfilled by staging guerilla attacks against the German columns retreating through the Polish countryside. These attacks would not attract the necessary attention and publicity and their political impact would then be marginal. To stage political demonstrations towns would need to be occupied. Within the framework of the July decision to occupy towns the Warsaw Rising was undertaken. It seems hardly credible that the leaders of the Home Army should take several months to arrive at the simple truth that the occupation of large towns was essential to the realisation of their aims; Grot-Rowecki had suggested this policy as early as February 1943.[3]

This hesitancy seems to indicate that the leaders of the Home Army seriously doubted whether their badly-armed troops could attempt to wrest strongly-garrisoned towns from the Germans.[4]

Meanwhile, however, in February 1944 Bor-Komorowski's decision to reveal the Home Army to the Russians was approved by the Polish Cabinet in London.[5] At this moment, after two years of intermittent discussion, as one of the leaders of the underground state put it; 'the die was cast'.[6] Bor-Komorowski's Chief of Staff summarised the new situation as follows:

> The struggle against the Germans has to continue regardless of the Russian threat. An understanding with the entering Soviets should be sought while simultaneously stressing the sovereign rights of the Republic.[7]

The strategy adopted was the result of politics, and the politics in their turn were the result of sentiments and traditions adhered to by the London leaders. In the opinion of its commanders, the Home

[1] Cf. T. Bor-Komorowski, *op. cit.*, p. 202.
[2] Cf. *Polskie Siły Zbrojne*, *op. cit.*, p. 573.
[3] Cf. p. 143 of this study.
[4] Report No. 243 from the Commander of the Home Army to the C-in-C 14 July 1944, Ldz. 6302/44, APUST.
[5] For details see pp. 187ff of this study.
[6] Zygmunt Zaremba, *Wojna i Konspiracja* (London, 1957), P. 224.
[7] Tadeusz Pelczynski, *Geneza i przebieg 'Burzy'*, (London, 1949), p. 7.

Army's operations would result either in securing political power in Poland for the London Government or in Western intervention on their behalf; as Bor-Komorowski remarked, they still thought that the Western Allies would defend their cause against Russia.[1]

[1] Cf. T. Bor-Komorowski, *op. cit.*, p. 180.

6

The London Poles and 'Tempest'

1. *Mikolajczyk's Response*

Bor-Komorowski's decision to reveal to the Russians the Home Army troops which were to take part in the 'Burza' operations met with mixed reactions among the Polish circles in London. Mikolajczyk was amenable to the idea as a sound and realistic political move and was determined that it should be officially sanctioned by his Cabinet and the C-in-C. There were two main considerations which prompted the Prime Minister to accept Bor-Komorowski's decision without reservation; his desire 'to manifest complete unity of opinion between the Government and the Home [authorities]' and his desire 'to provide the Government with an argument of great political importance in the current diplomatic talks with our Allies'.[1] The Premier believed that approval of Bor-Komorowski's order would permit him to declare to the Allies Poland's readiness to collaborate with the U.S.S.R., in spite of the severance of Russo–Polish diplomatic relations. He hoped that such an offer might lead to the establishment of Russo–Polish military co-operation and consequently pave the way for a more far-reaching political *modus vivendi* with the Kremlin. Indeed, in Mikolajczyk's opinion this co-operation might create the 'possibility of reaching an agreement with the Allies – Russia included – concerning the activities of the Homeland [i.e. the underground], securing arms, and taking over the administration of undisputed territories'.[2] The conclusion of this type of agreement with the Soviet Union would have been highly favourable to the pro-London movement in Poland; it would have secured sovereign status for the Home Army by turning it into a

---

[1] Minutes of the meeting of the Council of Ministers, 18 February 1944, GSHI–A.XII, 3/90–2 (hereafter referred to as the Minutes of the Council of Ministers, 18 February 1944.)

[2] Despatch from the Prime Minister to the Government's Delegate, 25–6 January 1944, Ldz. K. 519/44 GSHI–PRM, L.II (hereafter referred to as Despatch K.519/44).

legitimate Russian ally, and would have surrendered the administration of liberated territories to the agents of the secret state. It would have made the London Poles the undisputed master of the Polish territories west of the Curzon Line, and would therefore have amounted to a signal defeat for the Communists, their main rivals in the internal struggle for power. Mikolajczyk rightly sensed that he had everything to gain from such an accommodation with Moscow.

He was ready to conclude with the Kremlin a treaty similar to that made by Sikorski in July 1941. This treaty had provided for the restoration of Russo–Polish diplomatic relations and the establishment of military collaboration between the two signatories, while leaving the territorial dispute open and unresolved.[1]

The Premier's hopes of reaching so advantageous an agreement with the Kremlin rested on his belief that Stalin would, for strategic reasons, be very anxious to accept the Home Army's offer to collaborate with the Soviet forces, as this would greatly facilitate the Russian passage through Poland.[2] In this respect, it seems, Mikolajczyk tended to *overestimate* the potential strategic usefulness of the Home Army to the Russians, during the Soviet advance through his country, and to *underestimate* Russian military ability to expel the Germans without recourse to the pro-London Polish forces. Further, he seemed unable to contemplate another possibility – namely, that Stalin might refuse to accept the Home Army as his sovereign ally until the final solution of the Russo–Polish territorial dispute and the establishment of a *rapprochement* between the pro-London and pro-Soviet forces in Poland.[3] The Polish leader was convinced that the Home Army's offer of collaboration with the Russians would be bound to improve his Government's standing in London and Washington and secure for them more sympathetic treatment from Churchill and Roosevelt. The latter might then be persuaded that the London Poles were determined to settle their differences with Moscow in a reasonable and amicable way.

In brief, Mikolajczyk was very willing to approve the Warsaw authorities' decision because, at this stage, it appeared to coincide very closely with his own new approach to Russia. By this time he was firmly convinced that he must show at least a desire to reach wider understanding with Moscow, even though he intended to do his utmost to postpone the ultimate solution of the territorial

[1] Woodward, pp. 200ff.
[2] General Kukiel's oral evidence.   [3] *Ibid.*

dispute until the conclusion of an overall European peace settlement, following the German defeat.

With this idea firmly embedded in his mind, as early as the second half of January 1944 he announced to his followers:

> We have to endeavour to establish cordial relations with Russia and to abandon the demagogy of intransigence . . . In the opinion of the world our frontiers are an open question. The calculations connected with [the possibility of] a conflict between the West and Russia are illusory and dangerous. The West will not fight for our eastern frontiers and, in case of tension with Russia, would try to relieve it at our expense. But in the event of our coming to terms [with the U.S.S.R.] the Anglo–Americans would be ready to guarantee the defence of our mutually agreed territories and would even undertake to fight for them.[1]

Nevertheless, the Polish Premier showed no immediate desire to open negotiations with Stalin, because 'the Russian victories are creating a bad climate for talks with [Russia]. . .' He hoped, however that more favourable conditions would develop

> when the voice of our Allies will carry more weight. For that moment Poland must preserve all her trump cards – her untarnished ideological image – her unity and her struggle against the enemy – for these secure for us our moral standing and bind the Allies to us. The weakening of our standing means the weakening of [the Allies] obligations to us. Our trump card, our struggle against the Germans, must be played to the utmost at the moment of their collapse . . .[2]

Mikolajczyk was playing for time and hoped that the Home Army's attitude to the Germans and Russians would help him here. He needed time to be able to 'survive' until the moment when 'in the contest for Germany, the scales will tip in favour of the Western Allies – [at which time] they might become accessible to other arguments. . .' Meanwhile, he wished to create a situation in which 'the responsibility for failure to solve the [Russo–Polish] conflict, or even for aggravating it, would fall on the Soviets and not on Poland.'[3] To achieve this end he needed to display to the world Bor-Komorowski's willingness to collaborate with the Red Army and his own readiness to talk with Moscow.

---

[1] Despatch from the Minister of the Interior to the Government's Delegate, 24 January 1944, Ldz. K.495/44, APUST, File 50, Min. Spr. Wew.

[2] *Ibid.*

[3] Despatch from the Prime Minister to the Government's Delegate, 17 March 1944, Ldz. K.1775/44 APUST, File 50, Min. Spr. Wew. (hereafter referred to as Despatch K.1775/44).

At the same time he told Warsaw that the initiation of Russo–Polish talks 'does not pre-judge anything: it gives, us, however, a possibility of remaining within the family of Allied nations, of representing Poland unchallenged by other bodies and of surviving until the advent of better times for us.'[1]

His lack of enthusiasm for serious negotiations with Moscow at this stage was the result of two main considerations: first, a possibility that Stalin might adamantly refuse to talk with the Polish Government,[2] and secondly his fear that the U.S.S.R. was in reality aiming 'at the Sovietisation, not only of Poland, but of all Europe'.[3] He consoled himself, however, with the belief that the Polish question was becoming a thermometer of real Soviet intentions and that its 'unfavourable solution [for the London Poles] would not only discredit the United Nations, but would also fail to secure peace in the future'.[4]

Apart from Mikolajczyk's political and diplomatic reasons for accepting Bor-Komorowski's decision, there was another important consideration, of a more dubious nature; he wished to transfer at least some of the burden of responsibility for reaching a Russo–Polish *rapprochement* to the shoulders of the Home authorities. At the same time Mikolajczyk intended to instruct the Home authorities to prepare a second supplementary team of leaders who, in any event, would remain underground and would try to communicate with the Polish authorities about the fate of the representatives revealed to the Russians, that of the Polish population in general, and the behaviour of the Soviets in the territories occupied by them.[5] This instruction would seem to be illogical; Mikolajczyk could hardly present the Home Army to the Russians as their allies, willing to submit to their wishes, while at the same time ordering some of its personnel to spy on them. Sooner or later the activities of his 'shadow' force would undoubtedly have been detected by the Soviet security forces, and might have provoked Russian reprisals.

Nevertheless, he was very anxious to avoid possible Russo–Polish hostilities which, in his opinion, would only tend to provoke the existence of a 'factual state of war' between Poland and the U.S.S.R. and produce a new senseless slaughter in Poland, culminating in her

---

[1] Despatch K.519/44.
[2] Despatch K.1775/44.
[3] Despatch K.519/44.
[4] *Ibid.*
[5] Letter from the Prime Minister to the C-in-C, 1 February 1944, Appendix No. 1, Ldz. 138/XV/44, GSHI, File XV, N.W.

being abandoned by the Western Allies.[1] Mikolajczyk believed that Bor-Komorowski's November order 'categorically excluded any possibility of a struggle with the Soviet Army'.[2] The Premier failed, however, to repeal the self-defence clause of his own October instruction and to issue to the Home Army an order specifically forbidding any anti-Soviet measures.

In some respects, then, the Premier departed from the policies of his predecessor, Sikorski, who had been convinced that, should the victorious Russians enter Poland in force, the reconstruction of the Polish state could be brought about only with their good will and the help of the Western Allies.[3] Yet Mikolajczyk, engaged in mortal combat for Poland, was grimly determined to use any weapon, real or imaginary, which might help him to emerge victorious.

The Premier proposed that

> should it become known that ... Polish representatives have been arrested the Home authorities will issue an order prohibiting [other units] from coming into the open in other territories.

He continued:

> Before the issuing of this ban it will be necessary to ascertain the Soviets' behaviour, after their crossing of the frontier [the Curzon Line] of the territories regarded by the Soviet authorities as annexed to the White Russian and Ukrainian Republics respectively.
>
> Should the Soviet behaviour on as yet unquestioned territories not differ from that on those they regard as annexed, the Home authorities will make a final decision as to the banning of further coming into the open.[4]

Mikolajczyk was willing, therefore, to vary his response to the Russians in accordance with any differences between the Soviet attitude to the secret state and its organs on the territories east of the Curzon Line and their attitude on the areas west of the Line. What is more, to him the Soviet behaviour west of the Curzon Line would clearly be the more important index of Russian intentions. The Premier saw 'Burza' primarily as an opening move in his political and diplomatic endeavours to ensure the return of his

---

[1] Minutes of the meeting of the Council of Ministers, 18 February 1944, GSHI–A.XII, 3/90–2.

[2] *Ibid.*

[3] For details see p. 133 of this study.

[4] Letter from the Prime Minister to the C-in-C, 1 February 1944, Appendix No. I, Ldz. 138/XV/44, GSHI, File XV, N.W.

Government to Warsaw with the approval – indeed, the blessing – of London, Washington and even, possibly, of Moscow. Alternatively, should his attempts to reach an understanding with the Kremlin fail, he wished, by means of 'Burza', to expose, to the Western Powers, Soviet hostility to his conception of post-war Poland. To him, 'Burza' was a crucial political and military move in Russo–Polish polemics; a move which was 'at all costs to prevent Poland's finding herself in [diplomatic] isolation'.[1]

2. *Sosnkowski's response*

Mikolajczyk's enthusiastic reception of, and support for, 'Burza' failed to elicit a similar response from the C-in-C and other senior members of the Polish military establishment in London. In their view the Home authorities would have been well advised to stand by the original text of the Government's directive of 27 October 1943. This instruction had made no provision for the emergence of the Home Army into the open, much less for its co-operation with the Russians, without a prior political *rapprochement*.[2]

The C-in-C was clearly disturbed by Bor-Komorowski's independent decision, which contradicted the letter and spirit of the October instructions, and he intended to secure its revocation, or at least to minimise its possible consequences.

He first expressed his profound misgivings concerning the 'Burza' plan on 4 January 1944, in a letter to the Premier:

> The complications which might result from the Homeland's decision to reveal the A.K. units to the Russians are obvious.
>
> I consider the above-mentioned decision . . . to be the result of a desperate all-consuming impulse on the part of the Homeland to manifest Poland's right to existence.
>
> Under such conditions and in view of the entry of the Soviet Army into Poland, which took place without any understanding with the Polish Government, the immediate submission of a [Polish] protest to the United Nations . . . is becoming imperative. . . . It would be difficult to alter the Home [authorities'] decision unless the Polish Government's protest meets with a wholly positive response from the British and American Governments.

[1] Despatch from the Prime Minister to the Government's Delegate, 17 March 1944, Ldz. K. 1775/44, APUST, File 50 Min. Spr.
[2] For details, see pp. 160ff of this study.

By positive response I mean a public declaration by these two Governments:

1. – that they take note of our protest,

2. – that they reaffirm that in the existing situation they will not on their part recognise any territorial changes arising out of military operations,

3. – that they will use all their influence to ensure the safety and protect the rights of the population of our territories being occupied by the Soviet Army.

In the event of any Soviet outrages, and in view of the Government's order for self-defence under such circumstances, further silence on the part of the Allied Governments might lead at Home to a struggle on two fronts. At best, the intensified diversionary activity might develop, because of the universal hatred of the Germans, into an attempt to launch an armed insurrection – unfortunately without arms and on the territories flooded by numerous German armies.

In these circumstances it might soon be my duty to be with . . . the AK. In consideration of the political aspects of this step I ask you, Prime Minister, to make it possible for me to go [to Poland] with the knowledge and approval of the Polish Government and of the British and American Governments.[1]

The aim of Sosnkowski's representation was obvious. Knowing that it would be almost impossible to alter Bor-Komorowski's decision, he was urging his Government to do its utmost to secure official Anglo–American support for 'Burza'. He rightly sensed that the underground authorities' decision would, in a matter of a few months, lead to a great tragedy for the London camp and Poland as a whole, yet he felt unable to declare himself against it in plain terms. He tried, however, to point out, first to Mikolajczyk and later to Bor-Komorowski, all the possible dangers involved in the implementation of the 'Burza' plan.

He involved himself in certain inconsistencies. First, he feared that 'Burza' – 'intensified diversionary activity' – might, if carried out openly, escalate into a forlorn spontaneous 'insurrection'; but was there any way of ensuring that any large-scale Home Army operation would not transform itself into an uprising, even if it were not followed by the Home Army's coming into the open to receive the Russians as their guests? The risk of mass uprising was latent in the Government's and the C-in-C's directives of October 1943, stating

[1] Letter from the C-in-C to the Prime Minister, 4 January 1944, Ldz. 7/GNW/tj/44, APUST. The C-in-C wrote another letter to the Prime Minister on this subject on 9 January 1944. Ldz. 38/GNW/tj/44. APUST.

that the Home Army's operations would be intensified during the German retreat from Poland. In fact, the risk could have been avoided only be proscribing any intensification of anti-German operations by the Home Army. This, however, Sosnkowski was unwilling to do. Secondly, it is difficult to see how the Home Army could have 'manifested Poland's right to existence' without revealing its identity to friend and foe alike. As to the C-in-C's argument that the 'further silence of the Allied Governments' might lead to a struggle on two fronts in Poland, he himself had added to this danger by agreeing to the inclusion of the 'self-defence' clause in the Government's directives of October 1943.[1] The observance of this clause by the Home Army in the face of Russian attempts at suppression would automatically have led to sporadic Russo–Polish fighting regardless of the Allied Governments' reaction. Such eventualities could have been entirely avoided only by issuing a categorical order to the effect that in no circumstances were the Home Army soldiers to fire on the Russians. The C-in-C adamantly refused to issue such an order. Indeed he was soon trying to inspire Bor-Komorowski to resist the Russians if they refused to accept the London Poles as their sovereign hosts in Poland.[2]

Although he clearly foresaw all the risks and dangers involved in 'Burza' the C-in-C was hardly helping to reduce them. Instead, he seemed to be acting in a way most likely to aggravate them, in spite of his dark forebodings. This was primarily due to his exalted conception of his military duties and honour, and to his stubborn adherence to his opinion that 'Burza' should have a clearly anti-Soviet as well as anti-German character.

On 11 January 1944, Sosnkowski told Bor-Komorowski: 'The motives behind your decision to come into the open to represent the Republic and Her legitimate authorities to the Russians . . . are worthy of the highest respect.' But the C-in-C's admiration of the motives behind his subordinate's independent decision did not prevent him from reminding the Home Commander that the Government's Instruction had made no provision for Russo–Polish military co-operation prior to the restoration by the U.S.S.R. of diplomatic relations with Poland, 'on a basis acceptable to us.'[3]

---

[1] For details see p. 160 of this study.
[2] For details see pp. 181ff of this study.
[3] Despatch from the C-in-C to the Commander of the Home Army, 11 January 1944, Ldz. 281/tjn, APUST.

Further, Sosnkowski told Warsaw that in his opinion the Russians would not tolerate the existence of the Home Army east of the 'Molotov–Ribbentrop Line', let alone 'recognise . . . [its] right to act as their hosts' in these regions, which the Soviets regarded as an integral part of the U.S.S.R. The C-in-C believed that the Russians would attempt to incorporate the Home Army units into Berling's army, and that the real aim of Soviet policy was to transform Poland into a 'vassal communist republic, or even the Seventeenth Soviet Republic'.[1] Sosnkowski hoped to dissuade Bor-Komorowski from revealing the Home Army to the Russians by stressing the risks which this would involve. Above all, the C-in-C was trying to convince Bor-Komorowski that he should not expect anything good from the Soviets as, in his opinion, they were hostile to the pro-London military establishment in Poland and abroad.

His arguments failed to produce the desired effect in Warsaw. The Home Army leaders were firm in their determination to proceed with 'Burza' as planned, regardless of the possible consequences. This was clear in Bor-Komorowski's reply to the C-in-C's January despatch, when he wrote that he was not prepared to alter his plans, though he had 'no illusions about the Soviet hostile attitude' to the pro-London circles in Poland. He stated that his November decision had been taken after a long analysis of the situation and had been determined by the following circumstances:

1. . . . Our will to manifest our struggle against the Germans.

2. . . . Our will to manifest to the Soviets the presence [in Poland] of elements representing the sovereignty of the Republic, so placing before the Soviets a threshold on which they will have to reveal their attitude to our Statehood;

3. . . . A conviction that failure to reveal our units, in the eastern territories in any case weak and few in number, would enable the Soviets to argue that these regions are not Polish in character and to assign the credit for our armed actions [against the Germans] to the Soviet partisans or the units of the PPR.

4. The opinion of the local Commanders concerning the impossibility of hiding our units from the Soviets.

I have determined in great detail the degree of intensity and the character of the struggle against the Germans; I have issued directives aimed at preventing our diversionary activities from becoming a spon-

---

[1] Despatch from the C-in-C to the Commander of the Home Army, 11 January 1944, Ldz. 281/tjn, APUST.

taneous attempt at an armed insurrection launched under unfavourable conditions.

My orders . . . exclude armed struggle against Russia, that is, struggle on two fronts. But they do not preclude armed self-defence in the case of Russian terror. The Soviet behaviour towards the Polish population and our units on the territories occupied by them will dictate any eventual alterations in the orders already issued. I ask you, General, for your instructions as to whether our units coming into the open should lay down their arms when faced with categorical Soviet demands to do so, or [whether they should] put up armed resistance in this event.[1]

Although this explanation failed to convince Bor-Komorowski's C-in-C of the wisdom of the 'Burza' order, his determined tone seems to have prompted Sosnkowski to express qualified approval of his subordinate's independent decision; on 12 February 1944 the C-in-C felt compelled to say to Bor-Komorowski:

. . . You have acted independently of the Government's and my own instructions, which were the result of protracted discussions. . . . *The Government and myself consider that the will of the country . . . can hardly be disregarded.* Finally, the Government has accepted your order . . . Further on 6 February 1944 the *Premier communicated it to the British Prime Minister, identifying it with the will of the Polish Government.*[2]

Notwithstanding his qualified acceptance of Bor-Komorowski's order, Sosnkowski remained sceptical about its chances of success:

Since you have no illusions about the hostile attitude of the Soviets to you and the AK you should have no illusions about the effects of revealing your units to them without a previous political understanding between Russia and Poland.[3]

More important, Sosnkowski was grimly determined to impose his own interpretation of 'Burza' upon its authors in Warsaw:

I interpreted your decision as signifying your readiness to accept an imposed fight within the limits of self-defence, should Russia fail to respect our sovereignty and our rights as hosts . . . You are expecting from me instructions as to whether your units, which will come into the open in accordance with your own decision, ought, if faced with categorical Soviet demands, to lay down their arms or put up armed resistance.

It may be claimed, of course, that it is the C-in-C's duty to issue

[1] Despatch from the Commander of the Home Army to the C-in-C, 3 February 1944, Ldz. 957/tjn/44, APUST.
[2] Despatch from the C-in-C to the Commander of the Home Army, 12 February 1944 Ldz. 1217/tj/44, APUST. My italics.   [3] *Ibid.*

appropriate orders, though your question arises from your independent alteration of the Instruction of 27 October 1943. I do not fully understand you. On the one hand your orders wisely exclude the possibility of a struggle on two fronts, on the other you state that you do not exclude armed self-defence. Is armed self-defence not armed struggle? Do you not think that the necessity for self-defence will arise? We all exclude the possibility of armed struggle on two fronts, where this depends entirely on our will. *Such a struggle might be imposed on us, however, by Soviet behaviour.*

In your order . . . you state that all attempts to incorporate your units into the Red Army or Berling units should be decisively resisted as an outrage. I ask you, what does it mean when a military unit resists an outrage decisively? Do you assume that the Soviet Command would tolerate, without a previous political rapprochement, the existence at its side of Polish units, owing allegiance to the legitimate authorities of the Republic? In your order you talk about armed self-defence against the Soviet terror, and at the same time you ask whether your units should lay down their arms at the Soviet request. Is armed self-defence possible without arms? [. . .] *The C-in-C cannot issue orders to lay down arms in the face of outrage and force.* I repeat once more: to the limits of human endurance avoid open struggle against the Soviets.

Everything which could be said on this subject is included in the principle of self-defence defined by the Government and reaffirmed in your order as a natural right of every human being. *Regardless of definitions, in the face of Soviet evil intensions the practical effect would be the same, if the real aim of your order . . . is to manifest our sovereign rights to act as hosts [to the Russians] on the whole territory of the Republic.*[1]

In spite of his reluctance to issue direct orders, Sosnkowski seemed here to be trying to inspire and encourage his subordinate in Warsaw to resist the Russians, should they refuse to come to terms with the exiled Government and to acknowledge its authority throughout the territories of pre-war Poland.

The C-in-C saw 'Burza', then, as a 'desperate all consuming impulse'[2] on the part of the Home Army to defend the interests and ambitions of the London camp in Poland, 'in spite of all and against all'.[3] Here he was opposed to his Prime Minister, to whom, in the

---

[1] Despatch from the C-in-C to the Commander of the Home Army, 12 February 1944, Ldz. 1217/tj/44. APUST. My italics.

[2] Letter from the C-in-C to the Prime Minister, 4 January 1944, Ldz. 7/GNW/tj/44. APUST.

[3] Despatch from the C-in-C to the Commander of the Home Army, 12 February 1944, Ldz. 1217/tj/44, APUST.

C-in-C's opinion, 'Burza' was 'a function of realism, which dictated co-operation with the Red Army to the point of submission to the orders of the Soviet Commanders, even without the previous restoration of [Russo–Polish] diplomatic relations'.[1]

To some extent, Sosnkowski tended to blame Bor-Komorowski for his own disagreement with Mikolajczyk, as in his opinion Warsaw's independent decision to alter the October directives had created 'political and psychological difficulties' between the Premier and himself.[2] To overcome these 'difficulties' the C-in-C was trying to persuade the Secret Army Commanders to follow his own, rather than the Government's policies.

As he saw it, two courses of action were open to the London Poles at this turning-point in Poland's war-time history.

> both based on the assumption that uncompromising struggle against the Germans will continue. The first consists in the strict implementation of the Instruction of 27 October 1943 which insists on the defence of our rights *in spite of all and against all*. Under pressure from the Allies, our Government has, as it were, compromised this course. What is more, it wants to use your independent decision to justify a policy of gradual concessions leading to the abandoning of the essential point of the Instruction ... that we are not going to co-operate with the Soviets without previous political understanding with them.
>
> The alternative course would be to make concessions in the face of Russian pressure, at present strengthened rather than restrained by the policy of the Anglo–Saxon Powers. [. . .] We should not deceive ourselves that this way does not lead to the Sovietisation of Poland.
>
> I am a confirmed supporter of the first course . . .[3]

Even on this occasion the C-in-C did not restrict himself entirely to the field of theoretical speculations and personal opinions; he advised Bor-Komorowski:

> 1. As far as possible stand by the Instruction of 27 October 1943.
>
> 2. Avoid armed conflict with Russia, apart from acts of self-defence and opposition to Soviet outrages.
>
> 3. In the event of (Soviet) outrages, forbid emergence into the open in other territories, and if possible withdraw endangered units. *Above all else ... together with the Government's Delegate and the Home Political Representation, you have to decide a basic question: – whether military co-operation with the Soviets is advisable, without a previous political understanding, as in such circumstances – it would mean the subordination [of*

---

[1] *Ibid.*   [2] *Ibid.*   [3] *Ibid.* My italics.

the Home Army] *to the orders of the Red Commanders and in consequence its probable incorporation into Berling's units.* Political understanding, if at all possible in the existing situation, would mean our acceptance of the Soviet territorial demands.

My attitude to this question is consequently negative. Nevertheless, I am not certain whether in the Cabinet there are not some supporters of [a policy of] co-operation [with the Soviets] in any eventuality, who would quote British opinions and *use your order as an argument to support their case.*[1]

Sosnkowski's words suggest that he expected Bor-Komorowski's experiment in co-operation with the Red Army to end disastrously, and intended to make Warsaw fully aware of this probability. The C-in-C was endeavouring to convince the underground leaders that the twin aims of 'Burza' were incompatible: that they could hardly expect the Russians to help them to stage what in reality amounted to an anti-Soviet demonstration in return for nominal military assistance in the struggle against the Germans. Sosnkowski was right in his insistence that 'Burza' could not be expected to solve all the problems of war-time Poland and that it would only lead to further 'difficulties and complications' in the already inflamed Russo–Polish relations. Yet he continued to dismiss any idea of a compromise with the U.S.S.R. The question arises of why Sosnkowski adopted so dangerous an attitude. There is a number of possible answers. First, he appeared to be convinced that regardless of orders people in Poland would 'resort to self-defence tactics; taking to arms spontaneously if Soviet troops enter Poland as enemies or in an ambiguous character'.[2] Secondly, until the middle of 1944 the C-in-C was convinced that his country would be liberated by the Anglo–American, rather than Soviet, forces.[3] Hence, he thought that the Russo–Polish conflict would not extend beyond the Curzon Line, but would assume only a limited form and simply demonstrate the Home Army's readiness to defend Polish claims to the pre-1939 eastern borderlands. The General's rather low opinions of the Red Army's offensive capabilities sprang from the assumptions that Russia might be 'less strong and confident than she appears to be',[4]

[1] Despatch from the C-in-C to the Commander of the Home Army, 12 February 1944, Ldz. 1217/tj/44, APUST. My italics.
[2] Letter from the C-in-C to the Minister for Foreign Affairs, T. Romer, 5 October 1943, Ldz. III/43/tjn, GSHI–PRM. L21.
[3] For details see pp. 281–2 of this study.
[4] Despatch from the C-in-C to the Minister of National Defence, 25 November 1943, Ldz. 7571, GSHI–PRM, L45/47.

and that the *Wehrmacht* would 'stubbornly defend the access to Germany'.[1] Thirdly, he believed that 'sooner or later Great Britain might be compelled to face a showdown with Russian imperialism'.[2] He believed that in consequence, not only might the war last longer than expected, but 'many unforeseen changes' might take place during its course.[3] Thus, it seems that the C-in-C was already anticipating a new conflict between the West and the East, and therefore saw no reason for Poland to adopt a conciliatory attitude towards Russia.

Moreover, he was convinced that Poland's dilemma was primarily due to the fact that Great Britain and the U.S.A. were 'temporarily allowing Russia too much scope' in Eastern Europe. The C-in-C was trying to involve the Anglo–Saxon Powers in the affairs of Eastern Europe with all the means at his disposal. These attempts were motivated by his profound belief that the London camp's cause would 'achieve total victory only when Germany and Russia have weakened themselves to such an extent that final victory falls into the hands of the Anglo–Saxon Powers, who will occupy Germany and Poland'.[4] Sosnkowski was fervently hoping for a repetition of the events of 1917 and 1918, which had led to the creation of the inter-war Polish State, when both Germany and Russia had been considerably weakened as a result of the First World War.

In essence, the C-in-C's aims were similar to those of Mikolajczyk, but he wished to realise them by more ruthless means. Further, he did not share Mikolajczyk's fear that Polish intransigence and the flaring up of Russo–Polish fighting would lead to Poland's being abandoned by her Western allies. Consequently, the Premier's attitudes to the U.S.S.R. and the Anglo–Saxon powers appeared to him to be too meek and conciliatory. Sosnkowski believed that as the London Poles could influence neither Soviet policy nor the outcome of military operations they were left with only one alternative; 'to defend [their] interests . . . stubbornly and openly . . . and demand the same from the Anglo–Saxon Powers. . .' He wished to turn the Polish question into 'a problem for the conscience of the world', a test-case for the future of European nations.[5]

---

[1] Despatch from the C-in-C to the Commander of the Home Army, 7 July 1944, Ldz. 5480/44, APUST.
[2] Despatch from the C-in-C to the Commander of the Home Army, 12 February 1944, Ldz. 1217/tj/44, APUST.   [3] *Ibid.*   [4] *Ibid.*
[5] Despatch from the C-in-C to the Commander of the Home Army, dated 1 February 1944, sent to Warsaw 3 February 1944, Ldz. 877/tjn, APUST.

Though anxious to persuade the Home Army circles to accept his interpretation of the situation and the tactics he recommended, Sosnkowski deliberately refused to order them to do so. Indeed, he explicitly informed Bor-Komorowski that he was deliberately not issuing him with conventional orders because he feared that it might be impossible to execute them.[1] This refusal to issue direct orders could also mean that the C-in-C was deliberately inviting the Home Army leaders to act on their own initiative and rely mainly on their own judgement without paying too much attention to the instructions issued by the Cabinet in London; this, in spite of the fact that London – one of the three main centres of Allied war-planning and effort – was a better vantage-point for high-level decision-making than occupied Warsaw.

Sosnkowski's approach to the Home Army leaders seemed inconsistent, for while reproaching them for acting independently he was deliberately advising them to do so; unable to influence the Cabinet in London, the C-in-C was consciously attempting to undermine its authority in Warsaw by suggesting that its directives might be far from viable, though he himself continued to serve under this Government. Under such circumstances his resignation from his post as C-in-C might have been appropriate. He was unwilling to resign at this stage because such a drastic step would have removed him from the centre of events and would have left the entire field to Mikolajczyk, whom he distrusted. Instead, he was determined to remain at his post, for he still hoped that he might be able to exercise a considerable influence on Polish affairs. He hoped that by maintaining his control of the Army at home and abroad he would be able to restrain Mikolajczyk from submitting, under British pressure, to Russian demands. The C-in-C wished to act as the main pillar of possible political opposition to Mikolajczyk's Cabinet. This became clearer in the second half of July 1944, when the fate of Warsaw was in the balance and the Polish Premier was on his way to see Stalin in Moscow.

Meanwhile, though in practice Sosnkowski had deliberately relinquished, at least in part, his subordinates in Warsaw, preferring to assume the role of trusted and informed adviser, he continued to press his views upon them. He suggested that, circumstances per-

---

[1] Letter from the C-in-C to the Commander of the Home Army, dated 2 March 1944, sent to Poland by courier, probably Capt 'Cozas' (J. Kamienski), parachuted into Poland on 8–9 April 1944. APUST.

mitting, it might be advisable to 'transfer as many as possible of the most valuable and threatened elements of the Home Army' to the interior of Poland, or even, in extremity, to Hungary.[1]

This suggestion was rejected by the Home Army leaders,[2] in spite of Sosnkowski's assertion that as, sooner or later, Hungary would find herself on the side of the Allies, any Polish troops sent there would always be able to return to Poland at the time of the rising. The acceptance of the suggestion would undoubtedly have led to the wholesale dispersal of the Home Army and would have precipitated an internal crisis within its ranks, a crisis which would have tended to help the Communists to assume undisputed control over the resistance forces in Poland. The C-in-C was to return to this idea once again, at the end of July 1944 – on the eve of the Warsaw rising.[3] It is an idea which strongly suggests that in Sosnkowski's prolific and lively mind there was a certain amount of confusion as to the precise role of the Home Army in the events to come; Bor-Komorowski's forces could not have pursued all the different and conflicting policies proposed within a short space of time by their C-in-C; to fight against the Germans, to resist the Red Army if necessary, and to evacuate their most valuable elements abroad. Sosnkowski wanted the Home Army to play too many roles at the same time, and in reality he was merely confusing his hard-pressed subordinates in Warsaw by suggesting courses of action which stood in flagrant opposition to those recommended by the Cabinet. A unity of command was sadly lacking in the London camp on the threshold of its greatest trial.

It was paradoxical that almost at the time when Sosnkowski was trying to inspire Bor-Komorowski to start withdrawing parts of the Home Army from Poland the Polish Cabinet should send to Warsaw an amendment sanctioning the 'Burza' order.

3. *The amendment to the Government's Instruction of 27 October 1943*

On 18 February 1944 the exiled Government passed a resolution amending their October directives. This amendment read as follows:

> The Home authorities will issue orders to the local representatives of administrative organs to approach, together with the Commander of

[1] *Ibid.*
[2] Bor-Komorowski's oral evidence.
[3] For details see p. 300 of this study.

the local sector or Home Army unit, the Commander of the entering Soviet troops with the following declaration:

'Acting on the orders of the Government of the Polish Republic I approach you ... with a proposal to co-ordinate military operations against the common enemy with the Soviet forces entering the territories of the Polish Republic.'

The declaration should emphasise that the Home Army units ... form a part of the Polish Armed Forces and continue to remain under the orders of the Polish Government ...

Should it happen that the Polish representatives are arrested the Home authorities will forbid the administrative authorities and Armed Forces to come into the open in other areas.

In any case, apart from the representatives, acting openly, a second subsidiary network of civil and military leaders will be organised, which will remain underground, trying to establish contact with the Polish authorities and inform them of the fate of the revealed representatives, of the fate of the Polish population and of the Soviet behaviour in their respective areas.

We call upon the Polish population to remain in their homes. In its political activity the Polish Government continues its efforts to safe-guard the sovereign rights of the Republic and the safety of her citizens, as well as its efforts to create the conditions necessary for the co-ordination of the Homeland's struggle with the strategic plans of the Allies and Soviet Russia.[1]

On the same day the Cabinet also approved the text of additional directives, which were duly communicated to Warsaw, though they were not included in the official amendment. First, the Government informed its followers in Warsaw that the Home Army must emerge into the open in at least one place in the territories west of the Curzon Line, in order to ascertain Soviet behaviour in these regions. This 'supplementary' emergence from underground was deemed necessary to 'obtain additional political arguments in our defence of the interests of the Polish Republic and her population'. Another directive stated that the Home leaders would themselves have to decide, in the light of current circumstances, which of the civil organs and military units would come into the open and which would remain underground. Thirdly, if the Russian's rejected the Polish offer to co-ordinate operations against the Germans, the

[1] Resolution of the Council of Ministers, 18 February 1944, GSHI–PRM, L21.

Home Army Unit involved should disband, store arms, and try to avoid a conflict with the Russian troops.

Finally, the Cabinet agreed that the C-in-C should eventually depart for Poland 'as soon as [he] decides that the general rising is imminent'. If necessary the Prime Minister was to follow suit.[1]

These amendments represented for Bor-Komorowski and his plans total victory and for Mikolajczyk partial victory over the ideas and suggestions of Sosnkowski. They were an uneasy attempt to reconcile the opinions of the Premier and of the C-in-C concerning Bor-Komorowski's order for 'Burza'.

Sosnkowski was clearly displeased with the outcome of the Government's deliberations on the 'Burza' plan, and communicated his dissatisfaction to Bor-Komorowski and Mikolajczyk. He told Warsaw that these resolutions were 'the outcome of protracted arguments', primarily between the Premier and himself, and that not all their provisions were mutually agreed.[2]

He advocated that the Government issue a 'simple acknowledgement' of Bor-Komorowski's decision, instead of incorporating it formally into the Cabinet directives.[3] He also told Mikolajczyk that he continued to stand by the principles of the October instruction and regarded the achievement of Russo–Polish military collaboration without a previous political arrangement as in practice impossible, and attempts to this end as detrimental to the Polish *raison d'etat*.[4] Finally, he proposed officially that any Russian attempts to disarm the Home Army should be resisted. The Premier categorically rejected this proposal.[5]

The amendments of 18 February 1944 gave the underground authorities the official conceptual framework within which they were to stage 'Burza' and the Warsaw rising. Unfortunately, they failed to fully define the Home Army's attitude to the Russians, and tended to leave too much scope to the Home authorities with regard to the formation of an anti-Soviet conspiracy.

They accentuated the fact that the initiative in the deployment of the underground force was passing from London to Warsaw.

[1] *Ibid.*
[2] Despatch from the C-in-C to the Commander of the Home Army, 20 February 1944, Ldz. 1427/167. APUST.
[3] Letter from the C-in-C to the Prime Minister, 3 February 1944, Ldz. 124/GNW/ tj/44. GSHI–A.XII/3/90–2.
[4] Letter from the C-in-C to the Prime Minister, 21 February 1944, Ldz. 190/ GNW/tj/44. GSHI–PRM, L21.
[5] Minutes of the Council of Ministers, 18 February 1944, GSHI–A.XII/3/90–2.

7

The 'Tempest' East of Warsaw

1. 'Burza' in Volhynia

In February 1944 Operation 'Burza' began in Volhynia – one of the disputed provinces of inter-war Poland, in 1939 incorporated into the U.S.S.R. by the Russians – when a Home Army partisan detachment allegedly of about 6,000 men, began its intensified guerrilla operations against the Germans and the Ukrainian nationalists who collaborated with them. This detachment consisted of most of the Home Army partisan and conspiratorial units in the region. They were grouped together because the Area Commander feared that if they fought as separate units their operations would fail to show any significant results. Further, if they were not organised into one unit they might easily be pulverised by the German punitive counter-measures. Bor-Komorowski approved these tactics.[1]

Thus, even at the initial stage of 'Burza', a serious departure was made from the original plan. From the beginning of 1944 'Burza' in Volhynia was planned and executed in the form of relatively large-scale guerrilla operations rather than, as originally outlined by Bor-Komorowski in November 1943, a number of loosely co-ordinated small-scale local attacks on the German rearguards.[2] Within the space of a few months more serious and portentous departures from the 'Burza' plan were to be made. It was becoming a highly elastic concept.

In March 1944 the partisan group in Volhynia assumed the name of the 27th Home Army Volhynian Infantry Division, which before the war had been stationed in this region. The assumption of this name was intended to stress the local connections of the unit and to impress on the Russians the fact that they were dealing with a powerful and viable movement, capable of entering the field with strong and well-organised detachments. In reality the Division

---

[1] Cf. *Polskie Siły Zbrojne, op. cit.*, pp. 584ff.
[2] For details, see p. 167 of this study.

lacked the heavy weapons and support-units normally associated with a military unit of this size. The Division was made up of two regimental battle groups – the 50th and 24th Infantry Regiments – Divisional Headquarters and a number of rudimentary divisional units, such as Signals, Engineers, quartermaster personnel, Military Police, two field-hospitals, etc. It was commended by Lt-Col 'Oliwa' Jan Wojciech Kiwerski, who was also the Home Army Area Commander for Volhynia. His orders were to shape his unit into a coherent battle group, to intensify the operations against the Germans and to establish contact with the regular Soviet Army.

Colonel 'Oliwa' intended to implement these orders by placing his group under the Soviet operational command and, in addition, by attempting to stage his own anti-German operations always slightly in front of the Russian advance. He also made preparations for taking two of the main towns in the region, Kowel and Wlodzimierz. During the period from 13 February to 20 March 1944 the Volhynian Division fought a number of successful engagements against the Germans and Ukrainians, taking prisoners and capturing arms.[1]

On 20 March 1944 Col 'Oliwa's' troops established their first contacts with the regular units of the Red Army. Two days later Bor-Komorowski told London that 'the regular Soviet troops have behaved up to now in a correct manner, they are willing to accept all help and to try to win the confidence of the Polish population'.[2] Nevertheless, at the same time it became known that the Russians were treating Volhynia as an integral part of the U.S.S.R.[3]

On 23 March 1944 Bor-Komorowski informed London that the deputy Commander of the Volhynia region had had talks with the Russian staff officers, by whom he was received with 'demonstrative cordiality'.

> The deputy Area Commander clearly defined our attitude [and stated] that he owes allegiance to the Polish military authorities and the Government in London, as well as to his superiors in Warsaw. He has orders to fight against the Germans and within the framework of this struggle he can co-operate tactically with the Soviet troops.

[1] *Polskie Siły Zbrojne, op. cit.*, pp. 587–9.
[2] Despatch from the Commander of the Home Army to the C-in-C, 22 March 1944, Ldz. 2692, APUST.
[3] Despatch from the Commander of the Home Army to the C-in-C, 15 March 1944, Ldz. 2481, APUST.

He declared himself against all possible attempts to merge his units with Berling's. The Area Commander was invited to see the Soviet Army Commander and has left for his [Soviet] Headquarters.[1]

The results of the talks between Col 'Oliwa' and the Red Army Commander, General Sergeev, were, taken at their face value, very encouraging. For a short period of time it seemed that Russo–Polish military co-operation would be established. On 4 April 1944 Gen Bor-Komorowski wired London:

I have received the following report from the Commander of the Volhynia area: 'On 26 March I talked with ... General Sergeev ... The Soviet Command, after consultations with their central authorities, are willing to co-operate with our Division on the following conditions:

1. Unreserved submission to the Soviet operational Command, locally and beyond the Bug [west of the Curzon Line].

2. They recognise that we are a Polish Division with its own authorities in Warsaw and London.

3. The Division may maintain unrestricted liaison with its own authorities.

4. We must re-organise ourselves from a partisan unit into a regular army division. [. . .]

5. The Soviet Command will not allow any partisan units at their rear.

6. In return we will receive complete field equipment for a division: weapons, ammunition, artillery, motor-transport and supplies.

I reserved for myself the right to reply on receipt of orders from my own authorities. I promised to reply within four days. I ask you to consider this matter as extremely urgent for the following reasons:

1. I assume that in the case of a negative reply I would be compelled to cross the Bug with about 2000 men, probably while fighting with the Soviets, because to leave partisan units at their rear would undoubtedly lead to a fight and, in my opinion, to the speedy destruction of our units.

2. All our units are revealed [to the Soviets].

3. In the occupied territories the Soviets are imposing official conscription, partly to the Berling Army. [. . .] At this moment necessity compels me to co-operate militarily [with the Soviets] on the territories of Volhynia – within the framework of this co-operation I move to the west.'

Bor-Komorowski continued: 'In view of the need for immediate reply I have transmitted the following order to the Commander of the

[1] Situation Report No. 2 of 23 March 1944, Ldz. 2694, APUST.

Volhynia Area after consultations with the Government's Delegate: [. . .]

'1. Backed by Soviet help you will re-organise yourselves into the 27th Volhynian Infantry Division. This Division will continue to remain under the command of the Commander of the Home Army . . . To maintain this subordination you must preserve, unhindered and uncontrolled by the Soviets, liaison with me.

2. The task of the 27th Volhynian Division is to fight against the Germans on the territories of the Republic. In implementing this task it will temporarily serve under the Soviet Command . . .

3. For the development of the Division you will use recruits from Volhynia. *You will yourself settle, in consultation with the Soviets, the call-up and enlistment procedures.* I reserve for myself the right to commission officers in the name of the Commander-in-Chief and to appoint commanders to battalion level; lower posts will be filled by you according to your personal decisions.

4. The Division will have the distinct character of a re-established unit of the Polish Army and will realise the war-aims as defined by the highest Polish state authorities. It must not be deported to Russia. [. . .]

5. In communicating your reply to the Soviet Command you will point out that your group is the first which they have encountered on the territories of the Republic and [that] as they advance further into Poland they will meet, fighting against the Germans, other Polish units . . . *In view of this there arises a strong need for the conclusion of a fundamental agreement between the Soviet Government and the Polish Government in London, leading to the possibility of consistent conduct of the war against the Germans by the Soviet Union and Poland on our territories.*

I assume that you will accomplish this difficult mission, imposed on you by the circumstances, with the dignity of a soldier of independent Poland . . .'

I based the above directive on a conviction that we must avail ourselves of any opportunity to re-establish units of the Polish Army subordinate to the C-in-C. If the Soviet offer is hypocritical its falsity will soon be revealed and will provide the Government with useful arguments.[1]

A closer examination of the Soviet proposals and Polish counter-proposals reveals a number of interesting points. It appears that at the end of March 1944 the Soviet High Command was willing to accept the Home Army as an independent ally in the struggle against

---

[1] Despatch from the Commander of the Home Army to the C-in-C, 4 April 1944, Ldz. 2797/tjn/44, APUST. My italics. See also: T. Sztumberk-Rychter, *Artylerzysta Piechurem* (Warsaw, 1967), pp. 193ff.

the Germans and to conclude a military convention with Bor-Komorowski to that end. The two conditions were to be: first, unqualified acceptance by the Home Army of the Soviet operational Command, and, secondly, the disbanding of all Polish units behind the Soviet lines. Clearly, the Russians wanted to see the Poles at the Russo–German front and not at their rear.

This second condition was of cardinal importance and its rejection by the Poles could have had serious consequences, especially in view of the explicit intention of the Home Army leaders to leave and operate a nucleus of the anti-Soviet resistance movement in the Russian-held territories, which might lead to a direct Russo–Polish clash. This condition could be interpreted as a Soviet warning to Bor-Komorowski that the Russians would not tolerate this kind of activity behind their lines. In framing their subsequent actions, the Polish leaders in Warsaw and London ignored this important Russian warning, in spite of the fact that, in their offer to Col 'Oliwa', the Russians had made it quite clear that they would not allow the existence of Polish partisan units on their side of the Russo–German front. At that time, the Polish authorities were not sure that the Russian offers were genuine; neither, however, had they decided that they were false. If genuine, they were realistic, consistent and worthy of the serious attention of the pro-London leaders. In essence, they represented an offer of a purely military nature which much to the regret of the London Poles, left the problem of the recognition of the exiled Government and its aspirations in Poland in abeyance. Yet these offers implied that Polish services in the common struggle would be welcomed, even if the Poles insisted on maintaining their connections with Warsaw and London instead of placing themselves unreservedly at the disposal of Gen Berling and the leaders of the Communist-sponsored resistance.

Without access to Soviet documentary sources, it cannot be ascertained whether the offers were genuine and had in fact emanated from the Kremlin, as Col 'Oliwa' claimed, or whether they represented the local initiative of a relatively junior Russian General anxious, for mainly tactical reasons, to use Home Army support in his passage through Volhynia.

It emerges only too clearly from Col 'Oliwa's' message to Warsaw that he entered into co-operation with the Red Army in Volhynia with extreme reluctance and grave misgivings, under the duress of circumstances. He was prompted to establish liaison with the

Russians primarily by the fear that otherwise his units would be destroyed by them. He was, however, determined to maintain only very loose contact with the Red Army, at least for the time being, in order to preserve his freedom of action, though by doing so he was exposing his troops to possible destruction by a German counter-attack. He was prepared, if necessary, to fight against the Russians and to seek refuge beyond the River Bug. He was anxiously awaiting Bor-Komorowski's reply to the Soviet offer.

Bor-Komorowski's counter-proposals extended far beyond the limits of purely military convention and stressed the need for a wider political and diplomatic agreement between Poland and the U.S.S.R. which, if concluded, would not only lead to the recognition of Moscow by the London Government, but would also extend that Government's authority to all the territories of pre-war Poland. His propositions were consistent with the tasks of 'Burza', which aimed, at this stage, at stressing the Polish character of the disputed territories and displaying the Home Army's determination to fight against the Germans throughout the territories of pre-1939 Poland. Whether this offer would have been acceptable to Moscow remains doubtful; in any case, his reply was probably never delivered to Gen Sergeev, for on 19 April 1944 Bor-Komorowski reported to London: 'So far the Commander of the Volhynia area has had no further talks with the Soviet Commander because my instruction was delayed in reaching him, and because of his preoccupation with the battle.'[1] He himself had considerable doubts as to whether his offer would be acceptable to the Soviets, because of its insistence on Soviet recognition of the exiled Government's authority in Volhynia. In reality he had always suspected the Soviet motives and intentions. He believed that 'because of the failure to re-establish diplomatic relations between our Government and the Soviets, it is not advisable hastily to contract liaison with the Soviet Command on our own initiative. Indeed, it would be better to implement 'Burza' tasks independently [of the Soviets] for as long as possible'.[2] Consequently, the General showed little marked enthusiasm for or impatience to conclude even a temporary and localised military agreement with the Russians in Volhynia.

[1] Despatch from the Commander of the Home Army to the C-in-C, 19 April 1944, Ldz. 3418, APUST.
[2] The Order of the Home Commander, 23 March 1944, No. 144/III/KSZ, Ldz. 6302/tjn/44. APUST.

It is also significant that Bor-Komorowski decided to rely on a hard-pressed field officer of relatively junior rank to maintain his contact with the Red Army. The circumstances would seem to have merited the immediate despatch to Gen Sergeev of a high-ranking Home Army staff officer endowed with wide discretionary powers and in possession of confidential cyphers, to establish direct liaison between Warsaw and the Soviet High Command. Probably this would have achieved better results and would give the Russians a more favourable impression. Possibly, this was not done because Bor-Komorowski was afraid that high-level contacts with Moscow might hamper his 'Burza' operations and restrict his independence. However, this did not stop the Polish Government from issuing a communiqué – relayed to Poland by the B.B.C. – on 7 April, stating that on 26 March Col 'Oliwa', following the Soviet initiative, had visited the Soviet Command in Volhynia, 'where the principles of co-operation sent from the central Soviet authorities were communicated to him'. The communique went on:

> The Polish Commander reserved for himself the right to reply within four days, after consulting his superiors.
> The reply of the Commander of the Home Army, issued in consultation with the Government's Delegate and the Government of the Republic in London, *was delivered to the Command of the Soviet Army*.[1]

This was not the case. The Government was obviously under the impression that Bor-Komorowski had managed to transmit his reply within the time-limit set by Col 'Oliwa'. On his part, Bor-Komorowski protested to London against the issuing of this communique, as in his opinion it tended to impinge on his authority, and might confuse Col 'Oliwa' and the people in Poland.[2] It was suggested to him, however, that though the ending of the communique was inaccurate, important political reasons nevertheless dictated its inclusion.[3]

Events in Volhynia led to a lengthy exchange of communications between Warsaw and London. Reactions in London to the Soviet

[1] Communique of the Polish Telegraphic Agency, 7 April 1944, Appendix to Ldz. 377, APUST. My italics.
[2] Despatch from the Commander of the Home Army to the C-in-C, 15 April 1944, Ldz. 3352, APUST, and despatch from the Commander of the Home Army to the C-in-C, 3 May 1944, Ldz. 3777/A/tjn/44, APUST.
[3] Report by Lt Pomian of an interview with the Polish Minister of Information, Prof S. Kot, 5 May 1944, Appendix to Ldz. 377, APUST.

offer of co-operation and Bor-Komorowski's counter-proposals were again conflicting. Mikolajczyk greeted them with undisguised enthusiasm and satisfaction, as might be expected. On 18 April he radioed the Government's Delegate in Warsaw:

> On 6 April 1944 the Polish Government accepted in full the very equitable dispositions which were issued by the Commander of the Home Army ... in reply to the Soviet propositions. We have immediately included them in our notes to the British and American Governments, [proposing] that they exploit this moment in their political activity, and demanding the dispatch of Allied missions [to the Home Army].
>
> Regardless of what the Soviets might do tomorrow, the propositions, once made by them, [even] if they change or fail to honour them, will remain an important political argument.
>
> At this moment the intensification of the operations in the Wilno region, as well as the meeting with the Red Army and collaboration with it in the struggle against the Germans, constitute an important political argument which displays the falsity of charges of co-operation with the Germans, the loyalty [of the Home Army] to the State authorities, and demolishes the conviction in Moscow ... that the Poles are bent on armed struggle against the entering Soviet Army.
>
> On behalf of the Government I am communicating our gratitude to you and the Commander [of the Home Army] for such a wise decision, and our appreciation to the Home Army units in the Volhynia and Wilno regions for their sacrifices, their heroic bearing and their action, which has overcome political deadlock.
>
> I believe that this proof of the heroism and loyalty of these units, as well as the fear that by disarming and shooting they [the Russians] might drive the desperate Poles into German arms, decided this last Soviet move.[1]

Mikolajczyk was, undoubtedly, convinced that, in accordance with his expectations, 'Burza' had started to pay political dividends, paving the way for a broader understanding with Moscow, providing London and Washington with tangible reasons for intervening in the Russo–Polish dispute and finally displaying to all Poland's good will and reasonable frame of mind. The Prime Minister's satisfaction with Bor-Komorowski's handling of the Volhynian affair was no surprise, for the day before, on 5 April 1944, he had told Warsaw that if the underground failed to come into the open and co-operate

[1] Despatch from the Prime Minister to the Government's Delegate, 18 April 1944, Ldz. 4046/tjn/44, APUST.

with the Red Army the 'Anglo–Saxon world' would interpret its actions as pro-German. Consequently, the Premier asked the Home authorities to continue as long as possible their policy of coming into the open, regardless of the immediate outcome of the Russo–Polish confrontation east of the Curzon Line. He added: 'Most important to the public here will be the Soviet behaviour after their crossing of the Curzon Line and hence the fact of our coming into the open behind this line will be crucial, as well as the methods which the Soviets will use there.' He reminded Warsaw that these two elements might sway the Anglo–Saxon world in favour of the pro-London camp.[1]

Mikolajczyk intended to exploit the sacrifices of the Home Army to gain Anglo–American support for his Government's ambitions and aspirations in Poland. Sosnkowski's response to the news from Poland was more pessimistic. His appraisal of the situation differed considerably from that of his Prime Minister. On 8 April he wrote to Bor-Komorowski:

> Realising your difficult situation, I acknowledge the accomplished fact in the shape of your Instruction to the Commander of the Volhynia Area concerning the establishment of the 27th Infantry Division. I doubt whether the Soviet Command's promise will be fulfilled, or alternatively whether the additional conditions in your instruction will be accepted, and even if they are I do not believe there will be a favourable outcome of this experiment; the subordination of the division to you and myself would probably be completely illusory. It would be useful if in this way you succeed in acquiring a certain amount of arms and save at least a part of these people and units, which, as you inform me, are completely revealed. I expect that at a certain stage attempts to incorporate the division into the Berling Army will be made, or repressions will be applied. I assume that the Area Commander is a trustworthy and experienced person. His whole skill will have to consist in his ability to know how to break off contact with the Soviet troops in the event of danger, and to undertake independent operations against the Germans in order to break through to an area which is under your direct orders.
>
> The possibility of an understanding between the Soviet Government and the Polish Government . . . about the tactical subordination of the 27th Infantry Division does not as yet exist, in spite of all the efforts on the part of the Polish Government. I would like to know your opinion; whether your appraisal of the military situation is such that [in

[1] Despatch from the Prime Minister to the Government's Delegate, 5 April 1944, No. 84, Ldz. 1270/tjn/44, APUST, File 50/I Min. Spr. Wew.

your estimation] *the Soviets would be able to defeat the Germans independently and, pursuing them, occupy the whole of Poland.* In Great Britain the preparations for the opening of the Second Front are in full swing. The timing of the invasion is unknown, I think it will depend to a large extent on developments in the east.[1]

Sosnkowski militated against the very idea of Russo–Polish tactical collaboration without previous political agreement between Mikolajczyk and Stalin. What is more, he still continued to be highly sceptical of Russian military ability to occupy his country. He still hoped that the Anglo–American invasion of the Continent would lead to the liberation of Poland by the Western, rather than Soviet forces. Indeed, in his communication with Bor-Komorowski he was implying that a race for Europe might take place between the Anglo-Saxon powers and the U.S.S.R.

Meanwhile, he was clearly disturbed by the developments in Volhynia. 'In general', he wrote to Bor-Komorowski on 17 April 1944,

the information about the co-operation of the Home Army with . . . the Soviet Army is creating so distorted an image that it would be difficult or even impossible to convince the public here that the real cause of the Soviet terror is the aggressive policy of Moscow. We should remember that our further sacrifices, resulting from coming into the open, might be senseless in regard to the defence of our territorial and political rights.

It might even be feared that the facts of [our] coming into the open may be used by Soviet propaganda as a proof that we are not determined to defend, ruthlessly, our Eastern borderlands . . .

The idea that the English and Americans might try to gain Soviet permission to send an Allied mission to the Eastern borderlands should also be discounted, as these territories are regarded by Moscow as unquestionably belonging to her.[2]

Sosnkowski feared that Russo–Polish military co-operation without the participation of the London Government might nullify the intent and purpose of 'Burza', as he saw it. Further, he was once again hinting to Bor-Komorowski that he should resist the Russians.

His fears met with a ready response in Warsaw. On 19 April

---

[1] Despatch from the C-in-C to the Commander of the Home Army, 8 April 1944, Ldz. 2880/tjn/44, APUST.
[2] Despatch from the C-in-C to the Commander of the Home Army, 17 April 1944, Ldz. 362/1–2, APUST.

Bor-Komorowski explicitly stated for the first time his real intentions and plans to Sosnkowski, and expressed his full agreement with the C-in-C's appraisal of Russo–Polish relations. He wrote:

> The Soviet attitude to us I appraise realistically. We expect nothing good from their side, neither do we delude ourselves that they will loyally co-operate with the independent Polish body.
>
> ... We regard it as essential that our every step should be consistent with the sovereign rights of the Republic ... Hence, my instruction to the Commander of the Volhynia Area included conditions of a kind which the Soviets would certainly refuse to honour. I have, in a separate order, instructed that, if this should happen, the Commander of the Volhynia Area must break through to the German rear to the territories under my direct orders. The military situation, as seen at Home, strongly indicates an independent, though slow, Soviet victory over the Germans, should the containment of the German forces continue in the West. In any case the occupation of the whole of Poland by the Soviets is considered by us here as a serious possibility. In consequence we must be prepared for an open collision between Poland and the Soviets, and on our part we would have to demonstrate to the full, in this collision, the independent position of Poland. Naturally, hand in hand with this, an [anti-Soviet] underground undercurrent of Polish life will appear. At this moment its extent and battle-worthiness cannot be assessed, but its possibilities should not be over-estimated.[1]

Bor-Komorowski and his immediate entourage regarded 'Burza' as one aspect of the approaching Russo–Polish 'collision' which they considered would be imminent if the Soviets should occupy the whole of Poland. They were, in fact, preparing to resist the Russians, thereby returning to the ideas postulated by Grot-Rowecki in his correspondence with Sikorski in the years 1942–3, a policy which Sikorski had described as 'sheer madness' which could only harm Poland.[2] Given this frame of mind on the part of the Home Commander and his Staff, it is only too obvious that ideologically they adhered to the doctrine of two enemies and that this doctrine coloured all their actions and inner thoughts. The Home Army inevitably entered on a collision-bound course, with regard to the U.S.S.R. though this 'collision' was to assume political rather than military expression.

[1] Despatch from the Commander of the Home Army to the C-in-C, 19 April 1944, Ldz. 3418, APUST.
[2] Despatch from the C-in-C to the Commander of the Home Army, 28 November 1942, Ldz. 5060/Tj/42, APUST.

In reality, by fighting against the Germans the Home Army was taking up its position for the approaching Russo–Polish confrontation. Its leaders refused to accept Sikorski's earlier advice – that if the Red Army entered Poland in force the restitution of the Polish State could take place only with Soviet goodwill. Yet the very same Polish leaders who, in the second half of April 1944 were plainly talking about organising both open and clandestine resistance to the Russians, were, less than four months later – during the Warsaw Rising – desperately clamouring for Russian help, which they expected to save them from German carnage and bestiality. They believed, however that their earlier approach to the Russo–Polish problem was right because it was prompted by their determination to defend the 'sovereign rights' of Poland. They believed that by their actions they were defending Poland's right to independence, as they understood it. This conviction motivated all that they did. They failed to add, however, that they also regarded 'Burza' as their contribution to the internal struggle for power which was raging in Poland, between the pro-London and pro-Communist forces. To them, inactivity on their part was tantamount to political suicide.

Finally, it must be said that the Home Army generals' assessment of the military situation was at this stage more realistic than that of their C-in-C in London. In the second half of April 1944 they felt that the occupation of Poland by the Red Army was highly probable, and this fact 'compelled' them to demonstrate their true attitude to the Russians. The Secret State's political representatives were also despondent and alarmed by the events in Volhynia. They distrusted the motives behind the Soviet offer and were demanding that the situation created in Volhynia should be exploited by the Government for the restoration of diplomatic relations.[1] Further, these despatches to London reveal a substantial difference of opinion on the 'Burza' plan between the political and military leaders of the underground. Apart from its obvious anti-German aspects, the politicians regarded it as a way of forcing clarification of the real Soviet intentions regarding the pro-London Poles, while the Generals saw it, not only as an anti-German operation, but also as a Russo–Polish collision. What is

---

[1] Letter from the Government's Delegate to the President of the Republic, 23 April 1944, Ldz. 3706, APUST, and Despatch from the Government's Delegate and the Council of National Unity to the Prime Minister, 2 May 1944, No. 36, APUST.

more, the underground leaders were fully aware that in their struggle for power they were losing some ground to their Communist rivals. More significantly, they were not at all certain of the Polish people's response to the entry of the Red Army into the country.[1] It seems that large sections of the people, desiring, above all, speedy deliverance from the German yoke, were ready to hail the Soviet Army as their liberators; as early as November 1943 Bor-Komorowski had told Sosnkowski that 'Among the masses a tendency to regard the Soviets as [their] rescuers from the German terror has begun to emerge.'[2]

The communications from Poland so far quoted clearly define, then, the attitude of the Underground leaders – political and military – to 'Burza' and the problem of possible Russo–Polish military co-operation, this time from the practical, rather than academic, point of view. While this protracted exchange of communications between London and Warsaw was taking place the military situation of the Russo–Polish forces in Volhynia was deteriorating rapidly. By 10 April 1944 the *Wehrmacht* had temporarily regained the initiative on this sector of the Russo–German front. The Germans started their counter-attack in the Kowel region, where the 27th Division was deployed. The German onslaught made direct contact between the Poles and the Russians very precarious. Nevertheless, the Division was in constant radio-communication with the Soviet units. Liaison with the Home Army Command in Warsaw was also sporadic, as the divisional radio-transmitter was constantly being bombed by the Germans.[3] Hence, it is very hard to reconstruct precisely the subsequent events and the fate of the 27th Division.

On 18 April the Germans encircled the Division and Lt-Col 'Oliwa' was killed. His Chief of Staff, Major 'Zegota' (Tadeusz Sztumberg-Rychter) took over command.[4] The battle continued. On the night of 21 April the Division, suffering heavy losses, managed to break through the German encirclement. The new Divisional Commander decided to leave the Kowel area, where the Russo–German battle was still raging, and to seek temporary refuge in the

---

[1] Letter from the Government's Delegate to the President of the Republic, 23 April 1944, Ldz, 3706, APUST, and Despatch from the Government's Delegate and the Council of National Unity to the Prime Minister, 2 May 1944, No. 36, APUST.

[2] Despatch from the Commander of the Home Army to the C-in-C, 30 December 1943. Ldz. 6793, APUST.

[3] *Polskie Siły Zbrojne, op. cit.*, pp. 595ff.

[4] *Ibid.*, and T. Sztumberk-Rychter, *op. cit.*, pp. 209ff.

neighbouring forests, where he wanted to re-group the rest of his troops.[1] In May the Division was in the Szacki Forest, west of Kowel, and again became involved in the heavy fighting against the Germans. In these circumstances, on 21 May Major 'Zegota' decided to move the Division to the Russian-held territory.[2] On 22 May, when the Division, split into two columns, was already on the move, Gen Bor-Komorowski ordered it to withdraw behind the Bug.[3] Only one of its columns was diverted in time; the other crossed the Russo–German Front.[4] The soldiers of the latter column were incorporated into Berling's Army.[5] On 24 June 1944 the remains of the Volhynian Division – that is of the diverted column – reached the Lublin area.[6]

Thus 'Burza' ended in the Volhynia region. From the point of view of Russo–Polish relations, it ended inconclusively; diplomatic relations between the Government in London and Moscow remained suspended, military co-operation between the Home Army and the Red Army was not established, and Soviet intentions towards the London camp were neither finally clarified nor exposed to the view of world public opinion. Only events to come could finally settle these questions.

This was admitted by Mikolajczyk, who pointed out that the Russo–Polish confrontation would enter into its most crucial phase west, rather than east, of the Curzon Line. Hence, at least in his opinion, the Volhynian episode was but a prelude to important future developments.

Nevertheless, during 'Burza' in Volhynia a certain pattern of events had emerged which was soon to reappear in other parts of Poland: it became apparent to all concerned, Russians, Germans and Poles alike, that immediately before the arrival of the Red Army into a particular area of the country some of the local Home Army units would be mobilised, concentrated and thrown into the battle against

[1] *Polskie Sily Zbrojne, op. cit.*, p. 596.
[2] Despatch from the Commander of the Home Army to the C-in-C, 8 June 1944, Ldz. 4581, APUST; and T. Sztumberk-Rychter, *op. cit.*, pp. 216–17.
[3] Despatch from the Commander of the Home Army to the C-in-C, 31 May 1944, Ldz. 4581, APUST.
[4] Despatch from the Commander of the Home Army to the C-in-C, 10 June 1944, Ldz. 4680, APUST.
[5] Cf. T. Sztumberk-Rychter, *op. cit.*, pp. 217–18; and *Polskie Sily Zbrojne, op. cit.*, p. 599.
[6] Despatch of the Chief of Staff of the Lublin Home Army Area, 24 June 1944, Ldz. 13270/tjn/44, APUST.

the Germans. During the fighting temporary contact and co-operation with the Russians would be established. Initially, relations between both sides would be cordial and friendly. After the fighting those of the Home Army units which found themselves in Russian-held territory would be disarmed and incorporated into the Berling Army.

With regard to the 'Burza' plan itself, four main lessons emerged from the Volhynia experiment; first that the local Soviet Commanders were more than anxious to collaborate with the Home Army while fighting was in progress; secondly that it might be very difficult to maintain contact with the Red Army in the field in view of possible German counter-action; thirdly, that it was pointless to try to emphasise to the Russians the Polish claims to the disputed territories, as they regarded them as an organic part of the U.S.S.R.; finally, it became more than ever apparent that the Soviets were not going to tolerate the existence of the Home Army units behind their lines.

In conclusion, it seems that the Home Army Command made only a half-hearted and belated attempt to establish military co-operation with the Russians. The Secret Army leaders failed even to deliver their reply to the Russians in time (if, indeed, it was delivered at all), let alone exploit their offer to the full.

After Volhynia it became clear that it would be essential to capture towns, in order to realise and accentuate the political aims of 'Burza'. In June 1944 the Home Army Command came to the conclusion that, if their forces were to act as hosts to the Red Army, large towns must be captured from the Germans before the arrival of the Russians. 'The Home Army had to accommodate itself to this fact in spite of the earlier intentions of its Command.'[1] Thus, the Home Army was soon to be faced with even more difficult and demanding military tasks. It should be stressed here that Bor Komorowski had in mind the capture of large urban centres only in the event of a 'general and simultaneous rising'. Indeed, it seems that the exclusion of towns from 'Burza' was mainly introduced to distinguish it from, and prevent it from becoming, a 'general rising'. In consequence of the June decision to take large towns, the distinction between the 'Burza' operations and the 'general rising' was becoming blurred and indistinct. 'Burza', as defined by Bor-Komorowski and his chief planners in November 1943, was destined to be relegated to the role of a mere staff exercise – 'Burza' in its

[1] General Pelczynski's oral evidence.

classical form was never put into practice. Only its political aims remained unaltered.

2. *'Burza' in the Wilno and Nowogrodek Areas*

On 12 June 1944, during the Staff briefing held by Bor-Komorowski in Warsaw for the Commanders of the Wilno and Nowogrodek areas, it was decided that their combined forces would be concentrated in the vicinity of Wilno with the object of capturing this city as the Red Army approached. At the same time Col 'Wilk' A. Krzyzanowski, the Commander of the Wilno area, was entrusted with the command of this operation.

At the end of June 1944 Col 'Wilk' received from Warsaw his detailed orders for 'Burza'. They confirmed the earlier decision – he was to take Wilno.[1]

On 7 July a similar instruction was received in Warsaw from the C-in-C: 'If, owing to a happy conjuncture, during the last moments of the German retreat, and before the entry of the Red units, a chance should arise to occupy, even temporarily, Wilno, Lwow and any other important centre or even a certain limited territory, we should do so and act there as the legitimate hosts [to the Russians].'[2]

The C-in-C's directives, though couched in less categorical form, in a sense, sanctioned and approved, Bor-Komorowski's independent decision. Sosnkowski felt these new directives were still within the framework of 'Burza'. They were prompted by his long-held belief that in the event of the occupation of Lwow, Wilno or any other part of Poland by the Red Army 'the creation of a "fait accompli" by the Home Country [the Home Army] would . . . be the right thing'.[3] It is interesting to note that Sosnkowski did not transmit this idea to Poland until July 1944, in spite of the fact that he had told Gen Kukiel of it as early as November 1943.

At the beginning of July 1944 the C-in-C finally became convinced that 'the occupation of a considerable part of Poland by the Soviet troops may be expected within a relatively short period of

---

[1] *Polskie Sily Zbrojne, op. cit.*, p. 609; and S. Truszkowski, *Partyzanckie Wspomnienia* (Warsaw, 1968), pp. 273–4.

[2] Despatch from the C-in-C to the Commander of the Home Army, 7 July 1944, Ldz. 5480/44, APUST.

[3] Despatch from the C-in-C to the Minister of National Defence, 25 November 1943, Ldz. 7571, GSHI–PRM, L45/47.

time'. What is more, at the same time he arrived at the conclusion that 'the Soviet Government has decided to apply, in regard to Poland, the policy of accomplished facts'.[1] Hence, for his part he was convinced that Soviet policy should be checked by the Home Army by the creation of obstacles in the Russian path in the form of its own accomplished facts. For the time being, he seems to have revised his previous attitude, which had been critical of Bor-Komorowski's decision to reveal his troops to the Russians; it appeared that at long last partial agreement was established between the two Generals.

There was, however, an important basic difference between them on the question of what tactics to employ. Gen Bor-Komorowski sanctioned a full-scale attack on the well-defended town of Wilno, while his C-in-C recommended the capture of towns only in quite exceptional and favourable circumstances – when the fortunes of war might make them easy prey – because he was more mindful of the Home Army's lack of weapons and equipment. Nevertheless, the somewhat ambiguous phrasing of Sosnkowski's July directives possibly created the impression, among the members of Bor-Komorowski's Staff, that their decision to capture towns from the Germans fully corresponded, in essence, with their C-in-C's orders.

Meanwhile, on 23 June 1944 the Red Army started its offensive in White Russia. In the first weeks of July the Russo–German front moved into the north-eastern territories of pre-war Poland. 'Burza' entered into its main phase. On the night of 2 July Col 'Wilk' decided, in accordance with his plans and orders, to begin preparations for his attack. The rapidity of the Russian advances compelled him to speed up the Home Army's attack on Wilno, as he intended to capture this important centre before the entry of the Soviet troops. The Home Army unit attacked the German garrison of Wilno on the night of 6 July; about 5,500 Polish soldiers took part in this operation.[2] The first attack failed to dislodge the Germans from the town. In the early hours of 7 July Col 'Wilk' reported to Warsaw: '. . . the Home Army forces attacked Wilno. The fighting lasted for twelve hours, the city was not taken. Heavy losses. . .'[3] At 4 p.m., on the same day, the Red Army units, which had in the

---

[1] Despatch from the C-in-C to the Commander of the Home Army, 7 July 1944, Ldz. 5480/44, APUST.

[2] *Polskie Siły Zbrojne, op. cit.*, pp. 609ff.

[3] Despatch from the Commander of the Wilno Area to the Commander of the Home Army, 7 July 1944, Ldz. 13340, APUST.

meantime approached the city, joined the battle. Cordial relations and collaboration between the Russians and the Poles were established and maintained while the fighting lasted.[1] The battle for Wilno continued until 13 July, when the last pockets of German resistance were crushed by combined Russo–Polish effort. On 14 July the Commander of the Nowogrodek Area reported to Bor-Komorowski that 'Wilno was taken with the considerable participation of the Home Army, which entered the city. Heavy destruction and losses. Relations with the Soviet Army temporarily correct. Wilno experienced a short but joyful moment of freedom.' He continued:

> The Polish character of the town is striking. It is full of our soliders. The Civil Defence is Polish. The hospitals are overflowing, all in Polish hands. In the factories and workshops Polish committees and managements are being formed. The administrative authorities will come into the open shortly.[2]

Soon, however, the Russo–Polish relations started to deteriorate. The Russians refused to admit into Wilno other Polish units, which were being concentrated to the south-east of the city. The tension between the Poles and the Russians was mounting. Col 'Wilk' told Bor-Komorowski he was convinced the Soviet authorities were determined to 'liquidate our units'. To prevent this he asked his superiors in Warsaw to arrange for an 'international arbitration mission, or at least Anglo–American liaison officers' to be sent to his Headquarters immediately. Further, he reported that his subsequent actions would be conditioned by the attitude of the Russians to his troops. The plan which he submitted to Bor-Komorowski for approval was:

> 1. To remain in the Wilno region by concentrating the majority of forces in the Rudnicki Forests – and, with the remainder, to support the Soviet Army in their struggle against the Germans. I want to achieve Soviet recognition of my force as the Home Army.
> 2. I will not allow myself at any price to be disarmed and in the event of a Soviet drive to destroy the Polish element I will defend it.
> 3. I will march to the west only on your explicit orders.[3]

[1] Despatch from the Commander of the Wilno Area to the Commander of the Home Army, 10 July 1944, Ldz. 13289, APUST.

[2] Despatch from the Commander of the Nowogrodek Area to the Commander of the Home Army, 14 July 1944, Ldz. 13191, APUST.

[3] Despatch from the Commander of the Wilno Area to the Commander of the Home Army, 13 July 1944, Ldz. 13199, APUST.

Col 'Wilk' was determined, therefore, to cling to Wilno – to remain in the Soviet rear – and, if necessary, to put up resistance to the Russians, should they refuse to acknowledge the sovereign status of his troops. Events moved rapidly. On 15 July 1944 the Polish Commander was invited to see Gen I. Cherniakhovsky the Soviet Commander of the 3rd White Russian Front. The latter accepted without reservation his offer to place at the Russo–German front, in the first instance, an infantry division and a cavalry brigade. Gen Cherniakhovsky agreed to provide heavy and light equipment for the Polish troops. The Russo–Polish talks were conducted in a cordial atmosphere. Political issues and the Home Army's attitude to Gen Berling's Army were not discussed.[1] A Russo–Polish briefing for Staff officers was arranged for 16 July, to discuss the reorganisation of the Home Army units, and Col 'Wilk' was invited to see Gen Cherniakhovsky again in Wilno.[2] Both these meetings ended in the arrest of the Polish officers, including Col 'Wilk'.

At the same time the Polish troops, about six thousand strong, were marching to their new assembly area in the Rudnicki Forest, where they intended to resist the Russians.[3] On the same day the Russians issued an ultimatum: the Poles were to 'lay down their arms' and were to be incorporated into the Berling Army. Many Home Army units complied, while others were dispersed by their own commanders.[4] In some instances sporadic Russo–Polish clashes developed, as a number of Col 'Wilk's' soldiers refused to lay down their arms without token resistance.[5] This was the sequel to 'Burza' in the Wilno region. For Col 'Wilk' and many of his troops the epilogue to 'Burza' in their area was tragedy.

3. *'Burza' in the Lwow Area*

On 23 July 1944 the Russo–German battle for Lwow – the capital of Galicia – begun. It lasted for four days. The Home Army units, consisting of 3,000 men, took part in the fighting for the city under

[1] Despatch from the Commander of the Wilno Area to the Commander of the Home Army, 15 July 1944, Ldz. 13167, APUST.

[2] Cf. *Drogi Cichociemnych* (London, 1961), p. 161ff.

[3] Despatch from Lt-Col 'Strychanski', 17 July 1944, Ldz. 13168, APUST.

[4] Despatch from the Commander of the Nowogrodek Area to the Commander of the Home Army, 17 July 1944, Ldz. 13102, APUST.

[5] Despatch from the Commander of the Nowogrodek Area to the Commander of the Home Army, 27 August 1944, Ldz. 13106, APUST.

the command of Col W. Filipowski ('Janka'), Home Army Commander for the Lwow Area.

Nevertheless, by 26 July the Russians had already ceased to use the Poles in the struggle because their 'units were untrained and badly armed, which, combined with their great zeal, had been causing them heavy losses'.[1] It is claimed that another 4,000 of Col Filipowski's soldiers fought against the Germans in the neighbourhood of Lwow.[2] While the battle was in progress Russo–Polish relations were correct, as in Volhynia and Wilno. Moreover, in Lwow as in Wilno, when the fighting had ended the Poles tried to stress, to the Russians, the Polish character of this town. The Soviet response to this was swift and unequivocal.[3] On 27 July Col Filipowski was told by the Russian General Grushko that

> for the time being Lwow is Soviet and Ukrainian ... a Polish government led by Morawski is in existence, and the Polish Army, under the command of Zymierski, is fighting against the Germans. The Home Army units fighting against the Germans will be incorporated into the Polish Army. The Polish administration ... will be subordinated to the Soviet organs.[4]

In his turn, Col Filipowski informed Gen Grushko that he would submit his own point of view to the Red Army Front Commander. On the following day – 28 July – Col Filipowski met the representative of the Soviet Front Commander, who told him that the region of Lwow 'belongs to the Soviet Union', and ordered him to instruct his troops 'to lay down arms within two hours and disband. The Soviet authorities will proclaim general mobilisation. The Poles will have the choice of joining either the Berling Army or the Soviet Army. The Home Army officers who are exempted from the mobilisation may retain their arms and voluntarily join the Berling Army.'

The Polish Commander, faced, as he put it, by 'compelling circumstances', ordered his troops to disband.[5] Two days later he told Warsaw that his units were already disarmed and their organisa-

---

[1] Despatch from the Commander of the Lwow Area to the Commander of the Home Army, 26 July 1944, Ldz. 13123, APUST.
[2] Despatch from the Commander of the Lwow Area to the Commander of the Home Army, 27 July 1944, Ldz. 13212, APUST.
[3] The Affidavit of Major 'Draza', APUST.
[4] Despatch from the Commander of the Lwow Area to the Commander of the Home Army, 27 July 1944, Ldz. 13212, APUST.
[5] Despatch from the Commander of the Lwow Area to the Commander of the Home Army, 27 July 1944, Ldz. 13163, APUST.

tion was dissolved.[1] He himself was leaving Lwow for talks with the C-in-C of the Polish Army serving under Russian Command. Col Filipowski intended to collaborate with this army provided that an agreement was reached between Mikolajczyk, who was then in Moscow, and the newly-formed Communist-sponsored Polish Committee of National Liberation. His plan was approved by the Government's Delegate for Lwow.[2] Col Filipowski considered this step to be 'the only realistic position to adopt'.[3] In fact, he was trying to reach an understanding with the Communists. Nevertheless, on 31 July the Russians arrested some Home Army officers in Lwow.[4]

At the same time Bor-Komorowski issued an order calling upon his soldiers east of the Curzon Line to enlist in the Berling Army, when faced with 'forced call-up' by the Soviets.[5] The issuing of this order by the Home Army Command plainly testified to the fact that, as an anti-Soviet demonstration east of the Curzon Line, 'Burza' had ended in unqualified disaster. This fiasco was only to be expected. Indeed, it had been predicted by Grot-Rowecki as early as 1943, in his dialogue with Sikorski. During this the then Premier and C-in-C had ordered the Home Army Command to evacuate its troops from the territories east of the Curzon Line if the Russians were to enter them in force and without a previous agreement with the exiled Government. In view of this prediction, it is hard to imagine why Bor-Komorowski decided to stage 'Burza' as a partly anti-Soviet operation in these regions, unless he wished to establish Polish claims to them 'in spite of all and against all', regardless of the consequences, prompted by his spirit of political intransigence, so assiduously encouraged and cultivated by Sosnkowski. By launching 'Burza' in the disputed territories Bor-Komorowski was adopting a course which was bound to antagonise the Russians even further, even though he managed, in the course of operations in these territories to display the genuinely anti-German character of his force and to enter into temporary qualified collaboration with the

[1] Despatch from the Commander of the Lwow Area to the Commander of the Home Army, 30 July 1944, Ldz. 6238, APUST.

[2] *Ibid.*

[3] Despatch from the Commander of the Lwow Area to the Commander of the Home Army, 30 July 1944, Ldz. 6257/tjn/44. APUST.

[4] Despatch from the Lwow Area to the Commander of the Home Army, 11 August 1944, Ldz. 6725, APUST.

[5] Despatch from the Commander of the Home Army to the C-in-C, 31 July 1944, Ldz. 6420/tjn/33. APUST.

Russians. What is more, the disastrous epilogue to 'Burza' in the east failed to lead to its abandonment or to the revision of its aims and methods. Instead, the failure of the plan in Volhynia, Wilno and Lwow convinced the Home Army leaders that even greater effort and sacrifice was needed. They must amplify its political and military aspects, even though they knew well that their decision to stage 'Burza' in the east had, in essence, simply precipitated the wholesale liquidation of their movement in the disputed territories.[1] 'An effort was needed', wrote General L. Okulicki, one of the authors of the Warsaw uprising, 'which would stir the conscience of the world . . . an effort which would display our extreme good will to Russia [and] which would even more strongly accentuate her behaviour towards us. The battles which our units fought in Volhynia, the Wilno region and Lwow could not accomplish this task – since, in spite of our heavy sacrifices, they were battles of a local character only, and consequently could not raise in the world even an echo commensurate with their military significance.'[2]

On 1 August 1944 Warsaw was to stage the supreme effort to which Okulicki referred.

There is, then, an obvious connection between the failure of 'Burza' east of the Curzon Line and Bor-Komorowski's decision to begin hostilities against the Germans in the capital of Poland. After Wilno and Lwow the Home Army High Command was fully convinced that only Warsaw could provide the ideal theatre for the final act of 'Burza'. In the second half of July 1944 the Home authorities finally discovered the political importance of Warsaw for their plans to act as hosts to the victorious Russians.

[1] The course of 'Burza' in other districts of pre-war eastern Poland cannot accurately be reconstructed due to the lack of sufficient data. Cf. *Polskie Sily Zbrojne, op. cit.*, pp. 621ff.
[2] Letter from Gen L. Okulicki to the President of the Republic, 9 December 1944, No. 1780/1, APUST.

8

The Fate of Warsaw

1. The Preliminary Decision

The decision to begin hostilities against the Germans in the capital of Poland was taken in Warsaw in the second half of July 1944. The preliminary decision was made between 21 July and 25 July, while the final order to begin Home Army operations in Warsaw was issued early in the evening of 31 July 1944.

Before 21 July, a battle for the city had been contemplated only as part of a 'universal and simultaneous rising'. The capture of Warsaw, at the moment of German collapse on the Eastern Front, was to be an essential feature of this operation. This is supported by ample evidence. In March 1944 Gen Bor-Komorowski decided to specifically exclude the capital from the 'Burza' operations to save the city from destruction and spare its population unnecessary suffering.[1] The Home Army troops in Warsaw were charged only with the duty of protecting the population from possible German excesses and forced evacuation during the German retreat from the city. In accordance with this plan, it was envisaged that a well-armed Home Army unit, about 4,000 strong, would leave Warsaw to fight against the Germans outside the city.[2]

What is more significant, from March 1944 weapons received from British sources, or made clandestinely, were not stored for future use in Warsaw, being directed instead to the Home Army's eastern regions, which were the first to shoulder the main burden of 'Burza'.[3] Hence, as late as 7 July 1944, on the direct orders of Bor-Komorowski

---

[1] An interview with Gen T. Bor-Komorowski, *Biuletyn Informacyjny Kola AK*, No. 10, July–August 1947; Gen 'Monter', 'Zeszloroczne Powstanie', *Polska Walczaca*, No. 46 (1945); Gen Tadeusz Pelczynski, 'Powstanie Warszawskie', *Polska Walczaca*, No. 31 (1946); Col Jan. Rzepecki, 'Jeszeze o Decyzji Podjecia Walki w Warszawie', *Wojskowy Przeglad Historyczny* (Warsaw, 1958), No. 4 (9) p. 333.

[2] *Polski Sily Zbrojne, op. cit.*, p. 651; Adam Borkiewicz, *Powstanie Warszawskie* (Warsaw, 1957), p. 20.

[3] Adam Borkiewicz, *op. cit.*, p. 20.

900 sub-machine guns and appropriate ammunition were sent from Warsaw's arms caches to eastern Poland.[1] Even during the fortnight immediately preceding the outbreak of the rising a further consignment of 60 sub-machine guns and 4,400 rounds of ammunition was despatched from Warsaw to the east.[2] Thus, the March decision to exclude Warsaw from 'Burza' led to the serious depletion of the city's clandestine armoury shortly before one of the greatest trials in its eventful history, in spite of the fact that the capital was poorer in arms than other regions, where direct drops from the British-held bases could be arranged, and where storage presented fewer problems. Furthermore, in June and early July 1944 the Polish authorities were seriously considering the idea of persuading the Germans, through Vatican and Swiss channels, to declare Warsaw an open city and thus exclude it altogether from the area of projected military operations.[3]

Finally, on 14 July 1944 the Home Commander reported to London:

> In view of the present state of the German forces in Poland and their anti-insurrectionary preparations, which consist of turning every building occupied by their units, and even offices, into defensive fortresses with bunkers and barbed wire, the rising has no prospect of success.
>
> It may be successful in the event of the German collapse and the disintegration of their troops. Under the present conditions the carrying out of the rising, even with outstanding support in arms and co-operation from the air-force and airborne troops, would have to be paid for in heavy losses.

However, in the same report Bor-Komorowski stated that the Soviet summer offensive in White Russia – against the middle sector of the German Eastern Front – which had started in late June, had 'achieved surprisingly rapid results'. In his estimation the German defences in this sector had been broken, and the German retreat there resembled a headlong rout. In his opinion the Russian breakthrough had created a highly dangerous situation for the German forces in the north, by making it possible for the Russians to isolate them from their bases in East Prussia and perhaps even to push them

---

[1] *Ibid.*, p. 34.
[2] Aleksander Skarzynski, *Polityczne Przyczyny Powstania Warszawskiego* (Warsaw, 1964), p. 202.
[3] Despatch from the Government's Delegate to the Prime Minister, No. 71, 5 July 1944, Ldz. K.4116/44, GSHI–PRM, L9.

to the Baltic. Hence, he argued, the Red Army had opened for itself *'the gateway to Warsaw'*. He felt that the Soviet offensive could only be halted by either Russian 'logistic difficulties' or by 'a German counter-offensive undertaken by their reserve units . . .' He also expected a new Soviet offensive in the northern part of the Ukraine.[1]

He claimed that the Germans had suffered a serious defeat in the middle sector of their Eastern Front, as a result of which they might be compelled to retreat even further to the West.

In this report Bor-Komorowski was concerned only with the possible national insurrection and not with Warsaw; nevertheless, it was obvious that before 14 July he had no intention whatsoever of starting hostilities in the capital, either within the framework of the 'universal and simultaneous rising' or of 'Burza'.

In the course of a week he changed his mind abruptly and by 21 July 1944 had become convinced that Warsaw should be liberated from the Germans by Polish effort before the anticipated entry of the Red Army into the city; he asked the Government's Delegate – Jan Stanislaw Jankowski – to approve his decision.[2]

The events leading to this important new decision are obscured by veiled innuendoes which it is difficult to disentangle. It is alleged that in the second half of July 1944 a meeting took place between three high-ranking officers of the Home Army Command – Gen T. Pelczynski, Bor-Komorowski's Chief of Staff, Gen L. Okulicki, the Chief of Operations and Col J. Szostak, the Chief of the Operational Bureau – during which Gen Pelczynski 'discussed . . . the problem of the need to undertake "Burza" in Warsaw . . . he stressed that he would try to convince Bor and Jankowski of the necessity for the struggle . . .'[3]

Thus it appears that within the Command of the Home Army, a small but influential pressure group was formed whose members favoured the staging of a battle in Warsaw and decided to urge their plans on their superiors. If this meeting took place, it can be described as the first step, allegedly taken on the initiative of Pelczynski, towards the insurrection.[4]

[1] Report from the Commander of the Home Army to the C-in-C No. 243, 14 July 1944, received in London on 8 August 1944, Ldz. 6302/44, APUST. My italics.

[2] Transcript of an interview with Gen Bor-Komorowski broadcast by Radio Free Europe on 15 November 1957, APUST.

[3] Adam Borkiewicz, *op. cit.*, p. 21, f. 3.

[4] In 1964 Gen Pelczynski stated that because his memory was weak on this point he could neither confirm nor deny that the meeting actually took place; Gen

On 21 July there was a meeting of the three Generals, Bor-Komorowski, Pelczynski and Okulicki, during which Okulicki submitted the proposal that Warsaw should be occupied by the Home Army before the Russian entry into the capital.[1] After a detailed discussion Okulicki's proposal was accepted by Bor-Komorowski.[2] It is interesting to note that Okulicki and Pelczynski were named by Borkiewicz as two of the three officers who allegedly had met to discuss the matter before this conference. Whatever may have happened before 21 July, it is obvious that the idea of launching a battle in Warsaw did not originate with the Home Commander who merely approved Okulicki's suggestion in consultation with Pelczynski.[3] Agreement between the generals represented the crucial step towards the preliminary decision to launch the rising. Bor-Komorowski still regards Okulicki as the originator and main protagonist of the idea that the Home Army should capture Warsaw.[4]

After the conference Bor-Komorowski sent to London a highly optimistic appraisal of the strategic situation in the east. He claimed:

On the Eastern Front the Germans have suffered a defeat. The three [German] armies holding the middle sector of the front have been crushed and the OKW [Oberkommando der Wehrmacht] have failed to

Pelczynski's oral evidence. In August 1969 Col Szostak wrote that this meeting did in fact take place and confirmed Borkiewicz's account of it, adding, however, that Gen Okulicki supported Gen Pelczynski's plan to take Warsaw. J. Szostak, 'Dziesiec dni przed wybuchem powstania w Warszawie 1944 r.', *Stolica*, No. 31 (1130), 3 August 1969. See also: J. Ciechanowski, *op. cit.*, pp. 253–5.

[1] Jozef Garlinski, 'Decyzja Podjecia Walki o Warszawe – wywiad z gen. Tadeuszem Borem-Komorowskim', *Tydzien Polski*, No. 31 (184), 1 August 1964.

[2] *Ibid.*

[3] *Ibid.*

[4] Maj-Gen L. Okulicki, born in 1898 of peasant stock, was a professional soldier with a fine war record. In 1914, at the age of sixteen, he joined Pilsudski's Legions, with which he served until they were disbanded in 1917. From 1918 he served in the Polish Army and fought with distinction in the Russo–Polish War of 1920. In the inter-war period he attended the Staff College and served on the General Staff. In 1939 he took an outstanding part in the defence of Warsaw. He was one of the thirteen military founders of the Underground Army. In January 1941 he was arrested in Lwow by the Russians and spent the next eight months in a Russian prison. On his release he re-joined the Polish Army and served with Gen Anders' troops in the U.S.S.R. and the Middle East. At the end of 1943 he again volunteered for Underground work and was parachuted into Poland in June 1944 as the special representative of Gen Sosnkowski, who charged him with the duty of explaining his ideas concerning the role of the Resistance to the Home Army leaders. Gen Bor-Komorowski appointed him his deputy Chief of Staff and Head of Operations. Gen Okulicki's File, APUST.

replace them by bringing in fresh forces in sufficient numbers to stop the Soviet Army. The slowing down of the Soviet advance on this sector is probably due ... to the temporary fatigue of the Soviet forces. I foresee that the Soviet advance ... will gather momentum when their fatigue is overcome.

... The Soviet offensive [started on 18 July] south of Prypet has forced a wide gateway for further advance to the West. The Germans had not sufficient reserves ... to stop the Soviet advance. ... The Soviet advance on this sector will be rapid and will reach and *cross the Vistula in a further advance to the West without any effective or serious German counter-thrust.*

The German hold on their northern front does not represent any serious idea of an operational counter-stroke on their part ... It appears certain that on the Eastern Front the Germans are incapable of wresting the initiative from the Soviet hands, or of successful opposition. Recently, we have observed more frequent signs of the disintegration of the German forces, who are tired and show no will to fight.

The recent attempt on Hitler's life, together with the military position of Germany, may lead at any moment to their collapse. This compels us to maintain a constant state of readiness for the rising [that is, the simultaneous general rising].

In view of this I have ordered a state of alertness for the rising from 25.VII., at 001 hours, without calling off 'Burza,' which is still being implemented.[1]

At this time the Command of the Home Army was planning to stage a 'universal and simultaneous insurrection' in the event of German military or political collapse while at the same time continuing 'Burza' which was synchronised with the Soviet offensive. The action in Warsaw might take place, therefore, either within the framework of a 'universal and simultaneous insurrection' or within that of 'Burza', as a localised uprising. In fact, the latter course was adopted though a 'state of alert' for a universal insurrection, introduced on 25 July, continued until the middle of August, when it was finally repealed. On 31 July the three Generals decided that Warsaw should rise alone.

As a result of fresh developments at the Eastern Front and in Hitler's Headquarters in East Prussia, the Home Army Commanders were convinced that the German collapse was imminent. They were in high spirits, relished the prospects of final victory and

---

[1] Despatch from the Commander of the Home Army to the C-in-C, 21 July 1944, Ldz. 5916/tj, APUST. My italics. Bor-Komorowski revoked this order on 7 August.

were determined to act swiftly. At this stage they even thought seriously of launching the national insurrection which would constitute the crowning event to their own long and arduous struggle against the Germans, and a fitting contribution to the Allied victory over Nazism.

Almost simultaneously Bor-Komorowski despatched another urgent communication to London, in which he explained to the exiled authorities his political conclusions and recommendations arising out of the appraisal of the military situation which he had sent to London on 21 July. The tone of this new despatch was coloured by his belief that the Germans were on the verge of imminent collapse under the combined Soviet and Anglo–Saxon thrusts. To him, his duty was plain; the Home Army's struggle against the Germans must be continued to the very end, even though he was convinced that the Russians, who were advancing through Poland, were aiming at the 'liquidation of Polish independence', or at least at the political subordination of Poland to their will, after the incorporation of the Polish inter-war eastern borderlands into the U.S.S.R. In his opinion it was imperative for the Polish people, especially their leaders, to realise fully all the implications of the predicament which was facing them, as otherwise it would be 'impossible to mobilise all Polish forces for a *political campaign against Russia which we must wage and win*. In this campaign we can count on Anglo–Saxon help only when we display our determination to win it and skilfully to throw on to the scales all our resources.'

He expected that the Russians might employ very artful and elastic tactics in Poland, ranging from 'brutal occupation and terror' to 'simulated leniency and official abstention from interference in Polish internal affairs, while at the same time stirring up a part of the population [against the pro-London authorities] and spreading anarchy in order to intervene later . . . to restore peace and order'.[1]

He concluded his despatch by imploring his superiors abroad:

1. Not to stop our struggle against the Germans, even for a moment.
2. To mobilise spiritually the entire population at Home for the struggle against Russia. . . .

[1] Despatch from the Commander of the Home Army to the C-in-C, 22 July 1944, Ldz. 59881/tj/44, GSHI–PRM, L6. My italics.

3. To crush the irresponsible activity of the ONR [extreme right-wing nationalists] . . .
4. To detach from the Soviets as many as possible of the Polish elements already standing at their disposal . . .
5. In the event of a Soviet attempt to violate Poland, to undertake open struggle against them.

In addition, Bor-Komorowski called upon the Government to issue, at once, a number of decrees initiating social reforms in Poland. These must be radical, he insisted, if they were to inspire the urban and rural masses with full confidence in the pro-London authorities. They should include the appropriation, by the State and without compensation, of large estates in order to implement agrarian reform; nationalisation of the main sectors of industry and creation of workers' councils; universal free education and social welfare; and finally the passing of new electoral laws regulating general and local elections. He also demanded energetic preparations for the suppression of right-wing and left-wing extremists.[1]

Thus, Bor-Komorowski was grimly determined to wage and win the struggle for power in Poland and was prepared to fight against all the forces which, in his estimation, threatened the future of the London camp. His resolution must have been further strengthened during the next few days, between 23 July and 26 July, by the signs of German collapse and panic in Warsaw itself, where the hasty evacuation of the German administrative, and security organs, and rear installations of the *Wehrmacht* was taking place.[2]

Discussions between Bor-Komorowski and members of his immediate entourage on the staging of a battle in Warsaw ended on 22 July. On the same day the Home Commander approached Jankowski, the Government's Delegate, with the suggestion that Warsaw should be included in 'Burza'. The talks between Bor-Komorowski and Jankowski were brief and they reached full agreement about the need to capture the capital before the Russians entered it.[3] This was not surprising, in view of the fact that Jankowski had been, as early as 12 July, fully convinced of the 'political

---

[1] Appendix to the Despatch from the Commander of the Home Army to the C-in-C, 22 July 1944, Ldz. 5988/tj/44, GSHI–PRM, L6.
[2] *Polskie Siły Zbrojne, op. cit.*, p. 697.
[3] Bor-Komorowski's statement of 18 April 1951, 'Czwarte zebranie relacyjne w inst. J. Pilsudskiego w Londynie: Decyzja walki o Warszawe w 1944 r, 18/4/1951', APUST. Hereafter referred to as Bor-Komorowski's statement of 18 April 1951.

importance'[1] of Warsaw for the London camp and their plans for capturing power in Poland; Bor-Komorowski's suggestion fell on prepared ground.[2]

After his initial meeting with Jankowski, and on the suggestion of his Chief of Staff, Bor-Komorowski asked the Government's Delegate to arrange a meeting between them and the Presidium of the Council of National Unity, at which he intended to present the Home Army's case to the leading representatives of the four main political parties forming the backbone of the secret State. Jankowski agreed to this suggestion, although he asked Bor-Komorowski to submit to him beforehand a draft of the questions he wished to put to the politicians about the need for the Home Army to take Warsaw. More significant and even somewhat sinister, Jankowski urged Bor-Komorowski to 'formulate the questions very concisely and say little'.[3] It was evident, therefore, that Jankowski was anxious to make the discussions with the Presidium as short as possible, wanting merely to solicit their approval for the plan to capture Warsaw. When the Presidium finally met it was confronted with two simple questions, formulated jointly by Bor-Komorowski and Jankowski. These questions were as follows: first, 'whether the representatives of the Council of National Unity believe that the entry of the Soviet troops into Warsaw should be forestalled by the seizure of the capital by the Home Army?' and secondly, 'What minimal period of time should, in their opinion, be secured between the seizure of the capital by the Home Army and the entry into it of the Red Army?'[4]

The Presidium answered the first question with a unanimous affirmative and, in reply to the second, decided after discussion that at least twelve hours would be needed to allow the civil administration to start functioning.[5] Bor-Komorowski presented the Presidium with an analysis of the military situation at the Russo–German Front,[6] though in view of Jankowski's insistence on brevity this cannot have been very detailed or extensive. It seems then, that when the Presidium was approving Bor-Komorowski's and Jankowski's decision they were hardly in possession of all the details concerning developments at the Eastern Front, let alone the battleworthiness of the Home Army troops in Warsaw.

---

[1] Despatch from the Government's Delegate to the Prime Minister, No. 74, 12 July 1944, Ldz. K.4775/44, GSHI–PRM, L9.

[2] Bor-Komorowski's statement of 18 April 1951.

[3] Bor-Komorowski's statement of 18 April 1951.

[4] *Polskie Siły Zbrojne, op. cit.*, p. 658.   [5] *Ibid.*   [6] *Ibid.*

Whether Jankowski's attempt to control the discussions at the wider political level was prompted by deliberate determination to keep the Presidium ill-informed, or was intended merely to secure their prompt and unequivocal decision without too much argument and waste of time, or was due to reasons of security, cannot be accurately ascertained due to lack of evidence; it might be argued that he was prompted to curtail the discussions of the Presidium by all these considerations. Whatever his motives, the approval of the Presidium for the launching of the Home Army's battle for Warsaw was easily secured by Bor-Komorowski and Jankowski. The politicians approved Bor-Komorowski's decision while making the following assumptions: that his units would act during the last hours of the German stay in Warsaw by attacking German rear-guards; that the Western Allies would support the struggle; and finally that Russo–Polish collaboration would be established and operations synchronised at the last moment.[1] The Home Commander regarded the Presidium's approval as an expression of full agreement between the political leaders and himself on the need to capture Warsaw.[2]

At a Staff meeting on 24 July Gen Okulicki and Col Rzepecki unsuccessfully pressed Gen Bor-Komorowski to decide finally when the battle in Warsaw should begin.[3]

On 25 July a full-scale meeting of Bor-Komorowski's Staff was held to discuss the proposed operations in the capital. Jankowski and Col 'Monter' – (A. Chrusciel)[4] – the Commander of the Home Army units there, attended this briefing.[5] All those present at this conference concluded that the Russo–German Front might soon move into the vicinity of Warsaw, and agreed on the need to stage a Polish battle for the capital.[6] Gen Okulicki and Col Rzepecki again pressed Gen Bor-Komorowski to decide, immediately, the date of

---

[1] St Dolega-Modrzewski's statement of 18 April 1951, 'Czwarte Zebranie Relacyjne w inst. J. Pilsudskiego w Londynie 18/4/1951: Decyzja Podjecia Walki o Warszawa w. 1944 r', APUST, – hereafter referred to as Dolega-Modrzewski's statement of 18 April 1951.

[2] *Polski Sily Zbrojne*, *op. cit.*, p. 658.

[3] Iranek-Osmecki's oral evidence.

[4] Colonel A. Chrusciel – 'Monter' – born in 1895 of peasant stock, was a professional soldier who had served with distinction in the First World War and the Russo–Polish War of 1920. In the inter-war period he attended the Staff College, where he was a lecturer in tactics from 1936 to 1938. In 1939 he commanded an infantry regiment. From April 1941 he was the Commander of the Home Army Warsaw Area. Gen Chrusciel's File, APUST.

[5] Adam Borkiewicz, *op. cit.*, p. 22.

[6] Aleksander Skarzynski, *op. cit.*, p. 215.

the Home Army's attack in Warsaw.[1] Once more, their hasty and impetuous representations were, to their dissatisfaction, rejected by their superior. This convinced them that the Home Commander was incapable of taking the final decision. Prompted by this unwarranted assumption, Okulicki and Rzepecki approached Iranek-Osmecki, during a break in the conference, and urged him to report the situation at the front to Bor-Komorowski in such a way as to make the outbreak of the fighting a foregone conclusion. They urged the Chief of Intelligence to present, if necessary, a distorted picture of the military situation to compel Bor-Komorowski to issue his final order.

Iranek-Osmecki rejected this request, as he considered such action to be unprofessional and unethical. He told Okulicki and Rzepecki that he would report what his conscience and his sense of duty dictated, although he did not inform Bor-Komorowski of their highly irregular request. The Chief of Intelligence's own opinion, which he expressed at the conference, was that the Germans would defend Warsaw and that there might be a German counter-attack against the advancing Russians, from the region of Wyszkow, north-west of the capital. He was convinced that on the approaches to Warsaw there would be a Russo–German battle which would affect the situation in the city and its neighbourhood. He urged that the timing of the Home Army's operations in Warsaw should be made dependent, to some extent, upon the outcome of this Russo–German encounter in the vicinity of the city. Hence, he was opposed to a premature decision on the date of the Home Army's attack. At the same time he believed that the German forces were too weak to rebuff the Russians decisively, and anticipated a repetition of the attempt on Hitler's life and German collapse. Iranek-Osmecki's arguments were accepted and the date of the attack was left undecided.[2] The briefing ended with a dispatch approved by Jankowski being sent to London from Bor-Komorowski. It stated: '*We are ready at any time to launch the battle for Warsaw*. The participation of the [Polish] Parachute Brigade [stationed in the U.K.] in this battle

[1] Oral evidence of Bor-Komorowski and Iranek-Osmecki.
[2] Iranek-Osmecki's oral evidence. See also: J. Ciechanowski, *op. cit.*, p. 265. Colonel Rzepecki denied, however, that he had ever tried to influence Col Iranek-Osmecki's reports in any way. Yet, he admitted that he had believed that there should be a battle for Warsaw, and that he and Gen Okulicki had repeatedly asked Bor-Komorowski when it would start. Col Rzepecki's oral evidence.

would have immense political and tactical significance. Prepare for the possible bombing of air-fields in the neighbourhood of Warsaw at our request. *I will report the commencement of the battle.*'[1] Thus the initial decision to throw Warsaw into the turmoil of battle was irrevocably made.

The decision to free Warsaw by Secret Army efforts was taken at a time when the Germans were hastily evacuating the capital and seemed to have lost their will to defend it. The German flight from Warsaw continued until 26 July, when it gradually began to die down.[2] The signs of a German collapse in the region of the city encouraged the Poles to rise and fight; the leaders of the Underground, spurred by the spectacle of the German flight, including that of their administrative and security organs, had decided to play *va banque* and present their superiors in London with a ready-made decision, arrived at independently of their Government and the C-in-C. At no stage of their official deliberations, which lasted at least five days – from 21 July to 25 July – did they seek the Government's opinions concerning their plans to capture Warsaw. Thus, the resistance leaders bear the heaviest responsibility for this momentous decision.

Bor-Komorowski's despatch to London was couched in such categorical terms that it left little scope for dissension among the Polish leaders abroad on the wisdom and perspicacity of the decision reached in Warsaw; they were simply told to 'expect the outbreak of hostilities in the capital at any time' and were asked to arrange for British support. There was to be no dialogue between Warsaw and London on this subject. Probably only a most categorical order forbidding the whole venture, issuing from the Cabinet and C-in-C, would have caused the Home leaders to revise their plans. Time was running out. But Bor-Komorowski's assertion that the underground authorities were 'ready at any time' to commence operations against the Germans in Warsaw, in reality only meant that an agreement had been reached between the military and political leaders of the pro-London movement in the city, concerning the need to begin fighting at some unspecified date, for no immediate military preparations for specific anti-German action were as yet being made. Indeed, on the day before the despatch – that is, on 24 July – the Home Commander

[1] Despatch from the Commander of the Home Army to the C-in-C, No. 1441, 25 July 1944, Ldz. 6024, APUST. My italics.
[2] Cf. Aleksander Skarzynski, *op. cit.*, p. 214 and Jerzy Kirchmayer, *Powstanie Warszawskie* (Warsaw, 1959), p. 92.

had rejected Col 'Monter's' suggestion that he should alert his troops and put them on a war-footing.[1] The all-round military preparations were to follow later. For the time being – that is, from 25 July onwards – the attention of the Home Army leaders was mainly preoccupied with the question of the skilful timing of their operations. This meant that the initiative was passing entirely into the hands of Bor-Komorowski and his Staff, as the military experts of the Secret State. The politicians in Warsaw could play only a minor role in these military calculations.

This is confirmed in an order sent by Gen Pelczynski to Col 'Monter' on July 26, stating:

> It might be necessary to begin the battle for Warsaw at any time. The H.Q. will issue the order to begin the struggle, perhaps on your instigation. You will have to be ready to attack within 8 (eight) hours from the moment of decision. . . .
>
> To gain the data necessary for making the decision I instruct you immediately to undertake intensive and adequate reconnaisance in the directions of Modlin, Wyszkow, Tluszcz, Minsk-Mazowiecki, Garwolin, Gora Kalwaria – Warka [that is, on the north-eastern, eastern and south-eastern approaches to the city]. It is required to find out:
>
> (1) whether the Germans intend to defend Warsaw,
>
> (2) which German forces from these sectors are withdrawing to Warsaw,
>
> (3) where there is contact between the Germans and Soviets.
>
> This information is necessary to calculate the moment of German withdrawal from Warsaw.[2]

The underground Commanders intended to start their armed attack on the Germans at a time when the Russians would be so near to Warsaw that they would be able to *'buttress our success'*, by their entry into the city.[3] Meanwhile, on 23 July the Red Army occupied Lublin and the same day Moscow publicly announced the creation of the Polish Committee of National Liberation, PKWN, which came into being as a result of a decree issued by the Communist-sponsored National Council of the Homeland on 21 July. This decree defined the PKWN as 'a provisional executive authority to lead the nation's struggle for independence and restore the Polish

---

[1] A. Borkiewicz, *op. cit.*, p. 22.   [2] A. Skarzynski, *op. cit.*, p. 221.
[3] T. Pelczynski's statement of 18 April 1951, 'Czwarte Zebranie Relacyjne w inst. J. Pilsudskiego w Londynie 18/4/1951: Decyzja Podjecia Walki o Warszawe w 1944 r', APUST – hereafter referred to as Pelczynski's statement of 18 April 1951. My italics.

state'.[1] Another decree, passed on the same day, announced the
establishment of a new Polish Army as the outcome of a merger
between the Polish forces recruited in the U.S.S.R. and the People's
Army, AL, over which the PKWN assumed full authority.[2] In a
manifesto to the Polish people dated 22 July the Committee claimed
full legal authority, denounced the exiled Government as an 'illegal
and self-styled authority' which was 'driving Poland to a new
disaster', and asked the nation to collaborate closely with the Red
Army in the liberation of their country.[3] The manifesto promised
widespread social reforms and the democratisation of Polish
internal life by a return to the provisions of the 1921 Constitution.
The reforms were to include the solution of the agrarian question and
nationalisation of the German-held or -controlled means of pro-
duction and distribution. The right to own property was to be
protected and free enterprise would be encouraged.

The words 'socialism' and 'communism' did not appear in the
manifesto, which indicates that the Committee was making a
deliberate effort to gain support among non-communists.[4] The
problem of the Russo–Polish frontiers was to be 'settled by mutual
agreement' between Poland and the U.S.S.R. The manifesto envisaged Poland's expansion to the west at the expense of Germany.[5]

The formation of the PKWN was a major step towards the eventual
assumption of political power by the Communists and their allies.

2. The Final Decision

On 26 July there was a Staff meeting, attended by Jankowski and
Col 'Monter', to discuss the timing of the Home Army's operations
in Warsaw.[6] Gen Pelczynski referred the military situation to the
assembled officers and stated that to start the battle at this stage
would be unjustified, although it was imperative to be prepared for it.

After the Chief of Staff's exposé all those present at the briefing
were asked by Bor-Komorowski to express their opinions on the

[1] *Polski Ruch Robotniczy*, p. 513.
[2] *Ibid.*
[3] *Polski Ruch Robotniczy*, p. 514.
[4] Cf. M. K. Dziewanowski, *The Communist Party of Poland – An Outline of History* (Cambridge, Mass., 1959), p. 177.
[5] *Ibid.*
[6] Colonel J. Rzepecki, 'W Sprawie Decyzji Podjecia Walki w Warszawie', *Wojskowy Przeglad Historyczny* (Warsaw, 1958), No. 2 (7), p. 322.

planned battle. All were unanimous in agreeing that political considerations made the battle essential. They were divided, however, on the question of timing. Col 'Kuczaba' (K. Pluta-Czachowski) the Chief Signals Officer, stressed the lack of operational liaison with the Red Army and proposed that they should begin fighting when the Russians forced the Vistula bridges. In the opinion of Col Rzepecki, the Head of the Information and Propaganda Bureau, the establishment of direct contact between the Home Army and the Soviet High Command was impossible; he expressed the view that the Government was probably trying to re-establish relations with Moscow and that, indeed, they might succeed 'at any time: a day before or after the beginning of the struggle'.[1] The Chief of Intelligence, Col 'Heller' (K. Iranek-Osmecki) pointed out that the situation east of Warsaw was far from clear, and that the Germans had reinforced their units in the neighbourhood of Warsaw by sending in three SS armoured divisions during the last few days. Therefore, he urged extreme caution and the postponement of the final decision. Three other officers spoke in similar vein. They were Gen 'Laszcz' (A. Skroczynski), Col 'Sek' (J. Bokszczanin) and Lt-Col 'Benedykt' (L. Muzyczka). Gen Okulicki and Colonels 'Sedzia' (J. Rzepecki), Szostak and 'Monter' demanded immediate action. Col 'Monter' argued that the German troops defending the Warsaw bridgehead were of low quality and that the Soviet reconnaissance units were already infiltrating it through gaps in the German defences. He claimed that there were no German fortifications east of Warsaw. Nevertheless 'Monter' admitted that his troops were very poorly armed.[2] Although it is possible to assess with great accuracy the amount of arms at Col 'Monter's' disposal during the last days of July 1944, it is claimed that on 29 February that year his troops, including the units directly subordinate to Bor-Komorowski's Headquarters, had, according to Home Army reports, 20 machine-guns, 98 light machine-guns, 604 sub-machine-guns, 1,386 rifles, 2,665 pistols and revolvers, two anti-tank guns, four 'P.I.A.Ts', 12 anti-tank rifles, 50,100 grenades and 5,000 'Molotov Cocktails'. The supplies of ammunition were also low. They included 35,049 rounds of ammunition for machine-guns, 15,800 for light machine-guns, 121,000 for sub-machine-guns, 234,000 for rifles, 52,000 for pistols and revolvers, 100 for anti-tank guns, 1,170 for anti-tank rifles and

[1] *Ibid.*
[2] Adam Borkiewicz, *op. cit.*, p. 23.

700 kilogrammes of explosives.[1] In addition some of the Home Army soldiers and units possessed a certain number of officially unregistered pistols and revolvers, which could easily be stored.[2] These figures amply reveal a conspicuous shortage of even light arms in Warsaw, and a virtual lack of the heavy support weapons, such as mortars, bazookas, anti-tank and anti-aircraft guns, so essential for offensive operations even of a guerrilla type, let alone an attack on well-fortified German objectives.[3]

Col 'Monter's' admission had a dampening effect on those present at the meeting.[4] He explained that the unexpected shortage of arms was due to the fact that the Germans had managed to detect some of the clandestine arsenals in Warsaw, and also to the fact that they had billeted their troops in the immediate vicinity of arms-caches, so making recovery impossible.[5] He believed, nevertheless, that with the means at his disposal he would be able to remain on the offensive during the first three or four days of the fighting, and added that even without help from the Russians he would be able to stay on the defensive for a further fortnight. He hoped to capture more arms from the Germans, or to acquire them from British and Polish air-drops while fighting was in progress. He calculated that the entry of the Red Army into the capital would settle the outcome.

Col 'Monter' also proposed that in order to surprise the enemy all the German-held objectives should be attacked simultaneously by his units. The main effort was to be directed, however, at the seizure of the city centre, together with the bridges across the Vistula and railway stations situated in this part of the capital. He intended to keep strong reserves at his disposal, to be deployed according to the demands of the situation.[6] His plan was ambitious and audacious.

Bor-Komorowski and Jankowski decided that the Home Army would stage its battle for Warsaw within the next few days, depending on the developments on the Russo–German front and the German behaviour in the city.

---

[1] *Polskie Sily Zbrojne*, *op. cit.*, p. 680.

[2] Cf. *Ibid.*, pp. 679ff.

[3] Skarzynski claims that on 1 August 1944 the Home Army troops in the Warsaw Area – which included the city and its immediate neighbourhood – possessed 39 machine-guns, 130 light machine-guns, 608 sub-machine-guns, 2,410 rifles, 2,818 pistols and revolvers, 21 anti-tank rifles, four mortars and 36,429 grenades. Aleksander Skarzynski, *op. cit.*, p. 339; for the state of the Home Army's armaments in Warsaw see also Adam Borkiewicz, *op. cit.*, p. 35.

[4] Aleksander Skarzynski, *op. cit.*, p. 220.

[5] *Ibid.*   [6] *Ibid.*

At the same conference it was arranged that from henceforth the Home Army Staff would meet twice a day – at 10 in the morning and 5 in the afternoon – to study the military situation. The Government's Delegate was to attend the afternoon briefings.[1]

On the following day – July 27 – Bor-Komorowski communicated his intentions to London, when he informed his superiors that he was determined to undertake his own operations in Warsaw pending the result of the Russo–German battle on the eastern bank of the Vistula. He stated that the German forces fighting on the approaches to Warsaw were 'considerably reinforced' by the arrival of one or two armed divisions and elements of the Herman Goering Division. He estimated their strength at ten divisions. He also reported that the Germans had started to counter-attack in the region of Siedlce-Lukow in the direction of Brest-Litovsk, to relieve their garrison. Nevertheless, he regarded the prospect of further Soviet attack on Radom and Warsaw, from the Deblin-Pulawy region, where the Russians were trying to establish their bridgehead on the western bank of the Vistula, as a 'strong probability'. He also told London: '*After the panic evacuation of Warsaw from 22 to 25 July the Germans have recovered. The German administrative authorities have returned and have started to function again.*'

Finally, he told the C-in-C that on 25 July the Russians had started to disarm his 27th Division.

> This fact, as well as the hostile attitude to our forces in the Vilna region, clearly indicates that the Soviets want to destroy the Home Army ... It is imperative to inform the English – drawing to their attention the fact that such an attitude on the part of the Soviets must lead to our decisive counter-measures. *It will compel us to resort to self-defence.*[2]

This message strongly indicates that on 27 July Bor-Komorowski was far from certain as to what would be the outcome of the Russo–German battle east of Warsaw, and that he considered further Soviet attack on the capital as a 'strong probability', rather than a foregone conclusion; finally, that he was planning to start his own operations in Warsaw the moment the Russian entry into the city was imminent. He was quite aware that the Germans fighting in the area of the capital were still capable of launching a counter-attack,

---

[1] Aleksander Skarzynski, *op. cit.*, p. 220. Col Iranek-Osmecki claims that this arrangement was made on 24, not 26 July, Iranek-Osmecki's oral evidence.

[2] Despatch from the Commander of the Home Army to the C-in-C, 27 July 1944, Ldz. 6114/tjn/44, GSHI–PRM, L6. My italics.

even though one of a localised and limited nature. He was apprehensive of Russian hostility to the Home Army and feared that an open Russo–Polish clash might soon develop.

The German recovery in Warsaw and its vicinity caused considerable disquiet among the political leaders of the underground, who began to fear that the Germans might try to defend Warsaw. The politicians were urging the Government's Delegate not to begin operations prematurely. They demanded that the final decision should be taken after a calm and cool assessment of the military situation.[1] This state of unease, or even despondency, among the politicians was reflected in their communication to Mikolajczyk on 28 July, demanding Anglo–American intervention in the Russo–Polish dispute:

> We have already been fighting against the German occupation for almost five years . . .
>
> The Soviets are running riot in Poland, they arrest those of the Polish military and civil authorities which have come into the open, and are creating a fictitious [Polish] Government with which they have concluded a treaty. [. . .] Our further military co-operation with the Soviets is synonymous with preparing for them the way to a new conquest of Poland.
>
> The Allies have failed to call to order this ally . . . and to guarantee Poland's independence. Under such circumstances every Pole is faced with a poignant question; what is he fighting for. Why is Polish blood flowing freely on all the battlefields . . .
>
> There must be an immediate fundamental clarification by the Allies of Poland's situation, her independence and the sovereignty of her frontiers.[2]

Meanwhile the military leaders continued their preparations for the battle. They were studying the developments at the Russo–German Front and trying to collect reliable data which would allow them to begin their hostilities against the Germans at the climax of the German withdrawal from the city. They made no attempt, however, to establish direct contact with the Soviet Command and inform them of their plans and intentions. It seems that they wished to surprise both the Germans and the Russians with their action in Warsaw.

[1] Dolega-Modrzewski's statement of 18 April 1951.
[2] Despatch from the Government's Delegate and Presidium of the Council of National Unity to the Prime Minister, No. 93, 28 July 1944, Ldz. K.4394/44, APUST, File 16, Min. Spr. Wew.

On 27 July there were further important developments. On that day Moscow published the text of an agreement reached the day before with the PKWN in Lublin, recognising the latter as the 'only lawful temporary organ of executive power' and charging it with the administration of the liberated territories and of Russo–Polish military co-operation. The agreement provided for Soviet control of military operations in Poland.[1]

Meanwhile, Ludwig Fischer, the German Governor of the Warsaw district, issued a proclamation dated 24 July instructing the Polish population to remain calm and desist from any sabotage activities which, from that date, would be punished by summary executions. The Governor asked the people not to believe the 'deceitful' allegations that the Red Army was approaching the city, and to work as usual. Further, he assured them that the *Wehrmacht* would drive the Russians back from the city as the Polish Army had in 1920.[2] At the same time strong German patrols reappeared on the streets of Warsaw, while tanks, armoured cars and military units began to patrol its main thoroughfares. The German troop movements around Warsaw continued. To the west of the city, in the Skiernie-wice-Zyrardow area, echelons of the SS armoured division 'Viking' began to de-train. In the south, in the region of the Piaseczno-Kabacki Forest, two Hungarian divisions arrived. From the Modlin-Mlociny area of the north came reports of the arrival of an unidentified German motorised division. The Germans were concentrating their artillery, on the West bank of the Vistula, near the town, while at the same time sending some infantry reinforcements to their 73rd Infantry Divisions fighting at the approaches to Praga, Warsaw's East End district. These troop movements suggested to the Home Army Commanders that the Germans were determined to defend Warsaw.

Also on 27 July Col 'Monter' told his subordinate Commanders to expect their final orders at any time and alerted the staffs of his formations in Warsaw. In the late afternoon of the same day, at about five o'clock, the Germans broadcast, over their street megaphone system, an order calling for 100,000 people to come forward to take part in the construction of fortifications around Warsaw. On the next day – 28 July – the same order appeared on street placards all over Warsaw.[3] Col 'Monter' was deeply disturbed by the German

[1] Cf. M. K. Dziewanowski, *op. cit.*, p. 177.
[2] Aleksander Skarzynski, *op. cit.*, p. 222.
[3] *Polskie Sily Zbrojne, op. cit.*, pp. 698ff.

announcement. He considered this request to be the prelude to the forced evacuation of the Polish population of the city. Further, he was fully aware that the possible deportation from Warsaw of 100,000 men and women of military age would disorganise his units and make the staging of any serious Polish military action virtually impossible.[1] To prevent such an occurrence, Col 'Monter' alerted his troops as from 7 p.m. on 28 July allegedly after consulting Bor-Komorowski.[2] He told them to concentrate in their assembly areas and to wait for their final battle orders. Meanwhile, they were to act against the Germans only in exceptional circumstances, primarily within their assembly areas.[3] In reality these directives were tantamount to issuing a preparatory order for the commencement of hostilities and in theory, like earlier instructions, could not be recalled.[4]

Col 'Monter' later explained that he had issued these instructions to set the minds of his soldiers at rest and to prevent independent acts which might have provoked a premature outbreak of hostilities.[5] In the afternnon of 28 July the order was, after all, recalled when it became obvious that the Germans were unable or unwilling to enforce their demand for volunteers to help in the construction of fortifications against the Russians.[6] In fact, this request had been virtually ignored by the citizens of the capital.[7] In the afternoon of 29 July the Home Army units were dispersed after their mobilisation, during which they had become aware of their lamentable shortage of arms. The absence of any energetic German counter-measure was, to say the least, puzzling, as it is hard to believe that the Home Army's mobilisation entirely escaped German notice. It is probable that the German authorities were still suffering from the shock of their earlier panic, or alternatively were reluctant to provoke a Polish uprising; hence, their inactivity in the face of Polish mobilisation.

Nevertheless, Bor-Komorowski and his Staff were expecting German reprisals in the immediate future and believed that forced

[1] Antoni Chrusciel ('Monter'), *Powstanie Warszawskie* (London, 1948), p. 6.
[2] W. Pobog-Malinowski, *op. cit.*, p. 652, f. 133. Bor-Komorowski claims that 'Monter' took this action without consulting him. Bor-Komorowski's oral evidence.
[3] Adam Borkiewicz, *op. cit.*, p. 25.
[4] Cf. Aleksander Skarzynski, *op. cit.*, p. 227.
[5] Antoni Chrusciel ('Monter'), *op. cit.*, p. 6.
[6] Adam Borkiewicz, *op. cit.*, p. 25.
[7] *Polskie Sily Zbrojne*, *op. cit.*, p. 698.

evacuation of the Polish population from the city was imminent and that it would take place during the Russo–German fighting for the capital.[1]

On 28 July the Home Army decided to start operations in Warsaw when the Russians broke through from the direction of Praga and began to attack from their newly-established Magnuszew bridgehead on the Vistula, south-east of Warsaw. These two developments were to signify that strategic conditions were ripe for the insurrection in the capital.[2] At the same time Stalin ordered Rokossovsky, the Commander of the Soviet armies fighting in central Poland, to occupy Praga – the East End of Warsaw – between 5 August and 8 August, and to establish bridgeheads south of Warsaw on the western bank of the Vistula.[3]

On the same day the Government's Delegate received a very important message from his Prime Minister, then en route for Moscow, empowering Jankowski to start the rising at a moment selected by him, without consulting the Cabinet in London. Mikolajczyk asked Jankowski merely to inform the Government beforehand 'if possible'.[4]

The following day another despatch arrived from London, informing the Home authorities of the political circumstances connected with Mikolajczyk's visit to Stalin.

These despatches, both highly important, were sent from London on 26 July. The first amounted to a *carte blanche* for the Home authorities' planned action, the second informed them that Mikolajczyk was making a crucial attempt to reach an understanding with Stalin.[5]

When, on 29 July, Bor-Komorowski's Staff again met to discuss the military situation the content of these messages was known to them. Although this meeting again failed to produce the final orders for the insurrection, two decisions were made which were soon to affect its course. One decision concerned the timing of the mobilisation which would precede the operation, and the other the timing of the operation itself. It was decided, on Col 'Monter's'

[1] *Ibid.* [2] Iranek-Osmecki's oral evidence.
[3] *Istoriya Velikoi Otechestvenoi Voiny Sovietskogo Soyuza 1941–1945 gg* (Moscow, 1962), vol. 4, p. 194.
[4] Despatch from the Prime Minister to the Government's Delegate, 26 July 1944, Ldz. 2088/tjn/44, GSHI–PRM, L11.
[5] Despatch from the Prime Minister to the Government's Delegate, 26 July 1944, Ldz. 2090/tjn/44, GSHI–PRM, L11.

suggestion, to stage the Home Army's attack at 5 p.m. rather than at night, as in the plan of 1942–3.[1] 'Monter' argued that switching the hour of the attack might help to surprise the Germans, as it would then take place at the height of Warsaw's rush hour, when the attention of their sentries and patrols would be distracted by heavy traffic on the streets. He also maintained that the earlier decision to start operatons at night was already known to the Germans.[2] He was reluctant to start operations at dawn as this would necessitate keeping the troops in the assembly areas throughout the night. This might lead to their being detected by the Gestapo and might force upon them heavy fighting during the long hours of daylight after their initial attack. By starting his attack in the late afternoon he hoped to gain the time necessary to re-group his forces and to consolidate their gains under the cover of darkness.[3]

This plan had two main weaknesses: first, the troops expected and had been trained to launch their attacks at night, and secondly the new plan meant that, by attacking in broad daylight, they would be fully exposed, at the moment of attack, to superior German fire-power.

The other decision taken that day was to limit the period allowed for mobilisation and occupation of jumping-off positions to twelve hours, so making it possible to issue the order to begin the insurrection on the evening before the day on which hostilities were to begin.[4]

After the briefing on the 29th a confidential meeting between the three Generals, Bor-Komorowski, Pelczynski and Okulicki, resulted in the decision that Okulicki would assume command over the Home Army 'should the present Commander be unable to perform his function for any reasons'.[5]

At the same time the Polish Deputy Chief of Staff, Gen Tatar ('Turski') sent a despatch to Warsaw dated 28 July, informing Bor-Komorowski that his request of 25 July,[6] for assistance from England for his intended operation in the capital had been submitted to the British 'highest authorities'. He saw, however, only 'slight possibilities in the field of bombardments and [little possibility] of

[1] Adam Borkiewicz, *op. cit.*, p. 25ff.
[2] Antoni Chrusciel ('Monter'), *op. cit.*, p. 7.
[3] Cf. Aleksander Skarzynski, *op. cit.*, pp. 233ff.
[4] Adam Borkiewicz, *op. cit.*, p. 26.
[5] *Polskie Sily Zbrojne, op. cit.*, p. 708.
[6] For the text of Bor-Komorowski's request see pp. 221–2 of this study.

handing over to you [that is, to the Home Army] a Polish squadron of Mustangs'.[1]

In the afternoon of the same day a proclamation appeared in Warsaw signed by Col Julian Skokowski, the Commander of the 'Polish People's Army', announcing that Bor-Komorowski and his Staff had fled from Warsaw, and that in consequence Skokowski was assuming the command of all underground forces in Warsaw and ordering their mobilisation for the struggle against the Germans.[2] Probably in response to this misleading and confusing proclamation, Bor-Komorowski ordered 'Monter' to be ready to commence hostilities, if necessary, on 30 July, at 5 p.m.[3]

Skokowski's appeal coincided with a Soviet war-communique announcing that 'in central Poland Marshal Rokossovsky's tanks, motorised infantry and Cossack cavalry, powerfully supported by the Red Air Force, have pressed on towards Warsaw and are heavily engaged about 20 miles S.E. [of Warsaw] against the German lorry-borne reinforcements rushed to the front of stem [the Russian] advance . . .'[4] In the evening of the same day, at 8.15 p.m., Moscow radio broadcast an appeal in Polish to the people of Warsaw which called upon them to rise against the Germans: 'No doubt Warsaw already hears the guns of the battle which is soon to bring her liberation. Those who have never bowed their heads to the Hitlerite power will again, as in 1939, join battle with the Germans, this time for decisive action. . . . *For WARSAW, which did not yield but fought on, the hour of action has already arrived.*'[5]

Meanwhile the people of Warsaw were waiting for the outcome of Mikolajczyk's visit to Moscow.

On 30 July Bor-Komorowski and Jankowski asked the exiled authorities to request London and Washington for speedy recognition of the Home Army as an integral part of the Allied armed forces. They also asked the Government to pass a resolution recognising the civil administration as the Polish section of the Allied Military Government, for the duration of hostilities. The aim of these requests was the protection of the military and civil

---

[1] Despatch from Gen 'Turski' to the Commander of the Home Army dated 28 July 1944, Ldz. 6113, APUST.

[2] *Polskie Siły Zbrojne*, *op. cit.*, p. 703.

[3] Aleksander Skarzynski, *op. cit.*, pp. 236ff.

[4] Soviet War Communique of 29 July 1944, as quoted by Stanislaw Mikolajczyk, *The Pattern of Soviet Domination* (London, 1948), p. 75.

[5] *Ibid.*, p. 76. My italics.

members of the pro-London movement from possible arrests by the Russians. Finally, Bor-Komorowski and Jankowski asked the Government to request the Allied authorities to take under their protection those of the London Poles who had already been arrested by the Soviets.[1]

On the same day Col Iranek-Osmecki told two high-ranking Home Army Intelligence officers, Lt Col F. Herman ('Boguslawski') and Capt Z. Miszczak ('Bogucki'), that the insurrection was imminent and might start at any time. Lt Col Herman argued that, in view of the state of the German forces in the Warsaw region, it would be madness to begin operations at that time. Col Iranek-Osmecki refused to discuss the matter, merely asking Capt Miszczak to tell the PPR in Warsaw that the fighting in the city was about to begin. He said that this was desirable as an act of courtesy, but that there was no question of consulting the Communists, or of trying to co-ordinate the Home Army plans with them. Capt Miszczak explained that he could not undertake the task as he was no longer in contact with the PPR in Warsaw. He claims that he had earlier been ordered by Col Iranek-Osmecki to break off all contact with the communists.[2] I have been unable to establish whether, in asking Miszczak to contact the Communists, Col Iranek-Osmecki was acting on his own initiative or on the orders of his superiors. This seems to have been the only occasion when it was even suggested that the Communists, and, through them, possibly the Russians, should be told of the impending insurrection.

July 30 was also the date on which Lt Jan Nowak, a newly-returned Home Army emissary between London and Warsaw, reported his recent findings in London to Bor-Komorowski and his Staff. He told them that Warsaw could not count on large-scale British help or on the arrival of the Polish Parachute Brigade. Nowak also told Gen Pelczynski that, although the insurrection in the city would improve Mikolajczyk's political position, its effect on the Allied governments and on Western public opinion would be negligible. Nowak realised, while delivering his lengthy report, that his listeners, although strongly affected and even depressed by his news, were still determined to act. His report was frequently interrupted by the arrival of couriers and messengers with reports on the

---

[1] Despatch from the Commander of the Home Army and the Government's Delegate to the Prime Minister and the C-in-C, 30 July 1944, Ldz. 6155, APUST.   [2] Miszczak's oral evidence.

military situation in the approaches to Warsaw. These reports were followed by discussions as to whether the final orders should be issued forthwith, or further postponed. One of the officers present, Col Bokszczanin, told Bor-Komorowski: 'Until the Russians open artillery fire on the city . . . we must not make a move.' Nowak was greatly impressed by this officer's coolness and assurance.[1] In his view, the opening of Russian artillery bombardment of the city centre would signify the beginning of the Russians' general attack on the Polish capital.[2]

On 30 July the Home Army Command again came to the conclusion that the military situation was not yet ripe for the commencement of their operations in the city,[3] though the tone of the Soviet communique and appeal of 29 July strongly suggested that the Russian battle for the approaches to the Polish capital was unfolding. On 29, 30 and 31 July the sound of artillery fire could be heard in the city and the Red Air Force was active over Warsaw. The population of the capital was in a state of high excitement, convinced that the Russo–German battle for Warsaw had begun and that the hour of liberation was at hand.[4]

In reality only the left flank of Rokossovsky's troops, the units of the Second Soviet Armoured Army, had by 27 July, begun its advance in the general direction of Praga and was moving forward along the Lublin–Warsaw road.[5] The main body of the Russian forces advancing in the direction of the capital was still trying to establish bridgeheads on the western banks of the Vistula, in the Deblin region about 100 kilometres south-east of the city.[6] The first Russian units started to cross the Vistula on 29 July.[7] Indeed, from that date the Soviet Second Armoured Army was fighting on the near approaches of Praga and became involved in one of the greatest tank-battles fought in Poland in the summer of 1944.[8]

The Soviet advance on Praga was opposed by five German armoured divisions and an infantry division of the German Ninth Army[9] with about 450 tanks and self-propelled guns[10] under the

---

[1] Interview with Capt Nowak in *Na Antenie* (*Wiadomosci*), No. 962, 6 September 1964.
[2] Bokszczanin's letter, 19 April 1965.
[3] Aleksander Skarzynski, *op. cit.*, p. 237.   [4] *Ibid.*
[5] Wlodzimierz Woloszyn, 'Wyzwolenie Wschodnich Ziem Polski przez Armie Radziecka i Wojsko Polskie w 1944 r'. *Wojskowy Przeglad Historyczny* (Warsaw, 1963), No. 3/4 (29) p. 85 (hereafter to be referred to as Woloszyn).
[6] Jerzy Kirchmayer, *op. cit.*, p. 62.   [7] Woloszyn, p. 65.
[8] Woloszyn, p. 91.   [9] Woloszyn, p. 87.   [10] Woloszyn, p. 91, f.67.

personal command of Field-Marshal Mödel.[1] Hitler had ordered that the German troops were to defend Warsaw.[2]

The strength of the Soviet forces advancing on Praga cannot be accurately assessed. It is alleged that on 18 July this force consisted of 808 tanks and self-propelled guns, while less than three weeks later, on 6 August, they had only 383 battle vehicles left.[3]

On 30 July the Second Soviet Armoured Army continued its advance in the direction of Praga with the units of its 3rd, 8th and 16th Armoured Corps.

The 16th Corps was attacking along the Warsaw–Lublin road, and in the evening of that day its forward units reached the region of Milosna Starts, about 12 kilometres south-east of Praga. The 8th Corps exploiting the Russian success at Milosna started its attack in the direction of Okuniew – one of the main centres of the German outer defences on the approaches to Praga. At 8 p.m. the 3rd Corps occupied Wolomin and Radzymin, about 16 and 20 kilometres north-east of Praga respectively.[4] In spite of its success the general situation of the 3rd Corps was difficult. In Radzymin and Wolomin isolated pockets of German resistance were still holding on. What is more, its brigades, well advanced to the fore, were fighting in isolation from the main body of their Army and were running short of ammunition and fuel for their tanks and self-propelled guns.[5]

Meanwhile, the Germans were starting to counter-attack in the region of Radzymin–Wolomin, under the impression that Rokossovsky's main effort was concentrated there.[6] The German Command decided to throw in all its reserves to stem the Russian advance and encircle the 3rd Russian Armoured Corps.[7] As a result of this decision, by the evening of 30 July the elements of five German armoured divisions were converging in this direction.[8]

At the same time the Commander of the Soviet Second Armoured Army ordered his 8th Corps to launch an attack, on 31 July in the direction of Okuniew with the main body of his troops, and to establish contact with the hard-pressed 3rd Corps.[9] The 8th Corps opened its attack at dawn and by the end of the day had managed

---

[1] Jerzy Kirchmayer, *op. cit.*, p. 75.   [2] *Ibid.*, p. 65.
[3] Woloszyn, p. 91, f.67.   [4] Woloszyn, p. 90.
[5] *Ibid*; Hans von Krannhals, *Der Warschauer Aufstand, 1944* (Frankfurt, 1962), p. 83, f. 11.
[6] Woloszyn, p. 90; Hans von Krannhals, *op. cit.*, pp. 81ff.
[7] Woloszyn, p. 90.
[8] Woloszyn, p. 91; Hans von Krannhals, *op. cit.*, p. 83.   [9] Woloszyn, p. 92.

to take Okuniew, but had failed to link up with the 3rd Corps.[1] Throughout the day the units of the 16th and 3rd Corps were resisting numerous German counter-attacks.[2] Thus, on the evening of 31 July the initiative on the Praga sector was passing gradually into German hands.

It is alleged that in the small hours of 1 August the Commander of the Second Soviet Armoured Army decided to break off his attack and ordered his troops to go on the defensive by noon that day.[3] The first Russian attack on Praga had failed when their spearheads at some points were only about 10 kilometres from Praga; by the afternoon of 1 August the initiative on this sector had passed entirely to the Germans with whom it remained for the next few days.[4]

Meanwhile, however, in spite of this reverse on the Praga sector, on the same day the units of the 8th Soviet Guards Army managed to cross the Vistula in considerable force at Magnuszew, about 60 kilometres south-east of Warsaw.[5]

When, in the morning of 31 July, the Home Army leaders had met to discuss the military situation, they had been only partially aware of the developments on the approaches to Praga. They knew, nevertheless, about the occupation of Radzymin by the Red Army, and heard that Soviet tanks were moving westwards from that town in the direction of Praga.[6] They were still waiting for clarification of the situation at the front and for a Russian attack on Warsaw from the Russian bridgeheads on the western banks of the Vistula south of the city.[7] The Chief of Intelligence reported that the Germans were concentrating their troops for the final battle on the approaches to Warsaw.[8] Gen Okulicki once again repeated, however, his by now customary demand for immediate action. He strongly argued that further postponement of the battle would jeopardise its chances of success, as it would make it impossible to capture the city before the Red Army entered. He even accused those present of cowardice and temporisation. He was supported by Col Szostak, who claimed that it would be preferable to begin the battle three days too early rather than an hour too late.

These emphatic requests for action were opposed by Col Chrusciel,

[1] *Ibid.* [2] *Ibid.* [3] Woloszyn, p. 92.
[4] Hans von Krannhals, *op. cit.*, p. 84. [5] Woloszyn, p. 94.
[6] Aleksander Skarzynski, *op. cit.*, p. 240.
[7] *Polskie Sily Zbrojne, op. cit.*
[8] Iranek-Osmecki's oral evidence.

who maintained that his badly-armed troops were too weak to engage a still-organised enemy. He proposed to strike at the moment of German retreat. In view of the division of opinion, Bor-Komorowski asked all those present – Pelczynski, Okulicki, Chrusciel, Rzepecki, Iranek-Osmecki, Pluta-Czachowski, Szostak and Bokszczanin – to say whether, in their estimation, the situation at the front was propitious for the battle. Only three officers, Okulicki, Szostak and Rzepecki, were in favour of immediate action. Four others, Bokszczanin, Chrusciel, Iranek-Osmecki and Pluta-Czachowski, were in favour of further delay. Bor-Komorowski and Pelczynski abstained.[1] The briefing ended at about noon with the conclusion that 'the struggle will not be undertaken on 1 August and it is not very probable that it will be undertaken on 2 August'.[2]

In the early afternoon of the same day another important meeting took place, between Bor-Komorowski, Jankowski and the Presidium of the Council of National Unity, to discuss the possibility of launching operations in Warsaw. During this conference Bor-Komorowski apprised the politicians of the military situation. It is claimed that he told them that in view of the state of the German forces in the Warsaw region, which he estimated at about twelve first class divisions, and of the Home Army's lack of weapons and ammunition, the operations planned for the last day of the German retreat from the capital were not feasible in the immediate future.[3] He allegedly stated that his ammunition supplies were so low as to be sufficient for only three or four days' fighting.[4] In his opinion the chances of capturing arms and ammunition from the Germans during the fighting were very small, as the Germans had already managed to evacuate the greater part of their stores from Warsaw to the west. The politicians, for their part, were urging extreme caution in order not to expose the population to unnecessary losses.[5]

The day before this conference K. Puzak ('Bazyli'), the chairman of the Presidium, and a prominent socialist, expressed to his close friends and associates his grave misgivings concerning the danger of starting the struggle without being certain when, and if, the Red Army would enter Warsaw or being able to secure air-cover for the

[1] Bokszczanin's letter, 1 April 1965.
[2] Adam Borkiewicz, *op. cit.*, p. 27.
[3] Aleksander Skarzynski, *op. cit.*, p. 246; cf. J. Rokicki, *Blaski i cienie bohaterskiego pieciolecia* (West Germany, 1949), p. 98ff.
[4] *Ibid.*   [5] *Ibid.*

insurgents. Puzak argued that the underground forces were capable of staging an armed demonstration which might lead to their occupation of the capital and the containment of the German garrison for two or three days, but he feared that the Russians might not enter the city within this period. He doubted whether the Home Army could hold its ground against the Germans in Warsaw for more than a week or two without support from the air, even if its demonstration assumed the character of a popular insurrection.[1]

Thus it is clear that in the early afternoon of 31 July the most important political and military leaders of the resistance had no intention of sending their troops into battle on 1 August. Even so, another late afternoon briefing of Bor-Komorowski's Staff was arranged for five o'clock. To begin with this was poorly attended because of the outcome of the morning conference. Those present at its beginning were: Generals Bor-Komorowski, Pelczynski, Okulicki and Major 'H.K.' (J. Karasiowna). They discussed the news of the capture by the Russians of the Commander of the 73rd German Infantry Division defending the access to Praga, the reported Red Army outflanking movements around Warsaw, and the arrival in Praga of the elite 'Herman Goering' Division.[2] In the meantime, the German military radio station had stated: 'Today the Russians started a general attack on Warsaw from the south-east.'[3] 'That same day we learned from the radio,' wrote Gen Bor-Komorowski in 1946,

> that Mikolajczyk . . . had left London for Moscow. This was the best of news. The Soviet Government had broken diplomatic relations with the Polish Government in April, 1943, and we had since been able neither to re-establish relations nor to co-ordinate our military actions with those of the Red Army. Now in Moscow, the Prime Minister could doubtless establish military co-operation between the Red Army and Home Army for us, while at the same time our military action in Warsaw would aid him in re-establishing diplomatic relations between our governments.[4]

At about 5.30 p.m. Col 'Monter' arrived at the briefing, reporting that the Russian tanks were already entering Praga and insisting on

[1] Zygmunt Zaremba, *op. cit.*, p. 238.
[2] Adam Borkiewicz, *op. cit.*, p. 27.
[3] Winston S. Churchill, *The Second World War*, vol. VI, *Triumph and Tragedy* (London, 1954), p. 115.
[4] T. Bor-Komorowski, 'The Unconquerables', *The Readers' Digest*, February 1964, p. 129.

the immediate launching of the Home Army operations inside the city as otherwise it 'might be too late'.[1] Prompted by 'Monter's' report, Bor-Komorowski decided that the time was ripe for the commencement of 'Burza' in Warsaw,[2] in spite of his earlier conviction to the contrary, twice expressed during the course of that day. The General immediately sent his aide-de-camp for Jankowski, whom he wished to consult before giving his final order to Col 'Monter'.[3] The Government's Delegate arrived promptly, to be met with Bor-Komorowski's demand that operations begin immediately in Warsaw. In his opinion this would transform the German defeat in Praga into a complete rout, as it would make the reinforcement of the German troops fighting on the eastern bank of the Vistula impossible and in this way would speed up the Soviet encircling movements which, he claimed, had already started to the east, north-east and north of the city.[4]

Jankowski, writes Bor-Komorowski, 'heard me out and then put questions to various members of the Staff. Having thus completed his picture of the situation, he turned to me with the words: "Very well, then. Begin." '[5]

Then, Bor-Komorowski turned to Col 'Monter' and gave him a brief but decisive order: *'Tomorrow, at 1700 hours precisely, you will start operation "Burza" in Warsaw.'*[6]

The Home Commander issued this order at about 6 p.m. on 31 July 1944.[7] Thus, the point of no return had been reached and a final, irrevocable decision made. In reality, then, this decision was taken by Bor-Komorowski and Jankowski on the instigation of Col 'Monter', in consultation with Generals Pelczynski and Okulicki and in the presence of Major 'H.K.' Their final deliberations were swift and concise. The fate of Warsaw was decided within not much more than half and hour. No attempt was made to verify Col 'Monter's' report.

Colonels Szostak, Iranek-Osmecki and Pluta-Czachowski, the heads of Operational, Intelligence and Liaison Departments of the Home Army Staff, arrived after Bor-Komorowski had issued his

---

[1] Adam Borkiewicz, *op. cit.*, p. 27.
[2] Antoni Chrusciel ('Monter'), *op. cit.*, p. 7.
[3] T. Bor-Komorowski, *op. cit.*, p. 214.
[4] T. Bor-Komorowski, 'The Unconquerables', *The Reader's Digest*, February 1946, p. 129.
[5] *Ibid.*   [6] *Ibid.* My italics.
[7] Iranek-Osmecki's oral evidence.

order. When Col Szostak asked his Commander whether, in making his final decision, he had not needed either his Chief of Intelligence or Szostak himself, he was simply told that Bor-Komorowski had feared that the Home Army might not be able to start its operations before the entry of the Red Army into the city.[1] Col Iranek-Osmecki claims to have reported, on his arrival at the briefing, at about 6 p.m., that the news brought by 'Monter' had been exaggerated, if not utterly false. He told his Commander that the Germans were still sending fresh reinforcements into Praga and massing their armoured units for the approaching tank battle with the Russians. The Colonel also says that he told Bor-Komorowski that the German troops defending the Praga bridgehead were holding fast; there was no question of their withdrawal. Gen Bor-Komorowski, he says, listened to his report, looked at his watch, and said 'It's done – "*Stalo sie.*" It is too late to repeal the order.' Col Iranek-Osmecki was surprised by Bor-Komorowski's decision.[2] However, Bor-Komorowski denied, in an interview with me, that his Chief of Intelligence had had anything new to report at this stage. He claimed, however, that the chief Signals Officer, Col Pluta-Czachowski, told him, at about 6 p.m., that the German counter-attack north-east of Warsaw had started. The General told Pluta-Czachowski that orders were already issued and that it was too late to change them,

Indeed, he later maintained that he had had no intention of altering his decision as it was technically impossible to do so and also because he believed that the German counter-attack would be unable to check the Soviet march on Warsaw. Bor-Komorowski stated that he attached little significance to the important news brought by Pluta-Czachowski as the latter was not especially designed to collect and evaluate information, and, hence, the news reported by him could have been a *canard*.[3] In view of the conflicting evidence it is difficult to say whether it was the Chief of Intelligence or the Chief Signals Officer who told Bor-Komorowski that his decision was premature, in view of the developments east of Warsaw. But it is certain that less than half an hour after making his decision, 24 hours before the insurrection, the Home Commander was told

[1] Adam Borkiewicz, *op. cit.*, pp. 27ff.
[2] Iranek-Osmecki's oral evidence, given to the writer in the presence of Prof J. K. Zawodny.
[3] Bor-Komorowski's oral evidence, given to the writer in the presence of Prof J. K. Zawodny.

that the Germans were counter-attacking in the vicinity of the capital, and therefore he should have been aware that there was little likelihood that the Germans would retreat from the city without putting up a stiff fight.

At 7 p.m. 'Monter' issued the battle order to his troops. Distribution of the order began early the following morning – that is, on the day of the insurrection – because of the early curfew hour in Warsaw, which at that time began at eight o'clock. The order could not be revoked because of the conditions under which the clandestine liaison had to work.[1]

The members of the Presidium of the Council of National Unity were surprised to learn, on 1 August, of the decision to begin hostilities.[2] That afternoon the Home Army struck against the Germans. The battle had begun.

[1] Aleksander Skarzynski, *op. cit.*, pp. 251–2.
[2] Despatch from 'Florek' and 'Grabowski' (leaders of the Peasant Party in Warsaw) to the Prime Minister, No. 31, 12 September 1944, Ldz. K.5341/44, GSHI PRM, L9.

9

Why Warsaw Rose

The Home Army's attempt to free Warsaw before the entry of the Red Army was prompted mainly by political and ideological reasons. The authors of the insurrection decided to act because they were convinced that, if the claims of the London Government to govern and represent Poland were to be established in the eyes of the world, Warsaw must be liberated by forces loyal to that Government. By taking Warsaw the Home Army was to clear the ground for the final, decisive confrontation with Stalin, the outcome of which was to determine who would govern Poland – the London Poles or the Polish Communists and their sympathisers. To Jankowski and Bor-Komorowski, this was the crucial moment of the war for Poland; they believed that she stood at historic cross-roads, that her destiny was about to be decided.

Their assumption that the strategic situation in Poland favoured their political designs strengthened their determination to act; they believed that military developments on the eastern front afforded them a singular opportunity to wrest control of Warsaw from the collapsing Germans shortly before the entry of the victorious Red Army. Thus they would create the necessary conditions for their political demonstration.

Had Bor-Komorowski and his Staff made a more realistic analysis of the military situation, they would no doubt have abandoned their plan to free Warsaw during the first days of August 1944. They were well aware, even before the outbreak of the insurrection, that the success of their enterprise would depend on the outcome of the Red Army's offensive on Warsaw. On 31 July – the day before the insurrection – Pelczynski told Jankowski that if the Russians did not *soon* enter Warsaw the insurgents would be massacred by the Germans. When making their final decision to rise, the Home Army Generals assumed that the imminent entry of the Russians into the city was a foregone conclusion.

The decision when to stage the rising therefore, – or whether, indeed, to stage a rising at all – was conditioned by factors in the wider military context of the Russo–German confrontation in Poland.[1] From the purely military point of view their decision rested on two fundamental and simple assumptions; their profound belief that the Russians were on the point of taking the capital and their impression that the Germans were no longer capable of halting for long the Red Army's advances in central Poland.[2] Indeed, at the moment of the final decision, those responsible for it were confident that the Russians would take the city within a few days, if not hours.[3] They reached this optimistic conclusion because of 'Monter's' report that Russian tanks were already entering Praga.[4] They expected the Soviet attack on the city to begin at any moment. 'We were convinced that the occupation of Warsaw was one of the aims of the Soviet offensive', said Pelczynski in 1951. '. . . On about 21 July we became convinced that the Russians would cross the line of the middle Vistula without any strong opposition from the Germans. . . The developments at the front between 21 and 25 July supported our supposition and strengthened our belief.'[5] 'We believed', he continued, 'that the Muscovites would exploit the fact that the German troops were badly shaken, and that they [the Russians] would enter Warsaw, not to help us, but to further their own tactical interests'.[6] Thus the Home Army generals were firmly convinced that the Russians were extremely anxious to capture Warsaw as soon as possible because of its strategic and military importance. They decided that 'Moscow must be anxious to advance as far to the west as will secure favourable jumping off positions for their next offensive, aimed at the interior of the Reich [and] intended to forestall the occupation of its territories by the Western Allies, who had landed in Normandy.'[7] In addition, they assumed that the Russians were

[1] *Polskie Sily Zbrojne, op. cit.*, p. 658.

[2] Despatch from the Commander of the Home Army to the C-in-C, 21 July 1944 Ldz. 5916/tj, APUST.

[3] Letter from Maj-Gen L. Okulicki to the President of the Republic, 9 December 1944, No. 1780/I, APUST.

[4] Letter from Col J. Bokszczanin to the author, 19 April 1965; 'Komendant Armii Krajowej: Wywiad z Generalem Borem Komorowskim', *Na Antenie* (*Wiadomosci*), No. 962, 6 September 1964; A. Borkiewicz, *op. cit.*, p. 27; Antoni Chrusciel ('Monter'), *op. cit.*, p. 7.

[5] General T. Pelczynski's statement of 18 April 1951, 'Czwarte zebranie relacyjne w inst. J. Pilsudskiego w Londynie 18/4/1951: Decyzja podjecia walki o Warszawe w. 1944r., Zalacznik No. 2', APUST. Hereafter referred to as Pelczynski statement of 18 April 1951.

[6] Pelczynski's statement of 18 April 1951.   [7] *Ibid.*

anxious to take Warsaw because this would enable them to pose as the true 'redeemers of the Polish capital', a role which could be exploited politically.[1]

The second supposition, that the Germans were no longer able to stem the Russian advance in Poland, rested on the belief that the German defeats in the East, which had led to the destruction of about twenty-five of their divisions, the Anglo–American successes in Normandy and the attempt on Hitler's life had all combined to produce a situation potentially catastrophic for the German Reich. 'In these circumstances', said Bor-Komorowski in 1949, 'the possibility of the collapse of the Germans at the front and in their own country had to be taken into account.'[2] Referring to the attempted assassination of Hitler, Gen Pelczynski said:

> We were greatly affected by this event, which showed that the conspiracy against Hitler embraced the highest circles of the Reich's armed forces and Hitler's entourage. It was difficult to assess who would win, Hitler or the conspirators. We believed that even if this internal struggle did not lead to the wholesale collapse of German discipline, it would in any case seriously weaken it and affect the front by reducing the army's battleworthiness. During the following days this appraisal of the situation was confirmed in the appearance and behaviour of the Germans in Warsaw.[3]

In fact, even on 25 July the Home Army Command was seriously admitting the possibility that there might very soon be another attempt on Hitler's life.[4]

Thus, von Stauffenberg's attempted *putsch* and the German panic in Warsaw led the Home Army Commanders to expect a repetition of the events which had taken place in Germany in November 1918; apparently, they felt that history was in the process of repeating itself. They even clung to this idea during the rising itself. On 6 August 1944 Col 'Monter' assured his embattled troops and the people of Warsaw that Germany was faced with imminent catastrophe.[5] Exactly a month later Bor-Komorowski was still asking his C-in-C

---

[1] *Polskie Sily Zbrojne, op. cit.*, p. 660.
[2] 'Elementy decyzji powstania Warszawskiego', Referat Gen. T. Bora-Komorowskiego na akademii w 5-ta rocznice, dnia 2–8–1949 w Londynie, B.II, No. 84, APUST. Hereafter referred to as Bor-Komorowski's speech of 2 August 1949.
[3] Pelczynski's statement of 18 April 1951.
[4] Colonel K. Iranek-Osmecki's oral evidence.
[5] 'Wywiad z Komendantem Monterem', *Biuletyn Informacyjny*, No. 43–250, 6 August 1944, APUST.

whether in his opinion 'operations in the West can bring the war to an end within the next few days'.[1]

These highly optimistic prognostications gave birth in the military field to the idea that the Home Army should exploit German reverses and Soviet successes by liberating Warsaw and, in so doing, making a contribution to the approaching Nazi defeat in Poland. Further, they led the three Generals to conclude that the opportunity for certain victory over the Germans in Warsaw was within their grasp. They expected their struggle to be short and virtually to assume the character of mopping-up operations. 'Their faith in certain victory was unshakeable', writes Col Bokszczanin, 'and any reservations were dismissed as signs of petty-mindedness and defeatism. . . The course and outcome of the projected battle did not arouse the slightest feeling of apprehension, to such an extent that no-one talked about it, considering it already won; at the most, a few scattered, possibly more serious engagements, followed by the disarming of the terrorised Germans [were expected].'

In any case, a hard struggle 'was not envisaged if for no other reason than because the Polish units had insufficient quantities of arms and ammunition. The Soviet troops were to deal with the German reserves and their main forces in Praga.' 'Only in the case of a premature outbreak of the rising were certain difficulties and greater effort contemplated, but no great importance was attached to this, as in any event victory [was considered] to be certain.'[2]

In short regardless of the timing of the insurrection 'only success was reckoned with'. 'The possibility of defeat was not taken into account and no provisions were made for it or for the prolonging of the fighting.'[3] Thus, before the outbreak of the fighting Bor-Komorowski was quite confident that by skilfully exploiting Soviet military successes he would be able to liberate Warsaw before the entry of the Red Army. Col Bokszczanin maintains that Gen Okulicki, the main advocate of the insurrection, imagined that there would be 'no real struggle, but only a finishing off of an already defeated and disorganised enemy'.[4] In the Colonel's opinion Okulicki's optimism was fully shared by his immediate superiors Bor-Komorowski and Pelczynski.[5]

---

[1] Despatch from the Commander of the Home Army to the C-in-C, 6 September 1944, Ldz. 8025, APUST.
[2] Bokszczanin's letter, 19 April 1965.
[3] *Ibid.*   [4] *Ibid.*   [5] *Ibid.*

Col Bokszczanin's views seem to be justified, as otherwise Bor-Komorowski's decision to fight in Warsaw would not make military sense, in view of the paucity of arms and ammunition at his disposal; he had no wish to stage a forlorn gesture, which endangered the lives and safety of over a million people. He himself stated that before the insurrection he had altogether discounted the possibility that it might fail. Its final outcome was to be determined by the entry of the Red Army into Warsaw. He estimated that the Russians would arrive in the city on the second or third or, at the latest, by the seventh day of the fighting.[1] His Chief of Staff also expected that the struggle would be short, lasting for a few days; in any event, no longer than a week. He estimated that 'Monter's' troops would be able, without much difficulty, to capture the greater part of the city and a number of less strongly defended German positions during their initial assault. Bor-Komorowski and Pelczynski appreciated that, because of the shortage of heavy weapons, the offensive power of their troops was weak. They intended that, during the initial attack, their troops should merely 'isolate' – encircle – rather than storm the more strongly-held and -fortified German positions, presumably leaving such objectives to be dealt with after the entry of the Red Army. In the event, all German-held positions in the city were attacked by the Home Army on 1 August; Gen Pelczynski has recently explained that this was due to an 'oversight'.[2] It must be assumed that, in the general confusion, there was no time to issue the appropriate orders to the troops concerned. Bor-Komorowski intended to open his attack during the first stages of an all-out Soviet assault on the city; the Home Army was to act during the last moments of the German stay in Warsaw, in accordance with the basic tenets of the 'Burza' plan. The Polish attack was to be directed against the German rearguards retreating from the bridge-head through the city 'under the pressure of the Soviet troops'. The Polish 'success' against the Germans would be 'buttressed by the entry of the Soviet troops'.[3]

However, after the event, Bor-Komorowski stressed other military reasons for staging the struggle in the city. 'We thought', he said in 1949, that a struggle undertaken inside the city at the moment of the Russian attack from outside would shorten the battle and spare

---

[1] Bor-Komorowski's oral evidence.
[2] Pelczynski's oral evidence.
[3] Pelczynski's statement of 18 April 1951.

Warsaw the fate of Stalingrad. . .'[1] In 1964 he enlarged this argument by saying that between 21 and 22 July 1944 Gen Okulicki convinced him that the Germans might try to defend Warsaw – which could lead to considerable destruction – and that it was essential to hasten the outcome of the Russo–German battle by means of the Home Army operations within the city, thus sparing the population undue losses and devastation.[2] This seems to suggest that the Home Commander was moved to act, not by a desire to exploit Soviet success, but by the fear that if he failed to attack the Germans in the city they might be able to turn it into their own fortress – a second Stalingrad. But Gen Pelczynski wrote in 1950 that, when making their own decisions, the Home Army leaders tried to take into account *two* possible eventualities with regard to the probable German plans for Warsaw. They were as follows:

> . . . the Germans would not be able to organise the defence of Warsaw and would abandon it *under the first Soviet attack*.' '. . . the Germans would be able to organise the defence of the Warsaw bridgehead and would turn it into a bastion of their overall system of defence of East Prussia and the lower Vistula, and would stage a battle for the city.
>
> Both eventualities considered led to the same conclusion: it was necessary to stage the struggle for Warsaw.'[3]

Should the first possibility apply, Pelczynski said, it would then be easy for the Home Army to capture the city. The second presented a threat of the prolonging of the Russo–German battle for the capital and the unavoidable destruction of the city. 'In that case there would be a need to shorten the struggle by means of a Polish attack, and to throw the Germans out of the city.'[4]

This implies that, to the end, the Home Army Command was uncertain of the German plans for Warsaw and believed that the occupiers might try to defend the city. This is not borne out, however, by Col Bokszczanin's revelations or by Bor-Komorowski's own report, sent by him to London on 21 July, stating that he was, on the whole confident that on the Eastern Front the initiative was entirely in Soviet hands and that the Russians were expected to cross the Vistula without much opposition from the Germans.[5] Only

---

[1] Bor-Komorowski's speech on 2 August 1949.
[2] 'Komendant Armii Krajowej: Wywiad z Generalem Borem-Komorowskim', *Na Antenie (Wiadomosci)*, No. 962, 6 September 1964.
[3] *Polskie Siły Zbrojne, op. cit.*, p. 661. My italics.   [4] *Ibid.*
[5] Despatch from the Commander of the Home Army to the C-in-C, 21 July 1944, Ldz. 5916/tj, APUST.

a week earlier, on 14 July, Bor-Komorowski himself has stated that he had no intention of starting large-scale hostilities in the capital because, in view of the formidable German anti-insurrectionary preparation '*a rising has no prospects of success*'.[1] Thus, only a fortnight before the insurrection he had considered his forces incapable of a sustained effort to capture the city. Within a week he had changed his mind, not because his forces had become stronger but because he no longer believed the Germans to be capable of effective resistance, even to his badly armed troops, provided that the Polish operations were well-timed.

It seems indeed, that the second possibility envisaged by Pelczynski was introduced after the event, to justify and rationalise the great losses suffered by the people of Warsaw, and the heavy destruction of the city during the course of the insurrection. Col Rzepecki wrote in 1958 that he considered this justification to be 'insincere'. He stated that he did not remember hearing this argument used during the July meetings of the Home Army Command.[2]

There is little doubt that the Home Army leaders decided to act because they assumed the Germans would abandon Warsaw under 'the first Soviet attack', rather than because they intended to frustrate the Nazi plans for a long and strenuous defence of the city. The operations planned were to be similar to those already undertaken east of Warsaw – in Wilno and Lwow – within the framework of 'Burza', although the battle for Warsaw was to be staged in accordance with a modified version of the plans prepared for the universal and simultaneous insurrection.[3] 'Monter's' troops were to occupy the whole of Warsaw and immobilise its German garrison,[4] thus paving the way for the establishment of a London-controlled administration which, as hosts, would receive the Russians.

With regard to tactics, the Home Army Command intended to open its attack at the moment the Red Army crossed the line of the Vistula, south of Warsaw, and disorganised the defence of the German bridgehead in the neighbourhood of the city.[5] The observance of these two tactical conditions was intended to reduce the risks involved in launching Polish operations without co-ordinating them

[1] Report from the Commander of the Home Army to the C-in-C, No. 243, 14 July 1944, Ldz. 6302/44, APUST. My italics.
[2] Col Jan Rzepecki, 'Jeszcze o Decyzji Podjecia Walki w Warszawie', *Wojskowy Przeglad Historyczny* (Warsaw, 1958), No. 4(9), pp. 333ff.
[3] *Polskie Sily Zbrojne, op. cit.*, p. 706.   [4] *Ibid.*, p. 707.
[5] *Polskie Sily Zbrojne, op. cit.*, p. 707.

beforehand with the Soviet High Command. The Warsaw leaders' belief that the Russian crossing of the Vistula and entry into Warsaw was a foregone conclusion prompted them to act in the capital. Without access to the Soviet archives it is difficult to say whether the Soviet failure to take Warsaw during the insurrection was due to military causes, to political considerations, or to a combination of both.

Yet there are indications that the Red Army's failure to take Warsaw at the *beginning* of August 1944 was due chiefly to military causes. This emerges from an examination of some Polish, Russian and German sources. In October 1944 the officers of Gen Okulicki's Staff in German-occupied Poland unequivocally ascribed the Russian failure to take Warsaw to 'the general collapse of the Soviet offensive on the Vistula'. They maintained that Rokossovsky's offensive had been halted at the gates of Warsaw by the arrival on the scene of fresh German armoured reinforcements.[1] More significantly, Generals Bor-Komorowski, Pelczynski and 'Monter' admitted, after the rising, that at the beginning of August the Russians had met with serious military reverses in the approaches to Warsaw. In 1965 Gen Bor-Komorowski wrote that the Germans managed to 'check the Russian attack on the capital' by 5 August.[2] In 1951 Gen Pelczynski said that 'the Muscovites intended to take Warsaw in the first days of August, in the course of their initial attack. This did not happen. They met with serious difficulties of a military nature. . . Rokossovsky's exposed flank near Warsaw encountered a localised attack from Mödel . . . but by 20 August Rokossovsky had freedom of action in this area.'[3] In the considered opinion of Bor-Komorowski's Chief of Staff, Rokossovsky could not have renewed his attack on Warsaw before the end of August, by which time the insurrection was already three weeks old. Gen 'Monter' conceded, as early as 1946, that it was 'possible to understand' Russian behaviour on the Warsaw sector of the front in August 1944.[4] These guarded words imply that 'Monter' was prepared to accept the fact that at that time the Red Army was militarily unable to capture Warsaw. Stalin and

---

[1] 'Bitwa Warszawska', B.II, No. 543, APUST.

[2] Tadeusz Bor-Komorowski, *Armia Podziemna* (London, 1966), p. 252.

[3] Gen Pelczynski's statement of January 26, 1951, 'Trzecie Zebrania Relacyjne w inst. J. Pilsudskiego w Londynie, 26/1/1951: Decyzja Podjecia Walki o Warszawe', APUST. Hereafter referred to as Pelczynski's statement of 26 January 1951.

[4] Antoni Chrusciel ('Monter'), *Powstanie Warszawskie* (London, 1948), p. 14.

Rokossovsky gave similar accounts of the situation. On 9 August Stalin told Mikolajczyk that he had expected the Red Army to take Warsaw by 6 August; its failure to do so had been due to the arrival of five German armoured divisions in the Praga sector.[1] On 26 August Rokossovsky said that the Russians would have taken Warsaw if this had been possible.[2] Indeed, Rokossovsky seemed very anxious to take the city; on 8 August he told Stalin that by about 25 August he would be able to stage a new attack on the Polish capital.[3]

The Germans, for their part, maintain that they managed to halt the Soviet advances on Warsaw during the first days of August 1944. General Heinz Guderian, then Chief of the German General Staff, wrote in 1951: 'We Germans had the impression that it was our defence which halted the enemy rather than a Russian desire to sabotage the Warsaw uprising.[4]

The general consensus of Polish, Russian and German opinions on the Russian failure to take Warsaw in early August – that it was due to military obstacles – does not, however, tell us why Stalin did not act upon Rokossovsky's suggestion to renew a major offensive on Warsaw after 25 August. It is possible that, preoccupied with his offensive in the Balkans, which had begun on 20 August, he felt unable to pursue the offensive on two fronts. Again his motives for not advancing on Warsaw may well have been more sinister. It is possible, and is often believed, that Stalin decided to abandon Warsaw to its own fate and thereby avoided a direct confrontation with the London Poles; that he left it to the Germans, his main adversaries, to crush his political opponents.[5] Without access to the Soviet archives, attempts to explain his behaviour can be nothing more than conjecture. It is worthy of note that, before the insurrection, only one high-ranking officer of the Home Army, Col Bokszczanin, argued that the Russians would deliberately halt their offensive if they realised that the uprising was initiated and directed by the pro-London leaders. Hence, Col Bokszczanin urged his Commander not to open the attack before it was quite clear that the Russians were so seriously committed to the capture of the city that

---

[1] Note on the conversation at the Kremlin between Premier Mikolajczyk and Marshal Stalin held on 9 August 1944, GSHI–PRM, L4.
[2] Alexander Werth, *Russia At War* (London, 1964), p. 878.
[3] Woloszyn, *op. cit.*, p. 101.
[4] Heinz Guderian, *Panzer Leader* (London, 1952), p. 359.
[5] Cf. Chester Wilmot, *The Struggle for Europe* (London, 1963), p. 501.

it would be impossible for them to pull out without suffering heavy losses.[1] He advised Bor-Komorowski not to make a move until the Russian artillery had begun to bombard the city, which might be taken as a direct sign that their general assault was about to begin.[2] His warning went unheeded.

Whatever the explanation, the fact remains that Polish hopes and expectations that Rokossovsky's troops would soon enter Warsaw were unfulfilled. What is more, the Germans managed to withstand the combined Allied blows from the east and the west, in spite of their shattering defeats and heavy losses. They finally collapsed in May 1945 and not, as the Polish leaders had anticipated, in the early autumn of 1944. The abortive attempt on Hitler's life failed to sap Germany's will and ability to resist; its effects on German discipline were negligible. Finally, the expected race for Germany between the Russians and the Western Allies also failed to develop in the summer and early autumn of 1944.

The absence of these developments sealed Warsaw's fate and turned the insurrection into an appalling and cruel tragedy for Poland. The faulty assumption that all three developments would emerge in August 1944 was primarily responsible for bringing about this disaster; as Gen Pelczynski stated: '. . . the military factors played a tremendous role in the timing of the struggle. . .'[3] Even the final impetus for the resistance leaders' hasty decision of 31 July 1944 was based on exaggerated hopes derived from Col 'Monter's' report and accompanying demands for immediate action on the following day.[4]

Col Iranek-Osmecki, who was 'Monter's' closest friend and long-standing colleague, describes his report as 'exaggerated', though whether consciously or not he cannot say. In his opinion 'Monter' yielded to the general wish to fight, and acted under the pressure of events. He could not 'control his nerves' sufficiently to wait any longer.[5] This explanation of the Colonel's behaviour on the afternoon of 31 July would seem to be plausible, as on two earlier occasions

---

[1] General T. Pelczynski's statement of 30 August 1964. A transcript of Gen Pelczynski's broadcast of 30 August 1964, Radio Free Europe. APUST.
[2] 'Emisariusz: Wywiad z Kapitanem Nowakiem', *Na Antenie (Wiadomosci)*, No. 962, 6 September 1964; Bokszczanin's letter, 19 April 1965.
[3] Pelczynski's statement of 18 April 1951.
[4] See also pp. 239–40 of this study.
[5] Colonel Iranek-Osmecki's oral evidence.

'Monter' had acted in a rather highly-strung and impetuous manner; on 24 July he had advised Bor-Komorowski to alert his troops and on 27 July he had alerted and mobilised his units when the Germans had made their request for a hundred thousand people to present themselves for work on fortifications.[1] The Colonel seemed ready to act in response to almost any provocation. But the Colonel is now dead and the reasons for his report and suggestion that the battle should begin on 1 August will therefore never be fully known.

It should be mentioned, however, that Col Bokszczanin, who knew 'Monter' well, has most strongly rejected the possibility that he could 'consciously have made an exaggerated or false report in order to speed up the outbreak of the rising', because, 'as the immediate commander of the troops who were to fight he was primarily pre-occupied with the problem of how to begin the battle under the conditions most favourable for quick victory'.[2] To support this, Col Bokszczanin points out that on the morning of 31 July 'Monter' was opposed to launching of the attack next day. In Col Bokszczanin's opinion 'Monter' knew only too well that his troops were incapable of fighting a long and strenuous battle; indeed he was against speeding up the outbreak of the rising, 'was very worried about its course, and as a soldier wished to carry out his orders to the best of his ability'. 'Whether the report was exaggerated or not, whether a few, or a number of the [Soviet] tanks were seen, was immaterial. In view of the great concentration of the German armoured forces it had no significance at all, as was seen a few days later, when those forces defeated and drove the considerably reinforced Soviet troops back far from Praga. Consideration of the trivial incident reported was Bor-Komorowski's duty, not that of 'Monter', who simply passed on to him the report received from Praga.'[3]

Thus, Col Bokszczanin places the entire responsibility for the acceptance and evaluation of the news brought by 'Monter' on the shoulders of his Commander. This view is justified as Bor-Komorowski himself has stated that, in accordance with the estab-lished practice, he was always finally responsible for the decisions; his subordinates merely advised him and expressed their opinions when asked to do so.[4] But even Col Bokszczanin admits that 'Monter' contributed considerably to the 'premature outbreak of the fighting'. He became affected by the general anxiety not to start the insur-

[1] Cf. A. Borkiewicz, *op. cit.*, 24ff.   [2] Bokszczanin's letter, 19 April 1965.
[3] *Ibid.*   [4] Bor-Komorowski's oral evidence.

rection too late, and made a number of mistakes.[1] Hence, there seems to be some agreement between the accounts of both Iranek-Osmecki and Bokszczanin of 'Monter's' behaviour in the afternoon of 31 July 1944; both officers stress his impetuosity.

Briefly, it was the uncritical acceptance by the three top Home Army Generals, Bor-Komorowski, Pelczynski and Okulicki, of his report and his suggestion that the attack should begin which led to the premature outbreak of the insurrection. Its outbreak coincided with the opening of the German counter-attack on the approaches to Praga. There was no news about the beginning of a Soviet out-flanking movement from the south-east. Thus, neither of the tactical prerequisites which, according to the plan, were to accompany Bor-Komorowski's final decision, was present. Paradoxically enough, the Home Commander knew, or at least had reason to suspect, approximately half an hour after issuing his order, that it had been premature. But he failed to realise the full extent of his mistake and it was, in any case, already too late to rescind the order. Further, he was still confident that the Red Army would soon be in Warsaw.[2]

What Machiavelli calls 'good fortune' was not on Bor-Komorowski's side. 'There is something in the nature of historical events', writes H. Butterfield, 'which twists the course of history in a direction that no man ever intended'.[3] In this case the 'something' was manifested through 'Monter's' report, and the delay of both Iranek-Osmecki and Pluta-Czachowski in getting to the decisive meeting of 31 July. 'One can foresee a revolution or a war', wrote Trotsky in an account of his own downfall, 'but it is impossible to foresee the consequences of an autumn shooting-trip for wild ducks.'[4] Yet, Bor-Komorowski did not take elementary precautions against misfortune. He failed to foresee the consequences of making his final decision without checking 'Monter's' report and without waiting for the arrival of other members of his Staff who might throw additional light on the situation.

The three Generals considered it unnecessary to check 'Monter's' report because of their explicit trust in his professional skill and acumen. On 26 July 1944 Gen Pelczynski had implied great faith in 'Monter's' judgement by telling him that the order to begin the

[1] Bokszczanin's letter to the author, 19 April 1965.
[2] Bor-Komorowski's oral evidence given to the author in the presence of Prof J. K. Zawodny.
[3] H. Butterfield, *The Englishman and His History* (London, 1944), p. 103.
[4] Leon Trotsky, *My Life* (New York, 1960), p. 498.

struggle might be issued at his instigation – on the basis of his appraisal of the military situation east of Warsaw.[1] In 1958 'Monter' wrote that Bor-Komorowski twice assured him, during the last ten days of July 1944, that he trusted his opinions more than his own.[2] It should here be stressed that Bor-Komorowski had little experience of or training in the conduct of large-scale operations. He lacked higher military training and was primarily a regimental officer.[3] His military knowledge was 'limited to the ability to command a cavalry regiment', writes Col Bokszczanin. Gen Pelczynski, also, 'had little experience of commanding troops in battle', as he was primarily an intelligence and counter-intelligence expert.[4] Hence, they were only too ready to listen to Col 'Monter', who, in the years 1936 to 1938, had been a lecturer in tactics at the Staff Academy. Okulicki, the third General present during the delivery of 'Monter's' report, appears to have been prepared to accept anything which tended to make the battle inevitable. From the beginning, he was determined that the Home Army should fight in Warsaw. On at least three previous occasions – on 24, 25 and the morning of 31 July – he had unsuccessfully pressed Bor-Komorowski to fix irrevocably the date of the insurrection.[5] On 25 July he urged the Chief of Intelligence to varnish his reports to secure the desired result – the speedy outbreak of the fighting.[6] He was prepared to deceive his Commander and was urging others to follow his example. Bor-Komorowski himself stated, in 1965, that Okulicki had tried to accelerate the outbreak of the fighting.[7] Okulicki was widely known in army circles for his impetuosity, *bravura*, dynamism, self-confidence, boundless optimism and zest for offensive.[8] In the last ten days of July 1944 he displayed these qualities to the full, thereby playing an important part in shaping of Bor-Komorowski's ill-advised decision.

Secondly, it is possible that all those present at Bor-Komorowski's

[1] Aleksander Skarzynski, *op. cit.*, p. 221.
[2] W. Pobog-Malinowski, *op. cit.*, p. 662, f.150.
[3] Cf. Wl. Michniewicz, 'Smierc Plk. Hanczy', *Kultura*, No. 10/1963, p. 88.
[4] Bokszczanin's letter to the author, 19 April 1965.
[5] For details see pp. 220ff of this study.
[6] Iranek-Osmecki's oral evidence, given to the author in the presence of Prof J. K. Zawodny.
[7] Bor-Komorowski's oral evidence, given to the author in the presence of Prof J. K. Zawodny.
[8] Bokszczanin's letter to the author, 19 April 1965. Bor-Komorowski's oral evidence, given to the author in the presence of Prof J. K. Zawodny.

headquarters, and not only 'Monter', were unable to control their nerves any longer or to act in a restrained, calm manner when confronted with the Colonel's report and his request for an immediate decision. Something of the kind was implied by Col Adam Borkiewicz, who himself served in the Home Army and later wrote a military history of the insurrection.

> It should be remembered [he observed], that the outbreak of the insurrection was preceded by five years of unparalleled nerve-racking terror. The older generation were more affected than the young by these conditions, especially classes 1895–1900, from which the majority of senior commanders and officers were recruited. Only this can explain why talented officers, such as Gen Monter and others, were unable to carry out their rationally and carefully prepared plans and maintain cool heads, and why they lacked sufficient will to stand by their original decisions.[1]

Similarly, Col Bokszczanin argues that Bor-Komorowski's decision of 31 July can only be explained either in terms of the Commander's 'recklessness' or his 'nervous exhaustion'.[2] The second suggestion seems more appropriate, for it is not difficult to see how a general climate of tension, induced by a high degree of nervous exhaustion, might have led the three Generals, especially Bor-Komorowski and Pelczynski, to accept uncritically the contents and implications of so unexpected and vehement an intervention as 'Monter's' report. None of them was strong or patient enough to wait for corroboration or denial of 'Monter's' findings by the other Staff officers, who were soon to arrive at the briefing, before committing their troops to action. On the contrary, after receiving the report they proceeded to devote their entire attention to contacting Jankowski and putting before him the case for the immediate launching of operations – a recommendation which the Government's Delegate, a civilian, could hardly reject, presented as it was by the top military experts.

The haste with which the final decision was taken may be explained further by the fact that all three Generals feared that undue delay in reaching it might rob them of their last chance to throw their troops into battle. They feared that the rapid occupation of Warsaw by the Red Army, or alternatively the heavy concentration within the city of German units retreating from the Praga bridgehead might soon

---

[1] Adam Borkiewicz, *op. cit.*, pp. 704–5.
[2] Bokszczanin's letter to the author, 19 April 1965.

make any large-scale and concerted Polish action impossible.[1] Such a development would have reduced the Home Army soldiers to the role of passive spectators during the final phases of the Russo–German battle for their capital. Indeed, on his own admission Bor-Komorowski feared, when giving his order to 'Monter', that it was already overdue, He was apprehensive that it might be too late to begin the battle before the Russians arrived in the city.[2] The Generals knew that, after the Russian occupation of Wilno and Lwow, only in Warsaw could they hope to stage a large-scale battle against the Germans at short notice. Warsaw was their last card and they were resolved to play it. 'In July 1944 the Warsaw Command of the Home Army had about 50 thousand organised soldiers and was numerically the strongest Home Army Command', wrote Gen Pelczynski in 1961.[3] Obviously, then, only in Warsaw could the Home Army stage a great and spectacular military operation. Indeed, in 1965 Gen Pelczynski himself stated that if the Home Army had failed to act in Warsaw it would never have acted, on a large scale, at all.[4] Further, Bor-Komorowski and Pelczynski later stated that at the time of the decision they feared that delay in opening their attack might increase the risk of German detection and suppression of their preparations,[5] a risk which had, it is true, become graver since 25 July, when the Germans had managed to restore a semblance of order in Warsaw, after their great panic of the previous few days. On the basis of existing and available evidence it is, however, impossible to ascertain objectively the full extent of this risk and how far, in reality, it influenced the decisions and responses of the Home Army leaders in the last days of July 1944. It may be that the possibility of a German pacification of the city has been used, post factum, to justify and rationalise the over-hasty decision of 31 July; even today, Bor-Komorowski's Chief of Intelligence claims that he had no especially alarming information about the German threat to the Underground at that time.[6] There is a conflicting allegation that in the second half of July 1944 reports were reaching Underground authorities that the Germans were preparing a great police attack against

---

[1] Tadeusz Bor-Komorowski, *op. cit.*, p. 216.
[2] Adam Borkiewicz, *op. cit.*, pp. 27–8.
[3] Tadeusz Pelczynski, 'General Antoni Chrusciel', *Dziennik Polski i Dziennik Zolnierza*, 1 January 1961.   [4] Pelczynski's oral evidence.
[5] Tadeusz Bor-Komorowski, *op. cit.*, p. 212, and T. Pelczynski, ('Grzegorz'), 'Powstanie Warszawskie', *Polska Walczaca*, No. 31, 3 August 1946.
[6] Iranek-Osmecki's oral evidence.

the Home Army, its command network and arsenals. This allegedly affected the timing of the insurrection.[1] Again, it is claimed that the identities of certain high-ranking Home Army officers, including that of its Chief of Staff, were known to the Germans, and that this affected the timing of the rising by contributing to the state of tension at Bor-Komorowski's Headquarters.[2]

Bor-Komorowski and his chief lieutenants also state that an additional reason for action was the risk that delay in staging the battle might have given the Germans time to enforce their earlier request for 100,000 inhabitants of Warsaw to help in fortifications work at the Russo–German Front, a request which was decisively ignored by the Poles. It is difficult to ascertain whether this fear did indeed operate at the time. According to Col Iranek-Osmecki's testimony, the absence of German attempts to enforce this request tended to promote among the Poles the idea that the Germans were weak.[3] Nevertheless, on 12 September 1944, in an interview with John Ward, Bor-Komorowski stated that these fears were real and affected the timing of the insurrection: 'If we had not taken up arms on or about 1 August, it would have been impossible to have done so at all, since all our manpower would have been swallowed up by the German system for digging trenches or sent to factories far from Polish soil. Warsaw would have been a deserted city.'[4] On the third day of the rising the same argument was used by Jankowski's representative at Col 'Monter's' Headquarters.[5]

On 25 September 1944 the *Biuletyn Informacyjny*, the official organ of the Home Army, gave a similar account of the situation which had existed in Warsaw a few days before the insurrection, and concluded that German anti-insurrectionary preparations affected the timing of the rising.[6]

An almost similar conclusion was reached by Gen Okulicki's Staff soon after the fall of Warsaw: 'The course of military operations on

---

[1] 'Powstanie Warszawskie', *Biuletyn Informacyjny*, No. 93(301), 25 September 1944, APUST.

[2] Aleksander Skarzynski, *op. cit.*, pp. 263–4.

[3] Iranek-Osmecki's oral evidence.

[4] Radio message from a British airman serving with the Home Army in Warsaw to the Air Ministry in London, 12 September 1944 – Interview with General Bor, Commander-in-Chief of the Polish Home Army, APUST.

[5] Z. Stypulkowski, *W Zawierusze Wojennej: Wspomnienia 1939–1945* (London, 1951), p. 216.

[6] 'Powstanie Warszawskie', *Biuletyn Informacyjny*, No. 93(301), 2 September 1944, APUST.

the Vistula in the last days of July was one decisive factor in the choice of a date for the beginning of the battle for Warsaw, but was not the only one. A second factor was the increasing tempo of German preparation for a terrorist pacification of Warsaw, which would render any Polish armed insurrection in the capital impossible.'[1]

Finally, it is claimed that Bor-Komorowski and his Staff feared that procrastination on their part might lead, at the moment of the Red Army's entry into the city, to a spontaneous or Communist-inspired outbreak of fighting, impossible for them to control or exploit.[2] They feared that if such a situation should arise hundreds of their junior commanders, together with their men, would desert their ranks and place themselves at the disposal of any leadership willing to direct the fighting.[3] Nevertheless, both Bor-Komorowski and Iranek-Osmecki stated, in 1965, that they did not receive any reports warning them that the Communists were, in fact, preparing an insurrection; indeed, they both knew that the Communists were weak in Warsaw and that some of their units and leaders had left the city shortly before the insurrection. Apparently they feared, however, that the Communists might still act when the Russians entered Warsaw.[4] All these fears, if they existed, were bound to increase the state of nervous tension among Bor-Komorowski's Staff and prompt some of its members to act prematurely rather than too late, especially as they felt certain that the Russians were about to enter the city.

The main flaw in the Home Army's plan was, in fact, the absence of operational liaison with the Russians. No attempt was made to inform the Russians, even indirectly, of the approaching insurrection.[5] Rokossovsky was right in saying, during the rising, that from the military point of view 'armed insurrection in a place like Warsaw could only have succeeded if it had been carefully co-ordinated with the Red Army. The question of timing was of the utmost importance The Warsaw insurgents are badly armed, and the rising would have made sense only if we were on the point of entering Warsaw.'[6] The difficulties were further accentuated by the complex nature of the

[1] 'Bitwa Warszawska', B.II, No. 543, APUST.
[2] T. Bor-Komorowski, *op. cit.*, p. 216.
[3] A. Chrusciel, *op. cit.*, p. 6.
[4] Bor-Komorowski's and Iranek-Osmecki's oral evidence.
[5] Bor-Komorowski's oral evidence.
[6] Alexander Werth, *Russia At War, 1941–45* (London, 1964), p. 877.

Home Army's plan of action in Warsaw. They needed time – about 24 hours – to mobilise, concentrate and deploy the troops for battle. Secondly, they needed time to destroy or overpower the German garrison and occupy the city, and no one could accurately predict, beforehand, how long these operations might take. Finally, the Home Army would have to hold the capital for at least twelve hours, to enable the political and administrative organs of the Secret State to start functioning in the liberated city. All this would have to be accomplished before the Red Army's entry. Therefore, ultimate success demanded swift and decisive action *at the right moment*, but even an approximately accurate calculation of this moment could have been made only after consultation with the Russians. The Polish plan was ambitious, audacious and hazardous, in view of the shortage of arms and ammunition; it involved a number of intricate moves, the success of which depended, not on Polish effort alone, but also on the state and deployment of the German, and, especially, the Soviet forces fighting on the outskirts of the city. As Iranek-Osmecki has revealed, they knew 'very little' about the size and state of the Soviet forces fighting in the vicinity of Warsaw.[1] Bor-Komorowski went further in saying that before the insurrection 'none of us knew exactly where the main Soviet forces were. . .'[2] It is my opinion, then, that in view of the total absence of liaison with the Russians, and the lack of reliable data concerning their deployment and intentions, the Home Army leaders were militarily unjustified in embarking on an insurrection against the Germans. The risks involved in carrying out the plan were seriously increased by the fact that the Home Army could expect to receive very little, if any help, in men and equipment, from British-held bases. Bor-Komorowski was given this disappointing news two days before the outbreak of the rising.[3] The fact that it failed to prompt the Home Army commanders to abandon or even modify their plans is evidence that their anxiety to secure material support from the West has been based on their high evaluation of its political importance rather than its usefulness, and is a further indication of their unshake-able belief that the Red Army was about to take Warsaw.

Bor-Komorowski hoped that the fury and *élan* of the initial Polish

[1] Iranek-Osmecki's oral evidence.
[2] Letter from Gen T. Bor-Komorowski to Prof J. K. Zawodny, 6 April 1965 – a copy of the letter is in the possession of the author of this study.
[3] 'Emisariusz: Wywiad z Kapitanem Nowakiem', *Na Antenie* (*Wiadomosci*), No. 962, 6 September 1964.

assault and the Poles' passionate desire for revenge would be a powerful factor in rapidly crushing German resistance in Warsaw and would off-set Polish material inferiority.[1] 'In Warsaw we saw', said Pelczynski, 'a great concentration of German military and police forces. We saw their material superiority over us. But . . . they were morally shaken by the approaching inevitability of their final defeat. . . All Germans knew that after the attempt on Hitler's life their discipline had already collapsed. The Polish people had the advantage of better morale.'[2] The idea that German discipline had collapsed was a fallacy, as events were to prove. Throughout, and well after the rising, the Germans maintained good discipline and a will to fight. Bokszczanin writes that before the insurrection he viewed Bor-Komorowski's plan to destroy the German garrison in Warsaw as unrealistic and too absurd in the existing situation, to merit serious discussion.[3] The Home Army generals knew that their soldiers were badly equipped, but consoled themselves with the thought that 'when the people of Paris were marching on the Bastille they did not count their clubs. . .'[4] Such a comparison, however laudable the courage which prompted it, would seem to be out of place in the context of the Warsaw Rising, which was initiated by professional soldiers fully acquainted with the laws of tactics, and not by desperate and hungry *sansculottes*. Indeed, a counting of clubs before embarking on the rising would seem to have been precisely one of their professional duties, omitted because they believed that the struggle would be short and the Russians would soon enter the city, and because of their overwhelming impatience to fight.

The Home Army commanders attached great importance to the element of surprise which they hoped to exploit in order to eliminate as many as possible of the German troops while they were still scattered on the streets of the city. They hoped, too, to capture considerable quantities of arms in the course of their initial attack. Bor-Komorowski intended to remain on the offensive during the few days immediately following the opening of hostilities, until the

[1] Bokszczanin's letter, 19 April 1965.
[2] 'Szef Sztabu Armii Krajowej: Fragment Wywiadu z Generalem Pelczynskim', *Na Antenie (Wiadomosci)*, No. 962, 6 September 1964.
[3] Bokszczanin's letter, 1 April 1965.
[4] General T. Pelczynski's statement, 18 April 1951, 'Czwarte zebranie relacyjne w inst. J. Pilsudskiego z 18/4/1951: Decyzja walki o Warszawe', B.II, APUST.

entry of the Soviet troops.[1] The first hours of the insurrection shattered these high hopes in a cruel and tragic manner and the inaccuracies in Bor-Komorowski's military calculations became apparent. The results of the initial attack on well-fortified German objectives were disastrous. The Poles met with resolute German resistance, suffered heavy losses and were compelled to call off their attacks.[2] Bor-Komorowski decided, however, to continue the struggle. He asked London for help in men and equipment. 'Monter' still believed that time was working on the side of the insurgents, but implored his superiors to hasten the Red Army's arrival in Warsaw.[3] Thus, as early as the second day of the insurrection it was dramatically clear that only the Red Army's speedy entry into the city could save it from destruction and carnage. This was patently evident to the Polish leaders in the West, who realised soon after the rising had begun that it was premature. Within a few hours of learning of it Gen Anders informed his superiors in London that he considered it to be 'a misfortune'.[4] Some days later he stated that he and his soldiers regarded the order for the rising as 'a serious crime'. In his considered opinion the capital was 'doomed to be annihilated' in spite of 'the heroism, unparalleled in history', of the insurgents.[5] The General was certain that the insurrection had not a 'half-chance' of success. He saw it as 'a madness', a 'flagrant crime'.[6]

On 13 August Mikolajczyk sent a telegram to Stalin imploring him, in the name of the future of Russo–Polish relations, to save Warsaw from destruction, by ordering the Red Army to enter the capital of Poland as its 'liberators' rather than as grave-diggers 'to bury the dead in a destroyed city'.[7] Five days later the Polish Premier sent another telegram to Moscow, in which he said that the insurrection seemed premature and that the Soviet High Command could not be held responsible for it.[8] On 16 August Gen Sosnkowski

---

[1] General T. Pelczynski's statement, 30 August 1964; transcript of Gen Pelczynski's broadcast on Radio Free Europe, 30 August 1964, APUST.

[2] For details see A. Borkiewicz, *op. cit.*, pp. 81ff.   [3] *Ibid.*, pp. 103–4.

[4] Despatch from Gen W. Anders to the Chief of Staff, 3 August 1944, No. 2049, GSHI, Kol. G.A/46.

[5] Despatch from Gen W. Anders to the Minister of National Defence, 23 August 1944, No. 2139, GSHI, Kol. G.A./46.

[6] Letter from Gen W. Anders to Col 'Hancza', 31 August 1944, Ldz. ADJ/318/Tj./44, GSHI, Kol. G.A./46.

[7] Telegram from Premier Mikolajczyk to Marshal Stalin, 13 August 1944, GSHI, Amb.R.P., London, A.XII, 73/7.

[8] Telegram from Premier Mikolajczyk to Marshal Stalin, 18 August 1944, GSHI, PRM–L49/197.

stated that the opening of the fighting in Warsaw had 'coincided with the German counter-attack against the Soviet units on the eastern banks of the Vistula'.[1] On 24 August Gen Kukiel was more outspoken when he wrote that the timing of the insurrection was a 'surprise' to the exiled Government. He was convinced that the Home Army Generals regarded their action to be an implementation of 'Burza'. 'They probably thought', he said 'that they were cutting off [German] rearguards and that they were anticipating the entry of the Soviets within a few hours. [But] Hitler's decision to throw in his strategic reserves brought about a complete change of the situation.'[2] In 1964 he said: 'They drew a false card – a joker – when they finally decided to act.'[3] In his opinion the fact that the Russians had reached the vicinity of Praga was not sufficient proof of their ability to cross the Vistula and take Warsaw. He said that as early as 30 July 1944 the news of the arrival of German tank reinforcements in the Warsaw area had convinced him that the Russo–German battle would last longer than expected and that this called for postponement of the Polish action. At the time, however, Kukiel omitted to communicate this view to Bor-Komorowski and his Staff.[4]

Not only were the highest Polish authorities abroad fully aware, from the beginning of the insurrection, that it had been ill-timed, but in Warsaw itself, a number of high-ranking Home Army officers also regarded the insurrection as premature. Col Bokszczanin wrote in 1965 that he had always considered Bor-Komorowski's decision of 31 July 1944 'as unjustified and premature'.[5] Col Iranek-Osmecki said in 1965 that he knew at the time that 'the timing of the insurrection was faulty'.[6] Both Rokossovsky and Guderian regarded the insurrection as premature. Rokossovsky said, in August 1944, that 'a fearful mistake was made by the AK leadership. ... Bor-Komorowski and the people around him have butted in – *kak ryzhy v tsirke* – like the clown in the circus who pops up at the wrong moment and only gets rolled up in the carpet. . . If it were only a piece of clowning it wouldn't matter, but the political stunt is going to cost Poland hundreds of thousands of lives. It is an appalling

[1] Despatch from the C-in-C to Gen W. Anders, 16 August 1944, No. 7005, GSHI, Kol. G.A./46.

[2] Despatch from the Minister of National Defence to Gen W. Anders, 24 August 1944, Ldz. 368/AMIN/tj/44, No. 2139, GSHI.

[3] General Kukiel's oral evidence.   [4] *Ibid.*

[5] Bokszczanin's letter, 19 April 1965.

[6] Iranek-Osmecki's oral evidence.

tragedy. . .'[1] Guderian, for his part, wrote that 'the Polish uprising . . . had, from the enemy's point of view, been begun too soon'.[2] The military error made by Bor-Komorowski sprang from his undue optimism as to the Russian chances of taking Warsaw in the first days of August, his underestimate of German defensive capabilities and, finally, his uncritical acceptance of Col 'Monter's' fatal report.

Although, in the military sense, the rising was directed against the Germans it would be wrong to conclude that it was launched primarily to help the Russians to capture Warsaw. As early as 14 July 1944 Bor-Komorowski told his subordinates: 'By giving the Soviets minimal military help we create for them political difficulties.'[3] A fortnight later the political leaders of the Secret State plainly told Mikolajczyk that they regarded their 'further military co-operation with the Soviets' to be synonymous with 'preparing for them the way to a new conquest of Poland'.[4] Thus, on the eve of the insurrection, the highest political and military authorities of the pro-London movement were not prepared to give unqualified support to the Red Army in its passage through Poland. They had decided to exploit the situation which they believed to be prevailing on the Eastern Front to stage their own battle for Warsaw which, although of some military assistance to the Soviets, would, in the political sense, hinder the Russians in their work of imposing what the Underground leaders suspected were the Soviet plans for Poland. In 1948 'Monter' himself pointed out that the Home Army Command's decision to begin hostilities in Warsaw was motivated not only by a wish to assist the Russians militarily, but also by 'considerations' which had little to do with this.[5]

Similarly, there are no grounds for believing that the insurrection was launched in response to Russian broadcast appeals for help in their task of liberating the Polish capital from the Germans. On the contrary, as early as 12 July 1944 Jankowski told Mikolajczyk that it was 'out of the question to start the insurrection on account of the fighting in the East'. Indeed, the Government's Delegate was

[1] Alexander Werth, *op. cit.*, p. 878.
[2] Heinz Guderian, *op. cit.*, p. 359.
[3] Report from the Commander of the Home Army to the C-in-C, 14 July 1944, No. 243, Ldz. 6302/44, APUST.
[4] Despatch from the Government Delegate and the Presidium of the Council of National Unity to the Prime Minister, 28 July 1944, No. 93, Ldz. K4394, APUST, File 16, Min. Spr. Wew.
[5] Antoni Chrusciel, *op. cit.*, p. 13.

expressly determined to ignore Soviet calls for an insurrection in Poland. The Underground leaders alone were to decide when and where the Home Army would fight against the Germans.[1] Jankowski's attitude was shared by the Home Army Generals. In 1950 Gen Pelczynski said that the Soviet appeals to the Poles to begin the struggle in Warsaw 'did not incite us to rise'.[2] Gen Bor-Komorowski himself implicitly confirmed this by saying that, on the whole, these appeals were 'nothing new'.[3] The General regarded them as part of general Soviet war propaganda and not as clarion calls which had specifically stimulated his action in Warsaw, although he did assert that they tended to persuade him that Moscow regarded the situation as ripe for insurrection in Warsaw, an impression which was of special significance to him because of his inability to co-ordinate his plans with those of the Soviet High Command. The appeals, then, were not directly responsible for the outbreak of fighting in Warsaw; at most, they merely strengthened the Home Army leaders' determination to act by convincing them even more that the Polish capital was about to fall into Russian hands.[4] In any case, they had already arrived at this conclusion a few days before the Soviet appeals of 29 and 30 July.[5] What is more, despite these appeals the Polish leaders made no attempt to establish at least tactical liaison with Rokossovsky in order to co-ordinate their own projected operations with him; they could have used the appeals as a convenient pretext for the establishment of Russo–Polish military co-operation. It seems clear that the Polish leaders hoped that their action within the city would surprise not only the Germans, but the Russians as well. This was a grave mistake, as their failure to inform the Russians of their intentions allowed Stalin, later, to disclaim any responsibility towards the insurgents. It should also be mentioned that Rokossovsky himself dismissed the Soviet appeals for the insurrection in Warsaw as mere 'routine stuff'.[6] On this point, at least, there was agreement between the Polish and Soviet Commanders. Even if Rokossovsky's

---

[1] Despatch from the Government Delegate to the Prime Minister, 12 July 1944, No. 74, Ldz. K4775/44, GSHI–L9.

[2] General Pelczynski's statement, 15 September 1950, 'Protokoly z Zebran Relacyjnych w inst. J. Pilsudskiego w Londynie n.t. Powstania Warszawskiego, Walk A.K. i Postawy Rosji Sowieckiej – Zebranie Pierwsze Odbyte 15/IX/1950', APUST. B.II.

[3] T. Bor-Komorowski, *op. cit.*, p. 214.

[4] Bor-Komorowski's oral evidence.

[5] For details see pp. 215ff of this study.

[6] Alexander Werth, *op. cit.*, p. 877.

opinions concerning Moscow's appeals were dismissed as unconvincing, or even insincere, this hardly proves that the broadcasts were instrumental in bringing about the insurrection, especially in view of Jankowski's, Pelczynski's and Bor-Komorowski's statements to the contrary.

We can only conclude that the Underground leaders' decision to try to capture Warsaw was dictated more by a desire to forestall occupation of the city by the Russians than by a wish to render unqualified support to the Red Army, as the Soviet appeals requested.

The Warsaw rising was to be the means by which the pro-London Poles were to assume power, initially in the capital and then in the whole of newly-liberated Poland. The pro-London leaders intended to forestall, with their rising, the assumption of power by the Russian-supported Polish Communists, that is, the newly-formed PKWN.

The immediate sequel to the rising was to be the emergence of the underground authorities as the popularly-acclaimed leaders of the nation. This was to be achieved by the political, military and administrative authorities of the Underground coming into the open, at the head of a powerful and dynamic movement, in the capital, a city of over a million inhabitants flushed with recent victory and in a state of post-liberation euphoria. In this manner the Underground leaders intended to capture the hearts and minds, not only of the people of Warsaw, but of the whole of Poland, and even hoped to detach 'as many as possible of the Polish elements hitherto standing at their disposal. . .'[1] from the Soviets and the PKWN. By striking against the Germans in Warsaw they intended to place themselves and their movement very firmly in the vanguard of the struggle for national liberation, and make a powerful bid for the loyalties and support of all patriotic forces in the country. 'National dignity and pride required', Korbonski has written, 'that the capital should be liberated by the Poles themselves, and that was accepted without any discussion.'[2] By providing a dramatic outlet on the streets of Warsaw for these potent and explosive patriotic feelings, the pro-London leaders tried to unite all their countrymen behind the exiled Government; leadership in the struggle against the Germans was to provide them with the key to undisputed power in post-war Poland. Con-

---

[1] Appendix to the Despatch from the Commander of the Home Army to the C-in-C, 2 July 1944, Ldz. 5988/tj/44., GSHI–PRM, L6.
[2] S. Korbonski, *Fighting Warsaw* (London, 1956), p. 347.

versely, the Home Army's failure to act decisively in Warsaw would, they feared, allow the Communists to assume the initiative and authority over all patriotic forces. In July 1944 Bor-Komorowski maintained that if the Home Army did not act the Polish Workers' Party would initiate a large-scale struggle against the Germans and that a considerable part of the people would join this movement. Then, the country would enter into unqualified collaboration with the Soviets. The newly-arrived Russians would be met, not by the Home Army loyal to the exiled authorities, but by their own supporters. The General believed at the time that the Communists were planning to launch their own insurrection in Poland when the Red Army entered the territories west of the Curzon Line. He feared that, if he failed to forestall it, the Communist-inspired insurrection would sweep aside the pro-London leadership, split the Polish people and would make the PPR the real masters of the situation.[1] As early as March 1944 Rzepecki warned his superiors that if they failed to act energetically the leadership of the patriotic but turbulent masses might pass into the hands of the Communists. He observed, rather pathetically, 'for incompetent leaders only contempt, or even hatred and . . . a lamp-post will remain'.[2]

In brief, Bor-Komorowski and Jankowski felt compelled, by the political rivalry between their own and the pro-Moscow forces, to rise in Warsaw. In addition, they believed that the Russian attitude to the insurgents would reveal conclusively whether an understanding between the pro-London authorities and Stalin, allowing for the exiled Government's return to and assumption of power in Poland, was possible. The recent establishment of the PKWN, which had been anticipated in discussions between the pro-London leaders, hardly surprised Bor-Komorowski and Jankowski, but strengthened their resolution to act.[3] Warsaw learned of the formation of the PKWN on 22 July 1944 at 8.15 p.m., that is, over twenty-four hours after the three Generals had agreed to fight in the capital.[4] The news convinced the pro-London leadership that a radical opposition to the PKWN was essential.[5] Otherwise, they predicted the triumphal entry

[1] Report from the Commander of the Home Army to the C-in-C, 14 July 1944, No. 243, Ldz. 6302/44, APUST.
[2] Jan Rzepecki, *op. cit.*, p. 268.
[3] Despatch from the Commander of the Home Army to the C-in-C, 17 June 1944, Ldz. 612/GNW/44, APUST.
[4] E. J. Rozek, *op. cit.*, p. 229.
[5] Iranek-Osmecki's oral evidence.

into Warsaw of the representatives of the Committee and Berling's troops, in the wake of the advancing Red Army, and consequently popular acceptance of the PKWN as the national authority. 'After five years of bloody German occupation the hearts of the inhabitants of the Polish capital would have been open to temptation', wrote Gen Pelczynski.[1] In order that the citizens of Warsaw might be shielded from such temptation, the authors of the rising deemed it essential to keep the PKWN away from the city during the days immediately following liberation, and this could only be done by capturing Warsaw from the Germans and establishing an openly-functioning pro-London administration.

Further, they hoped that, if Moscow should adopt a hostile and intransigent attitude to their rising and their subsequent claims to represent and govern Poland, the Western Powers – Great Britain and the United States – would intervene at the Kremlin on their behalf. Bor-Komorowski maintained that Soviet violence 'might lead to protests from the Allies who are friendly to us'.[2] But he believed that the pro-London forces could only 'count on Anglo-Saxon help' if they displayed their determination to win, and skilfully threw all their resources on the scales.[3]

The authors of the insurrection believed, therefore, that by capturing Warsaw they had everything to gain and nothing to lose; if the Russians accepted their *fait accompli* they would automatically become the rulers of Poland. If, however, the Russians tried to reverse it by force, this would lead to Anglo–American diplomatic intervention on their behalf, resulting, in turn in a *rapprochement* with Stalin. Therefore, both eventualities would have the desired result of placing power in the hands of the London Poles. The insurrection seems, then, to have been Bor-Komorowski's and Jankowski's exercise in *Realpolitik*, a gamble prompted by their strong desire not to surrender without a fight their ambition to govern post-war Poland. The struggle against the Germans was to be a dramatic prelude to the Russo–Polish confrontation; it was to be instrumental in securing pro-London control of the capital for at least twelve hours before the arrival of the Red Army and was thus

[1] General Tadeusz Pelczynski, 'O Powstaniu Warszawskim', *Bellona*, No. 3/1955, p. 9.
[2] Report from the Commander of the Home Army to the C-in-C, 14 July 1944, No. 243, Ldz. 6302/44, APUST.
[3] Despatch from the Commander of the Home Army to the C-in-C, 22 July 1944, Ldz. 5988/tj/44. GSHI–PRM, L6.

to allow the political and administrative authorities loyal to the exiled Government to start functioning in the newly-liberated city.[1]

According to Col Bokszczanin's testimony, during the days immediately preceding the insurrection the entire attention of the Home Army Staff was devoted to the problem of how to secure this essential twelve hours. 'This task', stated Bokszczanin, 'became, as it were, the sole aim of the rising; it decisively affected the moment of its outbreak and, in consequence, its course.'[2] Similar views were expressed by Gen 'Monter'.

> The political aim was to be achieved by the seizure of the capital by our own forces before the entry of the Red Army. In the liberated capital of the sovereign state power over the entire country was to be assumed by the legal authorities . . . The idea was, to manifest to the entire world that the Government was in its place and that there was no need for the installation of candidates imported from the East to govern the country.[3]

The Warsaw Rising was, therefore, part of a political campaign. In the spring of 1944 the campaign was first initiated, as part of 'Burza', in Volhynia, and in the summer of that year was subsequently extended to the other parts of pre-war Poland – the Wilno and Lwow regions – with disastrous results. On 25 July Bor-Komorowski and Jankowski decided to extend it to Warsaw. The insurrection in the capital was to realise the political aims of 'Burza' which the operations east of the capital had failed to achieve. Some years after the war Bor-Komorowski said of this time,

> '. . . even the very great sacrifices which the units of the Home Army had already made in the fighting in Poland had passed unnoticed and had aroused no response in the outside world. Thus we felt that the battle for Warsaw would have to call forth a response from the world and proclaim our will for independence.'[4]

His Chief of Staff supported and enlarged upon this idea:

> After the fighting in Wilno, which lasted from 7 until 13 July, the Muscovites started to liquidate the Home Army in this region. This lasted until 17 July. About 20 July it became obvious that our reports to London dealing with the events in Wilno had met with no response in the west. Our greatest battle in Poland, other than Volhynia, the

[1] Bor-Komorowski's oral evidence.
[2] Bokszczanin's letter, 1 April 1965.
[3] Antoni Chrusciel, *op. cit.*, p. 15.
[4] Waclaw Zagorski, *Seventy Days* (London, 1959), p. 10.

battle for Wilno, was completely sunk in the sinister morass of relations between Poland, Russia and the Allies. This fact led us to the conclusion that a greater armed action was needed at home, greater than in Volhynia and Wilno, [an action] which could not be ignored or interpreted in a pro-Soviet manner by political opinion in the West. . . . [by] about 20 July we became fully convinced of the need for armed action in Warsaw.[1]

Clearly, then, there was an organic connection between the tragedy in Volhynia and Wilno and the insurrection in Warsaw. After the failure of 'Burza' in eastern Poland to improve the position of the London Poles, the shots fired against the Germans by the insurgents in Warsaw were to echo throughout the entire embattled world and arrest the attention of the Allied leaders.

However, the anti-Soviet aspects of 'Burza' were mitigated by the fact that, in the military sense, it was directed against the Germans, with the Home Army ready to do its share in the task of expelling the Nazis from the country. Only by fighting against the Germans could the Home Army oppose the Russian politically. 'At this decisive moment', said Bor-Komorowski in 1965, 'the capital of Poland could not remain passive. Its liberation from the German yoke by the Red Army alone, without the participation of her own soldiers [the Home Army], would have been used by Russia as a proof that the Polish nation was expecting to be liberated only by Russia and that it wished to build its future with Russia's support. . .'[2] These words indicate the nature of Bor-Komorowski's predicament in 1944; to fight against the Germans successfully he had to co-operate with the Russians militarily, yet he was unable to do so whole-heartedly because he wished to oppose them politically or, at least, to stress his independence of them.

On 12 July 1944 the General ordered his subordinates to 'co-operate with the Soviets, but only in the struggle against the Germans'. Politically, they were to oppose them and manifest their allegiance to the exiled Government, with which the U.S.S.R. did not have diplomatic relations. Indeed, Bor-Komorowski was more than anxious to make certain that his troops' tactical collaboration with the Soviets could not be used by the latter as evidence that the Polish people wanted political co-operation with them. Consequently, to stress the independent character of his forces he ordered them to 'conduct their combat tasks against the Germans completely

---

[1] Pelczynski's statement, 18 April 1951.
[2] T. Bor-Komorowski, *op. cit.*, p. 203.

independently for as long as possible, without rashly establishing liaison [with the Soviets]'.[1] The General was guided by the same considerations when he was planning his operations in Warsaw, the political aims of which were to be similar to those which had guided the Home Army's attitude to the Soviets east of the capital. The underground leaders were determined to meet the approaching Russians as their rightful hosts.

At that time the Polish leaders in Warsaw were, on the whole, quite optimistic that this plan which was to give them political and administrative power in Poland would succeed. Stefan Korbonski, one of the top leaders of the pro-London movement, has said that their hopes rested on the assumption that, if the capital were liberated by Polish effort and the Underground authorities then assumed power in the name of the exiled Government, 'we would create an accomplished fact which the Russians would have to accept. At that time it seemed to us to be as . . . unthinkable that the Soviets would undertake any repressive measures against this allied government as against any other. Then, we were simply optimists.'[2] Bor-Komorowski himself thought that the Soviet attitude to the pro-London movement might be 'different' in the territories west of the Curzon Line, which Stalin accepted as an integral part of Poland, from the attitude they had displayed in the territories to the east of it, which the Russians regarded as belonging to them. The General believed that the Soviet attitude to the pro-London forces was as yet not fully crystallised; he still regarded it as an open question. From the reports reaching him from the territories already occupied by the Red Army he had gained the impression that Soviet commanders still had no specific directives from Moscow as to how to treat his troops.[3] The Home Commander still hoped to reach some kind of *modus vivendi* with the Russians in Warsaw: this fact is supported by the testimony of Col Bokszczanin, who has stated that the underground authorities were generally 'quite optimistic' about their chances of reaching an understanding with the Russians, with the help of London and Washington, although they did not entirely exclude the possibility of Russian hostility, and even Russian repression of

[1] Report from the Commander of the Home Army to the C-in-C, 14 July 1944, No. 243, Appendix 3, Ldz. 6303/tjn/44. APUST.
[2] S. Korbonski's statement, 23 August 1964. A transcript of S. Korbonski's broadcast on Radio Free Europe, 23 August 1964. APUST.
[3] Bor-Komorowski's oral evidence.

the agencies of the Secret State.[1] This suggests that not all the Underground leaders were quite as confident as Korbonski that hostile Soviet action was impossible, although, on the whole, all were hopeful that the Russians would not dare to arrest them or disarm their troops in Warsaw, the capital of a country allied to Great Britain and the United States. Even if they did so they would, the resistance leaders believed, have to relent under pressure from the West.

Moreover, all the resistance leaders agreed that Warsaw was to serve as an immense and dramatic stage on which the final and decisive act of the Russo–Polish confrontation was to be performed. Here, the ultimate clarification of Russo–Polish relations was to take place. Here also, the Western Powers were to be invited to define their attitude to the Polish question. It was also hoped that a successful insurrection would strengthen Mikolajczyk's bargaining position during his Moscow talks with Stalin; it was to enable him to conduct his negotiations with the Russians from a position of relative strength, and convince the Kremlin that he was the real representative of resurgent Poland. Bor-Komorowski himself made it clear, in 1946, that immediately before the rising he had had this in mind; '. . . our military action in Warsaw would aid [Mikolajczyk] in re-establishing relations between our two governments'.[2] Iranek-Osmecki stated that the insurrection was to be a 'trump card' for Mikolajczyk.[3] Pelczynski admitted that the insurrection was to be an attempt to buttress the position of the exiled Government.[4] In July 1944 this could only mean that the underground authorities were anxious to synchronise their struggle in Warsaw with Mikolajczyk's visit to Moscow. Indeed, on 3 August 1944 a high official of the underground stated that one of the direct causes of the insurrection was the intention to assist Mikolajczyk in his talks with Stalin.[5]

Five years later Bor-Komorowski stated that in the early days of the rising he and his Staff had eagerly awaited news from Moscow. 'We were waiting with impatience', he wrote,

> for the outcome of Premier Mikolajczyk's talks in Moscow. We knew that he had radio contact with London and that he was receiving daily reports concerning the situation in the capital. We also knew

---

[1] Bokszczanin's letter, 1 April 1965.
[2] T. Bor-Komorowski, 'The Unconquerables', *The Reader's Digest*, February 1946, p. 129.   [3] Iranek-Osmecki's oral evidence.
[4] Pelczynski's oral evidence.   [5] Z. Stylupkowski, *op. cit.*, p. 216.

that on 31 July . . . he had his first talk with Molotov, and that a few days later he saw Stalin. We had no doubt that the problem of the co-ordination of operations between the Soviet Command and the Polish side, and the problem of help for Warsaw would be discussed.[1]

As early as 26 July Rzepecki told his superiors and colleagues that the Government was probably working for a Russo–Polish understanding and that their endeavours might soon meet with success.[2] Jankowski also believed that the rising might improve Mikolajczyk's position in his negotiations in Moscow, as the accusation that the pro-London movement was not fighting against the Germans would then become ludicrous.[3] Further, it is maintained that, on 2 September 1944 Bor-Komorowski told the Presidium of the Council of National Unity that he had ordered the insurrection partly because 'Mikolajczyk was going to Moscow and it was necessary to back him up in his negotiations with Stalin.'[4] In 1965 the General denied this, however, saying that 'the matter of backing Mikolajczyk's action was simply not discussed'.[5] He also stated that Mikolajczyk's departure for Moscow had no bearing at all on his decision.[6] But, in view of his own categorical statement of 1946 that his military action in Warsaw had been motivated partly by the fact that it 'would aid [Mikolajczyk] in re-establishing Russo–Polish diplomatic relations' his 1965 statement does not seem entirely convincing. Probably in 1965 the General was referring to the fact that, as official news of Mikolajczyk's departure did not reach Warsaw until 29 July, the Premier's plan to visit Stalin had not affected the Underground leaders' *initial* decision to act in Warsaw, made between 21 and 25 July. It must, however, have strengthened their resolution to act – and in 1965 Bor-Komorowski said that it did – by convincing them that decisive action on the part of the Home Army was needed, as Russo–Polish relations were reaching a climax. The news about Mikolajczyk's departure, supported by Churchill, gave to the Underground authorities an added sense of urgency. It confirmed them in their view that their independent decision to fight in Warsaw was fully

---

[1] T. Bor-Komorowski, *op. cit.*, p. 243.
[2] Colonel J. Rzepecki, 'W Sprawie Decyzji Podjecia Walki w Warszawie', *Wojskowy Przeglad Historyczny*, No. 2/1958, p. 322.
[3] A. Skarzynski, *op. cit.*, p. 255.
[4] J. Rokicki, *op. cit.*, p. 101.
[5] Letter from Gen T. Bor-Komorowski to Prof J. K. Zawodny, 6 April 1965. A copy of the letter is in the possession of the author of this study.
[6] Bor-Komorowski's oral evidence.

justified by high-level diplomatic developments, which they hoped to influence by seizing Warsaw.[1]

Here, they acted on the assumption that, in spite of the formation of the PKWN, the final clarification of Russo–Polish relations would take place in Warsaw after the entry of the Red Army. Indeed, they were encouraged by the fact that the newly-formed Communist administration had only been accorded the title of 'committee' and not of 'Polish government'; this they interpreted as implying that Stalin was leaving himself an opening for an understanding with Mikolajczyk.[2]

Further, the authors of the insurrection were encouraged to act by the firm conviction that the people of Warsaw would enthusiastically and unflinchingly respond to their call to rise against the hated Germans, as, in the event, they did. From the time of the partitions Warsaw had played a significant part in the struggle for Poland's independence. In 1794 the city had risen against the Russians in response to the outbreak of Kosciuszko's insurrection; the 1830 rising began in Warsaw; during the years 1863–4 Warsaw was the seat of an insurrectionary underground Government; in the years 1904–7 the Warsaw proletariat played an important part in the struggle against Tsarism; in September 1939 Warsaw fought heroically against the Germans, and in 1943 there was an uprising against the Germans in Warsaw's Ghetto. Throughout the period of German occupation Warsaw was one of the main bastions of anti-Nazi resistance. Here, the Secret Army and administration were born, the pro-London resistance movement had its greatest and strongest concentration of manpower, and its political and military headquarters, which meant that only in Warsaw could the course of the battle and the process of emerging into the open be personally directed and controlled by the leaders of the underground state. Now, on their orders, the people of Warsaw were to be given an opportunity to fight again for the liberation of their city. Bokszczanin writes that Bor-Komorowski was certain that the inhabitants of Warsaw, moved by their hatred of the Germans, would rise against them and would crush them in an enormous avalanche.[3]

Indeed, in July 1944 feeling in Warsaw was running high and

---

[1] Pelczynski's oral evidence.
[2] Despatch from the Commander of the Home Army to the C-in-C, dated 17 September, sent 19 September 1944, Ldz. 8619/Tjn/44. APUST.
[3] Bokszczanin's letter, 19 April 1965.

popular demands for immediate action against the Germans were growing. An eye-witness, an officer of the Home Army, noted that on 31 July the atmosphere in the city was so tense and so highly charged with emotion and hopes of a speedy liberation that it was 'something of a miracle that Warsaw has been so highly disciplined up to now'. 'But can we count on what amounts to a miracle?' he asked.[1] This officer remarked that the only question which people seemed to be asking each other a few days before the insurrection was 'What are we waiting for now?'[2] In the last days of July 1944 the Polish capital was, Stefan Korbonski observed 'a volcano on the point of eruption'.[3] The question was, when to precipitate the eruption and how to turn it to political advantage. During the last days of July 1944 the leaders of the secret state were doing their utmost to raise the temperature of this 'volcano' and ensure that it was constantly kept close to eruption-point.

On 28 July 'Monter' alerted and concentrated his troops, who spent the entire day at their assembly points, waiting for their final orders. In some units the state of semi-alertness continued, in spite of the repeal of the general alarm. This was bound to create a state of high tension and excitement among 'Monter's' soldiers, whose situation – a prolonged period of mobilisation in a city still occupied and policed by the Germans – was unprecedented.[4] From 29 July *Rzeczypospolita* – the clandestine organ of the Government's Delegate – was openly sold in the streets of Warsaw by 600 newspaper vendors.[5] On 31 July the Underground authorities started discreetly setting up offices in the establishments which the Germans had abondoned.[6] This could only inflame popular feeling and convince the people that the hour of action was approaching.

Thus, Bor-Komorowski and Jankowski were virtually becoming the prisoners of their own designs, by releasing forces and emotions which they could control only with difficulty; they were unwilling to deliberately dampen the spirit of the masses who were impatiently awaiting the hour of confrontation with the Germans. The *Biuletyn Informacyjny* of 25 September was quite explicit on this point: 'It was

---

[1] Waclaw Zagorski, *op. cit.*, pp. 15–16. [2] *Ibid.*, p. 15.
[3] Stefan Korbonski, *Fighting Warsaw* (London, 1956), p. 348.
[4] Jerzy Kirchmayer, *Uwagi i Polemiki* (Warsaw, 1958), p. 107.
[5] Despatch from the Department of Home Affairs of the Government Delegate's Office to the Minister of Home Affairs, 30 July 1944, APUST.
[6] Despatch from the Department of Home Affairs of the Government Delegate's Office to the Minister of Home Affairs, 31 July 1944, APUST.

utterly impossible to allow an unorganised, spontaneous outbreak, provoked by the enemy. Again, it was impossible to oppose the natural urge of a soldier to resist.'[1] Thus, Bor-Komorowski's order to begin the insurrection was not only the result of an inaccurate assessment of Russian proximity and a consequently over-optimistic calculation of the rising's chances of success, but was also the function of forces which had been at work for a considerably longer period; during five years of painstaking and dangerous preparation there had developed a sense of anticipation so intense, and so diffused through all sections of the Home Army and the population at large that, at the climax, a decision not to rise would have been more difficult to make, and would have required more mastery of self and the situation, than the decision which Bor-Komorowski finally made on 31 July 1944.

Apart from the tactical and psychological factors, the context of Bor-Komorowski's decision also included prominent ideological elements. The General himself wrote, recently, that 'ideological considerations' played an important part in the shaping of his decision to try to capture Warsaw by Polish effort.[2] His Chief of Staff went so far as to say, in 1951, that the decision to fight in the capital was mainly motivated by 'ideological factors'.[3] But, as G. Barraclough has pointed out, 'ideologies are so closely bound up with interests that the part they play in events is extremely difficult to disentangle and to assess'.[4] Indeed, this was stressed by Bor-Komorowski himself, who, when asked, in 1965, to elucidate the 'ideological considerations' which had influenced his decision, merely replied that 'the ideological motives coincided with the political ones'.[5] 'Ideologies do not operate in a void', Barraclough has said, 'and the relationship between the ideological and the power factors in any situation is extremely complicated and usually beyond our power to unravel. . .'[6] Gen Bor-Komorowski's answer suggests the truth of this; expediency and ideology coincided in the motives of the authors of the insurrection. The political and ideological factors

[1] 'Powstanie Warszawskie', *Biuletyn Informacyjny*, No. 93 (301), 25 September 1944, APUST.
[2] T. Bor-Komorowski, *op. cit.*, p. 203. A similar view was expressed by Gen 'Monter' – A. Chrusciel, *op. cit.*, p. 13.
[3] Pelczynski's statement of 18 April 1951.
[4] Geoffrey Barraclough, *An Introduction to Contemporary History* (London, 1967), p. 199.
[5] Bor-Komorowski's oral evidence.
[6] Geoffrey Barraclough, *op. cit.*, p. 208.

not only coincided but also reinforced each other. In 1965 Gen Pelczynski stated that the Underground leaders decided to fight because 'they intended to defend moral values, should it prove impossible to safeguard the material ones'. He said that the insurrection was staged because its leaders felt 'a strong need for armed action in the name of independent Poland'. But he also stressed that political and ideological motives were closely intertwined.[1]

A significant element in the ideological background of the insurrection was the pledge of its authors, in March 1944, to introduce far-reaching social and economic reforms in post-war Poland.[2] These reforms were to include radical land-reform, the extension of ownership of industrial property, the nationalisation of key industries and public utilities and the introduction of a planned economy. In part it is true, these promises could be ascribed to their concern that they should not be embarrassed, in their struggle for power with the Communists, by appearing to represent die-hard reaction, defending the interests and privileges of landowners and the bourgeoisie; at the same time, their insistence that a return to the pre-war system was impossible was based as much upon their realistic acceptance and even approval of the inevitability of a considerable degree of social change, demanded by the popular masses, as upon their desire to improve their own image. It would therefore be an oversimplification to say that the ideological framework of their opposition to the PPR and the Soviet Union was an extreme right-wing, rooted antagonism to social change as such. At this stage the NSZ and the National Democrats – the party at the extreme right of the London camp's political spectrum – represented the ultra-conservative tendencies;[3] the pro-London resistance movement as a whole cannot be classified as a political and ideological emanation of Polish reaction determined to resist all attempts to transform the social and economic structure of the country. The leaders of the insurrection were very much aware that if they adopted such a policy they would be repudiated by the popular masses and even by their own followers. In January 1944 Bor-Komorowski assured his soldiers that they were fighting for a Poland 'governed in the interest of the wide working masses' who, forming the very basis of the nation, were entitled 'to determine its future'. The General insisted, however, that the London Poles alone

[1] Pelczynski's oral evidence.
[2] For details see pp. 125ff of this study.
[3] For details see pp. 85–7 of this study.

had the right to solve 'the problem of the political, social and economic reconstruction of Poland'.[1] Hence, he identified Poland with the pro-London movement, in accordance with the old-established principle of the Polish gentry, 'We are Poland', – '*Polska to my.*' Briefly, he was trying to place all the opponents of the London camp outside the framework of effective political life, by castigating them as enemies of Poland. To the pro-London leaders, the PPR and its followers were simply Soviet agents who were trying to turn Poland into Moscow's vassal. By resisting the PPR's plans for the solution of the Polish question they were opposing Russia herself.

Their resistance to the Soviet Union was, in turn, nourished on their profound mistrust of Russia – a classical Polish position whose genesis dated back to the time of the partitions in Poland – and their attachment to the doctrine of two enemies, which shaped their entire political and ideological outlook. 'In Poland we had decided to act in accordance with the following formula: armed struggle against the Germans and political struggle against the Muscovites', said Pelczynski in 1950.[2] Hence, the doctrine of two enemies served as the pro-London leaders' ideological compass when they were planning the insurrection. Indeed, this doctrine was never discarded or compromised by the top echelons of the underground, although its political validity was questioned by one of their leading Generals on a number of occasions during the autumn and winter of 1943, when it became apparent that Poland would be liberated by the Red Army and not by Anglo–American forces, as had previously been assumed in Warsaw. In the autumn of 1943 Gen S. Tatar ('Tabor'), then Chief of Operations of the Home Army, tried to convince his superiors and colleagues that Poland could not afford to conduct a struggle on two fronts or against two opponents (Germany and Russia) simultaneously, especially as, in his opinion, the Red Army was bound to have occupied the whole of Eastern Europe by the end of the war. Tatar therefore urged Bor-Komorowski to abandon the doctrine of two enemies by seeking accommodation with Russia, even at the cost of great political and territorial sacrifices, and, if necessary, without the knowledge of the émigré Government. 'Tabor' was neither pro-Russian nor pro-Communist; his representations were the result of his analysis of the political and military

[1] Order of the Day of the Commander of the Home Army, 12 January 1944, GSHI, File 121/44.
[2] Pelczynski's statement, 15 September 1950.

situation. He held that the pro-London circles must reach an understanding with Moscow if they intended to play a part in governing post-war Poland and wished to be in a position to mitigate the consequences of the approaching Soviet occupation of the country.[1] His suggestions were logical, realistic and sensible. Nevertheless, they were rejected by his superiors because, as Gen Pelczynski has explained, it was felt that to accept them would amount to a wholesale capitulation to Russia, an enemy and not a possible partner for those who were fighting for Poland's independence.[2] Further, Bor-Komorowski and his Chief of Staff still believed that, at the end of the war, the situation might become more favourable for the pro-London forces.[3] This could only mean that they still had hopes of assuming power in Poland, with the help of Churchill and Roosevelt. In April 1944 'Tabor' himself was sent to England, ostensibly to give the émigré authorities a fuller account of the Home Army's operational plans, but in reality because it was feared that his presence in Poland during the ensuing months might be a source of potential danger to Bor-Komorowski's policies. It was feared that 'Tabor' might attempt to realise his own plans and seek to establish accommodation with the Russians, even against the will of his superiors, and might thus compromise the pro-London movement's official line.[4] In 1965 Bor-Komorowski said that he had felt compelled to send 'Tabor' out of the country as some of his high-ranking officers had protested that the latter should not continue to be a member of his Staff;[5] they regarded 'Tabor' almost as a 'traitor', willing to betray 'the ideology of the Home Army'.[6] Thus, shortly before the outbreak of the rising, an attempt to persuade the Command of the Home Army to abandon the doctrine of two enemies and to adopt a more realistic attitude to Russia was an unambiguous failure.

Bor-Komorowski appears to have believed that the struggle for national independence must be conducted on three distinct levels; militarily against the Germans, politically against the Russians, while, on the diplomatic level, appeals must be made to Great Britain and the United States to support and protect the interests

[1] Bokszczanin's letter, 1 April 1965; and Bor-Komorowski's oral evidence.
[2] Pelczynski's oral evidence.
[3] Bor-Komorowski's and Pelczynski's oral evidence.
[4] Bokszczanin's letter, 1 April 1965.
[5] Bor-Komorowski's oral evidence.
[6] Iranek-Osmecki's oral evidence.

of the émigré Government in Poland. The Warsaw Rising was to provide an opportunity for the application of this plan nourished on the doctrine of two enemies in its classical form. 'By undertaking the struggle against the Germans', said Gen Pelczynski in 1965, 'the Home Army was defending the independence of Poland threatened by the Russians. . . If the Russians were our allies there would not have been so great an insurrection. . .'[1] To its authors the insurrection was 'a form of political struggle against the entering Muscovites'.[2] They were resolved 'to oppose the Muscovites and refuse to surrender the capital to them in silence . . . under their threat'.[3] But their adoption of such a policy revealed their failure to appreciate the truth of Gen Sikorski's warning of 1942, that if Russia were to emerge victorious from her struggle against Germany the reconstruction of Poland could take place only with Soviet support and good will; such circumstances would call for a conciliatory policy towards Russia.[4] In the middle of 1944, when the triumphant Red Army was pressing on Warsaw, the adoption of such a policy would have been the only realistic and viable approach to the solution of the Russo–Polish question.

However, Jankowski and Bor-Komorowski hoped that a strong, resolute and unconciliatory attitude to the Russians would produce more fruitful results. They believed that only by assuming an intransigent attitude to Stalin and by confronting him as the leaders of insurgent Warsaw would they be able to compel him to treat them as equals and allow them to govern the country after liberation. In their view, the adoption of any less robust course of action would amount to political suicide. The insurrection was to be their moment of triumph; in the event, it was precisely the absence of military co-operation between the Polish and Russian forces which turned it, instead, into a time of defeat and destruction.

[1] Pelczynski's oral evidence.
[2] Pelczynski's statement, 15 September 1950.
[3] *Ibid.*
[4] For details see pp. 133ff of this study.

10

Warsaw and the Émigré Leaders

To fully understand the attitude of the leading émigré political and military leaders to the Warsaw Rising, it is necessary to examine the directives they sent to Jankowski and Bor-Komorowski in July 1944; only by this means is it possible to determine to what extent, if any, they were responsible for the outbreak of the insurrection and how far it fulfilled their intentions.

From the beginning of July 1944 Polish authorities in London were acting under the impact of two important events: the launching of the Red Army's summer offensive on the Eastern Front and the breakdown of the informal Russo–Polish diplomatic talks in London in June 1944.[1] These developments influenced the directives sent to Poland during the last few weeks before the outbreak of the insurrection.

On 3 July the Polish Premier, the C-in-C and the Minister of National Defence attended a working dinner in London to review the recent strategic and diplomatic developments and, if necessary, to issue additional instructions to the underground. This high-level meeting was arranged by Kukiel, who considered it was essential to bring Mikolajczyk and Sosnkowski together to discuss again the role of the resistance during the approaching months. Relations between the two were strained because Sosnkowski suspected that the Premier was about to capitulate to Soviet demands. Sosnkowski intended to leave for Italy soon to inspect the Polish troops fighting there.[2]

At the meeting, political and diplomatic events were reviewed. With regard to the military situation on the Eastern Front, the two Generals agreed that it was very probable that the Red Army would occupy large parts of pre-war Poland during the next few weeks and that it would reach the approaches to Warsaw within a matter of months. The C-in-C talked of 'the impending danger of the occupa-

---

[1] For details see p. 58 of this study.
[2] General M. Kukiel's oral evidence.

tion of Poland by the Red Army' and urged the Premier to issue explicit directives to the Underground, defining the role it was to assume under Soviet occupation; but at this stage neither Sosnkowski nor Kukiel expected the Russians to take Warsaw at the end of July or the beginning of August.[1] Here, Sosnkowski at last admitted that the whole of Poland would be liberated by the Russians, not by Anglo–American forces.

In his opinion, the new directives to Warsaw should be based on three cardinal assumptions: that the struggle against the Germans must be continued, that armed resistance to the Russians must be forbidden, and finally that the possibility of a general anti-German insurrection, without a previous Russo–Polish political understanding, must be excluded. The directives should also make provision for the possibility that the Russians would refuse to recognise the pro-London forces as their legitimate hosts in Poland and would try to disarm them and incorporate them into Berling's Army. The C-in-C advised that if this were to happen the Home Army should comply with Russian orders, should be disbanded, and its cadres withdrawn to western – that is, German-occupied – Poland. The General warned, however, that unless the Russians decided to halt their advances in Poland – along the old Ribbentrop–Molotov Line, for instance – this dilemma would eventually face the entire movement, including its central authorities.[2] Clearly, the C-in-C was primarily preoccupied with the problem of the approaching Russo–Polish confrontation and its possible consequences, rather than with the scope, intensity and character of the Home Army's anti-German operations, although he did advocate that these should be continued on a limited scale, regardless of the Russian attitude to Bor-Komorowski's forces.[3]

Sosnkowski's concern about the Russo–Polish confrontation sprang from his firm conviction that Mikolajczyk would not be able to reach a *modus vivendi* with Stalin, in spite of his attempts to do so. In Sosnkowski's opinion the Polish Communists would certainly assume power in Poland if the Red Army occupied the entire country; he believed that Stalin wished to incorporate Poland into the Soviet Union as one of its republics. Here, he differed

[1] Precis of a talk between Mikolajczyk, Sosnkowski and Kukiel of 3 July 1944; contained in the Appendix to a letter from the C-in-C to the President of the Republic, 6 July 1944. Ldz. Osob./GNW/tj/44. APUST. (Hereafter to be referred to as talk between Mikolajczyk, Sosnkowski and Kukiel, 3 July.)
[2] *Ibid.*   [3] *Ibid.*

from Mikolajczyk, who still hoped to reach an agreement with the Kremlin. The Premier would not agree that it was a foregone conclusion that the Russians wanted to absorb Poland. After his return from Washington, he was under the impression that Russia was not bent on spreading Communism to other countries but intended, for economic reasons, to cultivate good relations with Britain and the United States. In his opinion Stalin would need the economic and financial help of the Western Powers to rebuild Russia's shattered economy and would therefore be reluctant to antagonise them by exporting revolutions to other countries. Furthermore, Mikolajczyk was convinced that, although Stalin favoured a policy of 'accomplished facts' with regard to Poland, her future would largely be determined by 'the attitude of the [Polish] people . . . during these testing hours'.[1] In brief, Mikolajczyk believed that, given the active support of the underground and the diplomatic backing of London and Washington, he still had a good chance of reaching an agreement with Moscow and of assuming power in Warsaw.

Mikolajczyk and Sosnkowski were divided on this issue and their differences were reflected in their respective attitudes to the underground and its role in the unfolding Russo–German battle for Poland. The Premier wanted the resistance to fight against the Germans in accordance with the 'Burza' plan; that is, to come into the open and try to collaborate with the Red Army, while its political representatives in Poland displayed to the Russians their readiness to co-operate with them in the administration of the country. Sosnkowski suggested that they should state that they were 'taking over the local administration in the name of the Polish Government'.[1] The Premier accepted this, although he felt that if the Russians tried to disarm the Home Army or incorporate it into Berling's Army it would have no choice but to comply, under protest.[2]

At this stage Mikolajczyk had no intention of ordering Bor-Komorowski to stage a general insurrection, and had no special plans for Warsaw. Both the C-in-C and the Minister of National Defence were fully aware of this. Indeed, during this meeting both Mikolajczyk and Sosnkowski were, for the most part, reiterating well-established and frequently-discussed views, each upholding his respective position.[3] The most radical departure, with regard to the

[1] *Ibid.*   [2] *Ibid.*   [3] *Ibid.*   [4] For details see Chapter 6 of this study.

use of the Home Army during the approaching Russo–Polish confrontation, was supplied by Kukiel, who advocated that if the German army collapsed the underground should stage a partial insurrection, aimed at the seizure of a limited part of the Polish territory, where 'the highest authorities of the Republic' would then be installed 'at the right moment'.[1] In his view, placing a limited part of the country under 'full Polish sovereignty' would undoubtedly 'present the Soviet Government with a difficult dilemma and help to clarify the real state of affairs in the eyes of the world'.[2] However, even this bold suggestion was in essence a slightly modified version of one of the points of the Government's Instruction of November 1943, which had provided for the staging of an insurrection at the time of Germany's collapse.[3] Kukiel pointed out that 'Burza' already amounted to an insurrection and must be recognised as such, especially in view of pressing 'moral, propagandist and political considerations'.[4] Kukiel was the first émigré leader to recognise the true nature and potentialities of 'Burza'. By the summer of 1944 it was turning into a series of localised insurrections and Kukiel urged that this fact should be recognised. By presenting 'Burza' to the warring world as a full-scale anti-German insurrection, he hoped to attract world attention to Poland and to secure the sympathetic support of the Western Allies for the insurgents. He also wished to use the Home Army to force Stalin to clarify his real intentions towards the émigré Government.[5]

Yet even Kukiel had no specific plans for Warsaw, although as early as October 1943 he had suggested that Bor-Komorowski's forces should devote their main effort to seizing the Polish capital before the Red Army entered the city.[6] In July 1944 he talked only of capturing certain limited areas of territory, which implied that he expected that the Home Army would be fighting in rural rather than urban districts. Strangely, at that time none of the top Polish leaders in London considered Warsaw's role in the Home Army's struggle against the Germans although, within less than a month, the capital was destined to become its greatest, its most demanding and its most tragic battlefield. This significant and revealing omission can

---

[1] Talk between Mikolajczyk, Sosnkowski and Kukiel, 3 July.   [2] *Ibid.*
[3] For details see pp. 156ff of this study.
[4] Talk between Mikolajczyk, Sosnkowski and Kukiel, 3 July.   [5] *Ibid.*
[6] The record of a meeting held by the President of the Republic, 25 October 1943. APUST.

only be attributed to the fact that none of them expected the Red Army to take Warsaw in the summer of 1944; *they assumed that the Soviet summer offensive would come to a halt at the city's 'approaches'*.[1]

Kukiel's opinions and suggestions introduced a number of new elements into this top-level discussion and had far-reaching effects. They inspired an important communiqué which Mikolajczyk sent to Poland the following day. Kukiel's views were strongly opposed by Sosnkowski, who maintained that the indiscriminate use of the term 'insurrection' (*'powstanie'*) might impel people in Poland to a 'badly calculated and premature outburst'.[2] The C-in-C wished to retain the established nomenclature and reserve the term 'insurrection' for 'the universal and simultaneous' uprising.[3] He also warned against the premature use of the term 'collapse of Germany', in anticipation of a possible repetition of the events in Germany of November 1918, as this might lead to a major disaster in Poland.[4] He rightly supposed that on this occasion, in contrast to the events of 1918, the Germans would fight to the bitter end, especially in Poland, for by holding the Polish plains they would be defending access to Germany. Under such circumstances, he argued, it would be difficult for the Home Army to hold on to a large area or an important centre for more than a few days. In any case, he anticipated that all such attempts if undertaken without genuine Russo–Polish military co-operation, were bound to fail and lead to 'the wholesale slaughter of the Polish population'. *'Insurrection without a previous fair understanding with the U.S.S.R. and honest and real co-operation with the Red Army would be politically unjustified and militarily nothing more than an act of despair'*, he said.[5] Nevertheless, he was prepared to consider whether, for purely propaganda purposes, it might not be advisable to refer to 'Burza' as 'the insurrectionary operations'.[6] Clearly, the C-in-C was opposed to anti-German operations on a large scale.

The dinner ended with Mikolajczyk and Kukiel imploring Sosnkowski to postpone his visit to Italy and to remain in England because of the developments on the Eastern Front. They argued that he would be able to control and influence events in Poland only from London, the main centre of communications with occupied

[1] Talk between Mikolajczyk, Sosnkowski and Kukiel, 3 July.
[2] *Ibid.*   [3] *Ibid.*   [4] *Ibid.*
[5] *Ibid.* My italics.   [6] *Ibid.*

Warsaw. In spite of these pleas he decided to go to Italy, promising to return to London at two days' notice if necessary.[1]

The following day – 4 July – Mikolajczyk, greatly impressed by Kukiel's suggestions and arguments, sent a telegram to Jankowski, the Government Delegate, urging him to act on the lines advocated by his Minister of National Defence. He wished to inspire Jankowski to adopt a very bold attitude towards the Russians and to intensify the Home Army's operations against the Germans, thus demonstrating that the entire nation was behind the London Government. He insisted: 'We cannot remain silent when the Soviets enter Poland'.[2] To stress still more the need for action he told his followers in Warsaw that the Russians intended to call for an insurrection in Poland and to set up a pro-Soviet administration recruited from the local population. At the same time, he was prepared to leave the final decision in regard to the scope and character of the Home Army's activities in the hands of its leaders in Warsaw, although he asked them whether they would be prepared to announce that 'Burza' was the insurrection for which the country had been preparing itself for some years, especially in view of the large-scale fighting already raging in Eastern Poland. He hoped that by this means the Home Army would be spared possible hostile accusations of 'secret connivance with the Germans'.[3] If his suggestion were unacceptable to Warsaw 'for security reasons' he proposed the publication, by the underground leaders, of a proclamation stressing their 'military efforts' against the Germans and their 'readiness to co-operate' with the Russians, while at the same time remaining loyal to 'the legitimate authorities of the Polish Republic in London'.[4]

Mikolajczyk intended that this proclamation would receive wide publicity abroad and would lay particular emphasis on the existence in Poland of a pro-London local administration which was already functioning. He tried to convince Jankowski of the need to establish London-controlled administration in the liberated areas by pointing out that even Russian attempts to remove such organs by force could be turned to diplomatic advantage: they advertised to the world the fact that Stalin was imposing Soviet administration on Poland against the will of her people. He tried to persuade the

---

[1] Kukiel's oral evidence.
[2] Despatch from the Prime Minister to the Government Delegate, 4 July 1944, Ldz. 1784/tjn/44. GSHI–PRM, L11.
[3] *Ibid.*   [4] *Ibid.*

Government Delegate that the Russians, initially at least, 'would not be able to ignore the representatives of the local population or do much harm'.[1] Even if Jankowski's men chose to remain underground they could not for long escape detection by the Russians. In Mikolajczyk's view, then, it was both unavoidable and desirable that the pro-London administrative organs should come into the open.

He also asked Jankowski whether he had considered the possibility, in the event of German collapse, of a general or partial insurrection which would enable the Government Delegate and the Home Commander to assume power before the Russians arrived. He asked whether such an operation would call for the return of the Government to Poland, to direct it.

Finally, the Premier asked that Jankowski's reply, possibly in the form of counter-proposals, should be made as soon as possible, as it would soon be time to take decisive action.[2]

The tone of this telegram was one of encouragement and persuasion to action; even at this late hour Mikolajczyk was reluctant to issue categorical orders to the underground, and the possibility of insurrection in Warsaw was not mentioned. *The whole question of the character and extent of the Home Army's operations was left open, for Warsaw to settle.*

Three days later, on 7 July 1944, Sosnkowski sent his own instruction to Bor-Komorowski. The General told Warsaw that he expected the Red Army to occupy a considerable part of Poland within a relatively short period, and warned that the country might become the theatre of fierce Russo–German battles for access to Germany, in which more than a hundred Nazi divisions might be involved. He expected that the Germans would fight 'stubbornly'.[3]

With regard to the Russians, he told Bor-Komorowski that with their new offensive their attitude to the London Government had hardened. In his opinion they were 'highly reluctant not only to reach an agreement but even to enter into talks with our Government'.[4] According to his interpretation, this indicated that Stalin had decided to establish a pro-Soviet administration in Poland. 'Under such military and political conditions a national armed rising would be unjustifiable, not to mention the lack of physical chances of

---

[1] *Ibid.*   [2] *Ibid.*
[3] Despatch from the C-in-C to the Commander of the Home Army, 7 July 1944, Ldz. 5480/44. APUST.   [4] *Ibid.*

success', he cautioned.[1] He added, however, that as, theoretically, these conditions might still change, it was necessary to maintain a state of readiness for insurrection. Meanwhile, Bor-Komorowski was to continue the 'Burza' operations, as defined in the winter of 1943, himself deciding their extent, on the basis of his own assessment of the situation. Sosnkowski stated that he disagreed with the Government's proposal that, for 'political purposes', 'Burza' should be referred to as 'insurrectionary operations', as this might lead to a badly-calculated insurrection, and confuse junior commanders.[2] Yet in the same communication Sosnkowski introduced a new element into Home Army tactics: 'If, owing to a happy conjunction of circumstances, in the last moments of the German retreat and before the entry of the Red units, the chance should arise of even temporary occupation of Wilno, Lwow or any other important centre, or of a limited part of the territory, this should be accomplished and we should act as rightful hosts [to the Russians]'.[3] Thus, Sosnkowski, who claimed to wish to limit the extent of 'Burza' to the guerilla-type operations originally envisaged, himself altered its character by instructing Bor-Komorowski to fight for the towns within its framework, circumstances permitting. He therefore provided the Home Army Command with inspiration for, and justification of the staging of 'Burza' in Warsaw; his phrase 'any other important centre' could be applied to Warsaw as well as to any other large town. At this stage he probably had the towns situated east of the Vistula in mind; he did not foresee that by the end of July the Russians would be in Warsaw. Similarly, the vague phrase 'owing to a happy conjunction of circumstances' was capable, under war-time conditions of several interpretations. Inevitably, this part of the C-in-C's instruction created in Bor-Komorowski's mind the impression that he was expected to fight for the large towns during the last moments of German retreat from them and before the Red Army arrived. Indeed, Bor-Komorowski believed that in issuing to 'Monter' his final order to fight for Warsaw, on 31 July 1944, he was acting in accordance with the C-in-C's instruction of 7 July, as he assumed that the Soviet entry into Warsaw was imminent and that the Germans were about to retreat.[4]

---

[1] Despatch from the C-in-C to the Commander of the Home Army, 7 July 1944, Ldz. 5480/44. APUST.

[2] *Ibid.*   [3] *Ibid.*

[4] Bor-Komorowski's oral evidence given to the author in the presence of Prof J. K. Zawodny; see also T. Bor-Komorowski, *op. cit.*, p. 204.

In the same instruction Sosnkowski stated that during the days to come he expected the Home Army to maintain 'the highest standards of discipline, calmness and self-control in the face of possible attempts to an internal strife which might later be exploited to compromise the Home Army in the eyes of the world'.[1] He warned Warsaw to be prepared for Soviet requests that the Home Army should lay down its arms, or join Berling's units. Such demands should be resisted in every way save armed struggle. As a last resort units should be dispersed among the general population and should 'keep quiet until further orders' while remaining in contact with the pro-London authorities who should be kept informed about the state of affairs in Soviet-occupied Poland.[2]

The communications from both Mikolajczyk and Sosnkowski were the outcome of the meeting between the two leaders and Kukiel on 3 July; both urged the Underground leaders to continue their struggle against the Germans, both were silent with regard to Warsaw and its possible role during the approaching days and, finally, the contents of both communications were known to the Underground leaders when they made their initial decision to fight for the capital.

Apart from these written instructions both Mikolajczyk and Sosnkowski sent verbal messages to Warsaw by a special courier, Lt Jan Nowak, who delivered them to Bor-Komorowski on 30 July, two days before the outbreak of the insurrection, when only its timing remained to be finally settled.[3] The messages reached the Underground leaders too late to affect their initial decision,[4] yet they throw additional light on the respective attitudes of Mikolajczyk and Sosnkowski to the Underground and on their hopes for the solution of the Polish question.

The Premier told Nowak to tell the resistance leaders that he believed it to be his duty to reach an understanding with Moscow with their active support and the diplomatic backing of Churchill and Roosevelt. He considered this task to be one of paramount importance, especially as he firmly rejected any possibility of a conflict between the East and the West within the foreseeable future. He asked Nowak to stress this point in Warsaw.

[1] Despatch from the C-in-C to the Commander of the Home Army, 7 July 1944, Ldz. 5480/44. APUST. [2] *Ibid.*
[3] 'Emisariusz: Wywiad z Kapitanem Nowakiem', *Na Antenie* (*Wiadomosci*) No. 962, 6 September 1964.
[4] *Ibid.*

Sosnkowski, on the other hand, expressed the view that such a conflict was bound to occur within the next five years and that its outcome would finally determine Poland's fate. This suggests that he attached relatively little importance, in terms of its immediate value to the London camp, to the Home Army's current operations against the Germans. He wanted the Home Army to fight against the Germans because he believed that by remaining faithful to the last to her Western Allies Poland would be preserving their future goodwill towards her. Once against he stressed the need to capture large towns from the Germans, if the opportunity presented itself.[1] Presumably, this was to help to publicise in the West the Home Army's anti-German effort.

The basic differences between these two contradictory messages reflected the fact that relations between Mikolajczyk and Sosnkowski were reaching breaking-point. Their views on the role of the Home Army and the general world situation were so diametrically opposed that further co-operation between them was becoming impossible. It was becoming clear to the resistance leaders in Poland that their central authorities in London were bitterly divided and no longer capable of providing them with united counsel.[2]

On 11 July 1944 Sosnkowski left for Italy, ostensibly to inspect the Polish Second Corps, but in reality to prepare the ground for the staging of a military mutiny against Mikolajczyk's Government, should it 'capitulate to the Russians' – that is, agree to territorial changes or to the inclusion of Communists in a reconstructed Cabinet.[3] On the day of his departure from London Sosnkowski sent a revealing communication to Bor-Komorowski. In it he expressed his growing dissatisfaction with Mikolajczyk and his policies. He wrote that in his opinion the Soviets were trying to make the Poles amenable to an understanding with Russia on conditions dictated by Stalin. To achieve this they were trying to eliminate from the Polish political and military *apparat* those who understand the fruitlessness of giving in to the Soviet demands, and to replace them with Communists. Because of this, he stated, it was necessary to create a 'Government of National Unity' which would exclude, Communists and would be capable of defending Poland's sovereignty

---

[1] Jan Nowak, 'Operacja "Whitehorne" ', *Kultura*, No. 4–5 (21–2)/1949, pp. 212–15.

[2] Pelczynski's oral evidence.

[3] Witold Babinski, 'Powstanie Warszawskie', *Zeszyty Historyczne*, No. 6/1964, pp. 59–60.

and her internal and territorial integrity against Soviet encroachments.[1]

The C-in-C was trying to stimulate the Home Army generals in Warsaw to press for the reconstruction of Mikolajczyk's Cabinet and thus become involved in political matters. It was unfortunate that less than three weeks before the outbreak of the insurrection in Warsaw Sosnkowski should have finally decided to stage and lead a military mutiny against his Government if it reached agreement with Russia on terms unacceptable to him, instead of either resolving to serve it loyally as its highest military adviser, or expressing his disapproval by resigning from his important post. The General's behaviour seems particularly irresponsible as he was aware of the difficulties and dangers facing the Home Army and of the need for firm and consistent guidance from London; he knew that the Red Army was about to occupy a large part of pre-war Poland and that the underground forces would soon be confronted with a 'difficult dilemma'.[2] Even this prospect failed to dissuade him from assuming a primarily political role and thereby potentially neglecting his military duties towards the hard-pressed and harassed Home Army.

In this way unity of command ceased to exist among the highest émigré authorities at this most crucial stage of the war for Poland and her capital.

Meanwhile, Mikolajczyk was anxiously awaiting the Underground leaders' reply to the tentative suggestions he had sent to Warsaw on 4 July. His anxiety must have been acute for on 14 July he asked Jankowski to keep him fully informed about the progress of the Home Army operations against the Germans, which he intended to publicise widely abroad; he stated that Anglo-American public opinion regarded these operations as Poland's 'contribution to this phase of the war'.[3] He believed that events in his country were coming to a climax.[4]

On 21 July Jankowski's reply, dated 12 July, reached London. He told Mikolajczyk that at the end of June the highest political and

---

[1] Despatch from the C-in-C to the Commander of the Home Army, 11 July 1944, Idz. 5679/tjn/44. APUST.

[2] Despatch from the C-in-C to the Commander of the Home Army, 7 July 1944, Ldz. 5840/44. APUST.

[3] Despatch from the Prime Minister to the Government Delegate, 14 July 1944. Ldz. 1921/tjn/44. GSHI–PRM, L11.

[4] Kukiel's oral evidence.

military authorities of the Underground had decided to come into the open in Warsaw in the event of the withdrawal or collapse of the Germans or of the entry of the Soviet army into the capital. The same would apply to other Underground authorities in other areas. Jankowski also stated that he was preparing for 'the critical period' by creating 'a central directing body' consisting of himself, Bor-Komorowski and Puzak, the Chairman of the Council of National Unity. This body and the Staffs it represented were to come into the open in Warsaw. One of Jankowski's deputies, with a part of his Staff, was to remain underground to organise and direct 'self-defence' against the Russians, should this prove necessary. The Government Delegate told the Cabinet that he was determined to frustrate Communist calls to insurrection; he was confident that he would manage to retain the power of decision as to whether and when to stage a rising. Jankowski and his colleagues were not prepared to stage an insurrection solely on the strength of the Russo–German fighting in the east, but would do so only in the event of 'German collapse', without which such action would cost too much in terms of sacrifice.[1] In Jankowski's opinion the Home Army had, after all, already amply demonstrated its attitude to the Germans. They rejected Mikolajczyk's suggestion of a partial insurrection in one of the provincial regions and suggested that a rising in Warsaw would have more political significance. They said that it would not be advisable for the Government to return to Poland to direct the insurrection, because there was a risk that the Russians might prevent it from discharging its functions. In any case, in their view the Government would be able to achieve more by remaining in London. Jankowski strongly urged the Government to announce officially that it had decided to extend its representation in Poland by creating an official agency in Warsaw comprising a deputy Premier and three or four Ministers. Finally, he emphatically asked that the exiled leaders should not publish anything concerning operations in Poland without first consulting Warsaw.[2]

This communication shows how determined the resistance leaders were to direct the underground operations themselves, without any interference from their Government in London. They hoped the latter would confine its attention to diplomatic matters and to organise material assistance to the Home Army. This meant that the

[1] Despatch from the Government Delegate to the Prime Minister, dated 12 July, received 21 July 1944, No. 74, Ldz. K4775/44. GSHI–L, 9.   [2] *Ibid.*

struggle in Poland was to be controlled solely by Jankowski's directorate, with Mikolajczyk's role, in regard to the deployment of the Home Army, even further reduced.

On 23 July Mikolajczyk received a dispatch from Bor-Komorowski, dated 21 July, which stated that the Germans had been defeated on the Eastern Front and that the Home Army would be alerted to stand ready for the insurrection as from 25 July.[1] Once again, the exiled Government was presented with an accomplished fact; Bor-Komorowski was alerting the Home Army without first consulting his superiors in London.

Now, convinced that the insurrection in Poland was about to begin, Mikolajczyk asked his Government to sanction it. On 25 July he told his Cabinet that while the Government Delegate still considered that the best moment for the insurrection had not yet arrived, the Home Commander was ready at any time to issue the order for it. Because of this the Cabinet empowered the Government Delegate to make all the decisions required by the rate of the Soviet advance, if necessary without first consulting the Government.[2]

The following day Mikolajczyk finally and categorically informed his Cabinet colleagues that reports received from Warsaw showed that the German position there was critical and that the final battle order for the insurrection might be issued at any moment. During the same Cabinet meeting Jankowski's proposal that the Government should establish, an agency in Warsaw which would come into the open was discussed and approved; the Government Delegate was duly appointed the Deputy Prime Minister to the London Government.[3] Further, on the same day the Premier, acting in accordance with the Cabinet decision of the previous day, authorised Jankowski to launch the general insurrection on his own initiative, when he considered it to be appropriate.[4] He also informed him that he (Mikolajczyk) was going to Moscow to negotiate with Stalin.[5]

All communications from Warsaw reported the conjunction of

[1] Despatch from the Commander of the Home Army to the C-in-C, 21 July 1944, Ldz. 5916. APUST.

[2] Record of the Cabinet meeting, No. 39, 25 July 1944. APUST; and St Kopanski, *op. cit.*, p. 326.

[3] Record of the Cabinet meeting No. 40, 26 July 1944. APUST.

[4] Despatch from the Prime Minister to the Government Delegate, 26 July 1944, Ldz. 2088/tjn./44. GSHI–PRM, L11. See also: J. Ciechanowski, *op. cit.*, pp. 352ff.

[5] Despatch from the Prime Minister to the Government, 26 July 1944. GSHI–PRM, L11.

two circumstances – the imminence of German collapse and the readiness of the Underground leaders to order a rising – in the face of which Mikolajczyk had only two alternatives; either to give his blessing to the Home Army's projected venture, or to try to restrain the Warsaw leaders. Had he chosen to do the latter he could not have been certain of success; time was running short and the situation might, of its own momentum, precipitate the insurrection at any moment. Further, the Premier believed that by adopting the former course he would improve his position during his talks with Stalin, as a successful rising might increase his chances of assuming power in Poland.[1] Finally, although it is true that the course of action adopted by the Warsaw leaders was consistent with the general tone of Mikolajczyk's telegram to them of 4 July, it should be stressed that, in the event, he did not himself initiate the plans for the rising, but merely approved those submitted by the resistance in Poland.

On the evening of 26 July, before leaving London for Moscow, Mikolajczyk received a despatch from Poland informing him that the rising was about to begin;[2] again the exiled leaders were presented with a ready-made decision, arrived at independently by their subordinates in Poland, and, moreover, a decision which was reached before the despatch of the *carte blanche* telegram of 26 July. The decision was legitimatised *post factum* by this telegram.

Between 27 July and 1 August, when the rising broke out, Mikolajczyk made no attempt to contact Warsaw, possibly another sign that he approved the plans of Jankowski and Bor-Komorowski, that he believed the whole problem of anti-German operations in Poland had been finally settled. He was now eagerly awaiting news from Warsaw. The idea of the city's being freed by Polish effort before the entry of the Russians, just as his negotiations with Stalin were about to begin, may have appealed to him: it would suggest to Stalin that the pro-London Poles had deliberately synchronised the two events in order to underline, dramatically the strength of support for Mikolajczyk.

Did Mikolajczyk act wisely in letting the resistance leaders proceed with their plans without urging them to co-ordinate their operations with the Soviet High Command, or asking them to wait for the

[1] Kukiel's oral evidence.
[2] Despatch from the Commander of the Home Army to the C-in-C, 25 July 1944, No. 1441, Ldz. 6024. APUST; and S. Korbonski's statement of 23 August 1964. A transcript of S. Korbonski's broadcast on the Radio Free Europe of 23 August 1944, APUST.

outcome of his talks with Stalin before committing Warsaw to battle? In retrospect, the answer to this question can only be negative. The risks involved were too great to justify the Home Army's embarking on such an undertaking without first trying to establish contact with the Russians. At the time, however, it probably seemed to Mikolajczyk that the rate of the Russian offensive was too rapid and the situation of the Germans too critical to allow time for such intricate, delicate and time-consuming moves. Further, within a matter of a few days Mikolajczyk was to see Stalin and discuss the entire situation with him personally.

But by the time of his first meeting with Stalin the rising had already begun.[1] Far from being a help to him in Moscow, the premature insurrection became a liability; it greatly compromised his position, for, instead of boasting of his forces' successes in the struggle against the Germans, he was largely reduced to begging for Russian help. He talked to Stalin, not as the leader of a powerful and victorious resistance movement, but as a desperate petitioner who well knew that only the Red Army could save Warsaw and its people from a cruel predicament.[2]

By his failure to warn the underground leaders, before the event, of the risks inherent in staging their battle without at least military liaison with the Russians Mikolajczyk incurred heavy responsibility for Warsaw's subsequent fate and destruction. He failed to realise the military risks involved in the policy of using the Home Army to buttress his diplomatic position. Yet it was up to his military experts, especially Gen Sosnkowski, to remind him, at this time, of the military weakness of Bor-Komorowski's forces and of the need for extreme caution at this dangerous and critical juncture. At the time when it would have been most appropriate this warning was not given; the C-in-C was with Anders' troops in Italy and Gen Kukiel, the Minister of National Defence, and Gen Kopanski, the Chief of the General Staff, probably felt themselves unable to make such representations without first consulting Sosnkowski.

[1] Mikolajczyk saw Stalin for the first time on 3 August 1944 at 9.30 p.m. Record of a conversation between Premier Mikolajczyk and Marshal Stalin at the Kremlin on 3 August 1944. GSHI–PRM, Z–4.

[2] On 9 August 1944 Mikolajczyk asked Stalin for 'the immediate assistance by the Soviet Union for Warsaw' where 'a mortal struggle' was taking place between the Poles and the Germans. Note on conversation between Premier Mikolajczyk and Marshal Stalin at the Kremlin on 9 August 1944. GSHI–PRM, Z–4.

The C-in-C did not return to England until 6 August, in spite of urgent and repeated requests from the Polish authorities to report back to London immediately, because of the critical state of affairs in Poland and in view of his own solemn promise to return at a few days' or even forty-eight hours' notice, if necessary.[1] On 24 July both the President – Wladyslaw Raczkiewicz – and the Chief of Staff despatched urgent messages to Sosnkowski asking him to return to London without delay.[2] A day later Kukiel told the C-in-C that both the President and the Government wanted him to return.[3] On 26 July Kopanski again relayed to Sosnkowski the President's urgent request, of 24 July, for his return.[4] Sosnkowski replied to these repeated demands on 27 July, stating that he could not leave Italy before 1 August because of his heavy commitments – such items as an audience with the Pope, visits to Gen Alexander and Gen Mark Clark and investitures in the Second Corps. Furthermore, he asked London for permission to prolong his stay in Italy until 5 August.[5] Clearly, he was in no particular hurry to return to London. He intended to remain with Anders' troops as long as possible, even though he was urgently needed by his President, Cabinet and Chief of Staff. Capt Babinski, his trusted aide and political confidant, has recently written that Sosnkowski was determined, when he left England, to remain in Italy for at least a month and there to await the outcome of Mikolajczyk's visit to Moscow. He has also revealed that the General was determined to rebel against his Government if it submitted to Soviet political and territorial demands. Indeed, Babinski writes that, as soon as he learned about Mikolajczyk's departure for Moscow, Sosnkowski began to prepare the text of the order for the day which he intended to issue from the field head-quarters of the Second Corps in the event of the Government's 'capitulation' to Stalin.[6]

These revelations fully explain Sosnkowski's rather strange behaviour and his reluctance to return to London a few days before

[1] Kukiel's oral evidence; and St Kopanski, *op. cit.*, p. 330.
[2] Despatch from the President of the Republic to the C-in-C, 24 July 1944, Ldz. 5941, APUST; and Despatch from the Chief of Staff to the C-in-C, 24 July 1944, Ldz. 5941, APUST.
[3] Despatch from the Minister of National Defence to the C-in-C, 25 July 1944, Ldz. 5938, APUST.
[4] St Kopanski, *op. cit.*, p. 317.
[5] Despatch from the C-in-C to the Chief of Staff, 27 July 1944, APUST.
[6] Witold Babinski, 'Powstanie Warszawskie', *Zeszyty Historyczne*, No. 6/1964, pp. 59–60.

the insurrection in spite of the repeated demands of the President, his ultimate constitutional superior; he was too preoccupied with his own potental 'mutiny' to return without delay. He appeared unimpressed by Kukiel's assurances of 27 July that the Government would not 'capitulate',[1] possibly preferring to give credence to Babinski's report from London, on 18 July, that the Government would accept 'any agreement' with the Russians if the latter would agree to talk with them.[2] 'Our politicians are afraid of one thing only', wrote Babinski, 'the attitude of the Army'.[3]

On 28 July Sosnkowski asked the President to reconstruct Mikolajczyk's Cabinet immediately and warned him that the armed forces would refuse to serve under a Government which made concessions to the Russians or agreed to co-operate with the Communists.[4] Briefly, the C-in-C was informing the President that he would contemplate mutiny if his demands were not met. He seems to have believed that he had a historical mission to perform, that, backed by Anders' troops, he must save Poland from 'new humiliations' which in his opinion were bound to follow the 'fruitless concessions' which he suspected the Premier was about to make during his stay in Moscow.[5] Sosnkowski believed that as the Supreme Commander of the armed forces he could not afford to dissociate himself entirely from politics.[6] He seemed unable to grasp that this was a particularly ill-chosen time for him to concentrate his attention on political problems, thereby neglecting his military duties

By prolonging his stay in Italy Sosnkowski was cutting himself off from the main centres of decision – Warsaw and London – and thus considerably reducing his own chances of influencing events on the Vistula. From Italy it was impossible for him to co-ordinate, with the Cabinet, his responses to the reports reaching him, after delay, from Warsaw. Indeed, the instructions he sent to Poland, via London, between 25 July and 1 August, had no influence on Bor-Komorowski's fatal decision; at this vital moment there was, between the C-in-C and his subordinates in Poland, no effective dialogue concerning the latters' hazardous plans. They were left to

---

[1] Despatch from the Minister of National Defence to the C-in-C, 27 July 1944, Ldz. 6077, APUST.
[2] Despatch from Capt Babinski to the C-in-C, 18 July 1944. Ldz. 5731, APUST.
[3] *Ibid.*
[4] Despatch from the C-in-C to the President of the Republic, dated 28 July 1944, received 1 August 1944, Ldz. 6241, APUST.
[5] *Ibid.*   [6] St Kopanski, *op. cit.*, p. 292.

their own resources and denied any meaningful advice from their C-in-C. This was the price which was paid for Sosnkowski's unnecessary and unjustified excursions into politics. He knew that, in his absence, the Cabinet in London would have to make far-reaching and irrevocable decisions with regard to the Underground; he also knew that all telegrams between himself and Bor-Komorowski had to pass through London, the main centre of radio communications with occupied Poland, and, hence, was fully aware that by staying in Italy he was bound to delay the flow of communications. Indeed, in the last days of July 1944, liaison between himself and Bor-Komorowski broke down almost completely because of faulty technical arrangements and the gross inefficiency of Sosnkowski's Staff. It is incredible, but sadly true, that some of the C-in-C's communications to Warsaw took as long as four days to reach London and that decoding there took, on average, 17 hours, as he used a special code known only to two officers, one of whom was in Italy. Meanwhile, the flow of communications between Warsaw and London was much more rapid and efficient, even though Bor-Komorowski and his Staff had to work under very difficult conditions and in constant danger of detection by the Germans.[1]

Only by obeying the President's orders to return immediately, then, could Sosnkowski have kept up-to-date with, and influenced, developments in Warsaw and London. On 28 July Gen Kopanski cabled him that the Cabinet was meeting to discuss the problem of the insurrection and was expecting him to take part in the talks.[2] In reality, this meeting was largely superfluous because the Cabinet had, on 25 July, already authorised Jankowski to act on his own initiative in the matter and Mikolajczyk had informed Warsaw of this crucial decision on the 26 July.[3] But, as he had failed to inform Gen Kopanski either about the decision or the telegram the General must, when he cabled Sosnkowski, have been under the impression that the whole problem was still open to further discussion.[4] During the meeting of the 28 July the text of the Premier's telegram to Jankowski was officially acknowledged and Gen Kopanski informed the C-in-C of

---

[1] For details see: Z. S. Siemaszko, 'Lacznosc Radiowa Sztabu N. W. w Okresie Powstania Warszawskiego', *Zeszyty Historyczne*, No. 6/1964, pp. 85ff.

[2] Despatch from the Chief of Staff to the C-in-C, 28 July 1944, Ldz. 6082/44. APUST.

[3] Despatch from the Prime Minister to the Government Delegate, 26 July 1944, Ldz. 2088/tjn/44. GSHI–PRM, L11.

[4] St Kopanski, *op. cit.*, pp. 320–1.

this the following day, so that Sosnkowski learned about the *carte blanche* telegram at least four days after it was sent.[1] Although it is not known exactly when he received Kopanski's telegram, it is known that he had not received it by 30 July.[2]

On 30 July Raczkiewicz told Sosnkowski that, in his absence, far-reaching decisions had been made in London because of the demands of the political situation and the impossibility of discussing it with him. He once again asked the C-in-C to return to England as soon as possible.[3] On the same day, still ignorant of Mikolajczyk's telegram to Jankowski of the 26 July, Sosnkowski told London that he would be leaving for England on 1 August and that the Cabinet 'should not discuss the insurrection without knowing the course and outcome of the talks in Moscow'.[4] This communication was received in London on 1 August, and decoded at 17.00 hours, by which time Warsaw was already fighting.[5]

On 31 July the C-in-C once again told London that he intended to start for England on 1 August,[6] but he did not arrive there until 6 August. He has since explained that this further delay was due to talks with General Wilson, the Commander of the troops fighting in the Mediterranean.[7] It should be noted, however, that on 31 July Capt Babinski sent Sosnkowski a telegram advising him to 'await the outcome of the Premier's journey [to Moscow] among the troops, rather than in London', warning him that the Russo–Polish talks were bound to end in Mikolajczyk's 'capitulation' and predicting that 'the Premier will not return to London but to Poland'.[8] Babinski further told him that the President was not prepared to reconstruct the Cabinet and was feared that Sosnkowski might, while in Italy, rebel against its authority.[9] Babinski was implying that the President was siding with Mikolajczyk and wanted Sosnkowski in London because he wished to frustrate his political plans. It is worth noting

[1] Despatch from the Chief of Staff to the C-in-C, dated 28 July, sent 29 July 1944, Ldz. 6089. APUST.

[2] Z. S. Siemaszko, *op. cit.*, p. 107.

[3] Despatch from the President of the Republic to the C-in-C, 30 July 1944, Ldz. 4111/6863. GSHI, KGA/46.

[4] Despatch from the C-in-C to the Chief of Staff, dated 30 July, received and decoded 1 August 1944 at 17.00 hrs, Ldz. 6239. APUST.

[5] *Ibid.*

[6] Despatch from the C-in-C to the President of the Republic, 31 July 1944, No. 2125. GSHI, KGA/46.

[7] K. Sosnkowski, *Materialy Historyczne* (London, 1966), pp. 612–13.

[8] Despatch from Capt Babinski to the C-in-C, dated 29 July, sent 31 July 1944, Ldz. 6165. APUST.   [9] *Ibid.*

that, on 29 July, Babinski asked President Raczkiewicz for permission for Sosnkowski to remain in Italy, as all the decisions regarding the Underground either had already been made or would be made in Warsaw; contact between London and Poland might be disrupted at any moment, attempts to secure British help for the insurrection would fail and it would be better if the General could remain with the Second Corps until they knew the outcome of the talks in Moscow.[1] The President's refusal of this request appears to have made Babinski suspicious of his motives, and even more determined to urge Sosnkowski to stay in Italy as long as possible.

Gen Sosnkowski sent three telegrams from Italy to Warsaw. In the first, dated 25 July, he discussed the sequel to 'Burza' in the Wilno region and the formation of the PKWN in Lublin, at a time when Bor-Komorowski was already notifying London of his readiness to begin the battle for Warsaw at any moment. It is indeed ironical that while the Home Army Generals were discussing the timing of their operations in the capital their Supreme Commander should be advising them, in this telegram, that he considered the 'burning issue of the moment' to be 'the rapid and extensive expansion' of the Polish forces fighting under British command, in preparation for possible conflict between Moscow and the Western Allies.[2] The C-in-C said that the London Poles must be ready for such an eventuality, which might well be brought about by 'Soviet ill-will' in spite of British and American intentions.[3] To save 'the biological substance of the nation' in the face of possible extermination by the Germans and the Russians, Sosnkowski authorised Bor-Komorowski to withdraw, in extremity, the most exposed elements of the Home Army to Western Poland or even abroad, with the proviso that they were then to join the Polish Army in exile at the first opportunity.[4] If necessary, the Home Army soldiers were to try to get through to the West by temporarily joining the Todt organisation,[5] or volunteering for agricultural work in Germany. Sosnkowski also authorised Bor-Komorowski to order into the Berling army 'certain carefully selected individuals or groups' who were to be provided with

[1] Despatch from Capt Babinski to the C-in-C, dated 29 July, sent 31 July 1944, Ldz. 6165. APUST.
[2] Despatch from the C-in-C to the Commander of the Home Army, dated 25 July, received in London 26 July, and sent to Poland with certain alterations 28 July 1944, Ldz. 6030. APUST.
[3] *Ibid.*   [4] *Ibid.*
[5] The Todt organisation was the German auxiliary building service.

suitable and realistic directives and tasks.[1] He reminded Bor-Komorowski of 'the need to create a new small and carefully selected clandestine organisation in the territories occupied by the Soviets, to perform realistic and, for the time being, modest tasks'.[2] He told Warsaw that he was pressing the Government to arrange with the British authorities for the sending of a British 'liaison and fact-finding mission' to the Home Army.[3] This mission was to help to save the Home Army soldiers from possible reprisals by the Russians.

The directives in the telegram were largely irrelevant and almost totally unacceptable to the Underground leaders, in view of their decision to try to expel the Germans from Warsaw and act as hosts to the Russians. The C-in-C's suggestion that the most exposed cadres of the Home Army should be sent abroad was contrary to the very spirit of the Polish resistance movement and its adoption, in the way he suggested, could have exposed the entire force to the accusation of collaboration with the Germans.[4] It is unthinkable that such ambiguous operations could ever have been contemplated by Bor-Komorowski and his soldiers, whose primary interest was fighting against the Germans.

These directives were relayed to Poland from London on 28 July, although some of Sosnkowski's most controversial passages – on the need to save the biological substance of the nation, and the withdrawal of the Home Army units to the west or abroad – were omitted by Kopanski, on his own initiative and responsibility, as being in some parts too general and in others too dangerous to be transmitted to Warsaw at this stage. He believed that, at this late juncture, only precise military orders should be sent to Poland,[5] in the circumstances a reasonable and practical view. Before the shortened version of Sosnkowski's telegram was despatched, Gen Tatar himself added to it a passage pointing out that the C-in-C had written it while still unaware of Bor-Komorowski's intention to stage the insurrection.[6] On 30 July the Home Commander replied to

[1] Despatch from the C-in-C to the Commander of the Home Army, dated 25 July, received in London 26 July, and sent to Poland with certain alterations 28 July 1944, Ldz. 6030. APUST. [2] *Ibid.* [3] *Ibid.*
[4] Cf. General T. Pelczynski's statement 17 October 1950, 'Drugie zebranie relacyjne w Inst. Jozefa Pilsudskiego w Londynie odbyte 17.X.1950'. APUST B.II. [5] St Kopanski, *op. cit.*, p. 326.
[6] Despatch from the C-in-C to the Commander of the Home Army, dated 25 July, received in London 26 July, and sent to Poland 28 July 1944, Ldz. 6030. APUST.

this censored despatch merely by stating that Gen Okulicki was to command the new anti-Soviet organisation.[1]

On the day that he despatched his telegram to Warsaw Sosnkowski sent to Kopanski a draft of his new instructions to Bor-Komorowski, with the request that the Chief of Staff would discuss them with the Cabinet before despatching them promptly to Poland.[2] These instructions dealt with the possibility of Soviet occupation of Warsaw, following the Red Army's spectacular advances on the Eastern Front. The C-in-C wrote that when the Soviet occupation of Warsaw appeared to be imminent, Bor-Komorowski was to divide his staff and headquarters into two echelons. One of these was to remain in the city to direct resistance against 'the Soviet policy of accomplish facts' in co-operation with that part of the Government Delegate's Staff which might be left in Warsaw.[3] The policy of coming out into the open was to be abandoned as 'senseless', in view of the creation of the PKWN and of the possibility that the Russians would arrest the revealed authorities.[4] The other part of the Home Army headquarters was to withdraw to south-western Poland, from where it was to direct the struggle of the entire force. 'This procedure should be followed', the C-in-C concluded, 'even if it proves possible to capture Warsaw before the entry of the Soviet troops'.[5] This directive was completely incompatible with the Government-approved decision of the underground leaders in Poland to reveal themselves and act as hosts to the Russians.

Although dated 25 July, this instruction was received and decoded in London on 28 July, and was discussed by the Cabinet on the afternoon of the same day. It was decided not to send it to Warsaw as it clashed with a decision the Government had already made and, in any case, could not be discussed with Sosnkowski. At this meeting the Cabinet decided to try to silence Sosnkowski; it empowered the Deputy Premier, Jan Kwapinski, to request that the President should tell the C-in-C not, for the time being, to issue any directives to Poland.[6] The result of this would be that all future decisions regarding the underground would be made in Poland – in accordance with

---

[1] Despatch from the Commander of the Home Army to the C-in-C, 30 July 1944, 6198. APUST.

[2] Despatch from the C-in-C to the Chief of Staff, dated 25 July, received in London 28 July 1944, Ldz. 6089. APUST.

[3] *Ibid.*   [4] *Ibid.*   [5] *Ibid.*

[6] Record of the Cabinet meeting No. 41, 28 July 1944, APUST; and St Kopanski, *op. cit.*, p. 321.

Mikolajczyk's telegram to Jankowski of 26 July – regardless of any objections that the C-in-C might make to them. In fact, between 28 July and his return to London on 6 August, Sosnkowski was merely a deeply-perturbed spectator of the unfolding drama in Warsaw, powerless either to avert or mitigate it.

On the day on which the Cabinet resolved to prevent him from sending further instructions to Warsaw, Sosnkowski replied to the despatch from Poland of 21 July, in which Bor-Komorowski had informed him that he was about to alert his troops for the general insurrection. The text of this telegram, or parts of it at least, had been transmitted to Sosnkowski by Kopanski on 24 July,[1] but he did not reply until 28 July, his reply did not reach London until 22.40 hours on 31 July, and decoding of it was not completed until 12.15 the following day – that is, a few hours before the first shots were fired in Warsaw.[2] 'In view of the Soviet policy of violence and accomplished facts', wrote the C-in-C,

> armed insurrection would be a politically senseless act which might lead to unnecessary sacrifices. If the aim of the insurrection is to occupy a part of the territory of the Republic, it should be realised that in such circumstances it will be necessary to defend the sovereignty of Poland [in these territories] against those who will violate this sovereignty.
>
> You understand what this would mean, as the experiment of coming into the open and co-operating failed because of the ill-will of the Soviets.[3]

After consulting President Raczkiewicz, Gen Kopanski decided not to transmit this communication to Bor-Komorowski. The President could hardly advise otherwise, in view of the Cabinet's resolution of 28 July.[4]

On 29 July Sosnkowski sent yet another telegram to Warsaw via London, replying to Bor-Komorowski's demand of 22 July for the proclamation of social and economic reforms in Poland.[5] This telegram was received in London at 12.47 on 2 August, was deciphered at 12.47 on 3 August, and was transmitted to Poland on 6 August,

---

[1] St Kopanski, *op. cit.*, p. 326.

[2] Despatch from the C-in-C to the Commander of the Home Army, dated 28 July, received in London 31 July, at 22.40 hrs, and decoded on 1 August 1944 at 12.15 hrs, Ldz. 6213. APUST.

[3] *Ibid.*   [4] St Kopanski, *op. cit.*, pp. 323–4.

[5] Captain Babinski writes that in this telegram Gen Sosnkowski was replying to Bor-Komorowski's decisions of 25 and 26 July. Witold Babinski, *Przyczynki Historyczne: Do Okresu 1939–1945* (London, 1967), p. 373.

almost a week after the beginning of the insurrection and on the day Sosnkowski finally returned to London.[1] It is very difficult to understand why it was sent to Warsaw at all, as, apart from the Cabinet resolution of 28 July, its contents were now neither relevant nor of great interest to the hard-pressed Bor-Komorowski and his Staff, who were already fighting a defensive battle against the Germans. Sosnkowski wrote:

> I have no doubt that the Government Delegate will accept your plan of action . . . especially your conclusions in regard to socio-economic problems. The struggle against the Germans must be continued in the form of Burza. *On the other hand, under the existing circumstances I am absolutely opposed to general insurrection, the historical consequences of which would [be] the exchange of one occupation for another.*
>
> *Your appraisal of the Germans' position must be very sober and realistic. A mistake in this sphere would be very costly.* At the same time you have to concentrate all your political, moral and physical forces for the defence against the aggressive policy of Moscow. The news of [Mikolajczyk's] journey to Moscow in spite of the recent Soviet moves has painfully affected the souls of the soldiers of the II Corps. I do not know or understand the . . . purpose of this journey. Without knowledge of its outcome I see no reason to consider the question of the insurrection.[2]

Sosnkowski's warnings to Bor-Komorowski were to be fully justified by future events, but they reached him at least a week too late. It emerges from the C-in-C's despatches from Italy that he was categorically opposed to a general insurrection. Instead he wanted the Home Army to continue with the 'Burza' plan to harass German rearguards as they withdrew. Secondly, he was determined that the Home Army should prepare to resist the Russians. His instructions took the form of exhortations and warnings, rather than of conventional military orders. Finally, and more significantly, he failed to comment directly and specifically on the underground leaders' decision to stage a battle for Warsaw, as distinct from a general insurrection, although Bor-Komorowski had informed London of his plan on 25 July;[3] there are strong grounds for

[1] Despatch from the C-in-C to the Commander of the Home Army, dated 29 July, received in London 2 August, at 12.47 hrs, decoded on 3 August, and sent to Poland 6 August 1944, Ldz. 6289. APUST. My italics.
[2] *Ibid.* My italics.
[3] Despatch from the Commander of the Home Army to the C-in-C, 25 July 1944, No. 1441, Ldz. 6024. APUST.

assuming that Sosnkowski was not fully aware of Bor-Komorowski's intention until 31 July, or even later, and hence, for some time was in no position to make any comment.[1] Further, it appears that almost up to the time the insurrection broke out he was under the impression that the Home Commander was planning to stage a 'general' insurrection on a national scale and therefore embracing Warsaw, rather than a local rising in the capital alone.[2] There appears, therefore, to have been a profound misunderstanding between the C-in-C and the Home Army Command, as to the latter's exact plans and intentions. Sosnkowski was not fully informed of them by Kopanski until 31 July; in the second half of July 1944 all communications between the C-in-C and Bor-Komorowski were exchanged via Kopanski. The Chief of Staff claims, however, that he transmitted the text of Bor-Komorowski's telegram to Sosnkowski on 28 July.[3] In fact, none of the telegrams sent by Gen Kopanski to Gen Sosnkowski between 28 and 31 July, accessible in the existing archives, includes the full text of Bor-Komorowski's crucial telegram of 25 July. In none of them is there any mention of its most important passage, stating that the Home Army was 'ready to commence battle for Warsaw at any moment', although less important passages, such as the Commander's request for aerial bombardment and the arrival of the Polish Parachute Brigade in Poland are mentioned.[4]

Unaware, then, of Bor-Komorowski's plan for localized insurrection, the C-in-C, when writing to Poland, constantly referred to 'general' insurrection, to which he was opposed. Indeed, Sosnkowski argues, even today, that because the rising took place in the capital – 'the seat of the central political and military authorities' – it was a general insurrection in the true sense, not merely a battle for Warsaw.[5] This seems to be a rather extravagant interpretation of Bor-Komorowski's action; the term 'general insurrection' had been reserved, in earlier plans, for insurrectionary operations in the country as a whole, and was not used to describe localised action in Warsaw alone.[6] Sosnkowski's application of the term to the Warsaw Rising suggests a desire, on his part, to dissociate himself entirely from

[1] Z. S. Siemaszko, *op. cit.*, pp. 104ff.
[2] Cf. *Polskie Sily Zbrojne*, *op. cit.*, p. 666.
[3] St Kopanski, *op. cit.*, p. 320, and *Polskie Sily Zbrojne*, *op. cit.*, p. 662.
[4] Cf. Z. S. Siemaszko, *op. cit.*, p. 109.
[5] K. Sosnkowski, *op. cit.*, p. 607.
[6] The Order of the Commander of the Home Army, 20 November 1943, Ldz. 2100. APUST.

Bor-Komorowski's decision. At the same time, it should be remembered that Bor-Komorowski had himself stated, as early as October, 1943, that his main effort, during a general insurrection, would be concentrating on seizing and liberating Warsaw.[1] Hence, it might be held that the C-in-C, who knew of this when he was declaring himself against general insurrection, was thereby automatically expressing his opposition to the idea of staging any large-scale operations in Warsaw. But such an interpretation could not be reconciled with Sosnkowski's instruction to Bor-Komorowski of 7 July, ordering him to capture large towns, within the framework of 'Burza', if circumstances permitted.[2] Further, on 25 July the C-in-C explicitly referred to the possibility of Warsaw being seized by the Home Army, again within the framework of 'Burza'.[3] He cannot, then, have been entirely opposed, before the event, to the idea of Bor-Komorowski's troops capturing Warsaw, provided that the risks involved were small, that the fighting was restricted to a bare minimum, and that the chances of success were very high.

When making his final decision, Bor-Komorowski believed that such a conjunction of circumstances existed, but was unable to discuss his plans and intentions with the C-in-C.[4] It is therefore impossible to say with certainty whether Sosnkowski would have approved them, had he been fully aware of them and of the Home Commander's appraisal of his force's potentialities and the situation of the Germans. By deciding to remain in Italy after 24 July, Sosnkowski lost his final chance of guiding and influencing Bor-Komorowski's conduct and decisions with regard to Warsaw, and thus, by default, he may also have contributed to that city's tragedy. His absence from his London headquarters left his hard-pressed, war-weary, yet over-optimistic subordinates entirely to their own counsels, resources and devices; it was his duty to issue them with firm, concrete and timely instructions rather than belated general warnings. It would seem that, at this crucial moment, Gen Sosnkowski discharged less than his military duty with regard to the Home Army, although he was its Supreme Commander.

---

[1] The Report from the Commander of the Home Army to the C-in-C No. 221, 14 October 1943, Ldz. 3269/44. APUST.

[2] Despatch from the C-in-C to the Commander of the Home Army, 7 July 1944, Ldz. 5480/44. APUST.

[3] Despatch from the C-in-C to the Chief of Staff, dated 25 July, received 28 July 1944, Ldz. 6089. APUST.

[4] Bor-Komorowski's oral evidence.

Nevertheless, it is open to speculation whether, if he had returned earlier to London, Sosnkowski would have been successful in any attempts to exert greater influence on events in Poland; after 25 July Bor-Komorowski was determined to act,[1] and three days later the Cabinet decided to stop the C-in-C from sending any further instructions for the time being to the Home Army, as his instructions were clashing with those of the Cabinet's and of the underground leaders'.[2] It is probable, therefore, that the Government would have acted in the same way, even if the C-in-C had been in London at the time, but he would, at least, have been better informed, able to discuss his views directly with the Cabinet and to ensure that his despatches to Warsaw were passed on without delay, failing which he could have resigned in protest. His absence from London merely resulted in the Cabinet's formal repudiation of his instructions to Bor-Komorowski.[3]

On 2 August Kwapinski wrote to Warsaw:

'In connection with the Commander-in-Chief's suggestion that the [plans for] coming into the open and armed action decided by you should be suspended . . . the Government . . . considers it impossible to alter its existing instructions and your decision. The question of armed action and coming into the open lies only in your hands. This applies also to the question of insurrection . . .'[4]

The Government in London hereby reaffirmed the *carte blanche* they had given to the underground leaders in Warsaw, although this was by now a superfluous move, for Warsaw was already fighting. News of the outbreak of the insurrection reached England late on 2 August.[5]

Bor-Komorowski was puzzled by Kwapinski's telegram. He saw no disparity between the instructions received from the Cabinet and those of the C-in-C which he had received. 'Acting in close co-operation with the Government Delegate', he wrote,

I am issuing orders which are demanded by the situation and loyally following the basic directives of the Government's and the C-in-C's orders. The whole area has been ordered to implement 'Burza'. In

---

[1] Despatch from the Commander of the Home Army to the C-in-C, 25 July 1944, No. 1441, Ldz. 6024. APUST.
[2] Record of the Cabinet meeting No. 41, 28 July 1944. APUST.
[3] *Ibid.*
[4] Despatch from the Deputy Prime Minister to the Commander of the Home Army, 2 August 1944, No. 629. GSHI, Kol. G.A./46.
[5] St Kopanski, *op. cit.*, p. 329.

spite of the hostile attitude of the Soviets to the military authorities
and civil administration . . . I have not suspended the order to come
into the open west of the Curzon Line . . . Eventual change of this
decision will depend on the developments which occur after the coming
into the open in the capital. I am determined to come into the open
together with the Government Delegate.[1]

The Home Commander believed, therefore, even after the outbreak of the insurrection in Warsaw, that he was implementing
'Burza', in accordance with the directives received from his Government and the C-in-C.

After his return to London Sosnkowski strongly repudiated
Kwapinski's allegations that he favoured the suspension of all anti-
German operations in Poland. The General maintained that he
wanted the Home Army to continue 'Burza' in the form of 'increased
diversionary activity' and was only opposed to the insurrection
being staged.[2] Kwapinski's allegations were groundless – Sosnkowski's telegram to Bor-Komorowski of 29 July, urging that the
struggle against the Germans be continued, is sufficient evidence of
this[3] – but, in the arguments he used to refute them, the C-in-C was
not entirely consistent with his own recent directives, for he had,
after all, on 7 July issued to the Home Army the order calling upon
it to capture large towns when circumstances permitted.[4] In such
operations, local insurrections, to which the General now insisted
he was opposed, were inevitable, even if they were launched only
in the last moments of the German retreat and immediately before
the entry of the Russians; large towns could hardly be captured in the
course of 'increased diversionary activities'.

Sosnkowski blamed the Government for the outbreak of the
insurrection in Warsaw. 'My efforts to treat in a sensible and
cautious manner the question of general insurrection, under the
existing political and military conditions, were torpedoed during
my absence by the Government', he wrote to Gen Anders on 11

---

[1] Despatch from the Commander of the Home Army to the Prime Minister,
3 August 1944, No. 629. GSHI, Kol. G.A./46.

[2] Despatch from the C-in-C to the Commander of the Second Corps, 16 August
1944, No. 7005, GSHI, Kol. G.A./46; and St Kopanski, *op. cit.*, p. 330.

[3] Despatch from the C-in-C to the Commander of the Home Army, dated 29
July received in London 2 August at 12.47 hrs, decoded on 3 August, and
sent to Poland 6 August 1944, Ldz. 6289. APUST. My italics.

[4] Despatch from the C-in-C to the Commander of the Home Army, 7 July 1944,
Lodz. 5480/44. APUST.

August.[1] A few days later he told Anders that on 26 July the Premier had given the authorities in Warsaw power to decide when and where the insurrection was to take place.[2] In this way the C-in-C denied any responsibility for the outbreak of the rising; he claimed that it was a manifestation of 'general insurrection', to which he was opposed, and that, in any case, its outbreak was the fault of the Government.[3] But at least he acknowledged that his absence from London had greatly contributed to his inability to influence events. It should be noted that Anders was under the impression that the C-in-C had sent a despatch to Warsaw from Italy, 'categorically banning the insurrection and warning against the tragic consequences which such a move might bring upon the Polish nation'.[4] Indeed, Anders had urged Sosnkowski to issue such an order when he had stayed at his headquarters.[5] In August 1944 Anders was anxious to discover who was responsible for 'the tragic decision of the Commander of the Home Army'.[6] 'All this', he confessed, 'is not clear to me'.[7] Only much later did he finally realise that his C-in-C had, in the second half of July 1944 failed to issue to the Home Army, the unequivocal orders which Anders had considered so essential.[8]

Anders' confusion was largely caused by the fact that his superior was not very forthcoming in explaining the whole situation to him, omitting to tell him that he had not issued an order forbidding an insurrection. Sosnkowski preferred to blame the insurrection on Mikolajczyk rather than on his own subordinates in Warsaw, who were its chief instigators.

On 2 August, as yet unaware that the rising had begun, he sent a telegram to Kopanski expressing his fear that the insurrection might start 'against my advice' and seemed greatly agitated at the

---

[1] Despatch from the C-in-C to the Commander of the Second Corps, 11 August 1944, No. 4274. GSHI, Kol. G.A./46.

[2] Despatch from the C-in-C to the Commander of the Second Corps, 16 August 1944, No. 7005. GSHI, Kol. G.A./46.

[3] Despatch from the C-in-C to the Commander of the Second Corps, 11 August 1944, No. 4274. GSHI, Kol. G.A./46.

[4] Letter from Gen Anders to Col Hancza, 31 August 1944, Ldz. ADD/318/Tj./44. GSHI, Kol. G.A./46.

[5] W. Anders, *Bez Ostatniego Rozdzialu* (London, 1959), p. 252.

[6] Despatch from the Commander of the Second Corps to the C-in-C, 10 August 1944, No. 2074. GSHI, Kol. G.A./46.

[7] Letter from Gen Anders to Col 'Hancza', 31 August 1944, Ldz. ADD/318/Tj./44. GSHI, Kol. G.A./46.

[5] W. Anders, *op. cit.*, pp. 252–3.

contemplation of such a possibility.[1] Even then he could not bring himself either to assume responsibility for it or, alternatively, to issue an order categorically banning it.[2]

In contrast, as soon as Mikolajczyk realised that the insurrection was imminent he sanctioned it in advance, hoping that he would be able to derive political and diplomatic capital from it. In reality, however, his prompt authorisation had little direct influence on the decisions of Jankowski and Bor-Komorowski; it reached Warsaw when the initial decision to fight had already been made and merely strengthened the resistance leaders' determination to act.

In conclusion, when the resistance leaders first decided to fight in Warsaw their only guidance from London consisted in Mikolajczyk's telegrams of 4 and 14 July and Sosnkowski's directives of 7 July. These communications left the final decisions to the discretion of the leaders in Warsaw, who, in the second half of July, 'received no detailed orders or counter-orders from London', in the words of Gen Pelczynski.[3] The General omitted to add, however, that in any case, such orders might well have been superfluous, as the Underground leaders were determined to act on their own initiative. This determination was conveyed to London in messages from Jankowski and Bor-Komorowski on 12, 21 and 25 July. During the second half of July all 'detailed orders' were issued in Warsaw, without consulting the émigré authorities. Consequently, only three courses of action were open to Mikolajczyk and Sosnkowski: they could have sanctioned the orders, tried to countermand them, or at least have questioned their feasibility. The Premier decided to adopt the first course, while the C-in-C prevaricated and, in so doing, forfeited any remaining chance to influence events in Warsaw.

[1] Despatch from the C-in-C to the Chief of Staff, dated 2 August, received in London 4 August 1944, Ldz. 6395. APUST.

[2] In 1950 Maj-Gen K. Wisniowski, the Chief of Staff of the Second Corps, claimed that the C-in-C failed to ban the insurrection as he believed that such an order would not prevent the spontaneous outbreak of the fighting in Warsaw, because of the psychological state of its population and general desire for revenge. The C-in-C allegedly feared that in spite of his ban Warsaw would rise against the Germans and this would be exploited by 'the Red elements'. Gen Wisniowski's statement 15 September 1950. 'Protokoly z zebran relacyjnch w inst. Jozefa Pilsudskiego w Londynie n.t. Powstania Warszawskiego, walk AK i postawy Rosji Sowieckiej. Zebranie pierwsze odbyte 17/IX/1950'. APUST. B II.

[3] General Pelczynski's statement 18 April 1951. 'Zalacznik Nr. 2 do protokolu z dn. 18.4.51 z IV relacyjnego zebrania w inst. Jozefa Pilsudskiego n.t. "Decyzja walki o Warszawe" '. APUST. B II.

Bor-Komorowski stated, after the war, that if Sosnkowski had ordered him not to fight in Warsaw he would, in accordance with the demands of military discipline have obeyed.[1] He received no such order.

[1] Bor-Komorowski's oral evidence. An identical view was expressed by Gen Pelczynski in 1950. Gen Pelczynski's statement 15 September 1950. 'Protokoly z zebran relacyjnych w inst. Jozefa Pilsudskiego w Londynie n.t. Powstania Warszawskiego, walk AK i postawy Rosji Sowieckiej. Zebranie pierwsze odbyte 17/IX/1950'. APUST. B II.

CONCLUSIONS

The decision of the Polish leaders to fight in Warsaw was prompted by political, diplomatic, ideological and military considerations. Politically, the insurrection was intended by its authors to achieve four basic objectives. These were, to facilitate the emergence in Warsaw of an administration loyal to the Polish Government in London, to ensure for this administration the highest degree of popular support; conversely, to prevent the Polish Communists and their sympathisers from establishing themselves in Warsaw, with Russian help, as the new leaders of resurgent Poland, and finally to compel Stalin to recognise London Poles as the rightful rulers of Poland. The authors of the insurrection were not prepared to relinquish their ambition to govern Poland without a fight. They identified Poland, her interests and future with themselves.

Diplomatically, the pro-London leaders hoped, by staging a successful anti-German insurrection, to assist Mikolajczyk in his forthcoming negotiations with Stalin and to invite Churchill and Roosevelt to reaffirm their support for the Polish Government in London and its agencies in Poland. However, no serious diplomatic preparations for the insurrection were made by Mikolajczyk even in London and Washington, let alone Moscow.

Idealogically, when making their decision to rise in Warsaw, the authors of the insurrection were guided by the doctrine of two enemies, that is, their belief that while the struggle against the Germans must be continued, political opposition to the Russians and the Polish Communists must be strengthened, and, that help for the restoration of independent Poland must be sought primarily in London and Washington. The Polish Communists and their followers wished to build post-war Poland in close alliance and co-operation with Moscow. This idea was anathema to the London Poles in whose opinion it represented a threat to Poland's independence and territorial integrity, as the Communists were ready to accept the Curzon Line as the new Russo–Polish frontier. The main point of disagreement between the London Poles and the Communists was their attitudes to Russia and the frontier question rather than the problem of immediate social and economic reforms. Most of the pro-London resistance leaders were convinced, at the time of the insurrection at least, that large-scale social and economic reforms were necessary and inevitable.

The military basis for the decision to fight in the capital was the belief that the Germans were decisively beaten on the Eastern Front and that the Red Army was about to enter Warsaw. Bor-Komorowski and Jankowski issued their final order for the insurrection when it was erroneously reported to them that the Soviet tanks were entering Praga. Hence they assumed that the Russo–German battle for Warsaw was approaching its climax and that this presented them with an excellent opportunity to capture Warsaw before the Red Army entered the capital. The Soviet radio appeals calling upon the people of Warsaw to rise against the Germans, regardless of Moscow's intentions, had very little influence on the Polish authorities responsible for the insurrection. These appeals merely strengthened Bor-Komorowski's conviction that the Russians were on the point of taking Warsaw. Further, in the last days of July 1944 the Home Army's High Command knew that only in Warsaw had they enough troops to mount at short notice a military operation on a scale large enough to be effective in a major urban centre.

Given these attitudes and beliefs it was morally easier for the authors of the insurrection to issue the order for the battle to begin than to refrain from doing so, especially as they were convinced that failure to act would lead to their abandonment by the masses and would therefore amount to political suicide. But by deciding to act without co-ordinating their plans with the Soviet High Command they assumed heavy responsibility for the fate of Warsaw and greatly contributed to the ensuing tragedy of this city and its people. They failed to realise that a badly armed Home Army could not, in the summer of 1944 successfully do battle with the Germans while simultaneously trying to oppose the Russians and the Polish Communists politically. Bor-Komorowski's and Jankowski's plans were too complicated and too hazardous to succeed in the existing political and military situation.

It should be stressed that all important decisions leading to the insurrection were taken by the resistance leaders in Warsaw without prior consultation with the Polish Government in London. The

Polish Prime Minister and his Cabinet, it is true, seemed to agree with and to welcome the plans of their subordinates in Poland; until the actual outbreak of the insurrection the Commander-in-Chief of the Polish Armed Forces was undecided as to whether he should sanction it or try to prevent it.

The absence of Russo–Polish military co-operation made the rising an unmitigated tragedy. As a result of the insurrection Warsaw was destroyed; in January 1945 the advancing Russians entered a city of ruins and graves. Nearly 200,000 of the city's inhabitants were killed during the fighting.[1] The Germans expelled the survivors – about 800,000 – from their city,[2] they were dispersed throughout the rest of occupied Poland or deported to Germany. In recent history no other European capital has suffered so heavily.

The defeat and destruction of Warsaw had a traumatic effect on the entire nation. National romanticism, so strong before 1944, was superseded by political realism. As a result of the insurrection many Poles became aware of the need for close alliance with Russia, although to many this idea had formerly been, and probably still is highly repugnant. For the London Poles the failure of the rising was a great political, military and psychological defeat from which they never recovered. After the fall of Warsaw the Underground State and the exiled Government began to disintegrate rapidly. The Home Army, in particular, failed to recover from the shock and consequences of the defeat. Many of its best soldiers were killed or captured in Warsaw. Many of the rest were afflicted by defeatist feelings which affected not only their own ranks but society at large. Soon after the insurrection the last Commander of the Home Army decided to demobilise many of his units because he feared that they might become completely demoralised or join the People's Army.[3]

Thus, the insurrection and its aftermath helped, rather than frustrated the Communist assumption of power in Poland. On 6 September 1944 Jankowski and Bor-Komorowski warned the exiled Government: 'It is obvious that with the fall of the insurrection in Warsaw control of the entire country will pass into the hands of the Communists.'[4] The defeat had to a certain extent been brought about by the political and military ineptitude and undue optimism of the

[1] 'Bitwa Warszawska', B.11, No. 543, APUST.
[2] *Ibid.*
[3] Letter from Maj-Gen L. Okulicki to the President of the Republic, 9 December 1944, No. 1780/1, APUST.
[4] Despatch from the Government Delegate and the Commander of the Home

pro-London leaders particularly by their inability to come to terms with Stalin as Churchill had advised. Such a *rapprochement* would have been very costly to Poland, but, in the second half of 1944, it was the only realistic course to adopt.

Army to the Prime Minister and the C-in-C, 6 September 1944, Ldz. 7991/ Tjn/44, GSHI, L7.

Select Bibliography

The history of Poland and the Polish resistance movement before and during the Warsaw Rising is the subject of a large body of literature. Yet the political and ideological background of the insurrection, from the moment Polish resistance began to the outbreak of the rising has received sparse attention.

In this bibliography I have included major works only, a selection of memoirs and studies dealing with political, ideological and military problems and finally controversial and polemical contributions which have emerged from or are pertinent to the continuing debate, in Poland and abroad, on the Warsaw Rising.

NOTE ON DOCUMENTARY SOURCES

Because of the historical circumstances of the Second World War and its aftermath the most complete and authoritative collection of official Polish documents pertaining to the plans and activities of the Polish authorities responsible for the outbreak of the Warsaw Rising is deposited in Great Britain. From 1940 until 1945 the Polish Government was exiled in London and after the war its records were not returned to Poland. It was in London, then, that, during the most crucial period of the war, the highest Polish political and military authorities considered and debated their country's most important war-time problems. In London were recorded not only all communications between them and their subordinates in occupied Poland, but also the diplomatic exchanges between the Polish leaders and their Allied counterparts. For the student of Polish war-time history and politics therefore, especially the student of developments leading to the outbreak of the insurrection, there exist no other set of Polish records comparable with those which after the war were deposited in the Archives of the General Sikorski Historical Institute and the Archives of the Polish Underground Movement Study Trust in London. These documents are essential if the political, ideological and military background of the insurrection is to be understood.

However, the existing documentation does not include the minutes or records of many important conferences and briefings which were held by the resistance authorities in occupied Poland, as records were not made for security reasons. In addition, in many instances the existing documents contain only the final decisions and intentions of the resistance leaders and fail to reveal the discussions which undoubtedly led up to them. The main difficulty for the student of the

underground organisation is inherent in his subject; in some areas the documentary sources left for him to study are limited in number.

To overcome this difficulty the proceedings of a number of important meetings
and briefings held by the underground leaders in Warsaw had to be reconstructed
from evidence collected from the surviving personalities who were involved in
these events.

In the Soviet Union there are excellent sources for the history of the Warsaw
Rising, but they remain inaccessible to the student. Until these sources become
available reliance must be placed upon the Polish documents and published
materials listed here.

Sources

1. UNPUBLISHED DOCUMENTARY SOURCES

GSHI. – Archives of the General Sikorski Historical Institute, London. The records of the following were used:
>The Prime Minister's Office.
>The Polish High Command – the Commander-in-Chief.
>the General Staff and the Ministry of National Defence.
>The Ministry of Foreign Affairs.
>The Ministry of Internal Affairs.
>The collected documents of Gen W. Anders.

APUST. – Archives of the Polish Underground Movement Study Trust, London. The records of the following were used:
>The Commander-in-Chief's Office.
>The Special or VI Bureau of the General Staff (responsible for Home military affairs).
>The Ministry of Internal Affairs (responsible for Home political affairs).
>Reference was also made to reports and personal accounts of the events under study by some of the senior commanders and leaders of the Home Army e.g. its Commander, Chief of Staff, Head of Intelligence, etc.

2. PRINTED DOCUMENTARY SOURCES

Armia Krajowa w Dokumentach 1939–1945, vol. I, *Wrzesien 1939 – Czerwiec 1941*, London, 1970, Studium Polski Podziemnej.

Correspondence between the Chairman of the Council of Ministers of the U.S.S.R. and the President of the U.S.A. and the Prime Minister of Great Britain during the Great Patriotic War of 1941–1945, Two vols in one, London, 1958.

'Depesze KC PPR do Georgii Dymitrowa (1942–1943)', *Z Pola Walki*, No. 4/1961.

Documents on Polish–Soviet Relations 1939–1945, vols I–II, London, 1961–9.

Dokumenty Vnieshnei Politiki SSR, vols II–III, Moscow, 1959.

'Dziennik Dzialan Niemieckiej 9 Armii', Ed. by Jozef Matecki, *Zeszyty Historyczne*, No. 15/1969.

Foreign Relations of the United States. Diplomatic Papers 1942, vol. III, *Europe*, Washington, 1961.

Foreign Relations of the United States. Diplomatic Papers 1943, vol. III, *The British Commonwealth, Eastern Europe, the Far East*, Washington, 1963.

Foreign Relations of the United States. Diplomatic Papers, the Conference at Cairo and Teheran 1943, Washington, 1961.

Foreign Relations of the United States. Diplomatic Papers 1944, vol. III, *The British Commonwealth and Europe*, Washington, 1965.

Jedrzejewicz, Waclaw, *Poland in British Parliament, 1939–1945*, vols I–II, New York, 1946–59.

318

Komunikaty Dowodztwa Glownego Gwardii Ludowej i Armii Ludowej. Dokumenty, Warsaw, 1959.

Ksztaltowanie sie podstaw programowych Polskiej Partii Robotniczej w latach 1942–1945, Warsaw, 1958.

'Meldunki sytuacyjne "Montera" z Powstania Warszawskiego', Ed. by Jerzy Kirchmayer, *Najnowsze Dzieje Polski 1939–1945*, No. 3/1959.

'Misja "Freston" ', Ed. by Jan Zamojski, *Najnowsze Dzieje Polski 1939–1945*, No. 9/1965.

Nazi–Soviet Relations. Documents from the Archives of the German Foreign Office, Ed. by Raymond James Sontag and James Stuart Beddie, Washington, 1948.

'Niemieckie materialy do Powstania Warszawskiego', Ed. by Stanislaw Ploski, *Najnowsze Dzieje Polski 1939–1945*, No. 1/1957.

Official documents concerning Polish–German and Polish–Soviet Relations, 1933–1939, ('Polish White Book'), London (1940). Published by authority of the Polish Government.

Polish–Soviet Relations 1918–1943. Official Documents, issued by the Polish Embassy in Washington by authority of the Government of the Republic of Poland. (1944).

Protokol pierwszego plenarnego posiedzenia Krajowej Rady Narodowej. Warszawa 31.XII – 1.I.1944, Warsaw, 1947. Biuro Prezydialne KRN.

Rozkazy i odezwy Dowodztwa Glownego Gwardii Ludowej (1942–1944), Maria Turlejska, Lodz, 1946.

Sprawozdanie sadowe w sprawie organizatorow, kierownikow i uczestnikow polskiego podziemia na zapleczu Armii Czerwonej na terytorium Polski, Litwy oraz obwodow Zachodniej Bialorusi i Ukrainy rozpatrzone przez Kolegium Wojskowe Sadu Najwyzszego ZSSR. 18–21 Czerwca 1945 r., Moscow, 1945.

Spychalski, Marian, 'Informacja przedstawiciela KC PPR na zebraniu komunistow polskich w Moskwie 8 czerwca 1944 r.', *Z Pola Walki*, No. 4/1961.

Zburzenie Warszawy, Zeznania generalow niemieckich przed polskim prokuratorem, czlonkiem polskiej delegacji przy miedzynarodowym trybunale wojennym w Norymberdze, Warsaw, 1946.

3. MEMOIRS

Anders, Wladyslaw, *Bez ostatniego rozdzialu, Wspomnienia z lat 1939–1946*, 3rd ed. rev. and corrected, London, 1959.

Avon, Earl of, *The Eden Memoirs. The Reckoning*, London, 1965.

Baginski, Kazimierz, ' "Proces Szesnastu" w Moskwie', *Zeszyty Historyczne*, No. 4/1963.

Benes, Eduard, *Memoirs*, Boston, 1954.

Bor-Komorowski, Tadeusz, *Armia Podziemna*, 3rd ed., London, 1967.

Chrusciel, Antoni ('Monter'), *Powstanie Warszawskie*, London, 1948.

Churchill, Winston S., *The Second World War*, 6 vols, London, 1948–54.

Ciechanowski, Jan, *Defeat in Victory*, London, 1948.

   Drogi Cichociemnych. Opowiadania zebrane i opracowane przes Kolo Spadochroniarzy Armii Krajowej, London, 1961.

Guderian, Heinz, *Panzer Leader*, London, 1952.

Hull, Cordell, *The Memoirs of Cordell Hull*, London 1948.

Janke, Z. W., *W Armii Krajowej*, Warsaw, 1969.

Karski, Jan, *Story of the Secret State*, Boston, 1943.

Katelbach, Tadeusz, *Rok zlych wrozb (1943)*, Paris, 1959.

Kennan, George, F., *Memoirs 1925–1950*, London, 1968.

Kirkor, Stanislaw, 'Urywek Wspomnien', *Zeszyty Historyczne*, No. 18/1970.

Kopanski, Stanislaw, *Wspomnienia Wojenne 1939–1946*, London, 1961.

Korbonski, Stefan, *W Imieniu Rzeczypospolitej* . . ., 2nd ed., London, 1964.

Kulski, Julian, *Zarzad Miejski Warszawy 1939–1944*, Warsaw, 1964.

Kwapinski, Jan, *1939–1945 (Z Pamietnika)*, London, 1947.

Maisky, Ivan, *Memoirs of a Soviet Ambassador. The War 1939–1943*; London, 1967.

Malecki, Jozef Sek, *Armia Ludowa w Powstaniu Warszawskim*, Warsaw, 1962.

Mikolajczyk, Stanislaw, *The Pattern of Soviet Domination*, London, 1948.

Mitkiewicz, Leon, 'Powstanie Warszawskie (Z mojego notatnika w Waszyngtonie)', *Zeszyty Historyczne*, No. 1/1962.

W najwyzszym sztabie zachodnich aliantow 1943–1945 London, 1971.

Moczar, Mieczyslaw, *Barwy Walki*, 3rd ed., Warsaw, 1963.

Moran, of Manton, Lord, *Winston Churchill. The struggle for survival 1940–1965*, London, 1966.

Nagorski, Zygmunt, *Wojna w Londynie*, Paris, 1966.

Pamietniki zolnierzy baonu 'Zoska', Warsaw, 1959.

Popiel, Karol, *Na mogilach przyjaciol*, London, 1966.

Od Brzescia do Polonii, London, 1967.

Pragier, Adam, *Czas Przeszly Dokonany*, London, 1966.

Raczynski, Edward, *W sojuszniczym Londynie. Dziennik ambasadora 1939–1945*, London, 1960.

Retinger, Joseph, *Memoirs of an Eminence Grise*, ed. by John Pomian, London, 1972.

Rommel, Juliusz, *Za honor i ojczyzne*, Warsaw, 1958.

Rowecki, Stefan ('Grot'), *Wspomnienia i notatki*, Warsaw, 1957.

Sosabowski, Stanislaw, *Najkrotsza Droga*, London, 1957.

Stypulkowski, Zbigniew, *W zawierusze dziejowej*, London, 1951.

Szostak, Jozef, 'Dziesiec dni przed powstaniem w Warszawie 1944 r.', *Stolica*, No. 31 (1130), 3rd August, 1969.

Sztuberk-Rychter, Tadeusz, *Artylerzysta Piechurem*, Warsaw, 1967.

Tokarzewski-Karaszewicz, Michal, 'Jak powstala Armia Krajowa', *Zeszyty Historyczne*, No. 6/1964.

Truszkowski, Stanislaw, *Partyzanckie Wspomnienia*. Warsaw, 1968.

Zabiello, Stanislaw, *Sprawa Polska Podczas II Wojny Swiatowej w Swietle Pamietnikow*, Warsaw, 1958.

Zagorski, Waclaw, *Seventy Days*, London, 1959.

Wolnosc w niewoli, London, 1971.

Wicher Wolnosci, London, 1957.

Zaremba, Zygmunt, *Wojna i konspiracja*, London, 1957.

4. BOOKS AND SPECIAL STUDIES

Babinski, Witold, 'Na marginesie polemiki', *Kultura*, No. 5 (127), 1958

'Powstanie Warszawskie', *Zeszyty Historyczne*, No. 6/1964.

'Refleksje rocznicowe', *Zeszyty Historyczne*, No. 7/1965.

Przyczynki Historyczne. Do okresu 1939–1945, London, 1967.

'Poklosie Dyskusji', *Zeszyty Historyczne*, No. 16/1969.

'Jeszcze o Powstaniu', *Wiadomosci*, vol. xxv, No. 3/4 (1242–1243), 8–25 January 1970.

'Losy Stolicy' *Wiadomosci*, vol. XXVII, No. 13–14 (1356–7), 26 March–2 April 1972.
'Na marginesie Ksiazki J. M. Ciechanowskiego', *Zeszyty Historyczne*, No. 22/1972.
Bartelski, Leslaw M., *Powstanie Warszawskie*, Warsaw, 1965.
Mokotow 1944, Warsaw, 1971.
Bethell, Nicholas, *Gomulka, his Poland and his Communism*, London, 1969.
Boratynski, S., *Dyplomacja okresu drugiej wojny swiatowej*, Warsaw, 1957.
Borkiewicz, Adam, *Powstanie Warszawskie, 1944. Zarys dzialan natury wojskowej*, Warsaw, 1957.
Bor-Komorowski, Tadeusz, 'The Unconquerables', *The Reader's Digest*, February, 1946.
Bromke, Adam, *Poland's Politics: Idealism vs. Realism*, Cambridge, Massachusetts, 1967.
Caban, I. and Mankowski, Z., *Zwiazek Walki Zbrojnej i Armia Krajowa w Okregu Lubelskim 1939–1945*, 2 vols (Lublin, 1971).
Chocianowicz, Waclaw, *W 50-lecie Powstanie Wyszej Szkoly Wojennej w Warszawie*, London, 1969.
Ciechanowski, J. M., 'Gdy wazyly sie losy stolicy: Notatka z rozmowy z gen. Tadeuszem Borem-Komorowskim, odbytej w maju 1965 w Londynie w obecnosci prof. J. K. Zawodnego', *Wiadomosci*, vol. XXVI, No. 39 (1330), 26 September 1971.
Powstanie Warszawskie: Zarys podloza politycznego i dyplomatycznego, London, 1971.
'Na Tropach Kleski', *Wiadomasci*, vol. XXVII, No. 24 (1367), 11 June 1972.
Cieplewicz, M., 'Generalowie polscy w opinii J. Pilsudskiego', *Wojskowy Przeglad Historyczny*, No. 1/1966.
Deborin, G. A., *Druga Wojna Swiatowa*, Warsaw, 1960.
Deutscher, Issac, *Stalin: a political biography*, London, 1961.
The Tragedy of Polish Communism Between the Wars, London (undated).
Dolega-Mondrzewski, Stanislaw, *Polskie Panstwo Podziemne*, London, 1959.
Duraczynski, Eugeniusz, *Stosunki w Kierownictwie Podziemia Londynskiego 1939–1943*, Warsaw, 1966.
Dziewanowski, M. K., *The Communist Party of Poland. An Outline of History*, Cambridge, Massachusetts, 1959.
Ehrman, John, *Grand Strategy*, vol. V, *August 1943–September 1944*, London, 1956.
Feis, Herbert, *Churchill–Roosevelt–Stalin. The war they waged the peace they sought*, New Jersey, 1957.
Garlinski, Jozef, *Miedzy Londynem i Warszawa*, London, 1966.
Zolnierze i Politycy, London, 1968.
'Powstanie Warszawskie', *Wiadomosci*, vol. XXIV, No. 42 (1229), 19 October 1969.
'Od Wrzesnia do Powstania', *Wiadomosci*, vol. XXV, No. 9 (1248), 1 March 1970.
Giertych, Jedrzej, *Pol wieku polityki polskiej*, Western Germany, 1947.
Gomulka, Wladyslaw, *W walce o demokracje ludowa*, 2 vols, Warsaw, 1947.
Gross, Feliks, *The Seizure of Political Power*, New York, 1958.
Iranek-Osmecki, Kazimierz, 'Zarys Rozwoju Armii Krajowej', *Niepodleglosc*, No. 1/1948.
'Znaczenie powstania warszawskiego', *Bellona*, No. 3/4, 1957.
Irving, David, *Accident: The Death of General Sikorski*, London, 1967.

Israelin, Wiktor, *Historia Dyplomatyczna 1941–1945*, Warsaw, 1963.
Istorija Velikoi Otechestvennoi Voiny Sovetskogo Soyuza, 5 vols, Moscow, 1960–3.
Kalinowski, Franciszek, *Lotnictwo polskie w Wielkiej Brytanii 1940–1945*, Paris, 1969.
Karasiowna, Janina, 'Pierwsze Polrosze Armii Podziemnej', *Niepodleglosc*, No. 1/1948.
Kirchmayer, Jerzy, *1939–1944, Kilka zagadnien polskich*, Warsaw, 1958.
Uwagi i polemiki, Warsaw, 1958.
Powstanie Warszawskie, Warsaw, 1959.
Kliszko, Zenon, *Z problemow historii PPR*, Warsaw, 1958.
Powstanie Warszawskie, Warsaw, 1967.
Komisja Historyczna Polskiego Sztabu Glownego w Londynie, Vol. i: *Polskie Sily Zbrojne w Drugiej Wojnie Swiatowej: Kampania Wrzesniowa*, London, 1951. Vol. iii: *Polskie Sily Zbrojne w Drugiej Wojnie Swiatowej: Armia Krajowa*, London, 1950.
Korbonski, Andrzej, *Politics of Socialist Agriculture in Poland 1945–1960*, New York and London, 1965.
'The Warsaw Rising Revisited', *Survey*, No. 76 (1970).
Kowalski, Wlodzimierz, *Walka dyplomatyczna o miejsce Polski w Europie 1939–1945*, Warsaw, 1967.
Kozicki, Stanislaw, *Historia Ligi Narodowej*, London, 1964.
Kozlowski, Eugeniusz, *Wojsko Polskie 1936–1939*, Warsaw, 1964.
Krannhals, Hanns von, *Der Warschauer Aufstand, 1944*, Frankfurt a. M., 1962.
Kukiel, Marian, 'Strategiczne koncepcje gen. Sikorskiego w drugiej wojnie swiatowej', *Bellona*, No. 3/1955.
General Sikorski, London, 1970.
Leslie, R. F., *Reform and Insurrection in Russian Poland 1856–1865*, London, 1963.
Lukasiewicz, Juliusz, *Polska jest mocarstwem*, 2nd ed., Warsaw, 1939.
Machalski, T., 'Wspomnienia a gen. Borze', *Horyzonty*, No. 126–127/1966.
Madajczyk, Czeslaw, *Generalna Gubernia w planach hitlerowskich*, Warsaw, 1961.
Sprawa reformy rolnej w Polsce 1939–1944. Programy, *Taktyka*, Warsaw, 1961.
'Wazna decyzja. Przyczynek do rozmow miedzy PPR a Delegatura w 1943 r.', *Najnowsze Dzieje Polski 1939–1945*, No. 4/1960.
Polityka III Rzeszy w Okupowanej Polsce, 2 vols, Warsaw, 1970.
Majorkiewicz, Felicjan, *Dane nam bylo przezyc*, Warsaw, 1972.
Malinowski, Marian, 'Ksztaltowanie sie zalozen programowych ruchu komunistycznego w latach 1939–1942', *Z Pola Walki*, No. 4/1961.
Margules, Jozef, *Przyczolki warszawskie*, Warsaw, 1962.
Boje l Armii WP w Obszarze Warszawy (sierpien–wrzesien 1944), Warsaw, 1967.
Michniewicz, Wl., 'Smierc plk. Hanczy', *Kultura*, No. 10 (192), 1963.
Mitkiewicz, Leon, 'Mikolajczyk, Eden, Powstanie', *Horyzonty*, No. 128/1967.
'Preliminaria Powstania Zbrojnego A.K. (1)', *Horyzonty*, No. 131/1967.
'Preliminaria Powstania Zbrojnego A.K. (2)', *Horyzonty*, No. 132/1967.
Z Gen. Sikorskim na Obczyznie, Paris, 1968.
Mulak, J., *Wojsko Podziemne, 1939–1945*, Warsaw, 1946.
Nowak, Jan, 'Operacja Whitehorne', *Kultura*, No. 4–5 (21–22), 1949.
Ostaszewski, Jan, *Powstanie Warszawskie*, Rome, 1945.
Pawlowicz, Jerzy, *Z dziejow konspiracyjnej KRN 1943–1944*, Warsaw, 1961.
Strategia Frontu Narodowego PPR III. 1943–VII. 1944, Warsaw, 1965.
Pelczynski, Tadeusz, 'Powstanie Warszawskie', *Polska Walczaca*, No. 31/1946.

'Geneza i przebieg "Burzy" ', *Bellona*, No. 3/1949.
'O powstaniu warszawskim', *Bellona*, No. 3/1955.
'Zagadnienie sowieckie w Polsce w latach 1939–1945', *Bellona*, No. 2/1957.
Pilsudski, Jozef, *Pisma Wybrane*, London, 1943.
Pobog-Malinowski, Wladyslaw, *Najnowsza Historia Polityczna Polski*, 1864–1945, vol. III, London, 1960.
Podlewski, Stanislaw, 'Tak rozstrzygal sie los Warszawy', *Za i Przeciw*, No. 31 (593), 4 August 1968.
Polonsky, A., *Politics in Independent Poland 1921–1939*, Oxford, 1972.
Pomian, A., *The Warsaw Rising*, London, 1945.
Pomian-Dowmuntt, A., *Powstanie Warszawskie 1944 (Zarys problematyki)*, London, 1946.
Popiel, N., 'Jak "unwalniano" Polske', *Zeszyty Historyczne*, No. 5/1964.
Pragier, Adam, 'Powstanie Warszawskie', *Wiadomosci*, vol. XIX, No. 31 (1957), 2 August 1964.
'Ostatni raz o powstaniu', *Wiadomosci*, vol. XXV, No. 14 (1253), 5 April 1970.
Prochnik, Adam, (Henryk Swoboda), *Pierwsze pietnastolecie Polski niepodleglej*, Warsaw 1957.
Przygonski, Antoni, *Z problematyki Powstania Warszawskiego*, Warsaw, 1964.
Polski Ruch Robotniczy: w okresie wojny i okupacji hitlerowskiej: wrzesien 1939–styczen 1945, Warsaw, 1964.
Puacz, Edward, 'Powstanie Warszawskie w Protokolach PKWN', *Zeszyty Historyczne*, No. 10/1966.
'Sprawa granic Polski w ukladach miedzy P.K.W.N. a ZSSR', *Zeszyty Historyczne*, No. 15/1969.
Rawski, Tadeusz; Stapor, Zdzislaw; Zamojski, Jan; *Wojna Wyzwolencza Narodu Polskiego w latach 1939–1945*, Warsaw, 1966.
Rechowicz, Henryk, *Aleksander Zawadzki: Zycie i dzialalnosc*, Katowice, 1969.
Rokicki, Jozef ('Michal'), *Blaski i cienie bohaterskiego pieciolecia*, Western Germany, 1949.
Rokossowski, Konstanty, 'O Powstaniu Warszawskim', *Zeszyty Historyczne*, No. 15/1969.
Roos, Hans, *A History of Modern Poland*, London, 1966.
Rose, William John, *The Rise of Polish Democracy*, London, 1944.
Rothschild, Joseph, *Pilsudski's Coup D'Etat*, New York and London, 1966.
Rozek, Edward J., *Allied Wartime Diplomacy: A Pattern in Poland*, New York, 1958.
Rzepecki, Jan, *Wspomnienia i przyczynki historyczne*, Warsaw, 1956.
'W sprawie decyzji podjecia walki w Warszawie', *Wojskowy Przeglad Historyczny*, No. 2/1958.
'Jeszcze o decyzji podjecia walki w Warszawie', *Wojskowy Przeglad Historyczny*, No. 4/1958.
Sesja naukowa poswiecona wojnie wyzwolenczej narodu polskiego 1939–1945, Warsaw, 1959.
Seton-Watson, Hugh, *Eastern Europe Between the Wars, 1918–1941*, Cambridge, 1945.
The East European Revolution, London, 1956.
Siemaszko, Z. S., 'Lacznosc Radiowa Sztabu N.W. w Okresie Powstania Warszawskiego', *Zeszyty Historyczne*, No. 6/1964.
'Lacznosc i Polityka', *Zeszyty Historyczne*, No. 8/1965.
'Retinger w Polsce', *Zeszyty Historyczne*, No. 12/1967.
'Powstanie Warszawskie – Kontakty z ZSSR i PKWN', *Zeszyty Historyczne*, No. 16/1969.

'Powstanie Warszawskie (Inne Sporjrzenie)', *Wiadomosci*, vol. xxvi, No. 3/4 (1243–1244), 18–25 January 1970.

'Rozmowa z gen. Andersem', *Kultura*, No. 7/8 (274–275), 1970.

Skarzynski,Aleksander, 'Cele polityczne "Burzy" a sprawa wybuchu powstania warszawskiego', *Najnowsze Dzieje Polski 1939–1945*, No. 2/1959.

'Niektore aspekty dzialalnosci BIP-u Komendy Glownej AK', *Wojskowy Przeglad Historyczny*, No. 3/1961.

Polityczne przyczyny powstania warszawskiego, Warsaw, 1964.

Slessor, J., 'Tragedia Warszawy', *Skrzydlata Polska*, No. 2/1958.

Sobczak, Kazimierz, 'Kilka uwag o zamierzaniach dowodztwa radzieckiego w rejonie Warszawy w lecie 1944 r.', *Najnowsze Dzieje Polski*, No XI/1967.

Sosnkowski, Kazimierz, *Materialy Historyczne*, London, 1966.

Szwejgiert, Boleslaw, 'Podziemne formacje zbrojne "Obozu Narodowego" w latach 1939–1945. Zarys materialowy', *Wojskowy Przeglad Historyczny*, No. 1/1961.

Talmon, J. L., *Political Messianism. The Romantic Phase*, London, 1960.

Toynbee, Arnold and Toynbee, Veronica M., *Hitler's Europe. Survey of International Affairs 1939–1946*, London, 1954.

Turlejska, Maria, 'Co wiedzial wywiad AK w przededniu powstania', *Polityka*, No. 41/1958.

O wojnie i podziemiu. Dyskusje i polemiki, Warsaw, 1959.

Rok przed kleska (*l wrzesnia 1938–1 wrzesnia 1939*), 2nd ed., Warsaw, 1962.

Prawdy i fikcje: Wrzesien 1939–Grudzien 1941, 2nd ed., Warsaw, 1968.

Werth, Alexander, *Russia at War 1941–1945*, London, 1964.

Wilmot, Chester, *The Struggle for Europe*, London, 1952.

Woloszyn, Wlodzimierz, 'Wyzwolenie wschodnich ziem Polski przez Armie Radziecka i Wojsko Polskie w 1944 r.', *Wojskowy Przeglad Historyczny*, No. 3–4/1963.

Na warszawskim kierunku operacyjnym, Warsaw, 1964.

Woodward, Sir Llewellyn, *British Foreign Policy in the Second World War*, London, 1962.

Zabiello, Stanislaw, *O Rzad i Granice*, 2nd ed., Warsaw, 1965.

Zawodny, J. K., *Death in the Forest. The Katyn Massacre*, Notre Dame, Ind., 1962.

'Wywiad z gen. Borem-Komorowskim', *Kultura*, No. 11 (229)/1966.

Zbiniewicz, Fryderyk, *Armia Polska w ZSSR*, Warsaw, 1963.

Zukow, G. K., 'O Powstaniu Warszawskim i Polsce', *Zeszyty Historyczne*, No. 16/1969.

Zweig, Ferdynand, *Poland Between Two Wars: A Critical Study of Social and Economic Change*, London, 1944.

Zych, J., *Rosja wobec Powstania Warszawskiego*, London, 1947.

5. NEWSPAPERS AND PERIODICALS

(i) Underground Press

Agencja Prasowa, 1942–4.

Armia Ludowa, 1944.

Biezaca Informacja Polityczna, 1942–4.

Biuletyn Informacyjny, 1939–44.

Gwardzista, 1942–4.

Informacja Biezaca, 1943–4.

Insurekcja, 1940–4.

Narodowe Sily Zbrojne, 1942–4.

Okolnik, 1942–4.
Polska Agencja Telegraficzna, 1944.
Przez walke do zwyciestwa, 1942–4.
Rada Narodowa, 1944.
Reforma, 1942–4.
Robotnik, 1940–4.
Rzeczpospolita Polska, 1942–4.
Agencja Polityczna Strop.
Szaniec, 1939–4.
Trybuna Wolnosci, 1942–4.
Walka, 1940–4.
Zywia i Bronia, 1944.

(ii) **Polish press published in Great Britain dusing the war**
Dziennik Polski i Dziennik Zolnierza, 1940–4.
Wiadomosci, 1940–4.

(iii) **Polish press published in the U.S.S.R. during the war**
Nowe Widnokregi, 1942–4.
Wolna Polska, 1943–4.

Index